Library of
Davidson College

# Fifteenth-Century Studies

# Fifteenth-Century Studies

## Recent Essays

*edited by*

Robert F. Yeager

ARCHON BOOKS

1984

© 1984 Robert F. Yeager   All rights reserved
First published 1984 as an Archon Book,
an imprint of the Shoe String Press, Inc.,
Hamden, Connecticut 06514
Printed in the United States of America

**Library of Congress in Publication Data**
Main entry under title:

Fifteenth-century studies.

Includes bibliographical references.
1. English literature—Middle English, 1100–1500—History and criticism—Addresses, essays, lectures. 2. English language—Middle English, 1100–1500—Addresses, essays, lectures. 3. English poetry—Middle English, 1100–1500—Bibliography. 4. Scottish poetry—To 1700—Bibliography. 5. English poetry—Scottish authors—Bibliography. I. Yeager, Robert F.
PR293.F53   1984         820'.9'002         84-3105
ISBN 0-208-01902-2

The paper in this book meets the guidelines for performance and durability of the Committee on Production Guidelines for Book Longevity of the Council on Library Resources.

# Contents

Preface vii
Acknowledgements ix

## Part One: Reviews of Scholarship

The Poetry of John Gower:
Important Studies, 1960–1983
R. F. Yeager 3

Lydgate Scholarship:
Progress and Prospects
A. S. G. Edwards 29

Hoccleve Studies, 1965–1981
Jerome Mitchell 49

Henryson Scholarship:
The Recent Decades
Louise O. Fradenburg 65

Studies in Douglas and Dunbar:
The Present Situation
Florence H. Ridley 93

## Part Two: Language and Paleography

Texts, Textual Criticism and Fifteenth-Century
Manuscript Production
Derek Pearsall 121

Taboo-Words in Fifteenth-Century English
Thomas W. Ross 137

Caxton and Chancery English
John H. Fisher 161

# Part Three: Literary Criticism

*The Drama:*
*Learning and Unlearning*
   Donald C. Baker   189

*"O Moral Henryson"*
   C. David Benson   215

*Courtly Love and Chivalry*
*in the Later Middle Ages*
   Larry D. Benson   237

*Hoccleve's* Series:
*Experience and Books*
   John Burrow   259

*The Coherence of Henryson' Work*
   Denton Fox   275

*Rhyme, Romance, Ballad, Burlesque, and*
*the Confluence of Form*
   Thomas J. Garbáty   283

*James Ryman and the Fifteenth-Century Carol*
   David L. Jeffrey   303

*The Ironic Art of William Dunbar*
   Edmund Reiss   321

*Lydgate's Canterbury Tale:* The Siege of Thebes
*and Fifteenth-Century Chaucerianism*
   A. C. Spearing   333

   Contributors   365

# Preface

The fifteenth century, it has been said, is the last, vast *terra incognita* of English literature. Pressed as it is between Chaucer on the one hand and Spenser on the other, bedevilled by a tumultuous political history (and scarcely illuminated by Shakespeare's kaleidescopic treatment of its events and figures), the fifteenth century has gotten comparatively little attention in the past from literary scholars. What notice its writings have received is often condemnatory and dismissive: "dull," "plodding," and "undisciplined" are adjectives frequently found scattered across critical surveys attempting to characterize the literature of these years. Indeed, such good as has been offered about fifteenth-century poetry and fiction has come for the most part indirectly, by virtue of its location in the geography of English letters. Like many a crossroads nation, the fifteenth century has been valued for its borders—the places toward which a venturesome traveler embarks, the origins of his departures. Thus we find best known and best praised of fifteenth-century writing the work of the "Scottish Chaucerians," so-called, and the vernacular drama: the first group highly regarded for a supposed ability to recall and continue techniques of a departed master, the second honored as anterior to a resplendent theatrical tradition as yet just beyond the horizon. Even Caxton and Malory—arguably the most familiar citizens of the period—are commonly treated not as natives, with bloodties in various senses to others about them, but rather as unique, somewhat superior outriders more at home in alternative climes.

There have been, of course, exceptions to this rule-of-thumb appraisal: one thinks of historians such as C. L. Kingsford and Arthur B. Ferguson particularly, followed by literary writers—H. S. Bennett, Roberto Weiss.

# Preface

Carefully considered and sought after, a body of fine work exists which illuminates many of the recesses of Britain's last medieval century. Yet so much more remains to be done before our understanding of the period equals what we know of the years bounding it on either side that exploration still remains a useful metaphor to fix on our current approach. The process of discovery has begun, nevertheless, and recent years have seen a slow but steady increase in the amount of scholarly effort expended on fifteenth-century topics and conundra.

It was, then, with full awareness of these convergent circumstances that the present volume has been prepared. The pieces collected here are fresh work, unpublished elsewhere and exemplary, in many ways, of the new and growing strength of fifteenth-century interest. By design, the ensuing pages seek to further this interest in two distinct but complementary ways. First, because firm foundations are required for the successful growth of knowledge, previously available scholarship is addressed directly. Thus, the first five essays are descriptive bibliographies. Their purpose is to identify the most significant work of the past two or three decades, giving a sense of its strength and relative weaknesses, with a view toward isolating current problems and pointing directions for stimulating new research. Figures selected are the major poets of the period: John Gower (perhaps the first after 1400 to give voice to a "public" poetry in the fifteenth-century sense), John Lydgate, Thomas Hoccleve, Robert Henryson, William Dunbar, and Gavin Douglas. The bibliographic studies are complemented by what might be termed summational pieces—open-ended work, ultimately, which both collects earlier research and adds to it current information and theory. These essays treat such salient fifteenth-century genres as the ballad and the drama and explore the relationships of contemporary chivalry to courtly love and the alliterative romances.

The second broad group of essays offers new facts and critical assessments; it represents in another form the type of scholarly examination which, it is hoped, this volume will help to foster. Again, the direction of these pieces is testimony to the wide range of concerns awaiting assessment. A great deal of attention has been paid in the past to describing and analyzing the language and manuscript traditions (as well as the literary merits) of the superb poets of the foregoing century: Chaucer, Langland, the author of *Sir Gawain and the Green Knight* and *Pearl*. Here, although their names necessarily arise as touchstones in discussion from time to time, focus is deliberately placed on other matters, writers, and traditions, beginning with three essays on language and paleography—the very places where, in fact, all responsible criticism must begin. These are followed by others, some

*Preface*

dealing with the major fifteenth-century "makars" who have already received bibliographic treatment, some with less-studied but significant figures, such as the Franciscan lyricist James Ryman.

Finally, it should be noted that in its breadth and variety of approach, this volume is intended to be of use to readers and students of all sorts and all levels. We have—and I believe I do no contributor injustice if I presume to speak for all of us—a certain unavoidable sense of "going before" which often accompanies an exploratory enterprise. If we have done it well, our work will encourage others (many of whom are now students in universities, colleges, and schools) to follow and to challenge. It is from them, alongside our present colleagues, that we bring together our separate learning in this collection; and, *mutatis mutandis*, it is at last to them (if we have done our work very well indeed) that we shall look for subsequent enlightening expeditions into the rich and variegated landscape that is English letters in the fifteenth century.

CAMBRIDGE, MASSACHUSETTS
1983

R. F. YEAGER

# Acknowledgments

Perhaps it is somewhat akin to hubris for an editor of a collective volume to offer acknowledgments. Invariably, behind everyone's effort there are many patrons and just as many indispensable "little, nameless, unremembered, acts/Of kindness and of love" which render possible every finished work. No doubt had I asked each contributor conscientiously for the names and services of those who helped with each essay included here, the list would have run long indeed. But perhaps, too, it is an editor's privilege to direct the gratitude extended formally in print. In this case it seems to me a great deal is owed especially to a small and patient band, some of whose names and long suffering I think it due—if monstrous slight—recompense to rehearse here. First there are the contributors themselves, all of whom bore with great good will and forbearance the struggles of a journeyman editor. From each of you I have learned much, and I thank you for it. To James Thorpe III of The Shoe String Press, another patient teacher, in many ways the fruition of this book is owed, for without his helpful equanimity and generous spirit this project might well have come to nought. But most of all I wish to thank Nancy Aleda Neale, for unflagging support and good humor when, in the course of this and other projects, "the fretful stir/Unprofitable, and the fever of the world/Have hung upon the beatings of my heart." Would that I might bring about for every editor such contributors, and such friends at press and at home.

## Part I
## Reviews of Scholarship

# The Poetry of John Gower

## Important Studies, 1960-1983

### R. F. Yeager

The twenty years past have been comparatively rich ones for John Gower studies. Interest in his work has increased steadily from 1960, so that, during this period, much of the scaffolding requisite for a major reappraisal of his poetry has been completed. Similarly, various attempts have been made to provide accessible texts for classroom use. While it would hardly be correct to claim that this activity amounts to a "Gower Renaissance," nonetheless the volume and quality of recent scholarship points toward a growing audience of informed readers at many levels, supplied with new tools of diverse sorts.

### Editions and Translations

For eighty years, the standard edition of Gower's poetry has been that of G. C. Macaulay.[1] Since his publication of the *Complete Works* between 1899 and 1902, no newly edited version has been attempted. In large part, the longevity of Macaulay's edition is due as much to the obscurity into which Gower's writing has fallen as to the perpetual currency of Macaulay's editorial product. For, although Macaulay's skills as an editor were considerable—particularly in textual matters—the four-volume *Works* has been for some time in need of careful revision, to bring the linguistic apparatus and the notes up to date with current scholarship. There has also been a problem of availability, since until the later 1960s Macaulay's edition was not reprinted. In 1968, however, four individual attempts were simultaneously made to remedy this latter difficulty.

The most ambitious of these was that of The Scholarly Press, which produced a photographic reproduction of the Macaulay edition, in four volumes.[2] Unfortunately, before many of these sets could be sold, the publisher became embroiled in a lengthy legal battle which prevented distribution of the books until quite recently, when a few became available in remainder catalogues. Thus, the Anglo-Norman *Mirour de l'Omme* and the Latin text of the *Vox Clamantis* remain relatively difficult to obtain, as do the shorter poems in those languages, most of which are published only in Macaulay's edition.

Some few examples of Gower's French balades and Latin lyrics appear in *Selections from John Gower*, edited by J. A. W. Bennett, but he, as others, lent most of his attention to the *Confessio Amantis*.[3] Bennett's edition was intended to fill the need for a text suited to the demands of British undergraduates: it is, consequently, modest in price and size, but broad in its range of selections and in its assumptions about its readers' polylinguality (the Anglo-Norman and Latin verses are neither translated nor glossed). The introductory material is brief but helpful, as are the notes; there is a glossary and much bibliographic citation throughout. The text, nonetheless, is Macaulay's, and the glossary depends heavily on his edition.

A classroom volume of another sort is Russell A. Peck's *The Confessio Amantis*.[4] Peck's designated audience was American university students. His edition, which also uses Macaulay's text, deals only with the *Confessio* and includes most of the poem, excepting various tales (summarized in modern prose), about half of the framing conversations between Genius and Amans, and nearly all the Latin headlinks and marginalia. Like Bennett's *Selections*, Peck's *Confessio* has a useful introduction and notes; unlike Bennett's text, it has a listed bibliography, and it lacks a glossary. (Difficult words are glossed on the page where they appear, in the margins.)

Finally, 1968 saw the reissue by the Early English Text Society of the two volumes of Macaulay's that contained the *Confessio Amantis* and the shorter English poem "In Praise of Peace."[5] These volumes remain the only available complete texts of Gower's English poetry. They are, however, quite expensive and—because they are reprints—are as dated as Macaulay's original publication.

Most recently, another selected text of the *Confessio Amantis* has been published by Carole Weinberg.[6] It contains a useful, short introduction, a bibliography (listing secondary works to 1979), and various tales chosen from Books I, III, IV, V, VI, and VIII. Difficult words are glossed in the page margin; there are approximately five pages of explanatory notes as well.

Translations of Gower's work also appeared in the 1960s, alongside the various editions. In 1962, Eric W. Stockton published an exacting translation of the *Vox Clamantis* and the *Chronica Tripertita* into modern English prose.[7] Stockton's notes and introduction, which reflect current scholarly criticism as well as linguistic and editorial information, are copious and illuminating, and they make the book valuable for those with a general interest in Gower's writing. Terence Tiller, in 1963, translated the *Confessio Amantis* into modern English prose, treating somewhat over half the poem carefully and giving summaries of the rest.[8] While Stockton's volume was intended primarily for a scholarly readership, however, Tiller's is a popularized edition with little in the way of introduction or notes; it therefore has serious deficiencies, even as a classroom text. Somewhat later, in 1970, William B. Wilson turned out a close, readable translation of the *Mirour de l'Omme* as a doctoral thesis.[9] Currently, this remains unpublished, although copies in microfilm or xerox may be purchased from University Microfilms in Ann Arbor, Michigan.

Translations of Gower's major poetry, then, are relatively well handled, and we may consider this work to have been completed. Of great use now, in order to spur Gower studies in general and to broaden most students' views of the range of poetry produced in late medieval London, would be a new, bilingual edition of the balade sequences, the "Traitié pour les Amantz marietz" and the "Cinkante Balades." Also helpful would be an available edition of the earliest-known translation of Gower's work, the Spanish *Confision del Amante*. Two editions of this prose translation of the *Confessio* exist, one edited by Adolf Birch-Hirschfeld in 1909, the other by A. D. Deyermond in 1973.[10] Both are out of print and difficult to obtain, although—surprisingly—that of Birch-Hirschfeld seems to be the more common. As Robert W. Hamm has shown, there are intriguing differences between the Spanish and English texts which richly repay study.[11]

## Bibliographies

Coincident with the increase in critical studies of Gower's poetry during the last twenty years has come a number of attempts to record those studies in accessible form. Brief, selective, working bibliographies helpful to students exist in the editions of Bennett, Peck, and Weinberg, noted above. These may be bolstered by several more thorough studies, beginning with J. E. Wells's *A Manual of the Writings in Middle English, 1050-1400* and its supplements.[12] More recent mention of studies involving Gower and Chaucer appears in bibliographies prepared by D. D. Griffith and W. R. Crawford.[13] A selective inventory by Derek Pearsall concludes his chapter "The English Chaucerians" in *Chaucer and Chaucerians: Critical Studies in Middle English*

*Literature*, published in 1966.[14] The first bibliography devoted solely to Gower was produced by T. E. Pickford in 1972.[15] Pickford's list, while highly selective, was briefly annotated and covered some dissertations and reviews. A better catalogue was *The New Cambridge Bibliography of English Literature*, which brought notation of materials—though in an incomplete and unannotated fashion—through 1974.[16] A more inclusive bibliography, and the first to attempt a complete, annotated collection of Gower studies then in print (thus excluding dissertations), was published in *Mediaevalia* by R. F. Yeager in 1977.[17] Currently, the most thorough bibliography of Goweriana, including book-length studies, articles, reviews, and dissertations submitted through the end of 1979, is also by Yeager and was published in 1981.[18]

## Biographies and Portraits

Interest in the life of John Gower is not new. Indeed, some of the clearest conclusions about his history and heritage were drawn as early as 1828, by Sir Harris Nicholas—and even earlier, if we look back as far as the perceptive commentary of Dr. Johnson.[19] Macaulay, in his four-volume edition, gave what still remains a valuable summary of what was known at the turn of the century about Gower the man.[20] There were several specific inquiries into Gower's past during the heyday of biographical criticism of the 1920s and 1930s.[21] It was not until 1955, however, that a major attempt was made to place Gower within the coordinates of his times. In a lengthy article, Dorothea Siegmund-Schultze brought together the facts and theories assembled by her predecessors and added some of her own, based on careful reading of Gower's three major poems.[22] Her conclusions are speculative, offering as they do a portrait of the temperament and directions of a man and a century. Perhaps more than anything else, they point out the need that then existed for solid historical research and documented findings. This need was filled consummately by John Fisher, whose *John Gower, Moral Philosopher and Friend of Chaucer* was a watershed in Gower studies.[23] His book consolidated an extensive review of all known evidence related to the life of the poet. Expanding on an article he published earlier, Fisher established firmly Gower's genealogical lines and answered as many questions as the record allowed about his education, business dealings, and intimate relationships. By printing the relevant documents in an appendix to his book, Fisher made them accessible to other scholars who might wish to dispute his conclusions. Few have, as of present writing; Fisher's study remains the cornerstone of modern biographical research on Gower.

Discussion of the portraits of Gower that appear in various manuscripts has not occurred often in the past twenty years. Earlier studies and collections include several such discussions as well as "real" and idealized versions of the poet's appearance.[24] Roger S. Loomis, in his *A Mirror of Chaucer's World* (1965), includes an excellent photograph of Gower's tomb, with effigy, in Southwark Cathedral.[25] Another suggestive note is struck by V. A. Kolve, Gareth Spriggs, and Malcolm Parkes and A. I. Doyle, in separate articles who argue that the illustrations in many manuscripts of the *Confessio* are standardized copies of exemplars, and not original designs.[26]

## Language Studies and Stylistics

Although studies of Gower's language have appeared with increasing frequency in the last twenty years, no concordance or satisfactory lexicon to his work has ever been published. There are, of course, glossaries in various editions, as has been noted above. For the most part, however, later glossaries tend to base themselves on Macaulay's. Yet, while Macaulay was a great editor, he did not lay to rest all the many ambiguities of Gower's langauge in his glossary, which, in the last analysis, was intended primarily as a tool to make possible a complete reading of the poetry. Not surprisingly, the English of the *Confessio Amantis* is the best studied of Gower's languages; little, however, has been done with the Anglo-Norman of the *Mirour* and the balades or with the Latin of the *Vox*, the *Chronica*, and the short poems. Such studies as exist of these are not recent, and suffer in many cases from a reliance on inferior texts. Probably the closest project to a lexicon of Gower's vocabulary now under way is the *Middle English Dictionary*, which (like the *Oxford English Dictionary*) cites Gower frequently. The only true attempt to provide a lexicon/concordance is incomplete and difficult to obtain, as well as—by now—somewhat dated: J. C. Horton Burch's Duke University doctoral dissertation, "A Combined Lexicon and Concordance of the English Works of John Gower, A-C Inclusive." When it is added that Burch's degree was granted in 1933, the deficiencies of this area of Gower studies become obvious.

On the other hand, specific aspects of Gower's language—particularly Middle English—have been the focus of several strong papers since 1960. For the most part, these are the efforts of Japanese scholars; some are written in English (or have English abstracts), but most are found in journals obtainable in but few libraries in the United States. Of special use are articles by Haruo Iwasaki and Masayoshi Ito. In "A Peculiar Feature in the Word-Order of Gower's *Confessio Amantis*," Iwasaki has pointed out several unusual word groups that occur regularly before and after prepositions in Gower's English poems.[27] Ito offers corrections to thirteen translations of the *Vox Clamantis* published by Eric Stockton.[28] The Japanese, however, do not possess exclusive rights to the study of Gower's language. Gero Bauer has applied statistical linguistic pattern analysis to Gower's verbs and verbal constructions, to compare his usage with that of other Middle English writers and with modern custom.[29] Bruce Harbert, in a comparative examination of Gower's and Chaucer's knowledge of Latin, has found Gower to be the more accurate translator. Harbert's basis of comparison is vocabulary selection and grammatical emphasis.[30] E. Talbot Donaldson has noted that Gower handled inflected adjectives carefully and apparently with conscious intent, for he never rhymes them with historically inflected forms.[31] In a similar study, Tauno F. Mustanoja argues that Gower, like Chaucer and other late medieval English writers, frequently rhymed on verbs.[32] The most comprehensive look at Gower's language, after Macaulay's introductions, remains that of Fernand Mossé, the fifth edition of whose *Handbook of Middle English*, in translation by James A. Walker, was published in 1968.[33] Mossé's painstaking consideration of Book V, 3945-4174, of the *Confessio Amantis* is extremely informative in its identification of characteristic elements of Gower's style and dialect.

More common than specific language studies, however, are attempts to scrutinize and describe Gower's poetic style. These may be grouped loosely according to whether they focus on placing Gower within the classical/medieval rhetorical tradition, or whether "style" is defined in them in primarily aesthetic terms. The past twenty years have produced important examples of both sorts. James J. Murphy, in "A New Look at Chaucer and the Rhetoricians," has argued at length that, of fourteenth-century English writers, only Chaucer and Gower seem to show acquaintance with rhetorical traditions in their works.[34] Masayoshi Ito has discussed Gower's wordplay in both Latin and Middle English in two articles. In the earlier, "Paranomasia in *Vox Clamantis*," he identifies numerous examples of annominatio, traductio, and significatio which Gower has drawn from rhetoric-book models.[35] Ito pursues the same argument and approach in his later work, "Wordplay in *Confessio Amantis*."[36] Here, he finds the English language itself acting to restrain Gower's attempts to make puns; hence, there are fewer in the *Confessio* than in the *Vox*. Nevertheless, few as there are comparatively, Ito lists instances of annominatio and traductio found in the *Confessio*. Finally, in an extensive study, Linda L. Greene has traced Gower's use of metaphor, simile, personification, metonymy, synecdoche, and oxymoron.[37] Backing her conclusions with charts, statistics of frequency, and counts of each figure type, she attempts to define the purposes toward which Gower applied his rhetorical learning.

Several valuable "aesthetic" approaches to Gower's writing habits also deserve mention. Donald G. Schueler contends that the *Confessio Amantis* is structurally derived from the dialogue of Amans and Genius which forms its fictive center.[38] Its "loose" development, then, is the result not of rhetorical influence, but of a desire on Gower's part for verisimilitude. Also looking primarily at the *Confessio,* Arno Esch finds it is constructed in the same way that the individual tales are: with the medieval principle of a balance between possible opposites, "utile/dulce," "prodesse/delectare," at its center.[39] Douglas Gray identifies a "genuine polish" about the *Confessio Amantis*, derived from the absorption by Gower of the English courtly style fostered during Richard II's reign.[40] This links Gower stylistically not only to Chaucer, but also to Froissart. In two studies of Gower's rhyming techniques, Masayoshi Ito demonstrates the frequency (with charts and figures) of Gower's use of rime riche in both the *Mirour* and the *Confessio*; he also seeks to demonstrate that Gower's rhyme royal, unlike Chaucer's, is intended as a "lyrical" interlude, or embellishment, to the narrative.[41] It is not rendered unobtrusive, therefore, but rather is emphasized for the artistic effect. Goetz Schmitz argues in his *"The Middel Weie": Stil- und Aufbauformen in John Gowers "Confessio Amantis"* that Gower uses rhetorical figures, but always with an eye on their aesthetic (and moral) value, and seldom (in the manner of many of his contemporaries) solely for the purpose of embellishing the text.[42] In a more recent study, R. F. Yeager attempts to prove that stylistic purpose dictated the Latin marginalia and headlinks in the *Confessio*; that they show Gower leavening the intentionally simple English verse of the poem with commentary and ornate Latin poetry; and that a possible model for a handling of this kind might have been the *Fasciculus Morum* and related works.[43] Finally, Judson B. Allen seeks to classify Gower's structure for the *Confessio Amantis*, calling that structure an "array" and linking it to models offered by rhetoricians and Ovid's *Metamorphoses*.[44] In using such broad-ranging and—at times—apparently digressive formal ordering, Gower in Allen's view is thoroughly within the tradition of late medieval poetics.

## Source Studies

Of all topics of inquiry pursued in the past twenty years, more labor seems to have been expended on the search for Gower's sources than on any other. As a result, much new information about Gower's writing and borrowing habits has recently come to light. Four areas in particular have benefitted from this modern activity: the relationships between Gower's poetry and medieval traditions of courtly love, sermon and penitential literature, and rhetoric, and the applications Gower made of the works of Ovid. In order to illustrate the range of this scholarship, these four areas must be discussed in turn.

For the most part, studies of Gower's debts to the conventions of courtly love trace their origins back to C. S. Lewis's discussions of the *Confessio Amantis* in *The Allegory of Love*.[45] Lewis's argument that Gower, like most poets of his time, was heavily influenced by the *Roman de la Rose* and the social habits of a nobility committed to acts of "gentilesse"—so heavily committed, in fact, that the *Confessio* according to Lewis is an effective, if slightly skewed, embodiment of those ideals—has found more echoes than dispute in modern Gower criticism. Thus, J. V. Cunningham in a 1960 essay claimed that the poem (and the "Tale of Rosiphelee" especially) is derivative of Jean de Meun's approach to dream vision;[46] so also have John J. McNally, J. A. W. Bennett, and Constance Hieatt, although these latter three make exceptions of various aspects of the *Confessio*. McNally, while noting Gower's indebtedness to de Meun and Andreas Capellanus, underscores as well how much the courtly is offset by elements of the penitential.[47] Bennett, in the well-argued chapter "Gower's 'Honeste Love,'" contends that Gower joins the courtly with spiritual love to transform the earthbound ethos of *amour courtois* and so promote marital, procreative love.[48] Hieatt, writing in 1967, suggests that Gower's dependence on the dream vision intrinsic to all love poetry derived from the *Roman de la Rose* is misleading, since he only flirts with the outline of dream, while never clearly committing Amans to sleep.[49]

"Balance," indeed, seems to be the way of contemporary writers describing the courtly aspects of the *Confessio*. Walter S. Phelan expresses it well in the title of his 1971 dissertation, "The Conflict of Courtly Love and Christian Morality in John Gower's *Confessio Amantis*."[50] Phelan traces ideas of transforming opposites back to the *Timaeus* via the School of Chartres, and shows how they reappear as Gower's structuring principles. In "Courtly Love and the Confessional in English Literature from 1215 to John Gower," John F. Fitzpatrick agrees with McNally that the poem is built around a union of two traditions—Lewis's *courtoisie* and rituals of penance.[51] David Byrd also affirms traditional notions of the courtly as a starting place for his research into the meaning of "blanche fever," a symptom of lovesickness for Gower and Chaucer.[52] Henry A. Kelly alone of recent critics attempts to show that the *Confessio* is in fact an anticourtly poem by suggesting that—*contra* Lewis—Gower turns what he knew all along was merely a convention against itself by the final lines, to make a case in the *Confessio* for the validity and value of proper, Christian marriage.[53] Finally, one further study should be mentioned in connection with the courtly love tradition and its portrayal in the *Confessio Amantis*. William A. Neilson published his *Origins of the Court of Love* in 1899, and it has remained a valuable source of information about, among other things, Gower's backgrounds. The volume, long out of print, was photographically reproduced in 1967, thus making it available once more as a tool for modern scholars.[54]

Like the tradition of the court, those of the pulpit and the confessional have also been the focus of several scholars' work, and these influences on Gower's writing have been newly assessed. In her rich essay on allegorical imagery, Rosamond Tuve pointed out in 1966 that the *Confessio* and the *Mirour de l'Omme* both depend heavily on penitential treatises like the *Somme le Roi*.[55] Tuve is especially concerned to show the derivation of opposed vices and virtues in Gower's two poems to be from such penitential works. Other readers published similar conclusions in 1966. In the more influential of these, G. R. Owst argues convincingly for the presence of sermon material throughout all of Gower's work.[56] His view is seconded by Edwart Weber, who sees Gower's didactic impulses leading him constantly to models in the homiletic and penitential traditions.[57] In a more recent study, Judith Shaw seeks to demonstrate that in fact Gower's effects as artist can be seen to culminate in the *Confessio* in an attempt to turn secular materials into exempla of the seven cardinal sins.[58]

The rhetorical tradition, too, influenced Gower's poetics, and it has been the function of much modern scholarship to illustrate the degree to which this is true. Most responsible for this reassessment, perhaps, is James J. Murphy, who built upon his 1957 dissertation to produce three illuminating articles between 1962 and 1965.[59] Throughout, Murphy argues that there was little consciousness of classical rhetoric—or even, in Gower's case, of medieval continental rhetorics—in England until the fifteenth century and that Gower shows small evidence of having read Geoffrey of Vinsauf, but rather borrowed most of what he appears to know from Brunetto Latini's *Trésor*. Murphy's conclusions are somewhat offset by Susan Gallick, who helps to clarify what manuscripts might have been available to Gower, and which he might have used in developing a background in rhetorical practice.[60] Patrick J. Gallacher also disagrees with Murphy, both in his 1966 dissertation and in his subsequent book, *Love, the Word, and Mercury: A Reading of John Gower's "Confessio Amantis."*[61] Gallacher points out that in fact Gower must have known more about the standard attitudes toward rhetoric than Murphy supposed. Finally, Kurt Olsson terms Gower's work "moral rhetoric" in a study aimed at showing how, in his poetry, he blends and adapts rhetorical and homiletic traditions for calculated effect.[62]

Of all the individual sources used by Gower, none has come under as much scrutiny during the past twenty years as have the works of Ovid. Like Chaucer, Gower went to Ovid frequently; he borrowed not only plots and characters, but, at times, a kind of Ovidian tone or cast to his storytelling style. Many attempts to show how much, and why, Gower drew on Ovid have been helpful in demonstrating this indebtedness anew. In an article published in 1961, John L. Mahoney concluded that Ovid was one of the major forces directing Gower's imagination—more so, indeed, than is true of many late medieval English writers.[63] While conceding Ovid's power of inspiration for Gower, Wolfgang Clemen, in his study of Chaucer's early work, argued that Gower drew on relatively few Ovidian loci.[64] Chaucer, according to Clemen, was far better read in Ovid than was his friend and fellow poet Gower.

Three other scholars, Louise Vinge, M. L. Lord, and Bruce Harbert, while pursuing specific topics, tend to corroborate Mahoney's findings regarding Gower's dependence on Ovid. In *The Narcissus Theme in Western European Literature up to the Early Nineteenth Century,* Vinge sees Gower beginning his portrait of Narcissus with Ovid, then blending it with elements derived from the *Roman de la Rose.*[65] Lord argues similarly for Gower's synthetic abilities, pointing out that the story of Dido as related by Gower comes essentially from Ovid, although it has been altered somewhat. Since, according to Lord, there were two traditional treatments of Dido known to the later Middle Ages, Gower's decision to employ a modified version of Ovid's is significant.[66] Like Vinge and Lord, Harbert makes the point that Gower's treatment of the tale of Tereus shows changes from its Ovidian original—changes that can only be the result of a confident poet remaking his material to suit his particular purposes.[67] One means of adaptation common in Gower's verse is to blend commentary or *moralitas* from the *Ovide Moralisé* with narratives originating in Ovid; or so argues Conrad Mainzer, in an article published in 1972.[68] John Fyler, in comparing Gower to Chaucer in his study of the latter's use of Ovid, has noted that Gower's borrowings from the Roman poet can include inspiration, as well as story lines. The topos of mating birds, Fyler argues, is taken from Ovid, who like Gower used it to contrast with unrequited love among humans. This, in turn, helps to set the framework for the entire *Confessio Amantis.*[69] Also concerned with Gower's development of Ovid is Peter G. Beidler, who has brought together a collection of essays, *John Gower's Literary Transformations* in the *"Confessio Amantis": Original Articles and Translations*, representing his own work and that of others.[70] The essays examine, briefly but pointedly, various stories Gower has borrowed from the *Metamorphoses*. Critical studies such as these, then, indicate a greater synthetic, or "plastic," potential in Gower's creative imagination than was recognized in the criticism of former decades, and it seems likely this is a trend future approaches to Gower's use of source material may soon take.

## Critical Studies

Such a great deal of new writing on Gower has taken place in the years since 1960 that the total volume of Gower studies has more than doubled. As a result, it is difficult to do justice to all that is both contemporary and of value. Most ambitious, certainly, are those efforts that attempt to draw conclusions concerning Gower's entire oeuvre. Foremost among these, considered both in terms of publication date and contribution, is John H. Fisher's *John Gower, Moral Philosopher and Friend of Chaucer*, mentioned earlier. In addition to establishing the details of Gower's life, Fisher's book also presents the thesis that Gower's three major poems, the *Confessio*, *Vox,* and *Mirour*, are all in some senses parts of the same vast poem. Gower's purposes never wavered, Fisher argues, but simply were presented in slightly different forms, or with different emphases. Always the moralist, always the mentor for nobility and kings, Gower strove to clarify the essential connections between the affairs of this world and the next. Social justice, for example, had its origins in God's ultimate justice; government of states was simply a "middle-cosm," if you will, suspended halfway between the larger model of heaven and the microcosmic universe of man's interior life. The first to attempt an assessment of all of Gower's writing, as well as the first to suggest it hangs together as a unified vision, Fisher still sets the standard for discussion of Gower's verse.

This is not to say, however, that subsequent studies have agreed with Fisher's conclusions. He presented, rather, an alternative position for Shingo Yoshida, who in 1965 proffered a notion of opposed passion and reason resolved in an ideal "Christian humanism" as the thrust of all of Gower's writing.[71] Unlike Fisher, for whom law and custom figure as vital correlatives in Gower's world view, Yoshida looks instead to the inner conflict, the psychomachia, for the key to the poetry. A somewhat similar approach is taken by Edwart Weber, who posits the divisibility of Gower's writing into two sorts of poem—those with essentially "moral" concerns (the *Mirour*, the *Vox,* and the *Chronica Tripertita*), and those with "amorous" ones (the *Confessio* and the balade sequences).⁷² In direct opposition to Fisher, J. Lawrence Badenyck claims in his doctoral thesis, "The Achievement of John Gower: A Reading of the *Confessio Amantis*," that there is no thematic continuity between Gower's major poems; that in fact, while they show certain relationships of idea and plan, they are no more cohesive than are any three large undertakings completed by a single personality.⁷³ Derek Pearsall, too, looks at the entire Gower corpus in his compendious *Old and Middle English Poetry*, setting Gower's output against that of his contemporaries and before the backdrop of history.⁷⁴ He, too, shows debts to Fisher when he enumerates Gower's virtues as economy of narrative and the desire to enlighten kings.

Close scrutiny was given to Gower's works in a number of individual essays, as well. The *Confessio Amantis* received the greatest portion of attention, but useful pieces were published about all of Gower's poetry. The *Mirour de l'Omme* was discussed by Siegfried Wenzel in his research into medieval attitudes toward the sin of sloth.⁷⁵ The *Mirour*, Wenzel points out, contains a representation of the sin unusually rich in iconographic detail. Sister M. Dominica Legge, in her broad-ranging treatise *Anglo-Norman Literature and Its Background*, attempts to place all of Gower's French poetry, including the *Mirour*, in historical perspective.⁷⁶ Legge sees Gower at the end of a tradition, a little archaic in consequence, but able to use older conventions to advantage while putting his own expressive stamp on the product. J. A. W. Bennett approaches the *Mirour* as an analogue, and perhaps a source, of Chaucer's *Hous of Fame*.⁷⁷ Like Wenzel to a degree, Beryl Rowland describes ways in which animals are used to illustrate sins in the *Mirour*, dwelling particularly on the clarity and fullness of Gower's iconography.⁷⁸ Finally, on a different level of interest, Howard Schless points out the references in the *Mirour* to Lombard merchants, in an effort to establish attitudes toward them in Gower's (and Chaucer's) London.⁷⁹

Two discussions of the shorter Anglo-Norman poems also deserve some mention. P. M. Kean makes much of Gower's apparent poetic self-consciousness and traces its origins to the balades.⁸⁰ Kean finds their model in the lyrics of Deschamps, who in her view was probably most influential on the final form of the "Cinkante Balades." John Fyler, in a volume mentioned above, looks specifically at borrowings from Ovid, discoverable in Balades XXV and XXXIIII.

The Latin works have also received attention in several papers. John A. Yunck describes Gower's approach to satire in the *Vox Clamantis* as conservative and traditional, pursuing it back to its models developed in the eleventh century.⁸¹ But perhaps the most significant addition to available studies of Gower's Latin poetry is the translation into English by Robert J. Meindl of Maria Wickert's insightful and learned volume, *Studien zu John Gower (Studies in John Gower)*.[82] Originally published in 1955 and long out of print, Wickert's examination of Gower's *Vox* has no equal for its treatment of this important poem, which Wickert sees as intimately reflective of political events and attitudes in the 1380s and 1390s in London. The book examines Gower's handling of homiletic sources, *speculum regis* material, and social class theory. Her final chapter, "Gower's Narrative Technique," looks closely at three tales from the *Confessio* and reflects back from them to the *Vox* and the *Mirour*. Masayoshi Ito, taking many of his grounding principles from Wickert, posits that the central organizing structure of the *Vox Clamantis* is a contrast of ideals and figures. Ito interprets the first book of the poem through discussions of peasantry and nobility, natural order and unnatural, notions of past and present, and notions of heaven and hell.[83] Joseph R. Keller proposes the *Vox* as one example of "complaint against the times," a genre which, he notes, was common throughout the Middle Ages in works of poets as diverse as Marcabru and Dunbar.[84] Looking especially at Books III and VII, Keller identifies elements of the "world turned upside down" motif in Gower's major Latin poem. Applying formulae found in Geoffrey of Vinsauf's *Poetria Nova* to the *Vox* (and, less thoroughly, to the *Confessio* and the *Mirour*), Christian J. W. Kloesel portrays Gower as an important, "successful" rhetorician, especially in his Latin writings.[85] Frederick C. Mish looks toward Ovid's verses as the models for Gower's, citing among other points in his 1973 dissertation nearly nine hundred instances of borrowing, from single words to entire lines.[86] Alongside, he lists the passages from Ovid, for comparison. Finally, Jill Mann, in her strongly presented investigation "Chaucer and the Medieval Latin Poets," concludes that Chaucer must have read the *Vox Clamantis* and known its approach to the satirical conventions of its time.[87]

The *Cronica Tripertita* has been the subject of two examinations, in addition to those mentioned above. Edwart Weber, in a book-length comparison of the *Cronica* and *Richard II*, attempts to isolate the stylistically essential characteristics of Shakespeare and Gower by considering the way in which each one treats the same set of events.[88] Masayoshi Ito approaches the *Cronica* through its use of "amor," and sets it against the use of that word in the context of the *Confessio*.[89] In the latter, Ito assumes, "amor" has several meanings, including earthly affection, In the *Cronica*, however, Gower employs it only in the sense of heavenly, or purely spiritual, love.

Because such a great deal, comparatively speaking, has been written about the *Confessio Amantis* in the two decades just past, it is perhaps best to divide it for purposes of discussion into broad topical areas. Elements of social criticism in the poem must surely be one of these, for much attention has been paid to it in modern studies. Historically, the outlines of the current debate were settled by a pair of influential treatments, each still necessary reading for anyone approaching the poetry of Gower. The first, Ruth Mohl's *The Three Estates in Medieval and Renaissance Literature*, offers all three of Gower's major poems up for critical scrutiny, although it places greatest emphasis on the *Confessio Amantis*. Mohl (whose work directly anticipates Jill Mann's look at the class structure) treats Gower's writing as evidence of a conservative social and political attitude prevalent in London at the end of the fourteenth century.[90] Gower, caught in the tide of the Peasants' Revolt and the royal abdication, seems to Mohl to react typically and defensively, condemning change and loudly demanding a return to an older status quo. This theme is echoed and given sharper focus by George R. Coffman. In "John Gower in His Most Significant Role," Coffman argues against attempts to find in Gower's work much poetic craft or grace; rather we should recognize that his real value is as social gadfly and advisor to kings.[91] John Fisher, in his important book on Gower, cited above, draws a good deal from Mohl and from Coffman. In an article published three years earlier than his book, Fisher furthers Coffman's position by showing how the classical-Christian principle of the "common good" is at the heart of Gower's political ideology.[92]

A culling of the better pieces written about Gower since 1960, then, demonstrates the centrality of these themes. Arthur B. Ferguson's *The Articulate Citizen and the English Renaissance* makes the point (excellently) that Gower's work represents strong evidence of a concerned Englishman's attitudes toward late medieval political questions, such as the rights of the estates, kingly prerogative, and the powers of the Commons.[93] Similar conclusions are suggested by Edwart Weber, Takero Oiji, and Albert B. Friedman, although in slightly dissimilar ways: Oiji and Friedman portray Gower as a conservative with a religious man's belief in hierarchy; Weber, on the other hand, depicts him as simply reactionary.[94] In a later study, Derek Brewer goes even farther, terming Gower "farsighted" in his attitude toward the Peasants' Revolt and prudent in his shifting of the dedication of the *Confessio Amantis* from Richard II in order to ensure its influence on the new king, Henry IV.[95] The most complete treatment of the *Confessio Amantis* in terms of inherent social criticism, however, is also the best recent study. *Kingship and Common Profit in Gower's "Confessio Amantis,"* by Russell A. Peck, is a close, book by book reading of the poem—as such, the first of its kind and of great value to undergraduates and others looking into Gower for the initial time.[96] Following a brief summary of issues facing Gower as a citizen and a moralist, Peck turns his attention toward demonstrating that the *Confessio* is most about moral behavior as an imperative not only for the individual (represented by Amans, who symbolizes the human will), but also for the ruler, the common people, and the commonweal itself. Peck articulately clarifies the position that, in Gower's mind, the moral citizen is also the best citizen, loyal as he is to God's laws mirrored in those of the state. Concurring obliquely with Peck, Paul Strohm attempts, in an article published in 1979, to delineate the sort of aesthetic principles such a believing citizen would have had, arguing from a broad definition of poetry as a "mediation" between levels of reality and art.[97]

Another point of focus for recent work on the *Confessio Amantis* has been the characters. These examinations are of two sorts: general papers, which address all the figures together or which seek to describe Gower's broad methods of peopling his writing; and studies that are limited to the discussion of a single character. The first sort of approach is taken by Donald G. Schueler, in an essay published in 1966.[98] Schueler dwells at length on the structural importance of dialogue between Genius and Amans, as well as on them as narrational figures. A quite broad study, "The Influence of Medieval Mythography on John Gower's *Confessio Amantis*," was completed by James J. Foster in 1973.[99] Foster shows, first, the standard mythographic treatments of the *Confessio*'s central characters Venus, Cupid, and Genius in the Middle Ages, and then argues that Gower deviates from this tradition somewhat, usually to reveal Genius's ignorance. This ignorance, alongside other intentionally humorous aspects of the *Confessio*, is also noted by Anthony Farnham. In "The Art of High Prosaic Seriousness: John Gower as Didactic Raconteur," Farnham reads the poem as ultimately moral, but pointedly comic.[100] To Farnham, the Narrator, Genius, and Amans are unconsciously purveyors of an ironic joke which, through laughter, leads us to God.

Individual character studies have had Genius as subject most frequently, but a number of valuable pieces have been published on Amans, as well. The best work on Genius has appeared since 1970. In that year, George Economou pointed out the similarities between Gower's priest and the Genius figures of Alain de Lille and Jean de Meun, finding in them basic models for the *Confessio Amantis*.[101] All subsequent studies have made essentially the same point, although sometimes less directly. In the most complete study of Genius figures from classical antiquity through the fourteenth century, Jane Nitzsche clarifies the two different conventions of Genius that Gower would have known (that is, generative force and priest) and contends that only through resolution of these two "faces" of Genius is Amans able to become whole once more.[102] This reunification of Amans, and of the two Geniuses, is briefly touched upon by Alice S. Miskimin, whose real focus nonetheless is with the impact of Gower—and Genius—on the two centuries following Gower's death.[103] Most recently, Denise N. Baker has urged us to read no conflict in Genius's twin roles by Gower's time, for, she notes, through appearances in the *Roman* and the *De Planctu*, the priest was understood to serve both Venus and God compatibly.[104]

Gower's intentions in naming Amans "John Gower," and, despite this, the little we know about Gower's own feelings and revelations, occupied the attention of D. W. Robertson, Jr., in 1962.[105] By telling us so little about himself, Robertson asserts, Gower was thoroughly representative of poets of his era. Donald G. Schueler, in a closely reasoned article, has argued that Gower's making Amans an old man is part of a plan to undermine the courtly tradition in the *Confessio*.[106] E. T. Donaldson briefly compares the character of Amans with that of Chaucer the pilgrim.[107] This is an idea that Samuel T. Cowling expands upon, in 1975, while claiming that Gower's self-portrait as Amans is one of several ironies contributing in the *Confessio* to parody of the psychological experience of courtly love.[108]

Two other areas treated by a significant number of modern studies involve what might be called Gower's didacticism and his "Ricardianism." Edwart Weber, in 1966, concluded from a careful examination of the *Confessio Amantis* against a background of contemporary confession literature that Gower's inspiration for the poem lay entirely with such material.[109] Patrick J. Gallacher, in the book-length study *Love, the Word, and Mercury*, mentioned above, investigated applications of *logos* in the *Confessio* and argued persuasively that Gower's models were ultimately didactic in purpose, as is his English poem itself. Examining the concept of righteousness in Gower's work, Pamela Gradon has found that for him "rihtwisnesse" reflected ideas of equity synonymous, in many ways, with medieval notions of charity.[110] So understood, "righteousness" helps bind together the elements of the *Confessio* by providing a working ground for private and public relations. Finally, in an article written in 1982, Kurt Olsson identifies five different meanings for "natural law" in the *Confessio*, pointing out that the poem represents a careful working-through of the confines of *jus naturae* in order to impress upon the audience the greater power of Divine Law.[111]

Since 1971, when John Burrow suggested "Ricardianism" as a term useful in categorizing poetry of the late Middle Ages in England, there have been a number of attempts to apply it to Gower's writing. Burrow himself appraised Gower as Ricardian, citing similarities of character depiction, frame story, and argument with other Ricardian poems: the *Canterbury Tales, Piers Plowman,* and *Sir Gawain and the Green Knight*.¹¹² While Burrow was not the last to link the *Confessio Amantis* with these poems, he was also not the first. Derek Brewer did so, in 1966, in a paper devoted to courtesy, and Derek Pearsall described the *Confessio*'s success in terms of frame story and movement very like Burrow's subsequent remarks.¹¹³ Even Gervase Mathew, in a volume more historical than literary, conjoins Gower with other poets writing in and about Richard's court at the end of the century.¹¹⁴ Taking a somewhat opposite view from Burrow's is Elizabeth Kirk, who believes Gower to have been far more influenced by the French poets than was Chaucer, with the consequence that, apart from superficial similarities of frame story, the *Confessio Amantis* and the *Canterbury Tales* are not much alike.¹¹⁵ In a more exploratory essay, Anne Middleton considers the *Confessio* and *Piers Plowman* together, to determine what—if any—idea of "public" poetry existed during the Ricardian years.¹¹⁶ And Patricia Eberle, in her Harvard dissertation (soon to be published by the Medieval Academy in its monograph series), argues with persuasive evidence the crucial role played by the frame narrative in Gower's plan for his major English poem, seeing it as an aspect of the *Confessio* long neglected by critics who, following the lead of Macaulay, chose to focus their attention primarily on the tales.¹¹⁷ Eberle quite usefully describes the *Confessio* as a riddle built of smaller riddles, all having common solutions in the moral, rational—and Christian—life, best described in true speech, and not in the debased language (and sensibility) of courtly love.

One final area of study ought to be mentioned. The portrayal of women in Gower's poetry has never been examined with any frequency or to any depth. This may be changing, however, as one article at least has been devoted to explaining the necessary role of women in the *Confessio Amantis*. Linda Barney Burke concludes that the tone of this poem is characterized by a "mellowness," a feature of which she feels the *Confessio* owes entirely to the presentation there of women as worthy figures.¹¹⁸ This is effected in a natural, unobtrusive manner, and it sharply contrasts with Gower's treatment of women in the *Mirour* and the *Vox*.

## Future Directions

As it has been the aim of this overview to demonstrate, much of value and importance has been written about the poetry of John Gower in the past twenty-three years. Yet viewed from another perspective, Gower studies have yet to be launched fully. A complete text of his works exists, but for reasons of expense or unavailability, it is not common in library holdings, public or private—and, in addition, it could well stand revision, particularly of the introductory matter and the notes. Very little work has been done on the poetry in languages other than Middle English. While much of it is quite good, it hardly goes far enough in presenting us a picture of that learned, trilingual poet and man of affairs Gower must have been. New effort might be spent well in critical examinations of the *Mirour*, the *Vox*, the balade sequences, and the minor Latin pieces. Indeed, it is unfortunate that no translation of any of the Anglo-Norman poetry is published. If it were translated, perhaps the criticism of it, so needed, would follow. Other large-scale studies of the *Confessio Amantis*, to be sure, are also called for. Particularly helpful would be an attempt to read this poem in the larger context of Gower's oeuvre, with more than passing comment being given to a reassessment of the shape and scope of that total work. Whole sections of the *Confessio*, too, need better explanation. What is the relationship, for example, of the lengthy "Apollonius of Tyre," both structurally and thematically, to the rest of the poem? What can be said, if anything, about the "digressions"? Is there evidence in Gower's sources to interpret them? In sum, looking backward over the past twenty years, we can be pleased at what has been accomplished—even as we take sharp note of how much remains to be done.

# Notes

1. *The Complete Works of John Gower*, ed. G. C. Macaulay, 4 vols. (Oxford: Clarendon Press, 1899-1902).

2. Grosse Point, Michigan, 1968.

3. *Selections from John Gower*, ed. J. A. W. Bennett, Clarendon Medieval and Tudor Series (Oxford: Clarendon Press, 1968).

4. *The Confessio Amantis*, ed. Russell A. Peck (New York: Holt, Rinehart, and Winston, 1968; reprint ed., Medieval Academy Reprints for Teaching series, Toronto: University of Toronto Press, 1980).

5. *The English Works of John Gower*, ed. G. C. Macaulay, Early English Text Society, ES 81-82 (London, 1968).

6. *John Gower: Selected Poetry*, ed. Carole Weinberg (Manchester: Carcanet New Press, 1983).

7. *The Major Latin Works of John Gower*, trans. Eric W. Stockton (Seattle: University of Washington Press, 1962).

8. *Confessio Amantis (The Lover's Shrift)*, trans. Terence Tiller (Harmondsworth: Penguin Books, 1963).

9. William Burton Wilson, "A Translation of John Gower's *Mirour de l'Omme*" (Ph.D. diss., University of Miami, 1970).

10. *Confision del Amante, por Joan Goer*, ed. Adolf Birch-Hirschfeld (Leipzig: Seele, 1909); *Apollonius of Tyre: Two Fifteenth-Century Spanish Prose Romances: Historia de Apollonio and Confision del Amante, Apolonyo de Tyro*, ed. A. D. Deyermond (Exeter: University of Exeter Press, 1973).

11. Robert W. Hamm, "An Analysis of the *Confision del Amante*, the Castilian Translation of Gower's *Confessio Amantis*" (Ph.D. diss., University of Tennessee, 1975).

12. *A Manual of the Writings in Middle English, 1050–1400*, ed. J. E. Wells (New Haven: Yale Univeristy Press, 1916, with supplements to 1951).

13. *A Bibliography of Chaucer, 1908–1953*, ed. Dudley D. Griffith (Seattle: University of Washington Press, 1955); *Bibliography of Chaucer, 1954–63*, ed. W. R. Crawford (Seattle: University of Washington Press, 1967).

14. Derek Pearsall, "The English Chaucerians," in *Chaucer and Chaucerians: Critical Studies in Middle English Literature*, ed. Derek S. Brewer (University, Ala.: University of Alabama Press, 1966).

15. T. E. Pickford, "A Bibliography of John Gower, 1925–72," *Parergon* 3 (1972): 27–36.

16. *The New Cambridge Bibliography of English Literature*, ed. George Watson et al., 5 vols. (Cambridge: Cambridge University Press, 1974–77), I, cols. 553–56.

17. R. F. Yeager, "A Bibliography of John Gower Materials through 1975," *Mediaevalia* 3 (1977): 261–306.

18. *John Gower Materials: A Bibliography through 1979*, ed. R. F. Yeager (New York and London: Garland Publishing, 1981).

19. See his preface to *A Dictionary of the English Language* (London: J. and P. Knapton, 1755).

20. See *Complete Works*, IV, pp. vii–xxx.

21. See, for example, Edith Rickert, "Was Chaucer a Student at the Inner Temple?" in *The Manly Anniversary Studies in Language and Literature* (Chicago: University of Chicago Press, 1923), pp. 20–31; John M. Manly, *Some New Light on Chaucer* (New York: Henry Holt, 1926), pp. 195ff. For an answer to Rickert, see further D. S. Bland, "Chaucer and the Inns of Court: A Re-examination," *English Studies* 33 (1952): 145–55.

22. Dorothea Siegmund-Schultze, "John Gower und seine Zeit,"

*Zeitschrift für Anglistik und Amerikanistik* 3 (1955): 5-71.

23. John H. Fisher, *John Gower, Moral Philosopher and Friend of Chaucer* (New York: New York University Press, 1964).

24. See, for example, Richard Gough, *Sepulchral Monuments in Great Britain* (London: J. Nichols, 1796), II, 24-26; *British Authors before 1800: A Biographical Dictionary*, ed. Stanley Kunitz and Howard Haycraft (New York: H. W. Wilson, 1952), p. 229. The latter contains an artist's idealized conception of Gower, done in an extremely romantic mode.

25. Roger S. Loomis, *A Mirror of Chaucer's World* (Princeton, N.J.: Princeton University Press, 1965).

26. Gareth Spriggs, "Unnoticed Bodleian Manuscripts, Illuminated by Herman Scheere and His School," *Bodleian Library Record* 7 (1964): 193-99; V. A. Kolve, "Chaucer and the Visual Arts," in *Geoffrey Chaucer*, ed. Derek S. Brewer, Writers and Their Background Series (Athens, Ohio: Ohio University Press, 1975), p. 295n; A. I. Doyle and Malcolm B. Parkes, "The Production of Copies of the *Canterbury Tales* and the *Confessio Amantis* in the Early Fifteenth Century," *Medieval Scribes, Manuscripts, and Libraries: Essays Presented to N. R. Ker*, ed. M. B. Parkes and Andrew G. Watson (London: Scolar Press, 1978), pp. 163-210.

27. Haruo Iwasaki, "A Peculiar Feature in the Word-Order of Gower's *Confessio Amantis*," *Studies in English Literature* (English Literature Society of Japan) 14 (1969): 205-20.

28. Masayoshi Ito, "On the English Translation (by E. W. Stockton) of *Vox Clamantis*," *Bulletin of the College of General Education* (Tohoku University) 18 (1973): 1-17.

29. Gero Bauer, *Studien zum System und Gebrauch der 'Tempora' in der Sprache Chaucers und Gowers*, Weiner Beiträge zur englischen Philologie, 73 (Vienna and Stuttgart, 1970).

30. Bruce Harbert, "Chaucer and the Latin Classics," in *Geoffrey Chaucer*, ed. Brewer, especially p. 147.

31. E. Talbot Donaldson, "The Manuscripts of Chaucer's Works and Their Use," in *Geoffrey Chaucer*, ed. Brewer, particularly p. 97.

32. Tauno F. Mustanoja, "Verbal Rhyming in Chaucer," in *Chaucer and Middle English Studies in Honor of Rossell Hope Robbins*, ed. Beryl Rowland (Kent, Ohio: Kent State University Press, 1974), pp. 104-10.

33. Fernand Mossé, *A Handbook of Middle English*, trans. James A. Walker, 5th ed. (Baltimore: Johns Hopkins University Press, 1968).

34. James J. Murphy, "A New Look at Chaucer and the Rhetoricians," *Review of English Studies*, n.s. 15 (1964): 1-20.

35. Masayoshi Ito, "Paranomasia in *Vox Clamantis*," *Bulletin of the*

College of General Education (Tohoku University) 6 (1967): 21-35.

36. Masayoshi Ito, "Wordplay in *Confessio Amantis*," *Shiron* 13 1-18; reprinted, with slight revision, in Masayoshi Ito, *John Gower, the Medieval Poet* (Tokyo: Shinozaki Shorin, 1976), pp. 232-49.

37. Linda L. Greene, "Lust and Lore: Figures of Speech in John Gower's *Confessio Amantis* (Ph.D. diss., University of Arkansas, 1978).

38. Donald G. Schueler, "Some Comments on the Structure of Gower's *Confessio Amantis*," in *Explorations of Literature*, ed. Rima D. Reck, Louisiana State University Studies, 18 (Baton Rouge, 1966), pp. 15-24.

39. Arno Esch, "John Gowers Erzählkunst," in *Chaucer und seine Zeit: Symposium für Walter F. Schirmer,* ed. Arno Esch (Tübingen: Niemeyer, 1969), pp. 207-39.

40. Douglas Gray, "Later Poetry: The Courtly Tradition," in *The Middle Ages*, ed. W. F. Bolton, Sphere History of Literature in the English Language, I (London: Barrie and Jenkins, 1970), pp. 312, 316-20.

41. Masayoshi Ito, "Gower's Use of Rime Riche in the *Confessio Amantis*, as Compared with His Practice in the *Mirour de l'Omme* and with the Case of Chaucer," *Studies in English Literature* (English Literature Society of Japan) 46 (1969): 29-44; idem, "Gower and Rime Royal," *Bulletin of the College of General Education* (Tohoku University) 12 (1971): 47-65.

42. Goetz Schmitz, *"The Middel Weie": Stil- und Aufbauformen in John Gowers "Confessio Amantis"* (Bonn: Grundmann, 1974).

43. R. F. Yeager, "'oure englisshe' and Everyone's Latin: The *Fasciculus Morum* and Gower's *Confessio Amantis*," *South Atlantic Review* 46 (1981): 41-53.

44. Judson B. Allen, *The Ethical Poetic of the Later Middle Ages: A Decorum of Convenient Distinction* (Toronto: University of Toronto Press, 1982), pp. 142ff.

45. C. S. Lewis, *The Allegory of Love* (London: Oxford University Press, 1936), especially pp. 198-222.

46. J. V. Cunningham, *Tradition and Poetic Structure: Essays in Literary History and Criticism* (Denver, Colo.: Alan Swallow, 1960), pp. 65-66.

47. John J. McNally, "The Penitential and Courtly Traditions in Gower's *Confessio Amantis*," in *Studies in Medieval Culture*, ed. John R. Sommerfeldt (Kalamazoo, Mich.: Western Michigan University Press, 1964), pp. 74-94.

48. J. A. W. Bennett, "Gower's Honeste Love,' " in *Patterns of Love and Courtesy: Essays in Memory of C. S. Lewis,* ed. John Lawlor (Evanston, Ill.: Northwestern University Press, 1966), pp. 107-21.

49. Constance Hieatt, *The Realism of Dream-Visions: The Poetic Exploitation*

of the Dream-Vision in Chaucer and His Contemporaries, De Proprietatibus Litterarum, Series Practica, 2 (The Hague: Mouton, 1967), especially pp. 47–49.

50. Walter S. Phelan, "The Conflict of Courtly Love and Christian Morality in John Gower's *Confessio Amantis*" (Ph.D. diss., Ohio State University, 1971); see also his "Beyond the Concordance: Semantic and Mythic Structures in Gower's 'Tale of Florent,' " *Neophilologus* 61 (1977): 461–99.

51. John F. Fitzpatrick, "Courtly Love and the Confessional in English Literature from 1215 to John Gower" (Ph.D. diss., Indiana University, 1978).

52. David Byrd, "Blanche Fever: The Grene Sekeness," *Ball State University Forum* 19 (1978): iii, 56–64.

53. Henry A. Kelly, *Love and Marriage in the Age of Chaucer* (Ithaca, N.Y.: Cornell University Press, 1975), pp. 121–63.

54. William A. Neilson, *The Origins of the Court of Love*, Harvard Studies and Notes in Philology and Literature, 6 (1899; reprint, New York: Russell and Russell, 1967).

55. Rosemund Tuve, *Allegorical Imagery: Some Medieval Books and Their Posterity* (Princeton, N.J.: Princeton University Press, 1966), pp. 57n, 80n, 81n, 92, 114.

56. G. R. Owst, *Literature and the Pulpit in Medieval England: A Neglected Chapter in the History of English Letters, and of the English People* (1933; 2nd rev. ed., Oxford: Blackwell, 1966), passim.

57. Edwart Weber, *Gower: zur literarischen Form seiner Dichtung* (Bad Homburg: Weber, 1966).

58. Judith Shaw, "*Confessio Amantis*: Gower's Art in Transforming His Sources into Exempla of the Seven Deadly Sins" (Ph.D. diss., University of Pennsylvania, 1977).

59. James J. Murphy, "John Gower's *Confessio Amantis* and the First Discussion of Rhetoric in the English Language," *Philological Quarterly* 41 (1962): 401–11; "A New Look at Chaucer and the Rhetoricians," *Review of English Studies*, n.s. 15 (1964): 1–20; "Rhetoric in Fourteenth-Century Oxford," *Medium Aevum* 34 (1965): 1–20.

60. Susan Gallick, "Medieval Rhetorical Arts in England and the Manuscript Tradition," *Manuscripta* 18 (1974): 67–95.

61. Patrick J. Gallacher, *Love, the Word, and Mercury: A Reading of John Gower's "Confessio Amantis"* (Albuquerque: University of New Mexico Press, 1975); see also his preliminary "The Structural Uses of the Theme of Speech in John Gower's *Confessio Amantis*" (Ph.D. diss., University of Illinois, 1966).

62. Kurt Olsson, "The Poetry of John Gower: The Art of Moral Rhetoric" (Ph.D. diss., University of Chicago, 1969).

63. John L. Mahoney, "Ovid and Medieval Courtly Love Poetry," *Classical Folia* 15 (1961): 14–27.

64. Wolfgang Clemen, *Chaucer's Early Poetry* (London: Methuen, 1963), pp. 63ff.

65. Louise Vinge, *The Narcissus Theme in Western European Literature up to the Early Nineteenth Century* (Lund: Gleerup, 1967), pp. 45ff.

66. M. L. Lord, "Dido as an Example of Chastity: The Influence of Example Literature," *Harvard Library Bulletin* 17 (January and April 1969): 22–44, 216–32.

67. Bruce Harbert, "The Myth of Tyreus in Ovid and Gower," *Medium Aevum* 41 (1972): 208–14.

68. Conrad Mainzer, "Gower's Use of the Medieval Ovid in the *Confessio Amantis*," *Medium Aevum* 41 (1972): 215–29.

69. John Fyler, *Chaucer and Ovid* (New Haven: Yale University Press, 1979), pp. 91–92.

70. Peter G. Beidler, ed., *John Gower's Literary Transformations in the "Confessio Amantis": Original Articles and Translations* (Washington, D.C.: University Press of America, 1982). The contributors, besides Beidler, are Carole Koepke Brown, Edna S. deAngeli, Patricia Innerbichler DeBellis, John B. Gaston, Douglas L. Lepley, Natalie Epinger Ruyak, Nicolette Stasko, and Karl A. Zipf, Jr. It should be noted as well that this volume contains useful translations from Thomas of Kent's *Roman de toute Chevalerie* and the *Res Gestae Alexandri Macedonis* of Julius Valerius, both of which were very likely known to Gower and may have served as sources for his "Tale of Nectanabus."

71. Shingo Yoshida, "Love and Reason in Gower's *Confessio Amantis*," *Studies in English Literature* (English Literature Society of Japan) 42 (1965): 1–11.

72. Edwart Weber, *John Gower, Dichter einer ethischpolitischen Reformation* (Bad Homburg: Weber, 1965).

73. J. Lawrence Badenyck, "The Achievement of John Gower: A Reading of the *Confessio Amantis*" (Ph.D. diss., City University of New York, 1972).

74. Derek Pearsall, *Old and Middle English Poetry*, Routledge History of English Poetry (London: Routledge and Kegan Paul, 1977), pp. 208–12, 225–26, 242–43, 296–98, and passim.

75. Siegfried Wenzel, *The Sin of Sloth: 'Acedia' in Medieval Thought and Literature* (Chapel Hill: University of North Carolina Press, 1960), pp.

117–20, 235–39, and passim.

76. M. Dominica Legge, *Anglo-Norman Literature and Its Background* (Oxford: Clarendon Press, 1963), pp. 221–23, 357–60.

77. J. A. W. Bennett, *Chaucer's Book of Fame: An Exposition of 'The House of Fame'* (Oxford: Clarendon Press, 1968), pp. 20–21, 40ff., 126–27, 152ff.

78. Beryl Rowland, *Blind Beasts: Chaucer's Animal World* (Kent, Ohio: Kent State University Press, 1971), especially pp. 19, 68, 118, 128, 131.

79. Howard Schless, "Transformations: Chaucer's Use of Italian," in *Geoffrey Chaucer*, ed. Brewer, pp. 195–96.

80. Patricia M. Kean, *Chaucer and the Making of English Poetry* (London: Routledge and Kegan Paul, 1972), pp. 196ff.

81. John A. Yunck, *The Lineage of Lady Meed: The Development of Medieval Veniality Satire* (South Bend, Indiana: University of Notre Dame Press, 1963), pp. 262–65, 298.

82. Maria Wickert, *Studies in John Gower*, trans. Robert J. Meindl (Washington, D.C.: University Press of America, 1981).

83. Masayoshi Ito, "A Midsummer Nightmare—An Interpretation of Book One of *Vox Clamantis*," *Shiron* 12 (1971): 1–16; reprinted, with slight revision, in *John Gower, the Medieval Poet*, pp. 121–38.

84. Joseph R. Keller, "The Triumph of Vice: A Formal Approach to the Medieval Complaint against the Times," *Annuale Mediaevale* 10 (1969): 120–37.

85. Christian J. W. Kloesel, "Medieval Poetics and John Gower's *Vox Clamantis*" (Ph.D. diss., University of Kansas, 1973).

86. Frederick C. Mish, "The Influence of Ovid on John Gower's *Vox Clamantis*" (Ph.D. diss., University of Minnesota, 1973).

87. Jill Mann, "Chaucer and the Medieval Latin Poets, Part B: The Satirical Tradition," in *Geoffrey Chaucer*, ed. Brewer, pp. 172–79.

88. Edwart Weber, *John Gowers Chronica Tripertita und William Shakespeares Richard II* (Bad Homburg: Weber, 1971).

89. Masayoshi Ito, "'Omnia vincit amor'—An Interpretation of Gower's *Chronica Tripertita*," *Studies in English Literature* (English Literature Society of Japan) 59 (1972): 3–15.

90. Ruth Mohl, *The Three Estates in Medieval and Renaissance Literature* (New York: Ungar, 1933), pp. 28ff., 105ff., 278–300, passim; Jill Mann, *Chaucer and Medieval Estates Satire: The Literature of Social Classes and the General Prologue to the Canterbury Tales* (Cambridge: Cambridge University Press, 1973).

91. George R. Coffman, "John Gower in His Most Significant Role," in *Elizabethan Studies and Other Essays in Honor of George F. Reynolds*, University

of Colorado Studies, Series B, II, 4 (Boulder: University of Colorado Press, 1945), pp. 52–61; see also Coffman's subsequent essay, "John Gower, Mentor for Royalty: Richard II," *PMLA* 69 (1954): 953–64.

92. John H. Fisher, "Wyclif, Langland, Gower, and the 'Pearl Poet' on the Subject of Aristocracy," *Studies in Medieval Literature in Honor of Albert Croll Baugh*, ed. MacEdward Leach (Philadelphia: University of Pennsylvania Press, 1961), pp. 139–57.

93. Arthur B. Ferguson, *The Articulate Citizen and the English Renaissance* (Durham, N.C.: Duke University Press, 1965), pp. 13–23, 44–63, 251.

94. Takero Oiji, "Wat Tyler's Rebellion and English Literature," in *Chaucer to sono shuhen* (*Chaucer and His Contemporary Poets*), ed. Takero Oiji (Tokyo: Kenkyusha, 1968), chapter 12; Albert B. Friedman, "'When Adam Delved . . .': Contexts of an Historical Proverb," in *The Learned and the Lewed: Studies in Chaucer and Medieval English Literature*, ed. Larry D. Benson, Harvard English Studies, 5 (Cambridge, Mass.: Harvard University Press, 1974), pp. 213–30; Edwart Weber, *John Gower und G. B. Shaw: Antipoden einer abendlandischen Entwicklung* (Bad Homburg: Weber, 1968).

95. Derek Brewer, *Chaucer and His World* (London: Methuen, 1978), p. 84 and passim.

96. Russell A. Peck, *Kingship and Common Profit in Gower's "Confessio Amantis"* (Carbondale and Edwardsville: University of Southern Illinois Press, 1978).

97. Paul Strohm, "Form and Social Sentiment in the *Confessio Amantis* and the *Canterbury Tales*," in *Studies in the Age of Chaucer,* ed. Roy J. Pearcy (Norman, Okla.: Pilgrim Books, for the New Chaucer Society, 1979), II, pp. 17–40.

98. Donald G. Schueler, "Some Comments on the Structure," in *Explorations*, ed. Reck.

99. James J. Foster, "The Influence of Medieval Mythography on John Gower's *Confessio Amantis*" (Ph.D. diss., Duke University, 1973).

100. Anthony Farnham, "The Art of High Prosaic Seriousness: John Gower as Didactic Raconteur," in *The Learned and the Lewed*, ed. Benson, pp. 161–73.

101. George Economou, "The Character of Genius in Alan de Lille, Jean de Meun, and John Gower," *Chaucer Review* 4 (1970): 203–10.

102. Jane Chance Nitzsche, *The Genius Figure in Antiquity and the Middle Ages* (New York: Columbia University Press, 1975), pp. 1–6, 63–65, 115–16, and especially 125–37.

103. Alice S. Miskimin, *The Renaissance Chaucer* (New Haven: Yale University Press, 1975), pp. 21ff., 230–45, 259–60, and passim.

104. Denise N. Baker, "The Priesthood of Genius: A Study of the Medieval Tradition," *Speculum* 50 (1976): 277–91.

105. D. W. Robertson, Jr., *A Preface to Chaucer: Studies in Medieval Perspectives* (Princeton, N.J.: Princeton University Press, 1962), especially pp. 276–80.

106. Donald G. Schueler, "The Age of the Lover in Gower's *Confessio Amantis*," *Medium Aevum* 36 (1967): 152–58.

107. E. Talbot Donaldson, *Speaking of Chaucer* (New York: Norton, 1970), pp. 9–10.

108. Samuel T. Cowling, "Gower's Ironic Self-Portrait in the *Confessio Amantis*," *Annuale Mediaevale* 16 (1975): 63–73; see also Cowling's doctoral thesis, "The Personages in the Major Narrative Works of John Gower" (Michigan State University, 1970).

109. Weber, *Gower: zur literarischen Form*.

110. Pamela Gradon, "John Gower and the Concept of Righteousness," *Poetica* 8 (1977): 61–71.

111. Kurt Olsson, "Natural Law and John Gower's *Confessio Amantis*," *Medievalia et Humanistica*, n.s. 11 (1982): 231–61.

112. John Burrow, *Ricardian Poetry* (London: Routledge and Kegan Paul, 1971), pp. 50–60, 73–84, 94–107, 122–40, and passim.

113. Derek Pearsall, "Courtesy and the *Gawain*-Poet," in *Patterns of Love and Courtesy*, ed. Lawlor, pp. 54–85; reprinted in *Chaucer and His Contemporaries: Essays on Medieval Literature and Thought*, ed. Helaine Newstead (Greenwich, Ct.: Fawcett, 1968), pp. 310–35.

114. Gervase Mathew, *The Court of Richard II* (New York: Norton, 1968), pp. 68–69, 74–82, 120–22, and passim.

115. Elizabeth Kirk, "Chaucer and His English Contemporaries," in *Geoffrey Chaucer: A Collection of Original Articles*, ed. George D. Economou (New York: McGraw-Hill, 1975), especially pp. 111–15.

116. Anne Middleton, "The Idea of Public Poetry in the Reign of Richard II," *Speculum* 50 (1978): 94–114.

117. Patricia Eberle, "Vision and Design in John Gower's *Confessio Amantis*" (Ph.D. diss., Harvard University, 1977).

118. Linda Barney Burke, "Women in John Gower's *Confessio Amantis*," *Mediaevalia* 3 (1977): 238–59.

# Lydgate Scholarship

## Progress and Prospects

### A. S. G. Edwards

The time seems to be slowly passing when Lydgate can be seen as a particularly arid stretch of desert interposed between the hanging gardens of Chaucer and the manicured lawns of Wyatt and Surrey. Ritson's strictures on the "voluminous, prosaick, drivelling Monk" have been astonishingly influential in moulding critical responses to Lydgate for much of the nineteenth and twentieth centuries, leaving him largely ignored by literary historians and critics. His reputation has, until recently, been in the custody of a small group of gifted editors—Eleanor Hammond, H. N. MacCracken, and H. Bergen—and a larger, much less gifted group of desperate thesis hunters.[1] Neither group has done much to encourage a balanced view of Lydgate's achievement: the former through (possibly) fatigue, the latter (in general) through incapacity.

The last quarter of a century has seen some encouraging signs of a change in attitude. There have been a variety of attempts to establish the "significance" of Lydgate, reflected in large measure in the differing approaches of the three major book-length studies by Schirmer, Renoir, and Pearsall.

Schirmer's book is subtitled *Ein Kulturbild aus dem 15. Jahrhundert*, a sufficient indication of his approach.[2] He attempts to set Lydgate in the context of his age and to account for his poetry as a product of that age. Both the strengths and weaknesses of his study derive from his attempts to define Lydgate in terms of this *Kulturbild*. He offers a useful biographical account and is particularly helpful in relating Lydgate's works to specific historical moments, particularly political ones. But the corresponding limitation on his work is his inclination to see the poems as simply products of such historical moments, and to be less than sensitive to Lydgate's verse as verse, to see it as the manifestation of particular trends and tendencies.

Specifically, Schirmer cannot resist the temptation to see Lydgate as a "transitional" figure, existing in an uneasy relationship to earlier medieval traditions and an emergent humanism; as he puts it, Lydgate is "the first tender shoots of a new literary epoch" (p. xiii). Unfortunately he never succeeds in fully defining his terms: "medieval," "transitional," and "humanism" tend to be deployed as self-referential terms that lead to a degree of circularity in Schirmer's discussion. But it remains an important book, both for its comments on particular works and for its general willingness to take Lydgate seriously.

The second book-length study, Alain Renoir's *John Lydgate: Poet of the Transition* (1967), has fewer virtues.[3] Renoir does not attempt the comprehensive survey of Lydgate's oeuvre essayed by Schirmer. He claims in his preface to be chiefly concerned with "the three great works unequivocally attributed to Lydgate: the *Troy Book*, the *Fall of Princes*, and the *Siege of Thebes*." But it remains unclear from his study whether "great" is intended to be a qualitative or a quantitative modifier. In fact, his discussion largely ignores the *Fall* (arguably the most important as well as the longest of Lydgate's poems) and is only really illuminating when it considers the *Siege of Thebes*. Most of the material in his discussion of this poem had already appeared in article form previously and gains little in contextual illumination as it is redeployed in his book.

Derek Pearsall's *John Lydgate* (1970) is a study of altogether different quality and significance.[4] It is a careful analysis of the intrinsic features of Lydgate's poetry that seeks to define and understand the characteristics of his vast corpus. His responses are generally both discriminating and sympathetic. He sees Lydgate as a poet firmly tied to tradition and convention, in particular to rhetorical traditions of amplification, and to a view of versification generally favored by his contemporaries who saw prolixity and overt didacticism as virtues. These qualities are often realized through Lydgate's emulation of the work of his "master," Chaucer. Many of Lydgate's poetic characteristics can be shown to be systematizations and elaborations of Chaucerian techniques, both stylistic and metrical.

These perceptions form a sensible corrective to earlier gestures toward a vague historicism. They are securely rooted in a careful reading of the vast bulk of Lydgate's corpus. This reading also enables Pearsall to comment perceptively on the merits of a surprising amount of Lydgate's verse when it is approached neither through historicist defensiveness nor through a dismissive modernism sensitized only to more recent literary virtues of compression and indirection. His accounts of the *Troy Book* and the *Siege of Thebes* relate them convincingly to Lydgate's attempts to place himself within a Chaucerian tradition, reworking and elaborating what Chaucer himself had created in ways that invite interest, sympathy, and (surprisingly often) praise. The real power of much of Lydgate's religious verse is demonstrated, as are the qualities of many of his shorter poems. But more important perhaps than any particular analysis is Pearsall's demonstration of the possibility of careful literary analysis of Lydgate, provided that it is undertaken in terms of his own apparent purposes, not the ones we might wish him to have had. Pearsall provides a standard for Lydgate criticism that few have been able to match.

There have been disappointingly few other general examinations of Lydgate. Pearsall's other studies are largely either anticipations or recapitulations of aspects of the argument of his book, deployed for different purposes.[5] Richard Firth Green has some scattered but sensible observations in his study of literature and the court in the later Middle Ages.[6] In addition, there have been one or two studies of particular aspects of Lydgate's oeuvre: C. Dedeyan has examined his allusions to Dante; Elizabeth Walsh has written on his treatment of the image of the tiger; and Renoir and Edwards have offered sharply divergent views of his attitudes to women.[7] One or two other pieces of research have proved more rewarding. Johnstone Parr in a helpful study has redated the *Siege of Thebes* (ca. 1421) and the *Title and Pedigree of Henry VI* (ca. 1426) on astronomical grounds and shown the implausibility of astronomical evidence for dating the *Temple of Glass* and *Troy Book*.[8] The recent exemplary bibliography by Renoir and C. David Benson has provided an admirable overview of all aspects of Lydgate scholarship.[9]

There has also been a paucity of editorial work on Lydgate. This is particularly regrettable since most of his texts are in need of some form of reassessment, if only to take account of new manuscripts that have come to light. Most of them would benefit from commentary volumes that give fuller annotation than generally exists. Indeed, in some cases, particularly the two Early English Text Society volumes of the *Minor Poems* (1911 and 1934), we have no commentary or annotation at all.

The most distinguished recent contribution to the editing of Lydgate has come from John Norton-Smith in his selected works for the Clarendon Medieval and Tudor series. He provides new editions of several of Lydgate's shorter works, particularly the *Temple of Glass* and the *Complaint of a Lover's Life*, with informed (if at times gratuitously erudite) commentary.[10] The limitations of his edition lie in the nature of his undertaking rather than his execution of it. The attempt to provide in about 3,400 lines a fair representation of Lydgate's total output of nearly 148,000 is an impossible task. What Norton-Smith offers is, in effect, a presentation of Lydgate as court poet and occasional versifier, with only very brief selections from the major religious and secular works that constitute the bulk of his oeuvre. One is simultaneously grateful for what is here in an impeccably edited form and sympathetic to the circumstances that underlay his selections. But the result is a misleading picture of Lydgate's career through a distortion of the nature of his corpus.

Other editions in recent times have been less successful in execution. Beverly Boyd has produced an edition of the *Legend of Dan Joos*, chiefly of value for some brief discussion of Lydgate's sources.[11] The two editions that have appeared of Lydgate's major saints' lives, the *Life of Our Lady* and the *Lives of Saint Alban and Saint Amphibel*, have serious limitations.[12]

Of the *Life of Our Lady* it is perhaps best not to say too much. A collaborative effort, the editors apparently failed to reach an accord on some basic matters. Thus the first two books are virtually without punctuation, while the remaining three have varying degrees of modern punctuation. There are no textual notes, and the commentary is at times more perfunctory than matters warrant. J. E. van der Westhuizen's edition of *Alban and Amphibel* has similar weaknesses. The reediting of much of Lydgate out of a clearer understanding of his versification, poetic conventions, and sources is a prime desideratum of fifteenth-century studies.

As for specific poems, all three of Lydgate's major works, the *Troy Book*, the *Siege of Thebes*, and the *Fall of Princes*, have received some useful study. The most extensive examination of the *Troy Book* has been in C. David Benson's *The History of Troy in Middle English Literature*, which has a chapter on Lydgate's poem (parts of which are adapted from earlier journal articles).[13] Like Pearsall, Benson stresses the importance of rhetorical amplification as a principle of Lydgatean technique. He also points to the importance of Chaucer in establishing the poem's tone and historical perspective. The great strength of Benson's study is that it is based on a careful comparison of Lydgate's poem with his major source, Guido delle Colonna. He is able to show that Lydgate's fidelity as translator is not slavish and uncritical. He attempts to mitigate, for instance, Guido's profound pessimism and makes additions that seek to offer more optimistic and practical perspectives, even if they are at odds with the "matter" of his source. Benson's claims for the overall unity and poetic quality of the *Troy Book* are sensibly limited, but he does establish a convincing case for Lydgate's "solid craftsmanship" and increases our understanding of some of the principles underlying that craftsmanship.

Benson concludes his discussion rather oddly by reproducing an earlier study of Lydgate's use of Christine de Pisan's *Epistre d'Othea* in the *Troy Book*. While this study adds little to his argument, it is one of several useful examinations of the minor sources of the poem supplementing the earlier work of E. B. Atwood.[14] R. A. Dwyer has pointed to Lydgate's evident use of Trevisa's translation of the *Polychronicon* both here and in the *Fall of Princes*.[15] And McKay Sundwall has suggested that Lydgate's adaptation of Chaucer's *Troilus and Criseyde* was itself adapted and "pared down" in the later *Destruction of Troy*—an interesting instance of the role Lydgate seems often to have played in the transmission and understanding of Chaucer in the later Middle Ages.[16] Gretchen Mieszkowski makes some perceptive comparisons between Lydgate's and Chaucer's treatment of Criseyde.[17]

There have been one or two brief bibliographical studies. Pearsall has investigated the provenance of Trinity College, Cambridge MS. 0.5.2., which contains the *Troy Book* and the *Siege of Thebes*.[18] C. van Buuren-Veenenbos has shown that parts of Bodleian Library MS. Douce 148 were written by John Asloan, the scribe of the Asloan manuscript.[19] But much more profitable codicological analysis could be made of the manuscripts of the *Troy Book*, particularly in terms of their illumination and illustration. Examination of the elaborate programs of decoration in such manuscripts as British Library MS. Cotton Augustus A. IV and Bristol Public Library MS. and Bodleian MS. Digby 232 might help us to understand more about the centers of production for such sumptuous copies, as would related efforts to identify the scribes who wrote them. One or two promising starts have been made by Gareth Spriggs, Kathleen Scott, and J. J. G. Alexander, who have all linked various copies of the *Troy Book* (as well as other Lydgate manuscripts) to identifiable ateliers.[20] But there is still abundant scope for further research in this area.

The influence of the *Troy Book*, particularly on Elizabethan literature, has prompted some enquiries. Ethel Seaton has shown that Marlowe read it with care.[21] It was probably used in *The Lamentation of Troy for the Death of Hector*, as E. C. Wilson suggests in his edition.[22] Less convincing are K. M. Merritt's attempts to suggest it as a source for John Pikeryng's *Horestes*; the evidence of parallel commonplaces that is presented does not constitute a compelling case for the influence of Lydgate's poem.[23] Mieszkowski has argued for its influence on Henryson's *Testament of Cressid*.[24]

Lydgate's *Siege of Thebes* was seen by medieval compilers as a companion piece to the *Troy Book* and a continuation of Chaucer's *Canterbury Tales*, as well as an independent poem. Both Renoir and Pearsall have commented on the implications of the conjunction of Troy and Thebes in medieval literature and its relevance to Lydgate. Renoir has identified Lydgate's immediate source as a prose version of the *Roman de Thebes* very similar to the *Roman de Edipus*.[25] But we are indebted to Lois Ebin for the most extensive discussion of the relationship between Chaucer and Lydgate in the *Siege*.[26] She initially examines Lydgate's poetic terminology (especially such terms as "rhetoric" and "eloquence") in terms of their relationship to Chaucer's and Lydgate's own innovative concerns. The Amphion legend in the *Siege of Thebes* is then seen as an exemplification of Lydgate's views on the function of the poet: a harmonizing role deriving from his capacity to create order out of chaos through his work. Lydgate's treatment of Amphion dramatizes this aspect of his concern, and his way of developing it differentiates his style from Chaucer's through its emphasis on amplification, on style, and on ornament. Her later study, "Chaucer, Lydgate, and the Myrie Tale," makes substantially the same point.[27] Both provide helpful considerations of the important question of Lydgate's relationship to Chaucer in the *Siege of Thebes*.

Apart from the writings of Renoir and Pearsall the most valuable contribution to criticism of the *Siege of Thebes* itself has come from Robert W. Ayers.[28] He has argued convincingly for the poem's fundamental unity in terms of a coherent moral design. Lydgate is writing (he contends) exemplary history in which plot and character are subordinated to and organized around the constraints of his formal purpose. This is a helpful, pioneering study, establishing a valid unifying principle for an interesting and important poem.

Other critical studies have been more limited in scope. Renoir has argued for the influence of Chaucerian nomenclature on the poem.[29] Johnstone Parr, in another study of Lydgate's astronomy, has examined Oedipus's horoscope, complaining that the poet "exhibited little insight into the darker and more intricate mysteries of genethliac astrology."[30] Joseph Marotta, like Ebin, explores the thematic importance of the figure of Amphion, who becomes "a mythic image for the power of eloquence" and, as such, central to the poem's meaning.[31]

Both Ebin and Marotta link their discussions of the figure of Amphion to Lydgate's treatment of him in Book VI of the *Fall of Princes*. But their work apart, the main interest in Lydgate's longest poem has been either in its sources or in bibliographical studies. R. A. Dwyer has examined Lydgate's treatment of King Arthur in Book VII, showing his debt to both Bartholomaeus Anglicus's *De Proprietatibus Rerum* and Boethius's *Consolatio*.[32] He had earlier shown Lydgate's use of Trevisa's *Polychronicon* in this poem. Susan Schibanoff has shown the use of Coluccio Salutati in Book I.[33] But study of the poem itself has languished, apart from the work of T. Kurose, who has examined the figure of Fortune at a length disproportionate to the significance of his conclusion that Lydgate's presentation of this figure is unsympathetic.[34] Edwards has briefly examined the poem's posthumous importance and influence in a variety of fifteenth- and sixteenth-century writings, and he has also written a few notes on various manuscripts of the poem.[35]

The vast bulk of the *Fall of Princes* has left it largely inviolate against critical and scholarly enquiry. This is a pity because there are a number of questions about the poem that need answering. The circumstances of its composition are still unclear in important particulars: to what extent was it influenced by Duke Humphrey's library of humanist texts, and by Duke Humphrey himself? How much of it was composed before Lydgate's return to Bury in 1432, "propter melioris vitae captandam"? What are the implications of the identification by Edwards of two distinct versions of the poem, one produced by an early scribe specializing in *de luxe* copies of his works?[36] Such historical problems have important bearing on our understanding of the *Fall*. It would also be of great interest to know more about Lydgate's techniques as translator of Laurent de Premierfait's prose version of Boccaccio's *De Casibus*; at present we are still dependent on the superficial study of Patricia Gathercole.[37]

There has been some interest in Lydgate's major saints' lives. As I have already noted, two of them, *The Life of Our Lady* and the *Lives of Saint Alban and Saint Amphibel*, have been reedited in modern times. In addition, another edition of the latter work (by George Reinecke) should appear shortly.[38] The third of Lydgate's lengthy verse hagiographies, the *Lives of Saint Edmund and Saint Fremund*, has not been reedited since Horstmann's 1881 edition, although an edition is projected by J. I. Miller based on his 1967 Harvard dissertation.[39]

As a preliminary to his edition, Miller has published several studies. His "Literature to History: Exploring a Medieval Saint's Legend and Its Context" defines the tradition of veneration of Saint Edmund in English medieval writings and relates it to Lydgate's poem.[40] In a later study he makes a careful case for Lydgate's skill as a "conscious literary artist . . . in design and control."[41] He has also, in collaboration with A. S. G. Edwards, studied the activities of the antiquary John Stow in transcribing and annotating manuscripts of this poem.[42]

But by far the most important article on this poem—indeed, a major contribution to fifteenth-century English codicology—is Kathleen Scott's discovery and identification of a new manuscript in Arundel Castle.[43] The manuscript contains fifty miniatures and can be linked to programs of decoration found in other manuscripts of *Saint Edmund*, particularly MS. Yates Thomson 47 and also the even more sumptuous MS. Harley 2278. Scott is also able to identify the scribal hand as that which produced a number of other *de luxe* copies of Lydgate's poems. Her researches afford important insight into the circulation and contemporary status of Lydgate's poem and provide a model for future studies of his manuscripts.

The *Lives of Saint Alban and Saint Amphibel* have received rather less attention. W. McLeod has offered an analysis of Lydgate's source, demonstrating its derivation from a late fourteenth- or early fifteenth-century lost Latin compilation.[44] Renoir has a brief note on the survival of an oral-formulaic theme in one passage.[45] There is, however, little other specific commentary or analysis. It would be of considerable value to know more about Lydgate's treatment of his source material, for example, and about the provenance and circulation of the poem's manuscripts. Can the latter be linked at all with Saint Albans, where Abbot Whethamstede commissioned the poem? Can it be linked by style or technique to Lydgate's earlier celebration of an East Anglian martyr? In these terms, at least, *Alban and Amphibel* deserve greater examination, even if the conclusions are unlikely to change the received critical view of the poem as a piece of uninspired hack work.

In contrast, while all have been united in their praise of Lydgate's earliest major saint's life, *The Life of Our Lady*, few have been moved to analyze or demonstrate its intrinsic merits. Pearsall has a sensitive analysis, and Norton-Smith makes some brief and suggestive comments in his selections, but there is little indication of other critical interest apart from an article by J. A. Lauritis.[46] The most significant item is Johnstone Parr's redating of the poem: on astronomical evidence he places it ca. 1415–16, rather than 1421–22 or post-1434, as Lauritis and Norton-Smith, respectively, have claimed.[47]

Other studies have been mainly textual. R. A. Klinefelter has argued that MS. Chetham 6709 was copied from the Caxton print.[48] Rossell Hope Robbins printed a fragment from a manuscript in Trinity College, Dublin,[49] and H. G. Jones, A. S. G. Edwards, and A. W. Jenkins have printed fragments of the same manuscript, one of which is in the University of Missouri Library, the others in Cambridge University Library.[50] Karl Reichl has pointed to the possible influence of the *Life of Our Lady* on a later verse life of the virgin which he has edited from Cambridge University Library MS. Add. 4122.[51]

But Lydgate's saints' lives have received little more broadly based generic or stylistic study in spite of the merits some of them have been shown to possess. The only general study is by Theodor Wolpers, who has examined the *Life of Saint Margaret*, the *Life of Saint George*, and the *Lives of Saints Edmund and Fremund* in the course of a broader survey of saints' lives.[52] But the historical importance of Lydgate's contributions to the genre has been largely ignored.

Lydgate's shorter religious poems have fared even less well. There have been few significant studies. The best is Rosemary Woolf's brief and incisive commentary on Lydgate's use of the *imago pietatis* in some of his religious lyrics.[53] J. B. Trapp has also done helpful work on this aspect of Lydgate's art by printing and discussing verses painted in the Clopton Chantry of Holy Trinity Church, Long Melford, from his *Testament* and translation of "Quis dabit meo capiti fontem lacrimarum."[54] Isabel Hyde has pointed to Lydgate's use of Alain of Lille in his *Ballade at the Reverence of Our Lady* and shown how his translational techniques enable an understanding of the basis of his "aureate" style.[55] Beverly Boyd has discussed *Dan Joos* in some detail in her "Literary Background to Lydgate's *Dan Joos.*"[56] It is surprising that the shorter religious poems have not been studied with more care. They need far fuller commentary than they have received, and the studies noted above suggest that such commentary can be rewarding. Further research might also enable us to arrive at a firmer sense of the influence of Lydgate's religious verse. Articles by Beck and Leach have noted the continued use of his imagery as late as the poetry of Herbert and Donne.[57]

Among Lydgate's secular poems the *Temple of Glass*, Lydgate's longest and most enigmatic dream vision, has been the subject of some scrutiny, particularly by John Norton-Smith.[58] His fine edition is based upon a careful study of the extant manuscripts, which differentiates several stages in the growth of the poem from early draft to final version. Once again, a study of the manuscript evidence yields fruitful results and a clearer appreciation of the quality of Lydgate's craftsmanship. Further evidence of the benefit of careful manuscript study has been demonstrated by David Fallows, who traces a text in an Escorial chansonnier of probable Neapolitan origin back to lines from the *Temple*.[59] Janet Wilson has carefully analyzed the poem, suggesting that it shows a "deflation of the courtly love ideal" and a "growth of realism" that may have been dictated by the poem's audience of "rising bourgeoisie." A. C. Spearing has examined the poem in terms of its relationship to Chaucer.[60] The value of Alice Miskimin's study of the *Kingis Quair* and the *Temple of Glass* is less easy to determine.[61] She argues that the *Temple* is a work built on "numerical decorum," organized around the significances of the number seven. Her argument, which is presented rather perfunctorily, to my mind lacks convincing evidential force and logical necessity. The aberrations of Ethel Seaton (see below) and the inevitable uncertainties of the surviving manuscript tradition ought to be sufficient caution against enquiries that seek to impose a preconceived, mathematical order on medieval poems.

Some of the shorter secular poems have received more attention recently and have demonstrated that they justify it. Lydgate's mummings have been carefully studied by Glynne Wickham, who has shown their importance in the evolution of the drama as transitional works looking forward to Tudor dramatic experiments.[62] This question is also explored by P. H. Parry.[63] The date of one of the mummings, the Mumming at Hertford, has been disputed by Renoir and Green, the latter making the more convincing case for a date of ca. 1426–27, rather than 1430.[64] W. A. Davenport discusses Lydgate in the context of East Anglian fifteenth-century drama.[65]

The question of the milieu of Lydgate's poetry has produced a number of substantial studies. J. W. McKenna has examined *The Title and Pedigree of Henry VI* as an aspect of Henry VI's propaganda in support of his claim to the kingdom of France, linking it to other contemporary manifestations in art and numismatology in the same vein.[66] V. J. Scattergood's *Politics and Poetry in the Fifteenth Century* contains a number of helpful observations on the historical context of various of Lydgate's poems.[67] Henry Hargreaves has studied some of the texts of *A Ram's Horn* and shows how the poem was transmitted from a courtly milieu "to entertain a more popular audience."[68] And David Lampe has perceived a hitherto-unremarked degree of originality in the *Horse, Sheep, and Goose* in the manipulation and ambiguity that commonplace elements acquire in Lydgate's hands.[69] These studies are important, particularly those by McKenna and Hargreaves, in that they examine manuscript evidence and contexts to arrive at a clearer sense of the ways in which Lydgate was perceived and adapted by his contemporaries. They point to a profitable and underexplored line of enquiry in Lydgate studies. Recently Renoir has perceived some of the obvious potential for such study in the multifarious versions of the "Verses on the Kings of England," as he has examined the principles of development of the unique "third" recension.[70]

It is curious that while so many of Lydgate's shorter poems have been ignored, his only prose work, the brief *Serpent of Division*, should have been the subject of a helpful study by Margaret Schlauch in which she carefully examines its "stylistic attributes."[71] She pays particular attention to such features as doublets and rhetorical amplification, concluding that Lydgate had been "a diligent student of rhetoric" but that his "heightened style" is marked by some apparently individual features. (This accords broadly with

Pearsall's sense of rhetoric in Lydgate's poetry.) In the only other modern study of this work, William Ringler briefly and convincingly explores the relationship of several of the printed editions, suggesting that the Rogers edition may have been edited by the ubiquitous John Stow.[72] It is a matter for regret that MacCracken's exemplary 1911 edition of this work has never been reprinted.[73]

Lydgate's prosody has been reassessed on several occasions recently, with varying results but generally similar conclusions. The point has been made more than once that his verse has, in the past, been either attacked or regularized to make it conform to eighteenth-century notions of metrical regularity, notions that have little or no applicability to verse of other periods, especially medieval verse. Even so, the highly schematic categorizations of Josef Schick in the nineteenth century have continued to find supporters.[74] Pearsall has argued for the general validity of Schick's five types of Lydgatean line, but others have sought to see him as a careful metrist who possesses a greater degree of flexibility than has previously been perceived. Mahmoud A. Manzalaoui has sought to reconcile Schick's views with C. S. Lewis's theory of irregular stress.[75] Lydgate becomes "the Chaucerian who emphasized the 'relaxed' element in Chaucerian versification."

Dudley Hascall has also emphasized Lydgate's debt to Chaucer, arguing that "if Lydgate reasoned that all the master had done was permitted by the disciple, we have an explanation for his poetic practice."[76] He attempts to demonstrate this view through a flexible application of Halle's and Keyser's theory of Chaucer's prosody.[77] Ian Robinson is rather less sympathetic. He sees Lydgate more straightforwardly as a "writer of bad verse," "a competent hack," and "rather a stupid writer."[78] These deficiencies are, he argues, due to Lydgate's misuse of Chaucer through a mechanical application of Chaucerian techniques. At the Leavisite nub of Robinson's argument is the indictment of Lydgate for creating a "barrier between himself and life." It might be more fair to say that Lydgate's sense of "life" and its relationship to verse, which was sufficiently broad to encompass treatises to laundresses and dietary tracts, is hardly reconcilable with any Leavisite formulation.

The problem with these positions—with the partial exception of Robinson's—is that there is an element of circularity underlying them. They attempt to discuss Lydgate in terms of texts that have already been edited (presumably) according to some notion of Lydgate's versification. They work not from the manuscripts but from more or less established texts. Without systematic study of all the most authoritative manuscripts it is hardly possible, and not terribly profitable, to formulate securely based arguments about Lydgate's versification.

As I have already noted, there have been other studies of the influence of specific poems, but we still lack any broad assessment of the influence of the Lydgate tradition on fifteenth- and sixteenth-century literature. Thus Gregory Kratzmann in his otherwise suggestive study of Anglo-Scottish literary relations ignores Lydgate's influence in spite of the evidence gathered by P. H. Nichols and R. D. S. Jack of his importance as a stylistic model to Dunbar.[79] He also ignores other evidence of the ownership, copying, and literary use of Lydgate's works in Scotland during this period. A more promising start on the question of Lydgate's influence on English literature has been made by Alice Miskimin in *The Renaissance Chaucer*.[80] Unfortunately her comments are brief (Lydgate is not the main concern of her book) and unsympathetic. I suspect that a more extended study would establish that such works as the *Temple of Glass* and the *Fall of Princes* were much more pervasive transmitters of models of style and diction than has been appreciated. Indeed, a careful study of the provenance and ownership of Lydgate manuscripts might well establish that he was read by a far broader social spectrum than was Chaucer.

The question of Lydgate's influence is obviously closely involved with the determination of his canon. Modern work on this problem has been sketchy, probably because of a disinclination to linger overlong contemplating Ethel Seaton's *Sir Richard Roos*.[81] In this lengthy study Seaton reapportions the canon of later medieval English literature, claiming for Roos, otherwise known only as the author of a translation of *La Belle Dame sans Merci*, large chunks of the oeuvres of Lydgate, Chaucer, Wyatt, and Surrey, among others. Much of this work of reattribution is based on very dubious cryptanalytic criteria. This is particularly unfortunate, since a responsible reassessment of the canon is urgently needed. We still rely on MacCracken's 1910 study to provide criteria for canonicity.

Increasingly there have been signs of discontent with MacCracken's formulations. Some of these have been quite minor (see the articles by Edwards in *English Studies* [1970] and Edwards and Jenkins in *Medieval Studies* [1973]).[82] More significant are the questions raised by Kathryn Walls about the *Pelerinage de la Vie Humaine*, which have not altogether been resolved by Richard Firth Green's efforts to rebut her arguments.[83] M. C. Seymour has manifested some doubts about the canonicity of the *Serpent of Division*,[84] and recently Gail Gibson has suggested that Lydgate may have been involved in the composition of the N. Town cycle.[85] Other works remain lodged uneasily in the interstices of the canon. *Reason and Sensuality* is the longest of these problem pieces, for which we are solely dependent on the attribution of the sixteenth-century antiquary John Stow. The latest account of the canon, in the revised Wells *Manual*, includes at least thirty-five items, among the two hundred associated with Lydgate, whose authorship is for some reason doubtful—and this list could well be extended. For example, the Wells *Manual* does not include at all the *Holy Meditation*, a poem whose merit inspired strenuous efforts in the 1930s to prove it was Chaucer's. In addition, several of the items I have noted above are not included.

Clearly, though Lydgate research has made some important advances during the last twenty-five years, there is still much to be done. I have tried to indicate some of the directions new research can profitably take and some of the strengths and weaknesses of recent activity. There is in Lydgate's vast oeuvre a great deal of unexplored or undeveloped territory. I hope what I have written may encourage others to devote their energies to exploring and developing it. The multifarious activities of Lydgate's prolix genius may prove most rewarding.

# Notes

1. Henry Noble MacCracken, ed., *The Minor Poems of John Lydgate*, 2 vols., Early English Text Society, ES 107, OS 192 (London, 1911 for 1910 and 1934); Henry Bergen, ed., *Lydgate's Fall of Princes*, 4 vols. (Washington, D.C.: The Carnegie Institution of Washington, 1923-27), and also Early English Text Society, ES 121-24 (London, 1924-27); Eleanor P. Hammond, "*English Verse between Chaucer and Surrey* (Durham, N.C.: Duke University Press, 1927).

2. Walter F. Schirmer, *John Lydgate: Ein Kulturbild aus dem 15. Jahrhundert* (Tübingen: Niemeyer, 1952); trans. Ann E. Keep, as *John Lydgate: A Study of the Culture of the XVth Century* (London: Methuen, 1961).

3. Alain Renoir, *John Lydgate: Poet of the Transition* (London: Routledge and Kegan Paul, 1967).

4. Derek Pearsall, *John Lydgate* (London: Routledge and Kegan Paul, 1970).

5. See his discussions in "The English Chaucerians," in *Chaucer and Chaucerians*, ed. Derek Brewer (London: Nelson, 1966), pp. 201-39, and in his *Old and Middle English Poetry* (London: Routledge and Kegan Paul, 1977),

pp. 226-36.

6. Richard Firth Green, *Poets and Princepleasers* (Toronto: University of Toronto Press, 1980).

7. C. Dedeyan, "Dante en Angleterre: John Lydgate," *Lettres Romanes* 13 (1959): 179-84; Elizabeth Walsh, "John Lydgate and the Proverbial Tiger," in *The Learned and the Lewed*, ed. Larry D. Benson (Cambridge, Mass.: Harvard University Press, 1974), pp. 291-303; Alain Renoir, "Attitudes to Women in Lydgate's Poetry," *English Studies* 42 (1961): 1-14; A. S. G. Edwards, "A Note on Lydgate's Attitude to Women," *English Studies* 51 (1970): 436-37.

8. Johnstone Parr, "Astronomical Dating for Some of Lydgate's Poems," *PMLA* 67 (1952): 251-58.

9. Alain Renoir and C. David Benson, "John Lydgate," in *A Manual of the Writings in Middle English, 1050-1500*, ed. Albert E. Hartung (Hamden, Ct.: Archon Books/The Shoe String Press for The Connecticut Academy of Arts and Sciences, 1980), VI, pp. 1809-1920, 2071-2175.

10. John Norton-Smith, ed., *John Lydgate: Poems* (Oxford: Clarendon Press, 1966).

11. Beverly Boyd, ed., *The Middle English Miracles of the Virgin* (San Marino, Calif.: Huntington Library, 1964).

12. *A Critical Edition of John Lydgate's Life of Our Lady*, ed. Joseph A. Lauritis, Ralph A. Klinefelter, and Vernon F. Gallagher (Pittsburgh, Pa.: Duquesne University Press, 1961); *The Life of Saint Alban and Saint Amphibal*, ed. J. E. van der Westhuizen (Leiden: E. J. Brill, 1974).

13. C. David Benson, *The History of Troy in Middle English Literature* (Ipswich: D. S. Brewer, 1980), pp. 97-129; see also Benson's "The Ancient World of John Lydgate's *Troy Book*," *American Benedictine Review* 24 (1973): 299-312.

14. C. David Benson, "Prudence, Othea, and Lydgate's Death of Hector," *American Benedictine Review* 26 (1975): 115-23; E. B. Atwood, "Some Minor Sources of Lydgate's *Troy Book*," *Studies in Philology* 35 (1938): 25-42.

15. R. A. Dwyer, "Some Readers of John of Trevisa," *Notes and Queries* 212 (1967): 291-92.

16. McKay Sundwall, "The Destruction of Troy, Chaucer's *Troilus and Criseyde*, and Lydgate's *Troy Book*," *Review of English Studies*, n.s. 26 (1975): 313-17.

17. Gretchen Mieszkowski, "The Reputation of Criseyde, 1155-1500," *Transactions of the Connecticut Academy of Arts and Sciences* 43 (1971): 71-153.

18. Derek Pearsall, "Notes on the Manuscript of *Generydes*," *The Library*,

5th series, 16 (1961): 205-10.

19. C. van Buuren-Veenenbos, "John Asloan, an Edinburgh Scribe," *English Studies* 47 (1966): 234-41.

20. Gareth Spriggs, "Unnoticed Bodleian Manuscripts, Illuminated by Herman Scheerre and His School," *Bodleian Library Record* 7 (1962-67): 193-203; Kathleen Scott, "A Mid-Fifteenth Century English Illuminating Shop and Its Customers," *Journal of the Warburg and Courtauld Institutes* 31 (1968): 170-96; Jonathan J. G. Alexander, "William Abell 'lymnour' and 15th-Century English Illumination," in *Kunsthistorische Forschungen*, ed. A. Rosenauer and G. Weber (Salzburg: Residentz Verlag, 1972), pp. 166-72.

21. Ethel Seaton, "Marlowe's Light Reading," in *Elizabethan and Jacobean Studies Presented to Frank Percy Wilson* (London: Oxford University Press, 1959), pp. 28-33.

22. E. C. Wilson, *The Lamentation of Troy for the Death of Hector* (Chicago: Institute of Elizabethan Studies, 1959).

23. K. M. Merritt, "The Sources of John Pikeryng's *Horestes*," *Review of English Studies*, n.s. 23 (1972): 255-66.

24. Mieszkowski, "Reputation of Criseyde," p. 142.

25. Alain Renoir, "The Immediate Source of Lydgate's *Siege of Thebes*," *Studia Neophilologica* 33 (1961): 249-56.

26. Lois Ebin, "Lydgate's Views on Poetry," *Annuale Medievale* 18 (1977): 76-105.

27. Lois Ebin, "Chaucer, Lydgate, and the Myrie Tale," *Chaucer Review* 13 (1979): 316-36.

28. Robert W. Ayers, "Medieval History, Moral Purpose and the Structure of Lydgate's *Siege of Thebes*," *PMLA* 73 (1958): 463-74.

29. Alain Renoir, "Chaucerian Character Names in Lydgate's *Siege of Thebes*," *Modern Language Notes* 71 (1956): 249-56.

30. Johnstone Parr, "The Horoscope of Edippus in Lydgate's *Siege of Thebes*," in *Essays in Honour of Walter Clyde Curry* (Nashville, Tenn.: Vanderbilt University Press, 1954), pp. 117-22.

31. Joseph Marotta, "Amphion: The Hero as Rhetorician," *Centrepoint* 2 (1977): 63-71.

32. R. A. Dwyer, "Arthur's Stellification in the *Fall of Princes*," *Philological Quarterly* 57 (1979): 155-71.

33. Susan Schibanoff, "Avarice and Cerberus in Coluccio Salutati's *De Laboribus Herculis* and Lydgate's *Fall of Princes*," *Modern Philology* 71 (1974): 390-92.

34. T. Kurose, "Notes on John Lydgate's Character—Drawings of the Goddess Fortune in the *Fall of Princes*," *Studies in English Literature* (English

Literature Society of Japan), English number (1975): 79–100.

35. A. S. G. Edwards, "The Influence of Lydgate's *Fall of Princes*: A Survey," *Mediaeval Studies* 39 (1977): 424–39. See also his "Selections from Lydgate's *Fall of Princes*: A Checklist," *The Library*, 5th series, 26 (1971): 337–42; "The Huntington *Fall of Princes* and Sloane 2452," *Manuscripta* 16 (1972): 37–40; "Lydgate's *Fall of Princes*: A 'Lost' Manuscript Found," *Manuscripta* 22 (1978): 176–78.

36. A. S. G. Edwards, "The McGill Fragment of Lydgate's *Fall of Princes*," *Scriptorium* 28 (1974): 75–77.

37. Patricia Gathercole, "Lydgate's *Fall of Princes* and the French Version of Boccaccio's *De Casibus*," in *Miscellanea di Studi e Richerche sul Quattrocento francese*, ed. F. Simone (Turin: Giappichelli, 1966), pp. 167–78.

38. Currently, see George Reinecke, "Saint Alban and Saint Amphibalus: An Edition" (Ph.D. diss., Harvard University, 1960).

39. James I. Miller, "John Lydgate's Saint Edmund and Fremund: An Annotated Edition" (Ph.D. diss., Harvard University, 1967).

40. James I. Miller, "Literature to History: Exploring a Medieval Saint's Legend and Its Context," in *Literature and History*, ed. I. E. Cadenhead, Jr., Tulsa Monograph Series, 9 (Tulsa, Ok.: University of Tulsa Press, 1970), pp. 59–72.

41. James I. Miller, "Lydgate the Hagiographer as Literary Artist," in *The Learned and the Lewed*, ed. Benson, pp. 279–90.

42. A. S. G. Edwards and James I. Miller, "Stow and Lydgate's *St. Edmund*," *Notes and Queries* 218 (1973): 365–69.

43. Kathleen Scott, "Lydgate's Lives of Saints Edmund and Fremund: A Newly Located Manuscript in Arundel Castle," *Viator* 13 (1982): 335–66.

44. W. McLeod, "Alban and Amphibal: Some Extant Lives and a Lost Life," *Mediaeval Studies* 42 (1980): 407–30.

45. Alain Renoir, "Crist Ihesu's Beasts of Battle: A Note on Oral Formulaic Theme Survival," *Neophilologus* 60 (1976): 455–59.

46. J. A. Lauritis, "Second Thoughts on Style in Lydgate's *Life of Our Lady*," in *Essays and Studies in Language and Literature*, ed. H. H. Petit (Pittsburgh, Pa.: Duquesne University Press, 1964), pp. 12–23.

47. Johnstone Parr, "The Astronomical Date of Lydgate's *Life of Our Lady*," *Philological Quarterly* 50 (1971): 120–25.

48. R. A. Klinefelter, "Lydgate's *Life of Our Lady* and the Chetham MS. 6709," *Papers of the Bibliographical Society of America* 46 (1952): 396–97.

49. Rossell Hope Robbins, "A New Lydgate Fragment," *English Language Notes* 5 (1968): 243–47.

50. H. G. Jones, III, "An Unedited Manuscript of John Lydgate's *Life of Our Lady*: Book V, Verses 344–64 and 372–92," *English Language Notes* 7

(1969): 93–96; A. S. G. Edwards and A. W. Jenkins, "A Hymn to the Virgin: by Lydgate?" *Mediaeval Studies* 35 (1973): 60–66. See also Edwards and Jenkins, "Lydgate's *Life of Our Lady*: An Unedited Manuscript of Part of Book III," *English Language Notes* 9 (1971): 1–3.

51. Karl Reichl, "Ein Mittelenglisches Marienleben aus der MS. Add. 4122 der University Library in Cambridge," *Anglia* 95 (1977): 313–58.

52. Theodor Wolpers, *Die Englische Heiligenlegende des Mittelalters* (Tübingen: Niemeyer, 1964), pp. 308–22.

53. Rosemary Woolf, *The English Religious Lyric in the Middle Ages* (Oxford: Clarendon Press, 1968), pp. 198–210.

54. J. B. Trapp, "Verses by Lydgate at Long Melford," *Review of English Studies*, n.s. 6 (1955): 1–11.

55. Isabel Hyde, "Lydgate's 'halff chongyd latyne:' An Illustration," *Modern Language Notes* 70 (1955): 252–54.

56. Beverly Boyd, "The Literary Background to Lydgate's *Dan Joos*," *Modern Language Notes* 72 (1957): 81–87.

57. R. Beck, "A Precedent for Donne's Imagery in 'Good Friday, 1613. Riding Westward,'" *Review of English Studies*, n.s. 19 (1968): 166–69; E. Leach, "Lydgate's *Dolorous Pyte of Crystes Passioun* and George Herbert's *The Sacrifice*," *Notes and Queries* 205 (1960): 421.

58. John Norton-Smith, "Lydgate's Changes in the *Temple of Glas*," *Medium Aevum* 27 (1958): 166–72.

59. David Fallows, "Words and Music in Two English Songs of the Mid-15th Century: Charles d'Orleans and John Lydgate," *Early Music* 2 (1977): 38–44.

60. Janet Wilson, "Poet and Patron in Early Fifteenth-Century England," *Parergon* 11 (1975): 25–32; A. C. Spearing, "Lydgate's 'The Temple of Glass,'" in *Medieval Dream Poetry* (Cambridge: Cambridge University Press, 1976), pp. 171–76.

61. Alice Miskimin, "Patterns in *The Kingis Quair* and the *Temple of Glas*," *Papers on Language and Literature* 13 (1977): 339–61.

62. Glynne Wickham, *Early English Stages* (London: Routledge and Kegan Paul, 1959), I, 191–207.

63. P. H. Parry, "On the Continuity of English Civic Pageantry: A Study of John Lydgate and the Tudor Pageant," *Forum for Modern Language Studies* 15 (1979): 222–36.

64. Alain Renoir, "On the Date of the Mumming at Hertford," *Archiv* 198 (1962): 32–33; Richard Firth Green, "Three Fifteenth Century Notes," *English Language Notes* 14 (1976): 14–17.

65. W. A. Davenport, *Fifteenth Century Drama: The Early Moral Plays and*

*Their Literary Relations* (Cambridge: D. S. Brewer, 1982).

66. J. W. McKenna, "Henry VI of England and the Dual Monarchy: Aspects of Royal Political Propaganda," *Journal of the Warburg and Courtauld Institutes* 28 (1965): 145-62.

67. V. J. Scattergood, *Politics and Poetry in the Fifteenth Century* (London: Blandford Press, 1971).

68. Henry Hargreaves, "Lydgate's 'A Ram's Horn,'" *Chaucer Review* 10 (1976): 255-59.

69. David Lampe, "Lydgate's Laughter: 'Horse, Goose and Sheep' as Social Laughter," *Annuale Medievale* 15 (1974): 150-58.

70. Alain Renoir, "A Note on the Third Redaction of John Lydgate's Verses on the Kings of England," *Archiv* 216 (1979): 347-48.

71. Margaret Schlauch, "Stylistic Attributes of Lydgate's Prose," in *To Honor Roman Jakobson* (The Hague: Mouton, 1967), III, 1757-68.

72. William Ringler, "Lydgate's *Serpent of Division*, Edited by John Stow," *Studies in Bibliography* 14 (1961): 201-08.

73. *The Serpent of Division*, ed. Henry N. MacCracken (London: Frowde; New Haven: Yale University Press, 1911).

74. See Josef Schick, *Prolegomena zu Lydgates Temple of Glas* (Berlin, 1889); Schick, ed., *Lydgate's Temple of Glas*, Early English Text Society, ES 60 (London, 1891).

75. Mahmoud A. Manzalaoui, "Lydgate and English Prosody," in *Cairo Studies in English*, ed. M. Wahba (Cairo: Costa Tsoumas, 1960), 87-104.

76. Dudley Hascall, "Lydgate and English Prosody," *Language and Style* 3 (1970): 122-46.

77. Morris Halle and Samuel J. Keyser, *English Stress: Its Form, Its Growth, and Its Role in Verse* (New York: Harper and Row, 1971).

78. Ian Robinson, *Chaucer's Prosody* (Cambridge: Cambridge University Press, 1971), pp. 199-212.

79. Gregory Kratzmann, *Anglo-Scottish Literary Relations, 1430-1550* (Cambridge: Cambridge University Press, 1980); P. H. Nichols, "Dunbar as a Scottish Lydgatian," *PMLA* 46 (1931): 214-24, and "Lydgate's Influence on the Aureate Terms of the Scottish Chaucerians," *PMLA* 46 (1932): 516-22; R. D. S. Jack, "Dunbar and Lydgate," *Studies in Scottish Literature* 8 (1971): 215-27.

80. Alice Miskimin, *The Renaissance Chaucer* (New Haven: Yale University Press, 1975).

81. Ethel Seaton, *Sir Richard Roos* (London: Hart Davis, 1960).

82. A. S. G. Edwards, "Lydgate's *Tyed With a Line* and 'The Question of Halsam,'" *English Studies* 51 (1970): 527-29; Edwards and Jenkins, "A

Hymn to the Virgin" (see note 50, above).

83. Kathryn Walls, "Did Lydgate Translate the *Pelerinage de la Vie Humaine?*," *Notes and Queries* 222 (1977): 103–05; Richard Firth Green, "Lydgate and Deguileville Once More," *Notes and Queries* 223 (1979): 105–06.

84. M. C. Seymour, review of D. Pearsall, *John Lydgate*, in *Neuphilologische Mitteilungen* 73 (1972): 729–32.

85. Gail Gibson, "Bury St. Edmunds, Lydgate and the *N. Town Cycle*," *Speculum* 56 (1981): 56–90.

# Hoccleve Studies, 1965–1981

## Jerome Mitchell

**M**y doctoral dissertation on Thomas Hoccleve was in its final form in the spring of 1965,[1] and in 1968, after much revision, rearranging, and excision, it appeared as a book entitled *Thomas Hoccleve: A Study in Early Fifteenth-Century English Poetic*.[2] In the present pages I am concerned mainly with the work of other Hoccleve scholars during the past fifteen years or so, but I would like to say just a few words about my own work as an introduction.

In one way or another my book brings together almost all previous critical and scholarly opinion about Hoccleve. Although he had his admirers over the centuries, most critics considered him a poet of little if any importance. Like earlier commentators I stressed the autobiographical element in Hoccleve—perhaps showing more convincingly than the others its uniqueness in comparison with the efforts of his contemporaries. I also paid attention to his handling of his sources, praising him for his lively direct discourse. I succeeded (I hope) in ridding us of the old notion that Hoccleve was a poor metrist. I showed that the negative opinion about his meter can be traced back to an unacceptable theory of pentameter line structure. Shakespeare and Milton would be labelled poor metrists also if they had been subjected to the criteria by which Hoccleve was judged. My brief last chapter—certainly not the last word on the subject—is concerned with aspects of Hoccleve's relation to Chaucer.

I have organized the present discussion somewhat along the same lines as I did the annotated bibliography that concluded my book. First I discuss publications of the past fifteen years that contain bibliographical material on Hoccleve. Next I call attention to editions that have appeared recently.

Then I comment on recent special studies, that is, articles that deal primarily with Hoccleve. I conclude with a miscellaneous section, in which I have included scholarly works that deal importantly with him although not primarily. The order within each section is chronological rather than alphabetical, but I vary from this procedure occasionally, and I have felt free to discuss unpublished papers and research in progress as well as published material. Indeed, a surprising amount of scholarly work has been done in recent years on this man who has so often been said to be a poet of little if any importance.

## Bibliographical Material (including Manuscript Studies)

William Matthews's helpful section on Hoccleve for the *Manual of the Writings in Middle English* appeared in 1972.[3] It consists of an account of Hoccleve's life, summaries of his important poems with concise literary-historical information about them, a list of shorter poems with brief summaries, a general critical discussion, and at the end a full bibliography. Apparently Matthews did his work independently of my own efforts. He unfortunately repeats the old error that the *Tale of Jereslaus' Wife* and the *Tale of Jonathas* are translations from the continental *Gesta Romanorum* (as represented in Oesterley's edition), though I believe my book has established pretty clearly that they are based on the Anglo-Latin *Gesta*. He has also repeated the time-worn commonplace that Hoccleve was a sorry metrist. Following H. S. Bennett, Matthews gives the date of Hoccleve's death as "ca. 1437"; most scholars now prefer an earlier date. While the summaries of Hoccleve's poems are useful, I find the critical discussion a bit too negative and sometimes too vague; it smacks too much of the old literary histories. The bibliography lists several items not included in my own bibliography, the most interesting of which are Wilhelm Kleineke's *Englische Fürstenspiegel* (Halle, 1937) and George Sewell's modernization in 1718 of the *Letter of Cupid*.[4] A very positive feature of Matthews' bibliography is his full information as to the Hoccleve manuscripts, albeit within a format somewhat cumbersome and confusing. Matthews gives full manuscript data about the poems often attributed to Hoccleve in Deguileville's *Pilgrimage of the Soul*, but like me he was unaware of Janet Smalley's important M.A. thesis on this subject.[5]

M. C. Seymour's long-awaited study "The Manuscripts of Hoccleve's *Regiment of Princes*" appeared in 1974.[6] It consists of a brief introduction on Hoccleve and the *Regement* followed by detailed descriptions of all the manuscripts in which the poem appears. Each description begins with a brief general description of the manuscript's physical appearance. This is followed by information as to watermarks, collation, contents, decoration, scribal characteristics, history, and printed notices. Seymour's monograph is a milestone in the study of the *Regement*—an indispensable guide—but his grouping of the manuscripts (pp. 262-63) is based on insufficient data, as he himself says, and is "necessarily tentative." Moreover, the descriptions themselves, while far more detailed and complete than anything that had appeared before, are not exhaustive. The *Regement* as included in Brit. Lib. MS. Harley 116 lacks lines 1065-92 and 1121-48, in addition to the missing lines that Seymour cites; Cambridge Univ. Lib. MS. Gg.vi.17 lacks lines 1387-93, 1527-33, 1541-47, 1611-17, 1667-80, 1751-57, 1863-69, and 1884-90, in addition to the lines cited by Seymour; Fitzwilliam Museum MS. McClean 182 lacks lines 1573-1631, in addition to those cited by Seymour; Univ. of Edinburgh MS. 202 does have the headless *a*, as Seymour says, but not always (see, for example, lines 1008, 1009, 1117, 1150, 1151); Huntington Lib. MS. HM 135 normally has the short *r*, as Seymour says, but occasionally has the long variety as well (see, for example, line 1476). My additions to Seymour's data are by no means exhaustive. I offer them only to point out the limitations of his fine and useful study.

For interesting addenda to Seymour's monograph one can consult Richard Firth Green's "Notes on Some Manuscripts of Hoccleve's *Regiment of Princes*," *The British Library Journal* 4 (1978): 37-41. Green describes two *Regement* fragments that formerly belonged to "the notorious collector John Bagford," and he points out that MS. Arundel 59 and the second part of MS. Harley 372 are in the hand of the same scribe.[7] Marcia Smith Marzec's current work on the *Regement* manuscripts goes beyond Seymour's. She has read papers on this subject at several meetings, most recently in October 1981 at the Eighth St. Louis Conference on Manuscript Studies.[8] In her 1980 Northern Illinois University doctoral dissertation, "Thomas Hoccleve's *De Regimine Principum*, Sections 12 and 13: A Critical Edition," she has established an invaluable stemma—this being a mammoth undertaking, in view of the fact that Hoccleve's magnum opus has come down to us in forty-three manuscripts. A revised version of the section of her dissertation dealing with the genealogy of the manuscripts will be published in *Studies in Bibliography*.

# Editions

Several important editions of Hoccleve have appeared in the past fifteen years or so; others are in progress. Working under the late William

Matthews, Mary Ruth Pryor reedited Hoccleve's "Series" poems as a UCLA doctoral dissertation, completed in 1968, which she entitled "Thomas Hoccleve's Series: An Edition of MS. Durham Cosin V iii 9."[9] The "Series" consists of Hoccleve's *Complaint*, his *Dialogue with a Friend*, the *Tale of Jereslaus' Wife, Lerne to Dye*, and the *Tale of Jonathas*. Most of the Durham manuscript is in Hoccleve's own handwriting, but the *Complaint* and the opening stanzas of the *Dialogue with a Friend* are in the hand of the sixteenth-century chronicler John Stowe. Pryor has collated the part of the manuscript done by Stowe with three fifteenth-century manuscripts in the Bodleian Library (Bodley 221, Laud Misc. 735, and Arch. Selden supra 53), and she has compared *Lerne to Dye* with the poem as it appears in Huntington Lib. MS. HM 744, which is also a Hoccleve autograph manuscript. Pryor claims that "the resulting text is therefore as accurate a representation of what Hoccleve intended as can be obtained from the manuscript itself without the imposition of modern theories of metrics and punctuation" (p. 4). The text is preceded by some 160 pages of introduction; it is followed by very brief explanatory notes, a glossary, and a bibliography.

In 1970 the Early English Text Society reissued the old Furnivall-Gollancz edition of Hoccleve's *Minor Poems* in a one-volume revised photographic reprint.[10] I made most of the textual corrections, and A. I. Doyle and I together added material to Furnivall's "forewards" to bring them up to date. Both Furnivall (especially) and Gollancz made numerous errors in transcription. In May 1970, I discussed the significance of this revised reprint, which was still forthcoming, in a paper that I presented at the Fifth Conference on Medieval Studies at Western Michigan University. Entitled "Hoccleve's *Minor Poems:* Addenda and Corrigenda," it has since been published in the *Edinburgh Bibliographical Society Transactions*, 5, pt. 3 (1983): 9-16.[11] With concrete evidence I show that many a line for which Hoccleve has been blamed is owing to his earlier editors rather than to himself.

Most of Hoccleve's *Complaint* has been freshly edited by John Burrow and included in his anthology, *English Verse, 1300-1500*.[12] The last fifteen stanzas are unfortunately omitted, perhaps because of the exigencies of space. Burrow's introductory comments are generally helpful, but some could prove misleading to an unwary student (especially the suggestions as to the best short critical discussions). The text is heavily edited and the annotations are copious, but such apparently is the procedure of the series in which the volume appears.[13]

The most significant editorial work on Hoccleve to appear in recent years is the volume *Selections from Hoccleve*, by M. C. Seymour. This was released in 1981 by the Clarendon Press. It includes the *Complaint of the Virgin*, the *Mother of God, La Male Regle*, several balades, excerpts from the *Regement of Princes* (from MS. Arundel 38), the *Address to Sir John Oldcastle*, the *Complaint*, two passages from the *Dialogue with a Friend*, and the *Tale of Jonathas*. Seymour's long-awaited book will no doubt be adopted by many professors for their graduate seminars on fifteenth-century poetry; it fulfills a long-standing need. See my review of it for *Speculum* 58 (1983): 477-78.

Still in preparation is a new edition of the *Letter of Cupid* by Douglas J. McMillan. It will take into consideration all known manuscripts and will be published together with the original poem of Christine de Pisan. Also in preparation is a new edition of the *Regement of Princes* by David C. Greetham, who is being assisted by Charles R. Blyth, Peter Farley, Marcia Smith Marzec, Gale Sigal, and myself. A. Compton Reeves will help with the introduction, and David Yerkes will do the glossary. MS. Arundel 38 is our base text, collated with the forty-two other known manuscripts. Marzec's doctoral dissertation is being incorporated into this larger project. A new, critical edition of the *Regement* is much needed, since the older editions by Thomas Wright (1860) and Frederick J. Furnivall (1897) do not take into consideration all the extant manuscripts.

## Special Studies

The first item I shall mention here is an unpublished paper on Hoccleve by Henry Noble MacCracken, which came into my hands during the Christmas holidays of 1967, shortly before Professor MacCracken's death. The paper is entitled "A Poet of No Importance." It was apparently written several years prior to 1967—perhaps as early as 1950—and it was intended for oral presentation. I hasten to say that the title is ironic. While MacCracken certainly had no grandiose illusions about Hoccleve's ability as a poet, he shows on almost every page of his typescript a deep appreciation for both Hoccleve the man and Hoccleve the poet. This charming essay foreshadows some of the critical opinion of the past fifteen years.

Another essay worth mentioning is R. G. Howarth's "A Rakish Rhymer, Thomas Hoccleve," included in his miscellany entitled *A Pot of Gillyflowers: Studies and Notes*.[14] Howarth stresses the autobiographical element in Hoccleve and his ability to write a good narrative, concluding that Hoccleve was "not a bad specimen of a poet." This essay gives further testimony to the reawakening of interest in Hoccleve in the mid 1960s.

Although Eva M. Thornley's article "The Middle English Penitential Lyric and Hoccleve's Autobiographical Poetry" bears the date 1967,[15] it actually appeared somewhat later, and too late for me to make use of in my book. The title is a bit misleading, since Thornley discusses only one of the autobiographical poems, *La Male Regle*; but in viewing it in the context of the medieval penitential lyric she breaks new ground, finding the poem "remarkable in virtue of the ingenuity with which it conforms to, parodies, and transcends this genre" (p. 296). She by no means rules out the possibility of genuinely autobiographical elements, but she sees a subtlety in Hoccleve's workmanship that had hitherto been unnoticed. Previous discussions of *La Male Regle*, my own included, seem rather naive in comparison.

Late in 1968 my "Hoccleve's Tribute to Chaucer" appeared in the collection *Chaucer und seine Zeit: Symposion für Walter F. Schirmer*.[16] I am mainly concerned in it with the question of Hoccleve's friendship with Chaucer (which I think unlikely), and while I have no further data to add to what appears in an earlier short article[17] and in my book (pp. 115-18), my statement here is the fullest and probably the most carefully wrought of my different attempts.

Paying careful attention to the Latin quotations to be found in the margins of four of the five manuscripts of Hoccleve's *Complaint*, A. G. Rigg, in a very important article for *Speculum*, shows that the poem is heavily indebted to Isidore of Seville's *Synonyma*.[18] "If we may hypothesize an episode in his biography," Rigg argues, "Hoccleve, after a period of insanity, realized its potentiality as a theological lesson for other men; at the same time he became acquainted with Isidore's *Synonyma*. He then adapted the latter; for the lamenting man's persecution by his enemies he substituted his own social estrangement from his friends; for the acceptance of Reason's advice he substituted his own acceptance of God's will" (p. 574). This discovery does not rule out the autobiographical element, but we know now that there is more to Hoccleve's account of his illness than had previously been realized. Like Thornley's article on *La Male Regle*, this splendid article on the *Complaint* advances all previous discussions significantly.

The *Letter of Cupid* has long been one of Hoccleve's best known poems, owing to its having been included in some of the early printed editions of Chaucer. In his essay "Hoccleve's 'Letter of Cupid' and the 'Quarrel' Over the *Roman de la Rose*," John V. Fleming argues that Hoccleve translates, abridges, and adapts Christine's *Epistre* with faithfulness (more or less) to her anti-antifeminist arguments and to the tone of her poem, but that in some of his additions to her work Hoccleve shows that he is actually on the side of her archenemy Jean de Meun.[19] During the course of his *Letter* Hoccleve refers respectfully to his mentor Chaucer, who was known to be a great admirer of Jean de Meun. To quote Fleming: "Hoccleve realizes a satiric and ironic end within the 'Letter of Cupid' without marring its glossy enamel finish with open parody or brash intrusion. The poem remains the elegant essay in anti-antifeminism it was for Christine, but for readers who held the memory of Chaucer dear, its force as a polemic against Jean de Meun must have been spent in gentle laughter" (p. 32). Fleming goes on to say in a complicated (and perhaps overly subtle) discussion that Hoccleve in another addition hints at shortcomings in Christine's critical judgment of Jean de Meun, whom she would equate too closely with his characters, mistaking their sentiments for his. It is Hoccleve's subtly satirical attitude toward Christine, then, that lies behind the accusation, related in the *Dialogue with a Friend*, that he (Hoccleve) had spoken badly of women. Fleming's article is important because it shows that there is a complexity to the *Letter of Cupid* that had not been noticed in previous discussions.

Penelope B. R. Doob concludes her fascinating book *Nebuchadnezzar's Children: Conventions of Madness in Middle English Literature* with a chapter on Hoccleve,[20] "a man thoroughly familiar with medieval attitudes toward madness and perhaps personally concerned with the disease, a man who recapitulates the past and anticipates the future in his writings on madness" (p. 230). She shows that throughout his writings Hoccleve demonstrates a marked interest in the relationship between sin on one hand, and disease, melancholy, and madness on the other—this interest, or rather "preoccupation," culminating in his *Complaint* and *Dialogue with a Friend*, in which he describes what he says was his own recent experience with madness, its symptoms, the reactions of his friends, his suffering, and his eventual recovery. These poems and the others that comprise the "Series" have as their central theme "the usefulness of physical disorder for recalling men to spiritual sanity" (p. 220). Like Thornley and Rigg, Doob sees more of literary convention than do many previous scholars, and she presents her case very convincingly. What matters in Hoccleve, as she correctly realizes, is not the factual truth of his "autobiographical" poetry but rather its convincing illusion of truth.[21] Much of what Hoccleve says about disease and madness is conventional, "but in treating conventional ideas freshly by using himself as exemplum, in creating the appearance of tortured introspection, in illustrating dramatically the destructive moral tensions experienced by a would-be man of virtue living in the world, and in presenting a detailed study of the melancholic as more than just a sinner, he looks forward to the Renaissance—to *Hamlet*, to Robert Burton, to humoural psychology on the stage, and to the Jacobean preoccupation with madness" (p. 231). This is indeed high praise for our poet "of little if any importance."

One noteworthy article in German has appeared on Hoccleve in the past fifteen years. It is Gerd Dose's "Sozialkritische Literatur im spätmittelalterlichen England: Thomas Hoccleve."[22] First Dose summarizes the state of Hoccleve scholarship, and then he examines Hoccleve's view of English society, drawing his information mainly from the *Regement of Princes*. What is most important in this article is Dose's careful placing of Hoccleve's work in the context of other social criticism in the late English Middle Ages (*Piers Plowman*, for example, and the anonymous *Mum and the Sothsegger*) and his recognizing certain tendencies and ideas in Hoccleve that lead into the next century, namely, Hoccleve's unusually honest pointing out and appraisal of the problems in society as he saw them, with concrete examples drawn from contemporary life, and especially his forthright criticism of the nobility for their snobbery, pride, extravagance, and disrespect for the laws of the realm. Although in many ways deeply rooted in the Middle Ages, Hoccleve at the same time "ist ein nicht unbedeutender Exponent einer Phase englischer sozialkritischer Literatur, der ein ausgesprochener Übergangscharakter zukommt" (p. 26). Interestingly, both Penelope Doob and Gerd Dose, from totally different perspectives, view Hoccleve to some extent as a poet of transition.

Hoccleve has always attracted the interest of historians, foremost of whom in recent years has been A. Compton Reeves. In 1964 Reeves completed an M.A. thesis at the University of Kansas entitled "The Political Thought of Thomas Hoccleve." In May 1970 he presented a paper on Hoccleve at the Fifth Conference on Medieval Studies at Western Michigan University. It was later published under the title "Thomas Hoccleve, Bureaucrat" in the journal *Medievalia et Humanistica*.[23] In this paper Reeves brings together in convenient fashion all that is known about Hoccleve's life as clerk of the Privy Seal, and he discusses Hoccleve's political thought as revealed mainly in the *Regement of Princes*, the *Balade to King Henry V on His Accession to the Throne*, and the *Address to Sir John Oldcastle*. Reeves argues that Hoccleve, unlike Sir John Fortescue, was not a "true political theorist"; that his "approach to the problems he perceived in government was consistently moralistic and religiously dogmatic"; and "though he may have had the innate ability, he assuredly did not have the discipline to mould his ideas into a closely reasoned political philosophy" (pp. 212–13). At the 1978 conference Reeves followed up the earlier paper with a paper focusing on Hoccleve's attitude toward the church and toward society and the world around him. This was published the next year in *Fifteenth Century Studies*, with the title "The World of Thomas Hoccleve."[24] In both papers Reeves argues that what Hoccleve has to say is articulate and valuable for the light it sheds on fifteenth-century England, but that Hoccleve was not a systematic or profound thinker. He is worth studying today because he was "one who left for posterity thoughts reflecting the feelings and attitudes of a segment of English opinion that was rarely recorded."[25]

Some unpublished studies deserve mention, among them Linda E. Stolz's "Satire and Defense: Antifeminism in the Poetry of Hoccleve and Lydgate" —a stimulating paper presented at the 1972 Midwestern Modern Language Association Conference in St. Louis, which provoked much lively commentary from the discussant, Catharine A. Regan. In 1978 Diane Fincher Horne completed an M.A. thesis at East Carolina University entitled "Thomas Hoccleve: A Biographical Study." Directed by Douglas J. McMillan, this work is valuable for its bringing together of everything that is known about Hoccleve's life. In preparing it, Horne had access to an early draft of a book on Hoccleve by McMillan which he prepared for Twayne but later withdrew. At present he is rewriting it for another publisher and is hopeful that it will appear soon. Having observed that there were studies of Hoccleve the bureaucrat and Hoccleve the scribe but few on Hoccleve as a poet, Charles R. Blyth presented a critically oriented paper entitled "Thomas Hoccleve, Poet" at the 1980 Modern Language Association Conference in Houston. To my knowledge this is the first major paper to have been read on Hoccleve at the Modern Language Association annual meeting. In the fall of 1982 John Burrow discussed autobiographical problems in Hoccleve in a British Academy Lecture.

## Miscellaneous

Hoccleve has come under interesting discussion, and has sometimes figured prominently, in a number of other works that have been published since 1965. In *The Court of Richard II* Gervase Mathew adds little to our knowledge about him, but what he has to say is eminently sensible. He thinks that the *Regement of Princes* "has been judged too harshly. It is an accomplished work, with the smooth style prized at the time, the occasional strong line and a cluster of concise classical anecdotes." He believes that "his [Hoccleve's] was an oddly unsuccessful life and an unmerited oblivion" (pp. 57-58). In a *PMLA* article written jointly by A. I. Doyle and George B. Pace and entitled "A New Chaucer Manuscript,"[26] Doyle calls attention to the Hoccleve poems, namely the *Regement of Princes* and the "Series" group, that are included in this long-lost manuscript that reappeared in 1955 in Coventry (p. 24). The portrait prefixed to the *Regement* was once thought to be of Hoccleve, but it is more likely of Aristotle or Egidio Colonna.

The historian A. L. Brown discusses the careers of Robert Frye, John Prophete, and Hoccleve in his attractive article "The Privy Seal Clerks in the Early Fifteenth Century," which is included in a volume entitled *The Study of Medieval Records: Essays in Honour of Kathleen Major.*[27] Brown argues again that Hoccleve died in 1426, as indeed he had suggested many years ago in his short notice of H. S. Bennett's *Six Medieval Men and Women.*[28] V. J. Scattergood refers here and there to Hoccleve in his book *Politics and Poetry in the Fifteenth Century.*[29] Hoccleve's rhythms are sensitively analyzed by Ian Robinson in his *Chaucer's Prosody: A Study of the Middle English Verse Tradition.*[30] Robinson is a defender of Hoccleve, but he observes that "if there are no thwarted stresses in Hoccleve's decasyllables he is still sometimes very far from what we recognize as iambic pentameter" (p. 192). He goes on to discuss "the expressiveness of Hoccleve's rhythms" in a way (as he rightly says) that no previous study has attempted.[31] In an important note published in the early 1970s, Elizabeth Morley Ingram calls attention to the specific mentioning of Hoccleve in the will of Guy de Rouclif, who had been a senior clerk in the Privy Seal.[32] Also in the early 1970s, several articles and notes appeared in the *Review of English Studies* arguing for or against the possibility that the "maister Massy" to whom Hoccleve refers in his *Balade to the Duke of Bedford* is the *Gawain*-Poet.[33] Those who advocated this identification have not found many supporters, but they have not conceded defeat. While the debate was going on, P. D. Roberts, in another part of the world, transcribed and published twelve previously unpublished lyrics from a manuscript now in Melbourne of prose adaptations of Deguileville's *Pilgrimage of the Life of Man* and *Pilgrimage of the Soul.*[34] Three of the lyrics are among those ascribed to Hoccleve by Furnivall (in the argument over the authorship of the poems in MS. Egerton 615), but in this manuscript they have "extra unique stanzas added to them." The question then arises as to whether these stanzas and the other nine poems are by Hoccleve. Roberts prefers not to take a stand, but does observe cautiously that they "reveal qualities which may be said to be in the Hoccleve style at least" (p. 105).[35]

In the first of "Three Fifteenth-Century Notes" Richard Firth Green calls attention to a previously unnoticed reference to Hoccleve in the accounts of the Keeper of the Great Wardrobe.[36] James H. McGregor provides a fresh slant on Hoccleve's famous portrait of Chaucer in his article "The Iconography of Chaucer in Hoccleve's *De Regimine Principum* and in the *Troilus* Frontispiece,"[37] but what he says is somewhat vitiated by his apparent unawareness of most twentieth-century Hoccleve scholarship. Hoccleve the poet receives a good bit of attention from Derek Pearsall in one of his most recent books, *Old English and Middle English Poetry*,[38] but the reader will find little that has not been said before.

In a very erudite article entitled "The Production of Copies of the

Canterbury Tales and the Confessio Amantis in the Early Fifteenth Century," A. I. Doyle and M. B. Parkes discuss Hoccleve's copying of a part of the Confessio Amantis in Trinity College, Cambridge, MS. R.3.2.[39] Specifically, Hoccleve's hand appears on folios 82 and 83 and the first column of folio 84[.] He was one of a team of five copyists who worked independently of each other from sections of an exemplar which had been parcelled out to them. Interestingly, one scribe was also the copyist of the Ellesmere and Hengwrt manuscripts of the Canterbury Tales; another was the copyist of the Tales as they appear in MS. Harley 7334 and Corpus Christi College MS. 198, as well as of several other manuscripts of the Confessio Amantis. While Hoccleve's hand is well known from the Huntington and Durham manuscripts of his own *Minor Poems* and from Brit. Lib. MS. Add. 24062 (the formulary that he prepared in his capacity of clerk of the Privy Seal),[40] the Trinity College manuscript is the only known instance of his having copied the works of another poet. It is an important discovery in the study of Hoccleve's copying activities.[41]

If Hoccleve the bureaucrat, scribe, poet and man died in ca. 1448, 1437, 1430, or 1426 (the last-named date being most probable), Hoccleve scholarship is alive, well, and thriving as never before. Moreover, Hoccleve's literary reputation has never been higher. Penelope Doob calls him "a minor but much underrated poet." She writes of "the charm and skill of the *Male Regle*," and she refers to the prologue to the *Regement of Princes* as "charming." Eva Thornley is impressed with Hoccleve's "superior artistry" in *La Male Regle*, and she describes his merging of the conventional complaint to one's purse with the penitential lyric as "ingenious"; she also uses the adjectives "masterly" and "brilliant." John Fleming finds the *Letter of Cupid* "a most skillful poetic acheivement," especially in its "subtle but telling" interpolation into the French source. Gone are the days when a learned professor could stand before a group of scholars at a convention, make a witty and disparaging allusion to Hoccleve's poetry, which he would probably not have read in a long time if ever, and expect to be greeted by a chorus of guffaws from his fellow scholars, who also would have had little or no knowledge of Hoccleve. We all know that Hoccleve was no second Chaucer or *Gawain*-Poet, but he was looked on as poet of importance in his own day—why else should there be forty-three manuscripts of the *Regement of Princes?*—and he is being considered so again, in the late twentieth century, at long last. Much valuable work has been done on him since 1965. The reawakened interest suggests that we may look forward to many more fine studies.*

# Notes

1. "Thomas Hoccleve: His Traditionalism and His Individuality: A Study in Fifteenth-Century English Poetic" (Ph.D. diss., Duke University, 1965).
2. (Urbana, Chicago, and London: University of Illinois Press, 1968).
3. (Hamden, Ct.: Archon Books/The Shoe String Press for The Connecticut Academy of Arts and Sciences, 1972), vol. 3, section 8, pp. 746–56, 903–08).
4. Entitled *The Proclamation of Cupid: or, A Defence of Women*. Shortly after the publication of my book I discovered this item myself, by accident, while I was in the British Library looking for something else. To my knowledge, it has never been discussed anywhere.
5. Janet Smalley, "The Poems of the Middle English *Pilgrimage of the Soul*" (M.A. thesis, University of Liverpool, 1954). This is an edition of the poems, with a connecting prose summary; there is a thirteen-page introduction followed by a list and description of the various MSS. The extra poems from the Melbourne MS. are included in an appendix. (See also n. 35 below.)
6. In the *Edinburgh Bibliographical Society Transactions*, 4, pt. 7 (1974): 253–297.
7. See also A. S. G. Edwards, "Hoccleve's *Regiment of Princes*: A Further Manuscript," *Edinburgh Bibliographical Society Transactions*, 5, pt. 1 (1978): 32. This is a description of Yale MS. 493.
8. The title of this paper was "Scribal Emendation in the Later Manuscripts of Hoccleve's *Regiment of Princes*." Others include "Thomas Hoccleve's *Regiment of Princes*: Toward a Genealogy of Manuscripts," presented in October 1977 at the Fourth St. Louis Conference on Manuscript

---

*I am indebted to a number of friends and colleagues for helpful suggestions, especially to Penelope B. R. Doob, A. S. G. Edwards, David C. Greetham, Marcia Smith Marzec, A. Compton Reeves, and Robert F. Yeager. All shortcomings are my own.

Studies; "Thomas Hoccleve's *Regiment of Princes:* The 'New' Yale MS. and Its Genealogical Affiliates," read at the Thirteenth Conference on Medieval Studies at Western Michigan University, in Kalamazoo, May 1978; and "Hoccleve's Use of Sources and the Editing of *The Regiment of Princes*," read in April 1981 at the Conference of the Society for Textual Scholarship at the City University of New York.

9. University Microfilms, No. 69-7257.

10. The original edition was published in two parts in the Extra Series, no. 61, ed. Frederick J. Furnivall (1892), and no. 73, ed. Sir Israel Gollancz (1925 for 1897).

11. The paper is based on a 34-page typescript of addenda and corrigenda completed for the E.E.T.S. in the winter of 1968-69. I have one copy of this; another copy is in the University of Durham Library. I mention it because not everything it contains could be included in the revised reprint.

12. (London and New York: Longman, 1977), pp. 265-80.

13. Longman Annotated Anthologies of English Verse; general editor, Alastair Fowler.

14. (Cape Town, 1964), pp. 1-10. The book is in typescript; no publisher is indicated. I used a copy from the University of Delaware library.

15. In *Neuphilologische Mitteilungen* 68 (1967): 295-321.

16. Ed. Arno Esch (Tübingen: Max Niemeyer, 1968), pp. 275-83.

17. "Hoccleve's Supposed Friendship with Chaucer," *English Language Notes* 4 (1966): 9-12.

18. "Hoccleve's *Complaint* and Isidore of Seville," *Speculum* 45 (1970): 564-74.

19. This is *Medium Aevum* 40 (1971): 21-40.

20. (New Haven and London: Yale University Press, 1974), pp. 208-31. Reviewed by me for the *Humanities Association Review* 26 (1975): 261-62.

21. In a footnote (p. 210, n. 2) she alludes to an examination of "late medieval autobiographical, pseudo-autobiographical, and first-person narrative in a subsequent study, which will contain further material on Hoccleve."

22. In *Literatur als Kritik des Lebens: Festschrift zum 65. Geburtstag von Ludwig Borinski*, ed. Rudolf Haas, Heinz-Joachim Müllenbrock, and Claus Uhlig (Heidelberg: Quelle & Meyer, 1975), pp. 9-26.

23. n.s. 5 (1974): 201-14.

24. 2 (1979): 187-201.

25. "The World of Thomas Hoccleve," p. 199.

26. 83 (1968): 22-34.

27. Ed. D. A. Bullough and R. L. Storey (Oxford: Clarendon Press, 1971), pp. 260–81.

28. *Review of English Studies*, n.s. 8 (1957): 217–18.

29. (London: Blandford, 1971).

30. (Cambridge: Cambridge University Press, 1971), pp. 190–99.

31. Karen Lynn glances at Hoccleve's prosody in her article "Chaucer's Decasyllabic Line: The Myth of the Hundred-Year Hibernation," *Chaucer Review* 13 (1978–79): 116–27.

32. "Thomas Hoccleve and Guy de Rouclif," *Notes and Queries* 218 (1973):42–43. Rouclif bequeathed to Hoccleve a book about the Trojan War.

33. Barbara Nolan and David Farley-Hills, "The Authorship of *Pearl*: Two Notes," *Review of English Studies*, n.s. 22 (1971): 295–302; C. J. Peterson, "*Pearl* and *St. Erkenwald*: Some Evidence for Authorship" and "The *Pearl*-Poet and John Massey of Cotton, Cheshire," ibid., n.s. 25 (1974): 49–53, 257–66; Thorlac Turville-Petre and Edward Wilson, "Hoccleve, 'Maister Massy' and the *Pearl* Poet: Two Notes," ibid., n.s. 26 (1975): 129–43; and a Letter to the Editor from David Farley-Hills, ibid., p. 451. See also William Vantuono, "A Name in the Cotton MS. Nero A.x.Article 3," *Mediaeval Studies* 37 (1975): 537–42; and "John de Mascy of Sale and the *Pearl* Poems," *Manuscripta* 25 (1981): 77–88.

34. "Some Unpublished Middle English Lyrics and Stanzas in a Victoria Public Library Manuscript," *English Studies* 54 (1973): 105–18.

35. Roberts was not aware of Janet Smalley's M.A. thesis (see n. 5, above). Only one poem appears here ("My souerayn saueoure to þe I call," from the *Pilgrimage of the Life of Man*) that had not already been transcribed by Smalley, who also transcribed the extra stanzas to the three Hoccleve poems.

36. *English Language Notes* 14 (1976–77): 14.

37. *Chaucer Review* 11 (1976–77): 338–50.

38. (London: Routledge and Kegan Paul, 1977), pp. 236–39 and passim.

39. This is in *Medieval Scribes, Manuscripts and Libraries: Essays Presented to N. R. Ker*, ed. M. B. Parkes and Andrew G. Watson (London: Scolar Press, 1978), pp. 163–210.

40. Elna-Jean Young Bentley, "The Formulary of Thomas Hoccleve," Ph.D. diss., Emory University, 1965.

41. Other recent scholarly works in which Hoccleve's handwriting is discussed and photographically reproduced are P. J. Croft's *Autograph Poetry in the English Language: Facsimiles of Original Manuscripts from the Fourteenth to the Twentieth Century* (London: Cassell, 1973), vol. I, units 3–4; and

Anthony G. Petti's *English Literary Hands from Chaucer to Dryden* (Cambridge, Mass.: Harvard University Press, 1977), pp. 54–55. Peter Farley is currently doing a computer study of the dialectal, orthographic, and paleographic features of the autograph manuscripts.

# Henryson Scholarship

## The Recent Decades

### Louise O. Fradenburg

Henryson scholarship has, in recent years, labored under a double burden: it must not only recreate the work of past scholars to serve the needs of our own time, but must also, often, pioneer. Henryson's sources and analogues have never been collected; Florence Ridley's entry on the Middle Scots poets in *A Manual of the Writings in Middle English* contains the first major bibliographical research on Henryson in decades.[1] Because study of the Middle Scots language is still in its infancy, work on Henryson's language has lagged badly, Bengt Ellenberger's recent piece on Henryson's latinisms being a helpful exception. Answers to some of the major scholarly dilemmas about his textual tradition and canon await further progress in this area.[2]

## The Canon

The question of Henryson's canon is of critical importance, partly because the generically diverse minor poems complicate so thoroughly our understanding of Henryson's poetic range. I. W. A. Jamieson has reminded us that, however uncertain the authorship of such poems as "Sum Practysis of Medecyne" and "The Garmont of Gud Ladeis," the work of time and the Reformation may have left to us a very imperfect "sampling" of Henryson's shorter poems.[3] Denton Fox's review of the evidence for the canon in his 1981 edition of Henryson's poetry reopens serious doubts about the authorship of much of this minor poetry while emphasizing the apparent diversity of Henryson's achievements.[4] Fox finds the authenticity of the major narratives secure; the only attempt in recent years to broaden the canon has been Donald MacDonald's suggestion, not firmly substantiated, that Henryson wrote *The Thre Prestis of Peblis* (preserved in the Asloan manuscript).[5]

## The Text

Recent decades have witnessed a welcome resurgence of interest in the discussion of Henryson's difficult textual tradition. In 1963 John MacQueen denounced Wood's (and Elliott's) choice of the Bassandyne print as a "best" text for the *Fables*, arguing that the Bannatyne manuscript should be used for the text of the ten fables it includes, and Bassandyne for the remaining three fables, "but only with extreme caution."[6] His work raised important questions about the order of the *Fables*, and hence about the overall design of the work.

Many scholars have followed MacQueen's lead in using the Bannatyne text as their base; but not all have accepted his arguments. In fact, Denton Fox's 1981 edition challenges both MacQueen's methods and his editorial assumptions. Fox contends that no truly "best" text of the *Fables* announces itself; editorial 'truth' cannot, in this case, be sought in a single witness (p. xxx). Fox's decision to base his text on the complete Bassandyne print while emending in the light of other witnesses seems, if not a miracle cure, the most satisfactory means of tracking this *selva oscura*.[7] The testimony of witnesses like Bannatyne on the ways in which Scottish literary culture interpreted the textuality of Henryson's *Fables* has also become increasingly valuable; W. S. Ramson's 1977 essay "On Bannatyne's Editing" offers an important pioneering interpretation of Bannatyne's reading of the *Fables*.[8]

In view of the textual difficulties with which Henryson scholars are faced, and in view of changing conceptions of the scholarly value of variant texts, it is pleasant to report the increasing availability, in recent years, of the witnesses themselves. Denton Fox has published a transcription, with apparatus, of the 1663 Anderson edition of the *Testament of Cresseid* in *Studies in Scottish Literature*.[9] The appendixes to his 1968 edition of the *Testament* also present transcriptions of fragments of the work found in the Book of the Dean of Lismore and in the Ruthven manuscript.[10] Henryson scholarship is also benefiting from the current general interest in manuscript facsimiles. D. S. Brewer has edited for Scolar Press a facsimile, published in 1969, of the Clare College copy of Thynne's 1532 edition of "Chaucer's" works, which of course includes the *Testament*; and Scolar also published a facsimile of the Bannatyne manuscript in 1980. Fox's 1977 essay, "Manuscripts and Prints of Scots Poetry in the Sixteenth Century," an invaluable introduction to the problems faced by editors of Henryson, demonstrates how important is the evidence of variant texts for our understanding of Henryson's literary reception and the extent of his reputation.[11] Richard Smith's 1577 "Englished" print of the *Fables* has virtually no authority but is of considerable critical and historical interest.[12]

## Reception

Important new scholarship has begun to make study of Henryson's reception more feasible; but we can still do little more than speculate about Henryson's immediate audience. John MacQueen has suggested that the *Fables* "were written for a middle-class professional audience of private readers, much interested in the state of contemporary Scotland."[13] Misunderstanding of the nature of Henryson's political poetry has, until recently, distorted our sense of the kinds of audience that may have welcomed his work. R. J. Lyall's "Politics and Poetry in Fifteenth- and Sixteenth-Century Scotland" redresses some naive conceptions of Henryson's political satire;[14] and Nicolai Von Kreisler, in "Henryson's Visionary Fable: Tradition and Craftsmanship in *The Lyoun and the Mous*" (1973), challenges the traditional view of this fable as an outsider's attack on the abuses of James III's reign by arguing that the poem's balance of the demands both of conscience and of tact makes it a truly courtly poem, the kind "that men to kynges write."[15]

Gregory Kratzmann, in *Anglo-Scottish Literary Relations*, contends that both *Orpheus and Eurydice* and the *Testament* were written with a court audience in mind (p. 30). Douglas Gray agrees that *Orpheus*'s concern with the aristocratic themes of right rulership and 'gentilnes' may suggest a noble audience, and he reads the *Testament* as a poem also sympathetic to aristocratic ideals.[16] Other critics try to account for the courtly features of the *Testament* while maintaining that Henryson was "no man of the court." MacQueen's view of the *Testament* as a poem whose "powerful realism" might have shocked its 'more feminine' courtly audience resembles W. S. Ramson's vision of Henryson as a grudging and grumpy court poet, forced to write for a depraved court and producing, in response, a satire of courtly literature meant to show wanton ladies the errors of their ways.[17] But there is no reason to suppose, as Ramson does, that the court would have sympathized overmuch with the renegade Cresseid.

In "Manuscripts and Prints," Fox has been able to argue convincingly for Henryson's popularity with later audiences, and his piece on "Reputation" in *Poems* provides a useful introduction to the study of Henryson's reception by English and Scots poets alike. Robert Kindrick, too, has a brief chapter called "Henryson and Later Poetry."[18] The most comprehensive work to be done in recent years on Henryson's reception is that of Gregory Kratzmann. Kratzmann sometimes pushes too far in arguing for specific indebtedness, but his study points to important ways in which Henryson's reception can reveal significant features of Henryson's own poetic practice; Douglas, for example, appears to have valued highly Henryson's work on narratorial presence.[19]

The English reception of the *Testament* is a particularly problematic subject, long neglected by students of English and Scottish literature alike. For scholars trying to combat views of Henryson as just another Chaucerian imitator, Thynne's appropriation of the *Testament* has seemed no friendly gesture. But the early reception of Chaucer's *Troilus* was, as a result of that theft, inextricably bound up with the English history of the *Testament*;[20] and "sudron" responses to Henryson's poetry may, as critical and literary-historical statements, illuminate Henryson's work. An important task awaits scholars willing to reevaluate the usefulness of the "Chaucer" allusions to Henryson studies.

Neglect of this area has resulted in uncritical estimations of the nature of Henryson's influence on Cresseid's reputation. H. E. Rollins's 1917 essay "The Troilus-Cressida Story from Chaucer to Shakespeare,"[21] until recently the definitive study in this area, held Henryson's poem solely responsible for Cresseid's degradation by Elizabethan writers. But Gretchen Mieszkowski's excellent study of Cresseid's literary reputation has demonstrated that unsympathetic portrayals long predated Henryson; and Rollins's own materials suggest that the Elizabethan response was not monolithic.[22] Larry Sklute's contention that English readers saw Cresseid as a false whore because Henryson intended that they should oversimplifies both the poem and the history of response to it; but he at least asks us to take that response seriously in our own interpretations.[23] Cresseid's treatment by the English is not likely, as Kratzmann asserts, "one of the most bizarre accidents of literary history" (p. 86). Misreadings are surely more interesting than that.

Thus, G. Bullough's "The Lost 'Troilus and Cressida'" suggests that Thomas Dekker's and Henry Chettle's Troy play of 1599 sentimentalized and valorized Henryson's version of the Troilus-Cressida story, and that Shakespeare's own play was a revisionist attempt to treat the same material with "modern realism."[24] John J. McDermott's contention that the *Testament* influenced Thomas Heywood's *A Woman Killed with Kindness* may suggest to Henryson critics the possibility that Troilus's generosity to Cresseid is no simple act.[25] The evidence of Dekker's, Shakespeare's, and Heywood's plays points to a far more varied and thoughtful English reception of Henryson's poem than has generally been granted by scholars.

## Life and Milieu

Since David Laing's exhaustive search for biographical evidence, scholars have added little to the historical record; but evaluation of the evidence available to us has changed in important ways. MacQueen's ground-breaking work in *Robert Henryson* pictured Henryson not as a provincial schoolmaster but as a learned poet, living in an age that was violent, but not unusually so; and in a milieu in which growing material prosperity and educational opportunities enabled culture to flourish. MacQueen's arguments for Henryson's travels to Italy, and for his acquaintance with the texts and trends of continental humanism—a subject also taken up in MacQueen's "Some Aspects of the Early Renaissance in Scotland"[26]—are based on no very firm ground. (R. D. S. Jack, in *The Italian Influence on Scottish Literature*, agrees with MacQueen that Henryson may have studied in Italy and styles Henryson as the "first Scottish poet whose verse seems to owe more to the Italian humanists than to the French courtly writers.")[27] But MacQueen's portrait of Henryson as a herald of the "Northern Renaissance" raises important questions about the periodicity of Henryson's culture, even if it answers few of them.

Some recent scholars have preferred to emphasize Henryson's medieval conservatism. Douglas Gray's chapter called "Dunfermline and Beyond," now the most detailed account of Henryson's milieu, finds "inconclusive" the evidence for Henryson's humanism, suggesting instead that Henryson—like Chaucer—"may be related to an older (and wider) tradition marked by an interest in classical antiquity, literature and mythography which is not at all uncharacteristic of the latter Middle Ages" (p. 25). Gray tries to locate Henryson within a fifteenth-century periodicity distinct from the Italian Renaissance; but he relies too heavily on Huizinga's nostalgic vision of a latter age in decline.[28] Denton Fox portrays Henryson as a "man of good general knowledge" whose "learning would have been considered very old-fashioned" by "contemporary continental humanists."[29] While Fox's view of Henryson's culture is perhaps overly conservative, he nonetheless makes an impressive, well-reasoned appeal to the coherence of contemporary witnesses on Henryson's life and an important attempt to review the evidence for Henryson's *floruit*.

## Sources and Backgrounds

Despite the work of such earlier scholars as G. G. Smith, A. R. Diebler, and Janet M. Smith,[30] the study of the European background of Henryson's poetry took on genuine vigor and continuity only in the early 1960s, when allied with revisionist views of Henryson as a learned medieval rhetorician. Perhaps because of this comparatively late bloom, the hunt for sources has continued to dominate comparative treatment of Henryson's poetry. Study of Henryson's relationship to Italian literature, for example, has concentrated on the search for humanist sources. Fox and Gray reject R. D. S. Jack's suggestion that the *Orpheus* was directly influenced by Poliziano's *Orfeo* (1480); MacQueen's detection of influences from Florentine Platonism is likewise dubious.[31] But MacQueen's suggestion that Boccaccio's *De Genealogia Deorum* was a source for both the *Testament* and the *Orpheus*, though questioned by Fox, is at least within the realm of possibility—especially in view of the mythographic temper of both poems.[32]

Henryson's use, in the *Fables*, of the continental Aesopic and Reynardian traditions has been freshly explored by a number of scholars, most notably by Jamieson and Gray; Gray's account is by far the richest now in print.[33] Regrettably, however, no major work has appeared in recent years on French contexts for Henryson's poetry. Most scholars, for example, now reject Janet Smith's suggestion that Olivier de la Marche's *Le Triumphe des Dames* (ca. 1492) was the source for the "Garmont of Gud Ladeis,"[34] though the parallels between the two poems remain of considerable interest, implying, as they do, that Middle Scots poetry kept well up-to-date with trends in fifteenth-century French literature. Indeed, the best recent work on backgrounds to Henryson's minor poetry—Jamieson's essay "The Minor Poems of Robert Henryson" and Gray's chapter "The Shorter Poems" are useful reviews—emphasize genre rather than source as a means to understanding Henryson's historical poetics. Fox's essay "Henryson's 'Sum Practysis of Medecyne'" and Edward Schweitzer's fine work "The Allegory of Robert Henryson's 'The Bludy Serk'" both focus on the critical and literary-historical implications of Henryson's use of European genres and traditions as disparate as those of medical burlesque and "Christ as Lover-Knight."[35]

The willingness to consider Henryson's participation in wider European traditions and genres promises also to redefine in useful ways the debate over Henryson's "Chaucerianism"—a debate that has obscured, quite as much as it has illuminated, the historical features of Henryson's art. Critics as divergent in their views as Kinsley, Marken, Elliott, and J. A. W. Bennett continue, in effect, to validate Henryson by comparing his "Chaucerian" poem, the *Testament*, to the *Troilus* or by pointing to the subtlety of Chaucer's rhetoric as a model for Henryson's own.[36] Critics, sometimes the same critics, also continue to complain that comparisons between the two poets have distorted our estimations of Henryson: Kinghorn argues the virtues of "independent" reading of the *Testament*; Bennett questions the habit of treating "scenes in Henryson as ironic variations on scenes in Chaucer" (and then treats scenes in Henryson as bungled variations on scenes in Chaucer); McDiarmid argues that the *Testament* should be discussed in relation, not to the *Troilus*, but to Henryson's other poetry and to earlier Scottish literature.[37] Florence Ridley's powerful review of scholarly opinion in "Scottish Chaucerianism" holds that malign term uniquely responsible for the "persistent neglect" and "underestimation" of Middle-Scots poetry throughout its critical history.[38] Though it recognizes the importance of *imitatio* in the fifteenth century, MacQueen's "The Case for Early Scottish Literature" justifies the study of Henryson's poetry by insisting on its originality; according to MacQueen, Henryson's *Testament* makes "five main criticisms of the *Troilus*."[39] MacQueen enriches the Henrysonian text by impoverishing the Chaucerian text.

Such applications of canons of textual autonomy will only obscure the challenges posed by Henryson's poetry to our concepts of textuality and intertextuality. We will be able to revalue Henryson not when we suddenly see how different he is from Chaucer (critics have seen that for quite some time) but when we cease to associate creativity with Romantic myths of originality. Thus, though Alice Miskimin's *The Renaissance Chaucer* values the *Testament* as "the first and greatest of the reinterpretations of Chaucer's *Troilus*" (p. 215), her reliance on Harold Bloom's Great Tradition problematics excludes Henryson from her history of "allegorical irony"—he "precludes uncertainty" (p. 214)—and locates him as "the most Chaucerian of all Chaucerians" (p. 210).

Much new work on Henryson's Chaucerianism has tried to take unprejudiced views of his historical poetics. Critics like Fox, MacDonald, Kratzmann, and Jamieson have documented and investigated Henryson's artistic use of Chaucer in the *Fables*—hitherto a largely taboo subject, since it was chiefly upon the purity of the *Fables* that Scottish-traditionalist views of Henryson stood or fell.[40] Study of the *Testament*'s use of the *Troilus* has also grown in sophistication. Spearing's essay on conciseness, which attempts to link the stylistic economies of the *Testament* both to the poem's revision of Chaucerian ambiguity and to a larger humanist rejection of medieval prolixity, remains one of the most provocative comparisons of Henryson's and Chaucer's stylistic projects.[41] Fox, in his 1966 essay "The Scottish Chaucerians," explains Middle-Scots praise of Chaucer as part of those poets' own aspirations to write "highly civilized and highly wrought" vernacular poetry (p. 169). This early attempt to define Chaucerianism as part of a larger poetics was followed, most recently, by Kratzmann's

*Anglo-Scottish Literary Relations*, which links comparative readings of Henryson and Chaucer to an extended thesis on the dramatic and performative qualities of Middle-Scots poetry. Walter Scheps reads Henryson's revisionist presentation in the *Testament* of a "love vision manqué" as a Caledonian poet's response to the "muted" nationalism of later fifteenth-century Scotland.[42]

Preoccupation with the "Chaucerianism" of the *Testament* has too often inhibited discussion of the poem's other sources and backgrounds—unhappily so, since the larger Troy tradition to which the poem responds is itself so rich and difficult. Eleanor Long recently reopened the question—first debated by Whiting and Kinsley—of the relation beween G. Myll's *Spektakle of Luf* (1492) and the *Testament* by speculating that both were influenced by a work derived from Guido delle Colonne's *Historia Destructionis Troiae*.[43] Gretchen Mieszkowski proposes that Henryson knew Lydgate's *Troy Book* and used it as a source for his description of Venus; Priscilla Bawcutt suggests instead a passage from *Reson and Sensuallyte*.[44] We cannot say whether Henryson used a Scots translation of Guido's *Historia* or the *Troy Book*, but the difficulty of identifying specific sources should not discourage comparative study. The last chapter of C. David Benson's *The History of Troy in Middle English Literature* suggests the importance of this traditional context: he estimates Henryson's response to the matter of Troy as a radical departure from the posture of historical fidelity so central to the strategies of earlier narratives.[45]

Such comparative study is thus beginning to play a role in reevaluations of Henryson's poetics. Mieszkowski's analysis, for example, of Lydgate's and Henryson's narrators questions the notion, put forth by Spearing (p. 182) and Miskimin (pp. 30–31), that fifteenth-century poets failed to appreciate Chaucer's use of narrative personae. Scholars are also beginning to suggest, through study of Henryson's historical backgrounds, ways of defining the periodicity of Henryson's art. Robert Kindrick proposes that Chaucer's influence on Henryson was only part of a larger "Ricardian" inheritance—a problematic but suggestive thesis.[46] Jamieson, through a fine exploration of animal-tale literature in the fifteenth century, suggests in "The Beast Tale" that such works in Middle Scots (the *Fables* among them) are distinctive in part "by their deliberate linking to particular events, personal and private" (p. 27).

The extension of comparative approaches beyond source hunting thus will also enable greater appreciation of Henryson's participation in Middle-Scots literary culture. In different ways, the privileging of the source and the emphasis on Henryson's originality have ironically isolated him from his peers. Though Fox is undoubtedly right to state that the *Testament*'s borrowings from the *Kingis Quair* are "unprovable," Matthew McDiarmid's suggestion that the opening of the *Testament* "owes its sombre setting to the *Kingis Quair*" and not to the *Troilus* is—however determined to ignore Chaucer's presence in both the *Testament* and the *Quair*—the kind of observation on which studies of Middle-Scots poetics may usefully (as with Kratzmann's work) be based.[47]

Perhaps because of the *Orpheus*'s classical appearance and ancestry, that poem, of Henryson's major narratives, has been least stereotyped as either "Chaucerian" or "Scottish," and it has profited greatly from recent interest in Henryson's medieval and Renaissance contexts. Dorena Wright, for example, has discovered a source in the *Graecismus* of Eberhard of Bethune for Henryson's depiction of the Muses; R. J. Manning has explored Henryson's use of materials from the emblem tradition; and MacQueen and Jack speculate on links to Italian humanism.[48] Henryson himself names the two chief sources for the poem: Boethius's *De Consolatione* and Nicholas Trivet's commentary, the latter of which Fox prints in full in his 1981 volume of Henryson's poetry (pp. 384-92).

Scholars generally agree in deriving the *Orpheus* from the medieval Orpheus tradition, which comprised medieval allegoresis of classical myth on the one hand and more "popular" elements from the romance tradition on the other. But they have not succeeded in identifying with any precision the popular influences on the poem. Henryson probably knew a version or versions of the story similar in kind to *Sir Orfeo*; Carol Mills has recently proposed, on no very firm ground, the Auchinleck manuscript text of *Sir Orfeo* as Henryson's source.[49] Because of the nature of the materials involved, scholars have engaged the question of the poem's romance origins more fruitfully from broader comparative perspectives. John Block Friedman's work on Henryson in *Orpheus in the Middle Ages* and Douglas Gray's chapter " 'New Orpheus' " account most fully and comprehensively for the diverse traditions behind the poem, though Friedman and Gray agree neither with each other nor with such scholars as Gros-Louis and Wright concerning the critical significance of Henryson's use of traditional materials.[50] Fox reviews the evidence for the other literary sources, such as Chaucer's *Book of the Duchess* and the *Gesta Romanorum*, but also suggests a new and challenging context for the *Orpheus*: the encyclopedic celestial journey—for which Chaucer's *House of Fame* might provide an earlier, and Douglas's *Palice of Honour* a later, example—which takes as a central concern the nature of the poetic calling itself (p. cix).

Source study of the *Fables* has been complicated by scholarly disagreement over both Henryson's text and his *floruit*. Too, the complex nature of medieval fabulary traditions—traditions at once popular and learned, oral and written—accounts for much scholarly confusion over the nature of Henryson's poem. Both the Aesopic and Reynardian traditions have extremely complicated histories. MacQueen, in *Robert Henryson*, remarks happily that the nature of Henryson's sources reminds us of the fable's "learned Latin background" and "international literary importance" (p. 206); but other scholars, such as Richard Baumann and Shirley Marchalonis, have also emphasized the *Fables'* kinship with popular materials. Fox has most recently argued that Henryson probably relied chiefly on his own powers of memory and invention when composing the poem.[51]

Earlier scholars succeeded in proposing a number of likely sources for the *Fables*: Gualterus Anglicus's version of the *Romulus* (ca. 1175), the *Nun's Priest's Tale*, Lydgate's *Isopes Fabules* (in a minor way), a fable in the *Disciplina Clericalis* of Petrus Alfonsi (ca. 1100). Here traditional consensus ended and the debates of recent years began. David Crowne discussed anew Henryson's debt to Caxton in his "A Date for the Composition of Henryson's *Fables*."[52] He argues "a distinct division" among three groups of fables: those borrowing from Gualterus and Lydgate; those borrowing from, and hence dated after, Caxton's *Reynard* (1481); and those borrowing from Caxton's *Aesop* (1484). In 1964, Jamieson's invaluable dissertation on Henryson's sources reviewed available evidence and unearthed fresh possibilities.[53] In 1966 Anthony Jenkins added to the brew a new discussion of parallels from the *Roman de Renart*; he argues that Henryson had used a written version of the tenth episode of the *Roman* for his "The Fox, the Wolf, and the Cadger."[54] MacQueen then published, in *Robert Henryson*, two important appendixes on Henryson's use of Aesopic and Reynardian materials. In "The *Morall Fabillis* and the Aesopic Tradition" (Appendix II), MacQueen proposes that Henryson knew and used the *Isopet de Lyon* (or a text similar to it), a French expansion of Gualterus. In "The *Morall Fabillis* and the Beast-Epic" (Appendix III), MacQueen argues that "The Fox and the Wolf" and "The Trial of the Fox" are indebted to Caxton's *Reynard*; that "The Fox, the Wolf, and the Husbandman," like "The Wolf and the Wether," draws on Caxton's *Aesop* as its chief source. In Appendix I, "The Text of the *Morall Fabillis*," MacQueen elaborates a complex theory of the composition of the *Fables*. Those chiefly indebted to Gualterus and the *Isopet* tradition and to Caxton's *Reynard* he dates from 1482 or 1483. Dated after 1484 are the two fables indebted to Caxton's *Aesop* and the fable indebted to the *Roman de Renart*, grouped together by MacQueen because all three are excluded from the "early" version of the *Fables* which he hypothesizes was used by Bannatyne in compiling his manuscript.

MacQueen's work on sources, better known than Crowne's, was generally well received. But in "Henryson and Caxton," Denton Fox attacked the reconstructions of both Crowne and MacQueen. He questioned the logic of dating the "Gualterus" fables before 1481 simply because they showed no sign of Caxton's influence; and he argued that the evidence for the *Fables'* indebtedness to the *Reynard* and the *Aesop* was too frail to support reliably any suppositions about date.[55] Fox, in his 1981 edition of Henryson's poems, also questions Henryson's direct knowledge either of an extended version of the *Roman de Renart* or of the French *Isopets*; his contention that Henryson was "a man of some age in 1462," "active in 1477-8," would make the 1480s an uncomfortably late date for the *Fables'* composition (pp. l, n. 1; xxi).

Since the publication of "Henryson and Caxton" scholars have been more wary of making enthusiastic assertions about Henryson's fabulary sources: Douglas Gray, for example, finds that Caxton's influence has not been "conclusively proved" (p. 32), but other scholars continue to believe that Henryson knew the *Reynard* and the *Aesop*,[56] and investigation of Henryson's materials still flourishes. Richard Schrader offers rhyme evidence to support Henryson's use of the *Isopet de Lyon* and argues that Caxton's *Aesop* may have influenced "The Fox and the Wolf."[57] R. D. S. Jack has recently reopened the question of Caxton's influence by proposing Caxton's *Mirrour of the World*, a translation of the French *Image du Monde*, as a source for "The Cock and the Jasp."[58] Important questions, then, remain to be settled about the implications of Henryson's use of source material.

## Criticism

Before the 1960s, interpretation of Henryson's poetry was chiefly of a discursive, appreciative kind; only critics' belief in Henryson's "orthodox morality" seemed to encourage attention to the logic of his narratives. Readings depended on a view of the representational qualities of Henryson's art that has continued to shape criticism. Thus, for Kinghorn, Henryson is (admirably) less artificial than either Dunbar or Douglas: "his animals speak in the manner of Dunfermline officials, lawyers, or schoolmasters like himself whose diction was precise and to the point" (p. 5). According to MacQueen, Henryson uses "courtly" diction only when he wants to point to the moral turpitude of characters who use such diction (p. 86). Such views have partly served a larger defense of Middle-Scots poetry against charges of rhetorical mannerism; but the dislike of verbal excess has too often inspired defense as well as accusation, and has had not a little to do with distaste for Henryson's *moralitates*. Henryson's poetry still suffers from the kind of critical disposition that finds Chaucer's *Miller's Tale* less artful than the *Knight's Tale*, and hence somehow more honest and plain-spoken. But Daniel Murtaugh, in "Henryson's Animals," reminds us how fully conscious Henryson was that speaking mice, by virtue of, precisely, their impossibly "realistic" speech, are creatures of conspiracy and artifice.[59]

Emphasis on Henryson's representational skills has also led to disproportionate emphasis on Henryson's narrative economy, at the expense of his generic diversity. It has, as well, fortified the view of Henryson's achievement as what Kinsley calls "the art of mirroring his own personality in his work" (p. 16). Kurt Wittig emphasizes the "austerity" of Henryson's "outlook" and language partly because that austerity "is also a national characteristic."[60] Henryson's personality helped, in effect, to guard the Scottish *Sprachgeist*. In view of these attitudes it is scarcely surprising that critical interpretations of Henryson's narrative "speakers" is still in its infancy.[61]

Some of the best recent historicist criticism has addressed the relationship between *moralitas* and tale in Henryson's poetry. Denton Fox's groundbreaking essay "Henryson's Fables" (1962) and I. W. A. Jamieson's "Henryson's 'Fabillis': An Essay towards a Revaluation" (1966) both reject treatment of Henryson's poetry as "documentary" or "autobiographical"; both instead describe Henryson's "basically moral and religious point of view" as the controlling feature of his poetry.[62] For Jamieson, Henryson transformed the earlier beast-fable—hitherto a "collection of much shorter and less sophisticated poems studying unrelated ethical problems"—into "a study of man's essential animality, his desire for the passing pleasures of this world" (p. 21). In this essay, Jamieson has banished historicity from his own discourse because it seemed to interrupt, even to disrupt, the symbolic economy of Henryson's text. Nor has Henryson criticism yet reclaimed the historical allusions that fell thus into disrepute.

Fox, in "Henryson's Fables," argues for that symbolic economy by supposing, on the basis of formalist canons, that the *moralitates* could not be arbitrary; and his supposition has enabled a rhetoric of resolution in which the critic marries tale to *moralitas*—no longer an inorganic "imposition" but "an essential and central part" of Henryson's work (p. 338). Fox thus locates the "fundamental conflict" of the *Fables* in the gap between the tale's world of fallen nature and the *moralitas*' invocation of timeless verities. The critical task, then, is to demonstrate how the reader is left, "at the end, with a single whole: the fable and the *moralitas*, the visible world and its significance, have become one" (p. 356). John MacQueen's thematic pairing, in *Robert Henryson*, of the "Preaching of the Swallow" and the "Lion and the Mouse" constituted a significant advance in criticism of the narrative structure of the *Fables*, simply by implying that there might be one. Like Fox and Jamieson he describes the *Fables*' overarching concern as "the carnal passions of fallen man" (p. 100) or the fall of intellect to appetite, themes which he also finds in the *Testament* and *Orpheus*. MacQueen insists that the *moralitates* were meant to present only a part of the narrative's potential meanings. Not surprisingly, the "virtue" of a fable like "The Cock and the Jasp" is "the satisfactory resolution of the apparent conflict" brought about by the interdependence of meaning between tale and *moralitas* (pp. 110, 100). MacQueen's view of Henryson's poetry is ultimately ahistorical—that nothing, save historical allusions themselves, distinguishes Henryson's allegoresis from that of earlier medieval, or later Renaissance, poets. But his work established Henryson's rhetorical artistry; it usefully treated his poetry as a canon; and it legitimated for some time to come the pursuit of historicism.

Later treatments of Henryson's allegoresis have tended to accommodate more largely its felt discords. Harold E. Toliver's essay "Robert Henryson: From *Moralitas* to Irony" (1965) marks the beginning of this trend. His work is grounded in the historicist revisionism of that era; but his insistence that Henryson sought, throughout his poetry, to resolve the claims of "sympathy and moral judgment in an ironic solution" offered a newly powerful perspective on the self-conscious nature of Henryson's didacticism and on the function of narrative disjuncture as a source of moral awareness.[63] These insights prepared for Jamieson's suggestion, in 1972, that Henryson experiments, in some of the fables, with tensions between the particularity of tale and the abstraction of *moralitas* to produce a new "relativism," one which "leads to tolerance, because it demands of those professing it knowledge and self-awareness" (p. 29). Douglas Gray similarly contends that Henryson's moralizations "are not presented as inevitable or all-inclusive 'messages' " (p. 129). The moral of the *Orpheus*, for example, only "draws attention to some (and to some unexpected) moral aspects of the philosophical tale"; the narrative itself remains a story about the heroism and tragic excess of human love.[64] Finally, for Gray, Henryson achieves complementarity between *moralitas* and tale through an "ironic vision" large enough to contain "sympathy and detachment, comedy and tragedy" (p. 113).

The reconciliation of tale and *moralitas* has thus come to seem a goal as much of discovery as of recovery. The particular pleasures of what Fox calls Henryson's "witty and paradoxical" allegory (*Poems*, p. cix), and Gray his startling " 'dark' moralities" (p. 124) has occupied the center of much recent criticism. Kratzmann has remarked on Henryson's contribution to the Scottish tradition of a "non-explicit species of allegory"; and Richard Schrader suggests that Rosemond Tuve's research into fifteenth-century tastes for "imposed" allegory may illuminate study of Henryson's *moralitates*.[65] Edward Schweitzer's essay on "The Bludy Serk" urges that we "recapture ... the typically medieval excitement of ... seeing the meaning we have perceived confirmed by the *moralitas* at the end" (p. 170). A. C. Henderson, in "Medieval Beasts and Modern Cages: The Making of Meaning in Fables and Bestiaries," goes further in discussing problems of "predictability" and surprise in engaging Henryson's *Fables*, in part by raising questions about the very authenticity of "medieval" meanings.[66]

Some recent critics reject the recuperation offered by the pleasures of allegory. In Murtaugh's fine essay on Henryson's self-conscious exploitation of the beast-fable's central fictive proposition—that of the speaking animal—"figurative technique," that touchstone of historicist reading, is itself undone when rational "beistis" return to the brutality of silence. The split between *moralitas* and tale suggested to Murtaugh, as the *Testament* had to Douglas Duncan, a Henryson torn between "deep humanity" and "strict moral sense."[67] The thematization of disjuncture is also central to Matthew McDiarmid's vision of a Henryson whose preoccupation with "the tragedy of sin" forms the obverse of his profound attachment to life, who feels "a strong tension between accepted doctrine and feeling response" (p. 31). The bleakness of vision which McDiarmid ascribes to an age of "indecision" also explains, in George Clark's "Henryson and Aesop: The Fable Transformed" (1976), the conflictual relations among tales and *moralitates* in the *Fables*. Indeed, for Clark, the *Fables*' stance toward the tradition of Aesopic moralism is fundamentally revisionist—as is Clark's own stance toward historicist readings that "treat Henryson's fables as emphatically Aesopian and moralizing and therefore good" (p. 1).

Such critical attention to the problems of Henryson's allegoresis has fostered interest in his poetics. The *Orpheus*, because it is, at least in part, about poetry, is being read more carefully. Fox describes it as a "defence of poetry" (*Poems*, p. cix); for McDiarmid, too, the poem states that "the experience of poetry ... [has] its proper effect 'Quhen our desyre with resoun makis pes'" (p. 32). Some of the best work to be done in the area of poetics—Ian Jamieson's "'To preue thare preching be a poesye': Some Thoughts on Henryson's Poetics" and "Some Attitudes to Poetry in Late Fifteenth-Century Scotland"—describes an awareness, central to Henryson's work, of the challenge posed to the "moral purpose of poetry" by its "sophisticated pleasures."[68] In the former essay, he describes the narrative structure of the *Fables* as a means of debating the "varying potentialities of poetry" to delight and instruct and likens this experimentation to the similarly "incomplete" essays of Chaucer's *Canterbury Tales* and *House of Fame* (pp. 31–32).

Critical discourse on the *Testament* similarly works through a polarity of judgment and sympathy. Uncertainty over the nature of the poem's attitude toward Cresseid has been furthered by debate over the nature of her crime, the symbolic status of the planetary gods, the truth value of her dream, and the significance to the poem of *fin' amors*, to name but a few of the poem's unresolved cruxes. Many critics believe that Henryson feels sympathy for his heroine. Jane Adamson's "'Fyre and Cauld'" is one example of this often-sentimentalizing view; most often the apparently retributive moralism of the poem is put to the service of an ultimately compassionate authorial purpose: Cresseid cannot be redeemed unless she is first punished with leprosy, poverty, and death.[69] Tatyana Moran's essay "*The Testament of Cresseid* and the *Book of Troylus*" will still refresh the scholar weary of such moralizing: though Henryson himself may not have taken "sadistic pleasure" in describing "Cresseid's transformation from her lovely former self into a repulsive leper," Moran's account does justice to some of the brutalities of Henryson's narrative and rejects the kind of prurient moralism that constitutes one of the poem's most powerful temptations.[70] Larry Sklute's "Phoebus Descending: Rhetoric and Moral Vision in Henryson's *Testament of Cresseid*" is a subtler reading than Moran's. Sklute argues that the sympathetic rhetorical gestures of Henryson's "hypocritical narrator" serve to disguise the poet's "stern sense of moral retribution," and he usefully urges the importance of the *Legend of Good Women* to the *Testament*'s treatment of the theme of judgment (p. 190).

The meaning of the *Testament* has habitually been located within the heroine's experience of a developing selfhood. Kratzmann, Ridley, and others have viewed Henryson's decision to grant Cresseid her own fate as central to the meaning of the poem and to its revision of the *Troilus*; and Jennifer Strauss remarks that "Henryson is unusual among medieval poets in treating a heroine seriously as the center of moral consciousness."[71] When the historicism of the 1960s valorized Henryson's tropology, the justification of Cresseid's crime and punishment became newly urgent; formal analysis thus centered around the trial scene, and larger questions of genre were deferred. In a reading similar in temper to Spearing's account, in "Conciseness," of the poem as "a relentless accumulation of misfortunes," Douglas Duncan tried to redeem Henryson by displacing the harshness of the poem onto the planetary gods, regarded as symbols of a "divine order," the justice of whose dispensation Henryson questioned "quite peremptorily."[72] Many critics have softened the impact of Cresseid's sentence by viewing that doom as a mere preliminary to redemption, her crime as merely a sign for other, more serious, faults. E. D. Aswell's essay "The Role of Fortune in *The Testament of Cresseid*" argues that Cresseid is justly punished by the planetary gods, themselves representations of "natural law," not for blasphemy but for a thorough misunderstanding of her own status as a creature; she atones by "becoming a model or type of the mortal creature subjected to Fortune's whims."[73] The narrator offers an exemplary contrast to Cresseid's presumption by his own Boethian "obedience" to the natural forces of time—a view of him shared by MacQueen and Ridley. MacQueen's allegorical interpretation in *Robert Henryson* viewed Cresseid's leprosy as punishment for "lightness in love." Fox, in his 1968 edition of the *Testament*, argued that Cresseid's leprosy brought her "into an understanding of herself and the world" because of the leper's specially close relationship to God. Fox's reading of the poem warns not so much against blasphemy or even infidelity as against "the vanity of sexual love," revealed through Henryson's ironic use of a courtly love "framework"—including a "stupid and passionately involved" "aged servant of love" as narrator (pp. 53–56, 23).[74]

Gretchen Mieszkowski agrees with Fox (and, ultimately, with Toliver) in reading this narrator as a Chaucerian ironic device meant to enable sympathy but demand educated judgment.[75] Both critics thereby rationalize the eccentric temper of this narrator's response to Cresseid. More recently, W. S. Ramson, in "'Quha falsit Cresseid?'" has suggestively interpreted the narrator as a condemnatory "parody" of Chaucer's own urbane, tolerant narrator (p. 33). C. W. Jentoft's extended comparison of Chaucer's and Henryson's narrators finds Henryson's exploitation of comic and ironic stances to be entirely in line with Chaucer's own, and sympathetic in character. Jentoft, moreover, argues that the *Testament* is not an exemplum illustrating the "wages of lust"; his own contention that Cresseid is judged by courtly, not orthodox, morality at least accounts for Henryson's use of the court of love tradition.[76] Robert Kindrick's reading of the *Testament* proposes that, partly because of changing conceptions of the courtly code in the fifteenth century, Henryson is able to reconcile Christian theology and courtly morality, "both *eros* and *agape*" (p. 148).[77]

Such restitutions of courtliness to Henryson's text often took place in reaction to the moralizings of what Dolores Noll, in her own exploration of Henryson's "courtly love premises," calls the "Christian School."[78] But these readings shared the narratological assumptions and idealizing tendencies of the allegorical ironists: for Del Chessell, the *Testament* teaches

Cresseid properly to value both Troilus's real nobility and the code of love whose virtues he exemplifies.[79] The work of the 1970s often, however, criticized exegetical readings and began to articulate more carefully the fifteenth-century cultural and intellectual context for Henryson's poetry. John McNamara, in "Divine Justice in Henryson's *Testament of Cresseid*," interprets Henryson's cautious ambiguity on the subject of divine justice as characteristic of late medieval theology: though Saturn's "sentence" may seem unreasonably cruel, it is vindicated, not by Christian salvation, but experientially by Cresseid's moral redemption.[80] Lee Patterson's "Christian and Pagan in *The Testament of Cresseid*" takes Cresseid from shame to guilt, from the parody of justice available in a limited pagan universe to true repentance and charity, and takes the pagan narrator from the false consolations of escapist love fiction to confrontation with the possibility of genuine spiritual renewal.[81]

Patterson's work exemplifies a growing interest in the poem's generic variety, in its inclusion of what MacQueen describes as "lyrical comments" on the narrative; Götz Schmitz's piece on Henryson's ironic transversion of the complaint form and Ralph Hanna's on Cresseid's "sleeping vision" demonstrate the usefulness of studying the poem's "lyrical comments" within their generic contexts.[82] But slow progress in this area has been part of a larger failure to explore seriously the overall genre of the poem, to treat it too automatically as a *Bildungsroman*. Though the early editors name the poem a "Testament," few critics have explored the potential significance of this title—Fox notes, however, that "the whole poem can be considered Cresseid's testament, just as the whole New Testament was regarded 'as the last will and Testament of Our Lord' " (*Poems*, p. civ). While critics arguing for Cresseid's redemption seem at times to be working with a comic paradigm, many have accepted the designation "tragedie"—Jane Adamson, for example, and Matthew McDiarmid, the latter of whom reads the poem as a Boethian tragedy whose heroine's last thoughts are of "unamendable wrong, disastrous folly, final loss" (p. 38). Paul Strohm, in "Storie, Spelle, Geste, Romaunce, Tragedie: Generic Distinctions in the Middle English Troy Narratives," also contends that "tragedie" is "the most instructive generic designation within the poem," pointing out that though Henryson and Chaucer share the term "tragedy," only Henryson completely eschews the generic designations common to Troy legend that claimed historicity.[83]

W. S. Ramson's " 'Quha falsit Cresseid?' " makes the question of genre central to its interpretation of the poem. Ramson argues, refreshingly, that the frequency of digressive episodes in the *Testament* belies modern critical emphasis on the linearity of the narrative. Ramson's own readings are too often reductive: the "worthie Troilus" is a blind idolator, Cresseid remains throughout a static symbol of "Wantonness." Nor does Ramson fully succeed in ridding us of notions of narrative development and moral enlightenment; he displaces *entente* from the text of the poem to the minds of those "deluded servants of Venus" who made up the poem's immediate audience. Thus, the poem seems a "tragedie" only from the unrecuperated "courtly" standpoint of the prologue; it becomes a "ballet schort" once the moral limitations of that standpoint have been transcended.

The reading of the *Testament* proposed by Douglas Gray is perhaps the most comprehensive attempt yet to account for the *Testament* as tragedy—in this case, as "a medieval tragedy in the Senecan mode" (p. 166). Gray, like McDiarmid, views Cresseid as both responsible and not responsible for her fate; this is simply the tragic dilemma, not proof of the poet's personal despair of divine justice. The narrator plays a "'choric' role," mingling moral instruction and "'piete'" (p. 172). Henryson thus exploits tragic tension between fate and responsibility, divine power and human pity, in a poem whose complexities of voice and gesture recall the shifting ironies of the *Fables* and remind us that Gray's Henryson is a poet of the fifteenth century, striving to achieve an elusive harmony.

Gray is thus, like his Henryson, very much a writer in search of balance among conflicting points of view. But critics are not likely to accept very widely his recuperation of their controversies, partly because the genre of the rival reading occupies a disproportionate place in the history of recent commentary on this poem. Perhaps only in Jamieson's most recent essays on poetics does the critic's experience of Henryson's poetry help to redefine at all boldly what Henryson's texts did with, and did to, fifteenth-century literature. Elsewhere the sense that history can lead us to Henryson, but that Henryson can lead us neither to history nor to ourselves, has been formalized in essays that must conclude with—not from—his text.

Still, the interpretive rivalries that have grown up around Henryson's poetry bespeak wealth as well as poverty. That critics have so frequently been urged to determine the indeterminacy of his text attests its power to disturb our notions of signification. It is a text that demands a criticism both self-aware and deeply at risk.

## Notes

1. Florence Ridley, "Middle Scots Writers," in Albert E. Hartung, ed., *A Manual of the Writings in Middle English: 1050-1500* (Hamden, Ct.: Archon Books/The Shoe String Press for the Connecticut Academy of Arts and Sciences, 1973), vol. 4. See also Priscilla Bawcutt's entry in George Watson, ed., *The New Cambridge Bibliography of English Literature* (Cambridge: Cambridge University Press, 1974), vol. 1; R. H. Carnie, "The Bibliography of Scottish Literature 1957-1967: A Survey," *Forum for Modern Language Studies* 3 (1967): 263-75; James Kidd and R. H. Carnie, eds., *Annual Bibliography of Scottish Literature*, supplement to *The Bibliotheck*, (1969— ). William Geddie's *A Bibliography of Middle Scots Poets*, Scottish Text Society, vol. 7 (Edinburgh and London: William Blackwood, 1912) is still necessary.

2. Bengt Ellenberger, *The Latin Element in the Vocabulary of the Earlier Makars Henryson and Dunbar*, eds. Claes Schaar and Jan Svartvik, Lund Studies in English, 51 (Lund: CWK Gleerup, 1977). Ellenberger provides important evidence for reconsideration of clichés about Henryson's "popular" diction; an example is Isabel Hyde, "Poetic Imagery: A Point of Comparison between Henryson and Dunbar," *Studies in Scottish Literature* 2 (1965): 183-197. Two useful essays on Middle Scots are by A. J. Aitken: "Variation and Variety in Written Middle Scots," in A. J. Aitken, Angus McIntosh, and Hermann Pálsson, eds., *Edinburgh Studies in English and Scots* (London: Longman, 1971), pp. 177-209; and "How to Pronounce Older Scots," in A. J. Aitken, M. P. McDiarmid and Derick S. Thomson, eds., *Bards and Makars: Scottish Language and Literature: Medieval and Renaissance* (Glasgow: University of Glasgow Press, 1977), pp. 1-21. For specialized work see J. W. Proctor, "A Description of the Fifteenth Century Scots Dialect of Robert Henryson Based on a Complete Concordance of His Works" (Ph.D. diss., University of Missouri, 1966).

3. I. W. A. Jamieson, "The Minor Poems of Robert Henryson," *Studies in Scottish Literature* 9 (1971-72): 125-47; see especially p. 126.

4. Denton Fox, ed., *The Poems of Robert Henryson* (Oxford: Clarendon Press, 1981). See especially "The Canon," pp. cxv-cxxii.

5. "Henryson and the *Thre Prestis of Peblis*," *Neophilologus* 51 (1967): 168-77.

6. "The Text of Henryson's *Morall Fabillis*," *Innes Review* 14 (1963): 3-9; reprinted, with alterations, as Appendix I to *Robert Henryson: A Study of the Major Narrative Poems* (Oxford: Clarendon Press, 1967), pp. 189-99; see p. 199.

See H. Harvey Wood, ed., *The Poems and Fables of Robert Henryson* (Edinburgh: Oliver and Boyd, 1933; rev. ed. 1958; 1933 ed. reprinted 1978 by the Mercat Press, Edinburgh). Charles Elliott's *Robert Henryson: Poems* (Oxford: Clarendon Press, 1963; rev. ed. 1974; reprint 1978) followed Wood's methods and incorporated his errors.

7. "The Order of the Fables," in Fox, *Poems*, pp. lxxv–lxxxi. Fox argues for the coherence of the Bassandyne order of the *Fables*, and notes the work of H. H. Roerecke in "The Integrity and Symmetry of Robert Henryson's *Moral Fables*" (Ph.D. diss., Pennsylvania State University, 1969). Scholars have, in general, badly neglected consideration of the *Fables'* narrative structure. But see A. C. Spearing, "Central and Displaced Sovereignty in Three Medieval Poems," *Review of English Studies* 33 (1982): 247–61, which supports the Bassandyne order, and contends that the need for mercy to temper royalty and triumph is a central concern of the *Fables'* center—"The Lion and the Mouse." For further discussion of the structure of the *Fables*, see p. 73 in this essay.

8. In Aitken et al., *Bards and Makars*, pp. 172–83. R. J. Lyall has also argued for the importance of the Bannatyne version of *Orpheus* in "The Bannatyne 'Additions' to Henryson's *Orpheus and Euridices*," *Neuphilologische Mitteilungen* 81 (1980): 416–23.

9. *Studies in Scottish Literature* 8 (1970): 75–96.

10. Denton Fox, ed., *Robert Henryson: Testament of Cresseid* (London: Thomas Nelson, 1968), pp. 131–32.

11. In Aitken et al., *Bards and Makars*, pp. 156–71; see especially p. 169.

12. See Fox, *Poems*, pp. lv–lvi; Gregory Kratzmann discusses the print's introductory dialogue between Smith and "Aesop" in *Anglo-Scottish Literary Relations: 1430–1550* (Cambridge: Cambridge University Press, 1980), pp. 102–03. The prologue and a list of contents are printed in David Laing, ed., *The Poems and Fables of Robert Henryson* (Edinburgh, 1865), pp. 267–73.

13. See John MacQueen's "The Literature of Fifteenth-Century Scotland," in Jennifer M. Brown, ed., *Scottish Society in the Fifteenth Century* (London: Edward Arnold; New York: St. Martin's Press, 1977), pp. 184–208; see especially p. 205.

14. *Scottish Literary Journal* 3 (1976): 5–29.

15. *Texas Studies in Literature and Language* 15 (1973): 391–403; especially p. 402.

16. See Douglas Gray, *Robert Henryson* (Leiden: E. J. Brill; Cambridge: Cambridge University Press, 1979), p. 228.

17. MacQueen, "Literature of Fifteenth-century Scotland," p. 206; W. S. Ramson, "A Reading of Henryson's *Testament*, or 'Quha falsit

Cresseid?'" *Parergon* 17 (1977): 25-35; see p. 27.

18. Robert Kindrick, *Robert Henryson* (Boston: Twayne Publishers, 1979); see especially pp. 182 and 185, where Kindrick notes Henryson's "synthetic genius" and his importance as a stylist to later poets.

19. Another important source for Henryson's influence on Douglas is Priscilla Bawcutt's *Gavin Douglas: A Critical Study* (Edinburgh: Edinburgh University Press, 1976), especially pp. 43-44. See Kratzmann, *Anglo-Scottish Relations*, p. 257, on Henryson and Lindsay's *The Testament of the Papyngo*.

20. Fox reviews the English textual tradition in *Robert Henryson* (1968), pp. 9-13. Ann Thompson's *Shakespeare's Chaucer: A Study in Literary Origins* (New York: Barnes & Noble, 1978) provides useful background on this subject and points to some important literary parallels (see especially pp. 136, 143). But Thompson views the *Testament* as a "distortion" of Chaucer's poem; and her definition of what constituted "Chaucer" for Shakespeare and his peers fails to take into account the contemporary textual situation and Henryson's central place within it. The same error to some extent mars Alice S. Miskimin's *The Renaissance Chaucer* (New Haven: Yale University Press, 1975). For consideration of Henryson's possible influence on Wyatt, see Kratzmann, *Anglo-Scottish Relations*, pp. 189-91; 270, n. 16; and Denton Fox's "A Scoto-Danish Stanza, Wyatt, Henryson, and the Two Mice," *Notes and Queries*, n.s. 18 (June 1971): 203-07.

21. *PMLA* 32 (1917): 383-429; Marshall Stearns first questioned Rollins's findings in "Robert Henryson and the Leper Cresseid," *Modern Language Notes* 59 (1944): 265-69; see p. 265, n. 2 and also "Henryson and Chaucer," in *Robert Henryson* (New York: Columbia University Press, 1949), p. 53, n. 16.

22. Gretchen Mieszkowski, "The Reputation of Criseyde: 1155-1500," *Transactions of the Connecticut Academy of Arts and Sciences* 43 (1971): 71-153.

23. "Phoebus Descending: Rhetoric and Moral Vision in Henryson's *Testament of Cresseid*," *English Literary History* 44 (1977): 189-204; see p. 198.

24. *Essays and Studies* 17 (1964): 24-40, especially pp. 38-40. See also John Bayley, "Shakespeare's Only Play," *Stratford Papers on Shakespeare*, ed. B. W. Jackson (Toronto: University of Toronto Press, 1963), 58-83.

25. "Henryson's *Testament of Cresseid* and Heywood's *A Woman Killed with Kindness*," *Renaissance Quarterly* 20 (1967): 16-21.

26. In *Forum for Modern Language Studies* 3 (1967): 201-22. Pace MacQueen, the *Orpheus* is not "proof enough" that Henryson was up on Greek studies (see *Robert Henryson*, p. 19). But see also MacQueen, "Neoplatonism and Orphism in Fifteenth-Century Scotland: The Evidence of Henryson's 'New Orpheus,'" *Scottish Studies* 20 (1976): 69-89.

27. (Edinburgh: Edinburgh University Press, 1972), p. 14; see also pp. 8-9.

28. Sergio Rossi, in *Robert Henryson* (Milan: Carlo Marzorati, 1955), similarly contended that Henryson synthesized the medieval period rather than anticipating the "tempi della Riforma" (p. 1); few scholars seem to have read his work. R. J. Schrader suggests we view Henryson as a "transitional figure" in "Henryson and Nominalism," *Journal of Medieval and Renaissance Studies* 8 (1978): 1-15; see p. 2.

29. Fox prints the most important evidence in full in *Poems*, pp. xiii-xiv.

30. G. G. Smith, *The Poems of Robert Henryson*, Scottish Text Society, 1st ser. 55, 58 (Edinburgh and London: William Blackwood, 1906-14; reprint New York 1968), 2 vols.; Diebler, "Henrisone's Fabeldichtungen" (Halle, 1885); Janet M. Smith, *The French Background of Middle Scots Literature* (Edinburgh and London: Oliver and Boyd, 1934).

31. Fox, *Poems*, p. cv, n. 2; Gray, *Robert Henryson*, pp. 219-20. For full discussion see R. J. Lyall, "Did Poliziano Influence Henryson's *Orpheus and Eurydices?*" *Forum for Modern Language Studies* 15 (1979): 209-21.

32. See MacQueen, *Robert Henryson*, pp. 46-47; idem, "Some Aspects," 209. Fox (*Poems*, p. 350, note to ll. 151-263) argues that some of the planetary portraits resemble the short chapters in pseudo-Albricius's *Libellus de imaginibus deorum*. R. J. Lyall argues against MacQueen that Henryson worked from medieval, not humanist, sources in constructing *Orpheus*, the *Testament*'s planetary portraits, and the Prologue to the *Fables*. See "Henryson and Boccaccio: A Problem in the Study of Sources," *Anglia* 99 (1981): 38-59. Priscilla Bawcutt's "Henryson's 'Poeit of the Auld Fassoun,'" *Review of English Studies* 32 (1981): 429-34, finds details in Henryson's portrait of Mercury that suggest the poet's familiarity with humanist pictorial traditions (p. 434).

33. Jamieson's "The Beast Tale in Middle Scots: Some Thoughts on the History of a Genre," *Parergon* 2 (1972): 26-36, documents the striking popularity of animal-tale literature in the fifteenth century. Gray's second chapter gives an account of the development of the fabulary tradition and incorporates material on wisdom literature and animal symbolism. See also John Block Friedman, "Henryson, the Friars, and the *Confessio Reynardi*," *Journal of English and Germanic Philology* 66 (1967): 550-61, for an account of Henryson's use of mendicant satire.

34. Smith, *French Background*, p. 101. For commentary, see Gray, *Robert Henryson*, p. 261; Fox, *Poems*, p. 442; Jamieson, "Minor Poems," p. 135.

35. Fox, "Henryson's 'Sum Practysis of Medecyne,'" *Studies in Philology* 69 (1972): 453-60; Schweitzer, "The Allegory of Robert Henryson's 'The Bludy Serk,'" *Studies in Scottish Literature* 15 (1980): 165-74. Schweitzer argues convincingly against George Peek's suggestion ("Robert Henryson's

View of Original Sin in 'The Bloody Serk,' " ibid. 10 [1973]: 199-206) that the source for the "Serk" was the Middle English version of the *Gesta Romanorum* in British Library MS. Harley 7333. For two fine readings of "The Annunciation," see John Stephens, "Devotion and Wit in Henryson's 'The Annunciation,' " *English Studies* 51 (1970): 323-31; and Charles A. Hallett, "Theme and Structure in Henryson's 'The Annunciation,' " *Studies in Scottish Literature* 10 (1973): 165-74.

36. James Kinsley, "The Medieval Makars," in Kinsley, ed., *Scottish Poetry: A Critical Survey* (London: Cassell, 1955), pp. 17-18; R. Marken, "Chaucer and Henryson: A Comparison," *Discourse* 7 (1964): 381-87; Elliott, *Henryson: Poems*; Bennett, "Henryson's *Testament*: A Flawed Masterpiece," *Scottish Literary Journal* 1 (1974): 5-16.

37. A. M. Kinghorn, ed., *The Middle Scots Poets* (London: Edward Arnold; Evanston: Northwestern University Press, 1970), especially pp. 23-24; Matthew P. McDiarmid, "Robert Henryson in His Poems," in Aitken et al., *Bards and Makars*, pp. 27-40; see p. 34.

38. Florence Ridley, "A Plea for the Middle Scots," in Larry D. Benson, ed., *The Learned and the Lewed: Studies in Chaucer and Medieval Literature* (Cambridge, Mass.: Harvard University Press, 1974), pp. 175-96; see p. 176.

39. In *Edinburgh Studies in English and Scots*, pp. 238-39, 240; Henryson, for example, finds Chaucer's poem too "prolix."

40. Chaucer's *Nun's Priest's Tale* had long been recognized as a source for "The Cock and the Fox," but the first real attempt to document the debt was Donald MacDonald's "Henryson and Chaucer: Cock and Fox," *Texas Studies in Literature and Language* 8 (1967): 451-61. Fox, "The Scottish Chaucerians," in D. S. Brewer, ed., *Chaucer and Chaucerians: Critical Studies in Middle English Literature* (University, Ala.: University of Alabama Press, 1966), 164-200; Kratzmann, *Anglo-Scottish Relations*, pp. 91-93; and Jamieson, "The Beast Tale," pp. 30-31, agree that Henryson's revisions of Chaucer enhance the moral *entente* of the tale. See also MacDonald's "Chaucer's Influence on Henryson's *Fables*: The Use of Proverbs and Sententiae," *Medium Aevum* 39 (1970): 21-27, an important attempt to broaden discussion of Chaucer's presence in the *Fables* beyond the confines of "The Cock and the Fox."

41. A. C. Spearing, "Conciseness and the *Testament of Cresseid*," in *Criticism and Medieval Poetry* (London: Edward Arnold, 1964; 2nd ed. 1972), pp. 118-44 (157-92, 2nd ed.); originally appeared as "The *Testament of Cresseid* and the High Concise Style," *Speculum* 37 (1962): 208-25.

42. "A Climatological Reading of Henryson's *Testament of Cresseid*,"

*Studies in Scottish Literature* 15 (1980): 80–87.

43. See "Robert Henryson's 'Uther Quair,'" *Comitatus* 3 (1972): 97–101; B. J. Whiting, "A Probable Allusion to Henryson's *Testament of Cresseid*," *Modern Language Review* 40 (1945): 46–47; James Kinsley, *TLS* (14 November 1952), p. 793. For comment, see Fox, *Poems*, p. xix; Kratzmann, *Anglo-Scottish Relations*, p. 85.

44. Mieszkowski, "Reputation of Criseyde," pp. 136–7; Bawcutt, *Notes and Queries*, n.s. 15 (1968): 435–36; see Fox, *Poems*, p. lxxxiii. A comprehensive review of the *Testament*'s backgrounds is in Sydney J. Harth's "Convention and Creation in the Poetry of Robert Henryson: A Study of *The Testament of Cresseid* and *Orpheus and Eurydice*" (Ph.D. diss., University of Chicago, 1960).

45. C. David Benson, *The History of Troy in Middle English Literature: Guido delle Colonne's Historia Destructionis Troiae in Medieval England* (Woodbridge, Suffolk: D. S. Brewer; Totowa, N.J.: Rowman & Littlefield, 1980), p. 143. The chapter is a slightly expanded version of "Troilus and Cresseid in Henryson's *Testament*," *Chaucer Review* 13 (1979): 263–71. Sergio Rossi, *Robert Henryson*, pp. 66–67, discusses Henryson's poem in the context of the *De Excidio Trojae Historia* and *Le Roman de Troie*, but his insistence on the "indipendenza di poeta" hampers his comparativism.

46. Kindrick, *Robert Henryson*, p. 29. John A. Burrow's "Henryson: 'The Preaching of the Swallow,'" *Essays in Criticism* 25 (1975): 25–37, compares Henryson's treatment of the theme of Prudence to the practice of the *Gawain*-poet in poems like *Patience* and *Purity*, but accounts for the resemblance only in general terms. For an extended treatment of Henryson as Ricardian, see C. David Benson's "O Moral Henryson," in this volume.

47. Fox, *Poems*, p. xx; McDiarmid, "Robert Henryson," p. 34. Both the *Quair*-poet and Henryson break apart the structure of the dream-vision without discarding the fragments, an important resemblance in revisionist practice. A. C. Spearing's *Medieval Dream-Poetry* (Cambridge: Cambridge University Press, 1976) contains helpful comparative work on Henryson's use of the dream-vision in "The Lion and the Mouse," pp. 188–89.

48. Dorena A. Wright, "Henryson's *Orpheus and Eurydice* and the Tradition of the Muses," *Medium Aevum* 40 (1971): 41–47; R. J. Manning, "A Note on Symbolic Identification in Henryson's 'Orpheus and Eurydice,'" *Studies in Scottish Literature* 8 (1971): 265–71. On MacQueen and Jack, see above, n. 26.

49. Carol Mills, "Romance Convention and Robert Henryson's 'Orpheus and Eurydice,'" in Aitken et al., *Bards and Makars*, pp. 52–60.

50. John Block Friedman, *Orpheus in the Middle Ages* (Cambridge, Mass.: Harvard University Press, 1970), especially pp. 195–211. Kenneth Gros-

Louis, "Robert Henryson's *Orpheus and Eurydice* and the Orpheus Tradition of the Middle Ages," *Speculum* 41 (1966): 643–55. See below, n. 68.

51. Richard Baumann, "The Folktale and Oral Tradition in the Fables of Robert Henryson," *Fabula* 6 (1963): 108–24, has been criticized for undervaluing written sources. See MacQueen, *Robert Henryson*, p. 214, n. 1; Anthony W. Jenkins, "Henryson's 'The Fox, the Wolf, and the Cadger' Again," *Studies in Scottish Literature* 4 (1966): 107–12; especially p. 108. Fox, *Poems*, p. xlvii. Shirley Marchalonis, "Three Medieval Tales and their Modern American Analogues," *Journal of the Folklore Institute* 13 (1976): 173–84. See also Evelyn S. Newlyn, 'Robert Henryson and the Popular Fable Tradition in the Middle Ages," *Journal of Popular Culture* 14 (1980): 108–18.

52. *Journal of English and Germanic Philology* 61 (1962): 583–90.

53. "The Poetry of Robert Henryson: A Study of the Use of Source Material" (Ph.D. diss., University of Edinburgh, 1964). See also Jamieson, "A Further Source for Henryson's 'Fabillis,'" *Notes & Queries*, n.s. 14 (1967): 403–05, which discusses Odo of Cheriton's *De asino nolente venire ad parliamentum leonis* as a source for "The Trial of the Fox."

54. Jenkins, "Henryson's 'The Fox.'"

55. *Journal of English and Germanic Philology* 67 (1968): 586–93.

56. Kindrick, *Robert Henryson*, pp. 63–64; Jamieson, "Beast Tale," p. 28.

57. Richard J. Schrader, "Some Backgrounds of Henryson," *Studies in Scottish Literature* 15 (1980): 124–138; see especially p. 125.

58. "Caxton's *Mirrour of the World* and Henryson's 'Taill of the Cok and the Jasp,'" *Chaucer Review* 13 (1978): 157–65.

59. Daniel M. Murtaugh, "Henryson's Animals," *Texas Studies in Literature and Language* 14 (1972): 405–21. See also Robert Pope, "A Sly Toad, Physiognomy and the Problem of Deceit: Henryson's *The Paddok and the Mous*," *Neophilologus* 63 (1979): 461–68, for a discussion of Henryson's use of physiognomic lore to emphasize problems of interpretation.

60. Kurt Wittig, *The Scottish Tradition in Literature* (Edinburgh and London: Oliver and Boyd, 1958), p. 36. Cf. Tom Scott, ed., *Late Medieval Scots Poetry: A Selection from the Makars and Their Heirs Down to 1610* (New York: Barnes & Noble, 1967), p. 24: "Henryson's language is probably the purest literary norm of the period."

61. But see Jamieson's "Some Attitudes to Poetry in Late Fifteenth-Century Scotland," *Studies in Scottish Literature* 15 (1980): 28–42, for important new work on the function of the narrator in the *Fables*; and especially George Clark's "Henryson and Aesop: the Fable Transformed," *English Literary History* 43 (1976): 1–18. Kindrick usefully compares the narrator to

Langland, (*Robert Henryson*, pp. 99–100). Cf. also MacQueen, *Robert Henryson*, p. 64.

62. Fox, "Henryson's Fables," *English Literary History* 29 (1962): 337–56; Jamieson, "Henryson's 'Fabillis': An Essay towards a Revaluation," *Words: Wai-te-ata Studies in Literature* 2 (1966): 20–31; the quotation is from Jamieson, p. 21. Cf. Rossi, *Robert Henryson*, p. 18. Burrow's important essay "The Preaching of the Swallow" similarly proposes the theme of Prudence as "the unifying principle" of the fable (p. 32). Sandra Whipple Spanier, "Structural Symmetry in Henryson's 'The Preiching of the Swallow,'" *Comitatus* 10 (1979–80): 123–27, argues for the fable's "subtle resolution" of "apparent conflict of tones," p. 124.

63. Harold E. Toliver, "Robert Henryson: From *Moralitas* to Irony," *English Studies* 46 (1965): 300–09; see especially p. 300.

64. Gray, *Robert Henryson*, pp. 235, 263. Critics have, of course, disagreed on this point. Dorena Wright suggests that Henryson either "wavered" between allegorical methods or intended the *moralitas* to be optional; Manning and Friedman both argue that the *moralitas* is meant to gloss an "emblematic" tale; Gros-Louis thinks Henryson forgot the *moralitas* while writing the tale.

65. Kratzmann, *Anglo-Scottish Relations*, pp. 249–50; Schrader, "Some Backgrounds," p. 131. Jamieson's "Henryson's *Taill of the Wolf and the Wedder*," *Studies in Scottish Literature* 6 (1969): 248–57, argues that the reader of this fable is surprised by sin.

66. *PMLA* 97 (1982): 40–49.

67. Murtaugh, "Henryson's Animals," p. 408, n. 3; citation from Duncan, "Henryson's *Testament of Cresseid*," *Essays in Criticism* 11 (1961): 128–35; see p. 133. See also Stephan Khinoy, "Tale=Moral Relationships in Henryson's *Moral Fables*," *Studies in Scottish Literature* 17 (1982): 99–115, who suggests that tensions between tale and moral teach the reader to seek consolation not in the world but in spiritual meaning.

68. Jamieson, "'To preue thare preching be a poesye': Some Thoughts on Henryson's Poetics," *Parergon* 8 (1974): 24–36; "Some Attitudes," p. 40.

69. "Henryson's *Testament of Cresseid*: 'Fyre' and 'Cauld,'" *The Critical Review* 18 (1976): 39–60.

70. *Litera* 6 (1959): 18–24; see especially p. 23. Kratzmann (*Anglo-Scottish Relations*, p. 71) defends Henryson against Moran's charges of misogyny; McNamara, in "Language As Action in Henryson's *Testament of Cresseid*," in Aitken, et al., *Bards and Makars*, pp. 41–51, speaks of the narrator's "profound human sympathy" as a means of establishing the reliability of his voice.

71. For Kratzmann (*Ango-Scottish Relations*, p. 71) the "all-important question" in the poem is "Cresseid's painful but intensely moving regeneration." Cf. Ridley, "Middle Scots Writers," pp. 182-83: whereas "Chaucer presents a static Criseyde who never learns and never changes ... Henryson traces the progress of Criseyde become Cresseid." Strauss, "To Speak Once More of Cresseid: Henryson's *Testament* Reconsidered," *Scottish Literary Journal* 4 (1977): 5-13.

72. Duncan, "Henryson's *Testament of Cresseid*," p. 129. Sydney Harth countered Duncan in "Henryson Reinterpreted," *Essays in Criticism* 11 (1961): 471-80, but Harth's own contention that the poem is "a little tale of a notorious fallen woman, told with tongue in cheek" has not attracted a following.

73. *Philological Quarterly* 46 (1967): 471-87; see especially p. 479. For a similar emphasis see also Craig McDonald, "Venus and the Goddess Fortune in *The Testament of Cresseid*," *Scottish Literary Journal* 4 (1977): 14-24.

74. Fox tempers his view of the poem's explicit Christian meanings in his 1981 edition. For debate over whether Cresseid's disease was leprosy or syphilis, see Beryl Rowland, "The 'Seiknes Incurabill' in Henryson's *Testament of Cresseid*," *English Language Notes* 1 (1964): 175-77; and Kathryn Hume's rejoinder, "Leprosy or Syphilis in Henryson's *Testament of Cresseid*?" ibid., 6 (1969): 242-45.

75. Toliver, "Robert Henryson," pp. 305-09, especially p. 305. Mieszkowski, "Reputation of Criseyde," p. 139: both narrators "dramatize at once the distortion of judgment brought on by emotion and the human validity of that same emotion."

76. C. W. Jentoft, "Henryson as Authentic 'Chaucerian': Narrator, Character and Courtly Love in *The Testament of Cresseid*," *Studies in Scottish Literature* 10 (1972): 94-102; see especially p. 100. Cf. also John McNamara, n. 70, in this essay.

77. The allegorical ironists often do a better job on this "coldness of edge." W. S. Ramson's essay " 'Quha falsit Cresseid?' " is a good example; cf. also Benson's chapter on Henryson in *The History of Troy*, one of the few essays to take a dim view of Troilus without being overly reductive in its approach.

78. Dolores Noll, "*The Testament of Cresseid*: Are Christian Interpretations Valid?" *Studies in Scottish Literature* 9 (1971): 16-25; see especially p. 24.

79. Del Chessell, "In the Dark Time: Henryson's *Testament of Cresseid*," *Critical Review* 12 (1969): 61-72; see especially p. 70.

80. John McNamara, "Divine Justice in Henryson's *Testament of Cresseid*," *Studies in Scottish Literature* 11 (1973): 99-107; see especially p. 107.

Richard J. Schrader's "Henryson and Nominalism," *Journal of Medieval and Renaissance Studies* 8 (1978): 1–15, addresses the problem "of placing [Henryson] . . . in his own time" by reviewing possible nominalist contexts for his poetry.

81. Lee Patterson, "Christian and Pagan in *The Testament of Cresseid*," *Philological Quarterly* 52 (1973): 696–714.

82. See MacQueen, *Robert Henryson*, pp. 45–46; Götz Schmitz's "Cresseid's Trial: A Revision. Fame and Defamation in Henryson's *Testament of Cresseid*," *Essays and Studies* 32 (1979): 44–56; Ralph Hanna III's "Cresseid's Dream and Henryson's *Testament*," in Beryl Rowland, ed., *Chaucer and Middle English Studies in Honour of Rossell Hope Robbins* (London: Allen and Unwin; Kent, Ohio: Kent State University Press, 1974), pp. 288–97; see especially p. 289.

83. Paul Strohm, "Storie, Spelle, Geste, Romaunce, Tragedie: Generic Distinctions in the Middle English Troy Narratives," *Speculum* 46 (1971): 348–59; see especially p. 358. Cf. C. D. Benson, *History of Troy* (see n. 45, above).

# Studies in Douglas and Dunbar

## The Present Situation

### Florence H. Ridley

None of the medieval Scots poets has ever approached Chaucer in popularity, as a quick glance at the 1980 PMLA bibliography with its approximately nine entries for eighty-six poems of Douglas and Dunbar, one hundred and fifty for five poems of Chaucer, might suggest.[1] One obvious reason for this is their language, and another is the lack of appropriate texts. The "makars" have never been represented in readily available, adequately annotated and glossed classroom editions of their work, such as those of Chaucer prepared by F. N. Robinson or John Fisher. In addition, they have been oppressed by the debilitating sobriquet, "Scottish Chaucerian."[2] It is difficult to illustrate the effect continual comparison with Chaucer has had upon the Scots' reputation without citing extensive critical commentary. Here it may suffice to note that as recently as 1976 J. A. W. Bennett turned a gimlet eye upon *The Testament of Cresseid*, found that it lacked Chaucer's narrator, Chaucer's topography, Chaucer's Criseyde, Chaucer's imagination, and concluded that it was in consequence a "flawed masterpiece."[3] As Louis Golding has observed, "happier had the fate of the Scottish Chaucerians been had they . . . been born in China, 'their virtues' blurred in the glory thrown about them by the sun of Chaucer . . . deriving their immortality alas! more from his name than from their own high merits."[4]

Yet despite such difficulties interest in the makars is increasing. During the last decade considerable attention has been devoted to their works at international conferences on Scottish language and literature, in journals published in this country and abroad and on programs of the Modern Language Association, New Chaucer Society, Congress of the International

Courtly Literature Society, and the Medieval Academy of America.[5] Hugh MacDiarmid has even gone so far as to assert "so great has been the volume of studies of these Medieval Makars in the past three to four decades that there seems to have been a veritable boom in this connection."[6] Only a Scotsman could speak of the limited popularity of Douglas and Dunbar in such terms. Yet we are at last inching toward fulfillment of the essentials for their study: preparation of adequate bibliographies and satisfactory editions, elucidation of their language, and the kind of critical commentary that alone can bring them adequate recognition.[7]

Tom Scott's well-annotated "Bibliographical Review" and a "Middle Scots Writers" fascicle, which includes a bibliography and a summary of and brief comments upon each poem, have now replaced the incomplete bibliography of William Geddie, once of some limited value as the only thing of its kind.[8] With the aid of the *Scottish National Dictionary*, the *Dictionary of the Older Scottish Tongue* (now complete through "Pavillion—"), and a stream of articles and brief notes on the lost language of the makars, we are recapturing something of its sounds and meanings.[9] Analysis of their diction is being facilitated by computer techniques and the *Older Scottish Textual Archive*, which at present includes the contents of the Bannatyne, Asloan, Reidpeth, and Maitland Folio manuscripts, and has served as the basis for concordances of Henryson and Dunbar.[10] Of course for students of literature the value of definitions, word counts, and catalogues of contexts, structural formations, and rhymes remains limited unless accompanied by analyses; the collected raw data should now be analyzed and the findings applied to literary interpretation.[11]

We also need an up-to-date grammar of early and Middle Scots for better understanding of the poetry, and Angus McIntosh suggests that a first step toward creation of such a tool would be to make a survey of local vernacular documents and literary texts, then from the material try to determine regional practices in inflection, syntax, and vocabulary. Similarly, profiles might be made of scribes from their orthographic and spelling variants, which might help in placing texts of unknown provenance, perhaps even in determining the authorship of some of the anonymous medieval Scots poetry.[12]

As for texts, until recently the poetry of Dunbar has been readily available primarily in W. Mackay Mackenzie's 1932 edition and, as is that of Douglas, in small volumes of selections.[13] Mackenzie's edition was a labour of love put together for students. The editor was not a specialist in Middle Scots; he based his text upon transcripts of the Scottish Text Society, not the early manuscripts and prints; and his notes are severely limited, as is his glossary. Now James Kinsley has provided a new edition, with a text judiciously compiled from original materials, an up-dated glossary, and a comprehensive commentary that for the first time takes special note of the influence upon or parallels between Dunbar's poetry, sculpture, and art, as well as music. For each poem, Kinsley chooses the early version that seems "closer to a hypothetical authoritative original" and follows it "with cautious fidelity," adopting variants that seem more likely to preserve meter and meaning (p. xvi). The resultant text is much better than any we have had before. Unfortunately, at this writing the edition retails in the United States for about a hundred dollars, which effectively puts it out of reach of most students.

The only complete edition of Gawin Douglas, that compiled by John Small in 1874–76, was admirable for its day, and its commentary is still drawn upon. But the glossary and notes are badly in need of revision, and the four volumes which comprise it are out of print, hard to come by, and expensive. The more recent separate editions of the *Eneydos* by Coldwell and "The Palice of Honour" by Priscilla Bawcutt both contain useful glossaries and a wealth of information on background and techniques.[14] The texts the editors provide are, however, quite different in value.

Coldwell's is based upon the authoritative Trinity College, Cambridge, manuscript of the *Eneydos*, compiled by Douglas's amanuensis, Matthew Geddes, annotated by the poet himself, and still in very good condition. The only weaknesses possibly worth mentioning with which his edition has been charged have to do with Coldwell's understanding of Vergil's Latin or that of the commentators Badius Ascensius and Servius, rather than with presentation of Douglas's translation.[15] In some ways, despite its brevity, the text of "The Palice of Honor" presented its editor with more problems because the poem does not survive in manuscript but only in a few fragments ca. 1530-40, one print from London, ca. 1553, and two copies of another from Edinburgh, ca. 1579. In her notes Bawcutt carefully evaluates discrepancies between the prints and lists marginalia from one of the Edinburgh copies which consist of readings from the London print, alterations of spelling, and apparent efforts to improve sense or meter.[16] Yet from this material, inexplicably, she does not produce a diplomatic text reflecting a choice of wording, but instead reproduces the London and Edinburgh prints on facing pages, the latter on the right with modern punctuation. This inevitably leads the reader to concentrate upon it, although in her introduction the editor is at pains to establish that the two prints are equally authoritative.[17] Thus as matters now stand there is still no generally affordable edition of the works of either Douglas or Dunbar that provides one sound text as well as an up-to-date commentary and glossary. If studies of these poets are indeed to flourish, someone must provide such editions.

Second only to the need for satisfactory editions remains that for comprehensive critical studies. In 1956 David Daiches asked, "Where is the great new critical book on Dunbar, or on any of the Middle Scots poets?"[18] Save for Douglas Gray's excellent work on Henryson, we are still waiting, even though at least two books have been devoted to Douglas and four to Dunbar.[19] Lauchlan MacLean Watt's, on the *Eneydos*, once described as "insubstantial," today is clearly outdated.[20] Priscilla Bawcutt's more recent study of Douglas attempts to relate him to his context and to other authors, and in doing so cites innumerable aspects of his experience, sources, style, and so forth. But the mass of data is not sufficiently interpreted. Is Douglas valuable only as a repository of words and images mined from other poets? Or only historically as the first British translator of the *Aeneid*? Does he have any unique character as a poet? Bawcutt's shorter pieces, notably on Dunbar, make it clear that she is quite capable of perceptive literary appraisal, yet here she leaves central questions such as these about Douglas's literary merit almost completely unanswered.

Neither Rachel Annan Taylor nor Tom Scott liked Dunbar, and it is odd that they chose to write about him. In her book Taylor regrets that he is not Chaucer, Dante, Shakespeare, Walter de la Mare, or T. S. Eliot; she praises his music, but neglects his satires, religious verse, and aureate poems. Scott struggles to make Dunbar share his own moral sense, to detect in him a "unit of perception" which is not "I-not-them" but "I-in-them," though to insist upon a consistently selfless motive in this most "I-centered" poet inevitably frustrates the critic and causes him to miss the main thrust of the poetry.

Edmund Reiss is similarly hampered in his study of Dunbar by a conviction that all the poems must have a moral end. When indeed they do, Reiss is persuasive and original; when they do not, like Scott he tends to discount obvious meaning, overlook humor, find irony where there is none, or lapse into puzzlement. Yet despite his efforts to force the poetry into a moral strait jacket, Reiss paradoxically seems aware that the poet "cannot easily be encompassed and classified" (p. 150). The differences among Dunbar's indecencies, petitions, treatments of love, moralizings and so forth are in fact too marked to be, as this critic would have them, "more superficial than real." On the whole it is better to acknowledge and explore the various voices of Dunbar than attempt to make them one.

Ian Ross's main problem in the latest Dunbar book is his consistent attempt to assign the poems more intellectual significance than they have.

Although he is really more concerned with the poet than with the poetry, Ross paraphrases content and cites sources and parallel representations in the visual arts, bringing together much valuable material, but stops short of working out the implications for the poems. He is prone instead to find what a critical book on poetry should address—"the processes of the excitation and exercise of the creative imagination"—"merely baffling" (p. 113).

To date, significant critical commentary on both Dunbar and Douglas has been in the form of articles or chapters rather than books and may be said to have begun with C. S. Lewis and John Speirs.[21] As Catherine Singh, Gregory Kratzmann, and Denton Fox were to do later, Lewis and Speirs stressed differences from, rather than affinities with, Chaucer.[22] They noted that Douglas utilized variation in language to contrast scenes of beauty and terror in a manner quite unlike that of the English poet, and that Dunbar is neither storyteller nor delineator of character, yet has qualities Chaucer lacks: a power of song, goblin energy, a command of the varied resources of language then available to him, meters adapted from medieval French and Latin verse coupled with native alliteration and assonance, and a tendency rarely seen in Chaucer to reflect the actual sights and sounds around him and his own morbid moods. Bawcutt, on the other hand, points to similarities between the Scots' and Chaucer's images, modes, and wording.[23]

Of course Douglas and Dunbar borrowed from their famous English predecessor. Douglas found the humorous, self-mocking narrator of his "Palice of Honour" in the *House of Fame*, Dunbar his model for "Sir Thomas Norny" in *Sir Thopas*.[24] And although he could scarcely have learned insight and compassion from another poet, Douglas is most like Chaucer in his ability to convey human emotion and in his knowledge of and tenderness for human nature.[25] Yet despite the Scots' praise for Chaucer's aureation, his "ornate, sugurit lippis," it is a far cry from their own aureate descriptions to his. Moreover, while Chaucer's greatest achievement is a framestory, Douglas's is a translation, and Dunbar's is short lyrics in French measures. On the whole, save for "The Palice of Honour," the effect of the Scots poetry is different from that of Chaucer's. As Kratzmann points out (pp. 135-36), even "Sir Thomas Norny" is a satire of a social climber; *Sir Thopas* is a parody of a genre, in its delicate irony a decided contrast to Dunbar's pungent deflation of an individual.

It is somewhat the same with their relation to Lydgate, from whom both Douglas and Dunbar took raw material.[26] Roland D. S. Jack, though noting their borrowings, stressed differences, contrasting particularly the precision and control of Dunbar with the loose verbosity of Lydgate.[27] It is more accurate, really, to speak of Lydgate as a source mined by Dunbar than as an influence upon him so great as to justify the designation "Scottish Lydgatian."

Perhaps Dunbar is most like Skelton, although Lewis dismisses both "Scotch Skelton" and "Scotch Chaucer" as inept nicknames for him.[28] In his intense lyricism, intricate measures, goliardic parodies, obsession with death, and poems such as "Lament for the Makars," whose refrain, like *"mais où sont les neiges d'antan,"* marshalls the procession of the dead, he is similar to François Villon, and the resemblance between them has frequently been commented upon.[29] Yet Dunbar is not exactly a "Scotch Villon" either. As Kinghorn notes, Villon cared more about dead people than death, had real affection for his comrades and sympathy for humanity. Dunbar evinces sympathy neither for humanity in general nor for any individual in particular. He was a "loner," and his poetry is warmed by love neither for woman, child, king, country—or even mouse or flower, as was that of Scotland's other premier poet, Robert Burns. Although Speirs believes that "Lament for the Makars" speaks to us "in the makar's concern about his friends and, finally himself" (p. 68), the poem's refrain, *"Timor mortis conturbat me,"* makes it quite clear that this particular makar was not "finally" but primarily concerned about himself and the grim fact that he had to share his dead friends' fate.

On the whole, what must be seen as outstanding in the poetry of Douglas and Dunbar results not from the influence of other poets, but from their utilization of their native setting, of alliteration and vernacular language, and of European Latin and French verse traditions.[30]

In *English Literature of the Sixteenth Century*, C. S. Lewis leaves little doubt that what he found to be of value in Dunbar's poetry was not content but technique (pp. 91–96). Speirs, similarly, admires his vigour, directness, intense vitality, and command of language and of varied modes and meters adapted from medieval French and Latin (pp. 54–55). Most commentators agree with these evaluations of the poet's art; James Kinsley, for example, sees him as a poet of "sheer style . . . original humor, and imagination," whose "eye seldom reached beyond the fringe, or his mind beneath the surface, of that now remote Stuart court."[31]

The often-cited appraisal is a bit unfair. Dunbar wrote at least twenty moral and religious poems, and he certainly looked beneath the surface of the court to attack its corruption.[32] Others beside Edmund Reiss and Ian Ross, who insist upon the poet's consistent morality, have attempted to demonstrate that his subject matter is indeed worthy of serious consideration.[33] Bryan S. Hay thinks Dunbar has apocalyptic motifs and deals with retributive justice and reassertion of right order on a scale larger than any personal vendetta; Ian Milner, that he is concerned with the overthrow of feudal social order and issues an "indictment of a corrupt and ailing society."[34]

Dunbar's aureate allegories, particularly "The Goldyn Targe," are most often cited in evidence of both his superficial thought and technical brilliance—as Walter Scheps, who surveys critical opinion on the poem says, lifelessness and brilliance characterize it for detractors and admirers alike.[35] Lewis found it to be a dazzling exercise in rhetoric, whose allegory was adapted to the purposes of "pure decoration;" Speirs (pp. 56-57) calls it "a monument to the fact that you cannot make a poem out of an interest purely in language, and the manipulation and arrangement of it."[36] But Denton Fox and Lois A. Ebin think you can, and see "The Goldyn Targe" as being about the creation of poetry, with excellence resulting from skilled workmanship, dazzling "enamelling," compression, richness, and a highly wrought pattern.[37] Others have tried to find in the poem even more significant themes: discrimination between higher and lower love; the dangers of sexual love or of an immoderate concern with sensual pleasure; or the artificiality of love-vision poetry.[38] Literally "The Goldyn Targe" draws a clear contrast between nature and artifice, presenting the personifications and gods of conventional vision as enemies of reason, whose overthrow makes the poet's paradise—the world of nature—seem a hell. Apparently, then, Dunbar means to suggest the illogic of love as it is celebrated in dream-vision poetry. But whatever his theme, he did not expend much effort on developing it, and whether his attack is aimed at unnatural courtly love, at the poetry that celebrates it, or at all love remains unclear.

Although arguments pro and con regarding the significance of his content continue, the poems themselves supply the cons with considerably more ammunition. Milner's view of Dunbar as a moral critic of corrupt society overlooks the petitions' pervasive tone of injured merit. "The Birth of Antichrist" and "The Feigned Friar of Tungland," which Hay cites, do not support his argument that here the poet's attack on a personal enemy gives way to universal considerations. Dunbar did write poems which are both serious and moving, but their seriousness is that of orthodox wisdom and their emotion derives from the skill with which it is presented. Then, too, in such poems he tends to strike the attitude of a medieval preacher, musing either on the transcience and rottenness of the world or his own pathos, when not concerned with himself, while hammering home *sententiae*.[39] In light of the actual poetry, one is finally driven to conclude that Dunbar was not an exceptionally original thinker but a court entertainer, moralist, and satirist, whose greatness lies in his ability to give the most effective statement possible to commonplaces, and in his extraordinary range.[40]

Perhaps most perceptively of all critics, Edwin Morgan describes the unique character of Dunbar's poetry, its methods and effect, noting particularly the unexpected yoking of dissimilar elements—aureate, satirical, lyric; Scots and French traditions; conventional Latin and original native phrases. He observes, for example, how when in a poem we get "fairly regular syllabic verse with rhyme and irregular alliteration . . . [then] excitement . . . breaks the structure down into a loose alliterative swing, . . . the older non-syllabic rhythms prevail, the verse takes on a flailing verve and momentum, and if it is satirical or fantastic. . . . an effect is produced which is a notable Scottish characteristic . . . wild, flamboyant, ludicrous, and 'fouthy' [rich] with words."[41]

Dunbar's extraordinary versatility, in treatment, subject, and genre has been widely recognized.[42] Morgan found this quality unsettling: "We are uneasy as we watch him turn from the Rabelaisian endearments of 'In secret place' to a religious 'Nativitie' or 'Resurrection,' . . . from fantasy to ethics, ethics to satire to stately elegy and eulogy"; "what disturbs us most perhaps, is the spectacle of such intense energy devoting itself indifferently now to a splendid hymn on the Resurrection . . . now to the scarifying jovialities of the 'Flyting' with Kennedy."[43] But there is nothing "indifferent" about the manner in which Dunbar celebrates Christ's victory over the black dragon of hell or attacks his enemy Kennedy. It seems to be the single-minded intensity with which he treats his themes rather than their variation which makes critics uneasy, and to which they respond in different ways, finding Dunbar a maker of fantastic blendings, as Speirs says (p. 61), "of the comic with the horrible, the ghastly, the macabre." Whether it is this sense of violence, or his extravagances—of aureation, obscenity, or brutal assault—or his egocentricity, Dunbar is, as Edith Sitwell points out, "one of those writers . . . whom it is possible to dislike quite strongly even while feeling the power of their work."[44]

No one dislikes Gawin Douglas, although comparatively few critics write about him and those who do tend to focus on the same things. "The Palice of Honour" was praised by C. S. Lewis as a "phantasmagoria of dazzling lights and eldritch glooms," reflecting delight in the "whole world of poetry."[45] That opinion has subsequently been expanded to demonstrate in various ways how the poem reflects Douglas's self-consciousness as an artist and his concern with the creation of poetry. Bawcutt interprets it as an allegory of his education in which aspects of the man as lover, churchman, and poet are woven together; Norton-Smith, as an allegory of the "turning-point" in Douglas's literary career toward the moral and political themes of the *Eneydos*. To Kratzmann, the poem is Douglas's response to

Chaucer's ideas about a poet's allegiances, the problem of reconciling art and life, and the "nature of poetic composition." Kinneavy reads it as a study of imaginative wit, the Dreamer's course representing its intitial barrenness, his concern with his own faculty of imagination, and its subsequent regeneration.[46]

Kratzmann does a good job of analyzing the poem as a *summa* of vision allegory and of arguing for its high quality. He seems misguided, however, in comparing "The Palice of Honour" to *The House of Fame* and finding it better on the grounds that honour is the higher goal, for both poems stress the hollowness of fame. And if, as Kinneavy says, "The Palice of Honour" brings recognition "that honour is achieved by virtue" or, as Kratzmann says, Douglas's quest is more admirable than Chaucer's because of its religious context, why does Douglas permit Zenobia, or more to the point, Medea, to succeed in that quest? Although Kratzmann (pp. 104-08) gives the best extended critical study of the poem to date, he still fails to reconcile the tedium of its extended catalogues with his conclusion that it is better wrought than Chaucer's poem. On the whole, neither he nor anyone else has yet sufficiently clarified the intent of "The Palice of Honour" in light of its ending.

Further study should be given to Douglas's persona, the "humorous self-mocker of the poet as dreamer," for he is the key to this piece, to its unevenness, its self-conscious metrical fireworks, its endless catalogues, and abrupt ending. The figure closely resembles the persona of *The House of Fame*; but Douglas goes a bit further in its use than does Chaucer, to present a would-be poet exploiting *ad nauseam* all the techniques of the genre, trying desperately, comically, and futilely to create his own dream vision.

Most of the commentary on Douglas has been occasioned by his great translation with its prologues of Vergil's *Aeneid*. Critics have commented upon the *Eneydos* as an aid to early students of Anglo-Saxon and a source of enrichment for the native tongue, and upon Douglas's theory and practice of translation.[47] They note that direct translation had its start in English tradition with him, for Douglas does not adapt the Latin for allegory or romance, as previous translators had done, but translates as closely as possible to make Vergil's meaning fully accessible to his audience.[48]

In attempting this he was certainly a humanist, a man of the Renaissance rather than the Middle Ages.[49] It is questionable, however, that he attempted to present a Renaissance Vergil, "instructor alike of first- and sixteenth-century princes."[50] If Douglas drew Aeneas as a "prototype of the ideal prince" and focused upon that ideal and the virtues to be imitated, the vices to be eschewed by him, it was not because he consciously reshaped Vergil's material to do so, but because he saw the *Aeneid* through sixteenth-century eyes and presented what he found. As Hall says, his translation is "not governed by a sense of Vergil himself."[51]

Douglas's problem was to make meaningful a Latin Augustan classic in sixteenth-century Scotland.[52] That required modifications, and critics have been concerned with their nature and the relative degree of success with which Douglas achieves both the meaning and effect of Vergil—or something different and even at times in limited ways better. One can, of course, approach the *Eneydos* by comparing it with the *Aeneid* or with other translations, such as Surrey's.[53] But from that point of view no translation can be said to be totally successful, for differences in language, time, and place will inevitably create differences in tone, effect, and even intent. The only way to gain real appreciation of the *Eneydos*' literary quality is to consider it as a work of art in its own right. John Campbell is correct in drawing an equation between Chapman's *Homer*, as "a wonderful Book . . . [whose] Excellency lies in the Author's Genius, and not in the Justness of the Translation," and Douglas's *Eneydos*; Fulton, in saying that a comparison should not be made between the relative success of Vergil and Douglas in achieving the same purpose in different languages; and Speirs, in concluding that "what is important here is that Douglas's *Aeneid*, though it could not be other than unsatisfactory as a translation of Vergil's, *might* be a better poem than Virgil's" (p. 69).[54] The question to be asked is, What is good about the *Eneydos* apart from faithfulness to the *Aeneid*?—and some progress has been made in answering it.

Kratzmann (p. 171) praises Douglas's "apparently effortless" combination of words from many sources, the alliteration and variety of his Scots; Wittig (pp. 77–78), his range in diction, style, and tone, his suiting of style to content; McLachlan (pp. 183–86), his exploitation of the language and of his own experience of life, which seems to have given him emotional insight somewhat greater than Vergil's, enabling him better to understand and suggest, for example, the emotion behind Dido's pathetic attempts to legitimize her liaison with Aeneas. McLachlan praises as well Douglas's vitality, his ability to visualize action concretely and create rhythm that follows movement; Fulton (pp. 125–26), his expansion for vigorous action and localizing of effects to make immediate the thing seen and so excite the imagination.

Douglas's "sacrifice" of conciseness or subtlety and his "particularizing tendency," as in describing a sea storm or birds preening in the sun, are weaknesses in Fulton's eyes. But here she seems wrong. Douglas does not so much "sacrifice" Vergilian qualities as add visuality and specificity. His descriptions are really evocative rather than descriptive; and the sights, sounds, and rhythms he manages to convey are an essential part of his very Scots *Aeneid*.[55] It is this aspect which first brought the work serious consideration as an original literary achievement.

Douglas has been praised by, among others, Ezra Pound for his dealing with ships and the sea,[56] but most often for his descriptions of a raw winter day, a soft May morning, and a luminous summer evening in Prologues 7, 12, and 13.[57] Efforts to demonstrate the Prologues' thematic relevance either to the book each precedes or to the translation as a whole have not been notably successful.[58] Bawcutt argues that they are to be seen as proper introductions to their particular books; and sometimes they can be. For example, Prologue 13 gives Douglas a chance to explain and defend his inclusion of the thirteenth book, by Maphaeus Vegius. But as a group the prologues vary too much in kind and degree of relevance to Vergil to be characterized as consistently suitable introductions. Moreover, the subject matter of the group as a whole is too heterogeneous to be seen as developing any one theme, even so broad a one as that proposed by Ebin: they define the role of narrator who as poet, priest, and translator introduces a series of conflicts questioning the value of poetry and representing a movement from uncertainty to renewed creativity, which complements Aeneas's journey. Coldwell's surmise probably should be accepted: at least some of the prologues of the *Eneydos* are separate poems, written elsewhere but "too good to waste."[59]

Most critics agree that the value of the "nature" prologues, at any rate, lies in their independent description of landscape as a subject in itself. That view, expressed nearly fifty years ago by Agnes Muir MacKenzie, has received strong support from commentary demonstrating how by sound, tone, diction, and rhythm Douglas causes us to relive his own experience and feel the effect of nature on man, animals, birds, plants, even rocks.[60] Pearsall and Salter have analyzed Prologues 7, 12, and 13 in terms of painting, finding them comparable to the landscapes of Bellini and Brueghel. As they suggest, these pieces are intricate, panoramic, accurate in detail and coherent, "organized with incomparable visualizing power, and charged with a sensuous response to detail."[61] The same is true of many sections in the body of the translation, as has been noted by Robin Fulton and John Speirs in illustrating, respectively, the Scot's knack for describing nasty weather and the essential "Scots-ness" of the *Eneydos*.[62] If all the passages these critics cite were scrutinized from the point of view of painting, we might gain greater insight into both Douglas's treatment of Vergil and the unique character of his translation as an independent poem.

Although neither poet's precise life dates are known, Douglas and Dunbar were near contemporaries, associated with the same royal circles and generally subject to the same traditions. Further investigation into the influences operative upon both at that time and place, of traditional genres, Gaelic poetry, Flemish painting, music, and literature, and the art of sculptor and pageant-maker could be revealing, as might further study of the relation between the rhythm, tone, and diction of their poetry and its content.[63] This last is particularly true of the verse of Dunbar, whose sensitive ear for music is well recognized, and who was capable of making an adroit use of contrast between literal statement and the vehicle of its expression to create intense irony.[64]

At present, then, we can say that while much has been accomplished in the study of the two poets a good deal remains to be done—particularly the providing of affordable texts and extended critical analyses—before the poetic achievements of Douglas and Dunbar receive the appreciation they so clearly deserve.

# Notes

1. For discussion of reasons for neglect of the early makars, difficulties in the way of their study, and what is needed to overcome them, see James Kinsley, "Scottish Literary Studies," *Lines Review* 10 (1955): 7–10; and John MacQueen, "The Case for Early Scottish Literature," in *Edinburgh Studies in English and Scots*, ed. A. J. Aitken, Angus McIntosh, and Hermann Pálsson (London: Longman, 1971), pp. 234–47.

2. For a survey of the history and influence of the term, see Florence H. Ridley, "A Plea for the Middle Scots," in *The Learned and the Lewed*, ed. Larry D. Benson (Cambridge, Mass.: Harvard University Press, 1974), especially pp. 175–81.

3. "Henryson's Testament: A Flawed Masterpiece," *Scottish Literary Journal* 1 (1974): 5–16.

4. "The Scottish Chaucerians," *Saturday Review of Politics, Literature, Science, and Art* 134 (1922): 782.

5. Such conferences were held at Edinburgh in 1975; Strassburg in 1978; and Stirling in 1981. There are annual meetings of the Association of Scottish Literary Studies in Scotland; *Studies in Scottish Literature* is published

at the University of South Carolina; *The Scottish Literary Journal* at the University of Aberdeen; the *Bibliothek* and *Supplement* at the University of Stirling. See also the dissertations listed by Jean-Jacques Blanchot, "William Dunbar and Francois Villon: the Literary Personae," in *Bards and Makars: Scottish Language and Literature: Medieval and Renaissance*, ed. Adam J. Aitken, Matthew P. McDiarmid, and Derick S. Thomson (Glasgow: University of Glasgow Press, 1977), p. 85.

6. "Gavin Douglas and the *Aeneid*," *Agenda* 14, no. 2 (1976): 90.

7. We probably know as much about the Scots' biographies, canon, and chronology as we ever shall. The available biographical information on Douglas was presented by John Small, ed., *The Poetical Works of Gavin Douglas*, 4 vols. (Edinburgh and London: William Paterson; H. Sotheran, 1874) vol. 2, pp. i–cxxvii, and has been revised by Priscilla Bawcutt, *Gavin Douglas* (Edinburgh: Edinburgh University Press, 1976), pp. 1–22. That on Dunbar is most comprehensively presented by J. W. Baxter, *William Dunbar* (Edinburgh and London: Oliver and Boyd, 1952). According to what we know about the canon, Douglas clearly wrote neither "King Hart" nor "Conscience," formerly assigned to him; see Priscilla Preston, "Did Gavin Douglas write King Hart?" *Medium Aevum* 28 (1959): 31–47; Ridley, "Did Gawin Douglas Write King Hart?" *Speculum* 34 (1959): 402–12. He signed the *Eneydos* and refers to his authorship of "The Palice of Honor" and translation of "Lundeys Lufe the Remeid" although the latter is now lost; see "Mention of the Principal Works," in *Virgil's 'Aeneid,' Translated into Scottish Verse by Gavin Douglas*, ed. David F. C. Coldwell, Scottish Text Society, 3rd ser., nos. 25, 27, 28, 30, 4 vols. (Edinburgh and London: William Blackwood, 1957, 1959, 1960, 1966), vol. 4, p. 139. On the possibility that "Lundeys Lufe" may be taken from Ovid, see Coldwell, *Virgil's 'Aeneid,'* I: 256. Dunbar's canon can be accepted as described by James Kinsley, ed., *The Poems of William Dunbar* (Oxford: Clarendon Press, 1979), with the caveat that there is no persuasive evidence for inclusion of "Gladethe thou, Queyne of Scottish Regioun" and "To the Quene"; cf. the review by Ridley in *Renaissance Quarterly* 34 (1981): 134–35. On the authorship of "London Thou Art the Flowre of Cytes All," see Curt F. Bühler, *Review of English Studies* 13 (1973): 1–9. On use of the poems to reconstruct a biography, see A. M. Kinghorn, "Dunbar and Villon," *Modern Language Review* 62 (1967): 198; and A. G. Rigg, "William Dunbar: the 'Fenyeit Freir,'" *Review of English Studies* 14 (1963): 269–73. Rigg argues that since "feigned friar" was an accepted literary device, the poem could not be used for reliable evidence about Dunbar's life. Since the term refers to a "lying friar," however, rather than to "one who pretends to be a friar," the argument is beside the

point. On chronology, see C. S. Lewis, *English Literature in the Sixteenth Century Excluding Drama* (Oxford: Clarendon Press, 1954), p. 91, who points out that inferences from internal evidence "usually involve hazardous assumptions," and Kurt Wittig, *The Scottish Tradition in Literature* (Edinburgh and London: Oliver and Boyd, 1958), p. 64, who notes the impossibility of arranging most of the poems in a fixed chronological sequence. But see also Denton Fox, "The Chronology of William Dunbar," *Philological Quarterly* 39 (1960): 413–25, who attempts to order them on the basis of references to James as king, his marriage, Dunbar's court service, his pension, or events such as the queen's visit to Aberdeen, or the poem's lack of reference "to the anarchy of the period after Flodden," and concludes that all of them should be placed "in the period 1500–13, while admitting the possibility that a few . . . may have been written before 1500."

    8. Tom Scott, *Dunbar: A Critical Exposition of the Poems* (Edinburgh and London: Oliver and Boyd, 1966), pp. 360–85; Florence Ridley, *A Manual of the Writings in Middle English*, ed. Albert E. Hartung (Hamden, Conn.: Archon Books/The Shoe String Press for the Connecticut Academy of Arts and Sciences, 1973), vol. 4, pp. 961–1060, 1123–1284; William Geddie, *A Bibliography of Middle Scots Poets*, The Scottish Text Society, no. 7 (Edinburgh and London: William Blackwood, 1912). See also Peter Heidtmann, "A Bibliography of Henryson, Dunbar, and Douglas, 1912–1969," *Chaucer Review* 5 (1970): 75–82; and Florence Ridley, "A Check List, 1956–1968, for Study of 'The Kingis Quair,' the Poetry of Robert Henryson, Gawin Douglas, and William Dunbar," *Studies in Scottish Literature* 8 (1970): 30–51.

    9. *Scottish National Dictionary*, ed. William Grant and David D. Murison, 10 vols. (Edinburgh: The Scottish National Dictionary Association, [1931–]1976); *Dictionary of the Older Scottish Tongue*, ed. William A. Craigie, A. J. Aitken, and James A. C. Stevenson (Chicago: University of Chicago Press; London: Oxford University Press, 1937–), vol, 1, part 29. In spring 1978 appeared the first number of the "Language Supplement" to *The Scottish Literary Journal*, designed to reflect interest and research in Scots. It contained several helpful articles, notably that by Angus McIntosh, "The Dialectology of Mediaeval Scots; Some Possible Approaches to Its Study," pp. 38–44. Important essays are those (in A. J. Aitken et al., *Edinburgh Studies*) by David Murison, "The Dutch Element in the Vocabulary of Scots," pp. 159–76: A. J. Aitken, "Variation and Variety in Written Middle Scots," pp. 177–209; and W. F. H. Nicolaisen, "Early Spellings and Scottish Place-names," pp. 210–33. See also Adam J. Aitken, "How to Pronounce Older Scots," in Aitken et al., *Bards and Makars*, pp. 1–21. For briefer notes see E. J. Dobson and Patricia Ingham, "Three Notes on Dunbar's 'The Tua Mariit

Wemen and the Wedo,'" *Medium Aevum* 36 (1967): 38–39; John Norton-Smith, "Ekphrasis as a Stylistic Element in Douglas's 'Palis of Honour,'" ibid., 48 (1979): 240–53; Catherine Singh, "Line 124 of William Dunbar's 'The Tretis of the Tua Mariit Wemen and the Wedo,'" *Notes and Queries* 219, n.s. 21 (1974): 163; David W. Lindsay, "Two Notes on Dunbar," *Forum for Modern Language Studies* 12 (1976): 367–69; Priscilla Bawcutt, "Gavin Douglas: Some Additions to O.E.D. and D.O.S.T.," *Notes and Queries* 208, n.s. 10 (1963): 289–90; Priscilla Bawcutt, "Lexical Notes on Gavin Douglas's 'Eneados,'" *Medium Aevum* 40 (1971): 48–55; John Norton-Smith, "Douglas's Venus and Martianus Capella," *Notes and Queries* 225, n.s. 27 (1980): 390–92.

10. The resource is described by A. J. Aitken and Paul Bratley, "An Archive of Older Scottish Texts for Scanning by Computer," *English Studies* 48 (1967): 60–61; and in *Studies in Scottish Literature* 4 (1966): 45–47.

11. Bengt Ellenberger, *The Latin Element in the Vocabulary of the Earlier Makars Henryson and Dunbar*, Lund Studies in English, no. 51 (Lund: Liber Läromedel/Gleerup, 1977) collects the Latinisms, tabulating and classifying them in the light of form, sense, and frequency. In an instructive review of this book John Norton-Smith pointed out the need for further study of the origins, literal meaning, and implications of the language; *Medium Aevum* 49 (1980): 151–53.

12. McIntosh, "Dialectology of Mediaeval Scots," especially p. 43.

13. *The Poems of William Dunbar*, ed. W. Mackay Mackenzie (London: Faber and Faber, 1932); revised by Bruce Dickins (London: Pitman Press, 1960; John Dickens, 1970); *Selections from the Poems of William Dunbar*, ed. Hugh MacDiarmid, The Saltire Society (Edinburgh: Oliver and Boyd, 1952); *William Dunbar: Poems*, ed. James Kinsley (Oxford: Clarendon Press, 1958). *Gavin Douglas: A Selection from His Poetry*, ed. Sydney Goodsir Smith, The Saltire Classics (Edinburgh: Oliver and Boyd, 1959); *Selections from Gavin Douglas*, ed. David F. C. Coldwell (Oxford: Clarendon Press, 1964). For listing of older, out-of-print editions and anthologies containing limited selections, see Ridley, *A Manual of the Writings in Middle English*, vol. 4, pp. 1182–94, 1207–68, and "A Check-list," pp. 36–48.

14. Priscilla Bawcutt, ed., *The Shorter Poems of Gavin Douglas*, The Scottish Text Society, ser. 4, vol. 4 (Edinburgh and London: William Blackwood, 1967).

15. See for example the review by a critic knowledgeable in Latin rather than Middle Scots, R. G. Austin, *Medium Aevum* 35 (1966): 154–57.

16. The marginalia were first noticed by W. Beattie, in *TLS*, 23 February 1946, p. 91, who printed only a few of them.

17. Cf. the reviews by P. J. Frankis, *Review of English Studies* 21 (1970): 75-76, who praises Bawcutt's thorough explication of obscurities, but objects to her method of presenting the two texts, and John Norton-Smith, *Medium Aevum* 37 (1968): 353-56, who first says it is useful to have them on facing pages, then finds it annoying that the Edinburgh alone is punctuated, and concludes with the wish that the edition had been purged "of the howler-ridden Edinburgh."

18. David Daiches, *Literary Essays* (Edinburgh and London: Oliver and Boyd, 1956), p. 137.

19. Douglas Gray, *Robert Henryson* (Leiden: E. J. Brill; Cambridge: Cambridge University Press, 1979).

20. Lauchlan MacLean Watt, *Douglas's Aeneid* (Cambridge: Cambridge University Press, 1920; reprint, New York: AMS Press, 1975): Priscilla Bawcutt, *Gavin Douglas*; Rachel Annan Taylor, *Dunbar*, The Poets on the Poets Series (London: Faber and Faber, 1931); Scott, *Dunbar*; Edmund Reiss, *William Dunbar* (Boston: Twayne Publishers, 1979); Ian Simpson Ross, *William Dunbar* (Leiden: E. J. Brill, 1981).

21. C. S. Lewis, *English Literature in the Sixteenth Century*, especially pp. 66-99; John Speirs, *The Scots Literary Tradition* (London: Chatto and Windus, 1940; rev. 2nd. ed., London: Faber, 1962), pp. 54-76, 165-97. All quotations from C. S. Lewis cited by page numbers in the text are from this work. See also the much briefer comments in Lewis, *The Allegory of Love* (London: Oxford University Press, 1936; reprinted with corrections, 1936, 1953), passim.

22. Catherine Singh, "The Alliterative Ancestry of Dunbar's 'The Tretis of the Tua Mariit Wemen and the Wedo,'" pp. 22-54, especially p. 22; Lewis, *English Literature in the Sixteenth Century*, especially pp. 79, 97; Speirs, *Scots Literary Tradition*, especially pp. 54-55, 60-68. Gregory Kratzmann, *Anglo-Scottish Literary Relations, 1430-1550* (New York and Cambridge: Cambridge University Press, 1980), passim, found the Scots to be "Chaucerian" in their situation as court poets and their mode of adapting material to create new poetry, taking Chaucer to have been their example rather than model, and cited differences in matter, style, scale, creative treatment. Denton Fox, "The Scottish Chaucerians," in *Chaucer and Chaucerians*, ed. D. S. Brewer (University, Ala.: University of Alabama Press, 1966) pp. 164-200, attempts to demonstrate that the poets were not "submerged in Chaucer, and trying vainly to imitate him," but might be called "Chaucerians" in the sense that they were aware of and influenced by the change in English poetry he had brought about.

23. Priscilla Bawcutt, "Gavin Douglas and Chaucer," *Review of*

*English Studies* 21 (1970): 401–21, works principally with the *Eneydos* and its prologues (see also her "The 'Library' of Gavin Douglas," in Aitken et al., *Bards and Makars*, p. 120). In "Dunbar's 'Tretis of the Tua Mariit Wemen and the Wedo' 185–187 and Chaucer's 'Parson's Tale,'" *Notes and Queries* 209, n.s. 11 (1964): 332–33, she cites an image possibly taken by Dunbar from Chaucer. J. A. W. Bennett, in a review of Alice S. Miskimin, *The Renaissance Chaucer* (New Haven and London: Yale University Press, 1975), *Renaissance Quarterly* 29 (1976): 266, cites an echo in "The Palice of Honour" of "The House of Fame," perhaps by way of Lydgate.

24. Kratzmann, *Anglo-Scottish Relations*, pp. 29, 137–38, noted the resemblance between the naive or reluctant persona-narrators of Douglas, Dunbar, and Chaucer. See also Bawcutt, "The 'Library' of Douglas," p. 120; and "Gavin Douglas and Chaucer," especially pp. 401, 419–20. On the resemblance between "Sir Thopas" and "Sir Thomas Norny,' see Elizabeth Roth Eddy, "Sir Thopas and Sir Thomas Norny: Romance Parody in Chaucer and Dunbar," *Review of English Studies*, n.s. 22 (1971): 401–09.

25. Cf. Speirs, *Scots Literary Tradition*, pp. 180–81.

26. See A. S. G. Edwards, "Selections from Lydgate's 'Fall of Princes': A Checklist," *The Library*, Ser. 5, 26 (1971): 217–42; and "Douglas's 'Palice of Honour' and Lydgate's 'Fall of Princes,'" *Notes and Queries* 219, n.s. 21 (1974): 83; Nichols, "Lydgate's Influence on the Aureate Terms of the Scottish Chaucerians," *PMLA* 46 (1932): 516–22; and "William Dunbar as a Scottish Lydgatian," *PMLA* 46 (1931): 214–24.

27. "Dunbar and Lydgate," *Studies in Scottish Literature* 8 (1971): 215–27. See also Kratzmann, *Anglo-Scottish Relations*, pp. 139–49, who finds Dunbar to be a very different kind of poet, while noting some parallels between the two in genres, themes, techniques, and some details; and Lois Ebin, who in reviewing Kratzmann's book asserts the importance of Lydgate as "a catalyst" for many fifteenth century poems, *Speculum* 56 (1981): 881–82. Bawcutt, *Gavin Douglas*, p. 42, cites Lydgate as a transmitter of Chaucerian themes and wording, who has an occasional symbol or phrase in common with Douglas, while acknowledging that "in few cases can Douglas be definitely said to be indebted to Lydgate"; at most the English poet illustrates "themes, genres, phrasing and *topoi*" fashionable in the fifteenth century.

28. On the likeness see Kratzmann, *Anglo-Scottish Relations*, pp. 149–53 and passim; on the ineptness of the terms, see Lewis, *English Literature in the Sixteenth Century*, p. 97.

29. On the relation between Dunbar and Villon see Nichols, "William Dunbar as a Scottish Lydgatian," p. 214; Speirs, *Scots Literary Tradition*, pp.

62-68; A. M. Kinghorn, "Dunbar and Villon—A Comparison and a Contrast," pp. 195-208; and Blanchot, "William Dunbar and Francois Villon," pp. 72-87. Blanchot gives a useful bibliography of relevant comment and seeks to demonstrate the distinction between the poets by cataloguing the kinds of personae each adopts.

30. On another possible influence upon Douglas, that of Dunbar, see Alicia K. Nitecki, "A Note on Dunbar and Douglas," *Notes and Queries* 225, n.s. 27 (1980): 389-90; but also Priscilla Bawcutt, "Gavin Douglas: Some Additions to O.E.D. and D.O.S.T.," *Notes and Queries* 208, m.s. 10 (1963): 289-90, who finds no evidence of it. On their ability to make innovative use of traditional modes and material, see Lewis, *English Literature in the Sixteenth Century*, p. 97; Kinghorn, "Dunbar and Villon," p. 205; Singh, "Alliterative Ancestry," pp. 22-54, who appropriately cites Janet M. Smith, *The French Background of Middle Scots Literature* (Edinburgh and London: Oliver and Boyd, 1934), passim; Kratzmann, *Anglo-Scottish Relations*, p. 140, and Fox, who rather unjustly characterizes Dunbar's use of traditional genres as "almost parasitic" ("The Scottish Chaucerians," p. 187).

31. *William Dunbar: Poems*, p. xviii. Thomas D. Hill, "Dunbar's Giant: 'On the Resurrection of Christ,' Lines 17-24," *Anglia* 96 (1978): 451-56, demonstrates Dunbar's concern with pattern and points out the manner in which he carefully designed the poem so that its structure reflects its meaning. See also Fox, "Dunbar's 'The Golden Targe,'" *English Literary History* 26 (1959): 233: "in all Dunbar's poems the prose sense is negligible and the decoration, the poetic artifices, are everything."

32. T. S. Dorsch, "Of Discretioun in Asking: Dunbar's Petitionary Poems," in Arno Esch, ed., *Chaucer und Seine Zeit: Symposion für Walter F. Schirmer* (Tübingen: M. Niemeyer, 1968), pp. 285-92, dismisses these poems as "a handful," finding Dunbar to be essentially a court and occasional poet, his petitions tactless, lacking in variety and poorly designed to achieve their object. Yet it is impossible to discount the devoutness of poems such as "Ane Orisoun," "Of the Passioun of Christ," or "On the Resurrection," even though Dunbar's faith seems coupled with fear, lacking the depth and strength that could bring calm reassurance; cf. Wittig, *Scottish Tradition*, pp. 55-56; Speirs, *Scots Literary Tradition*, p. 66.

33. In addition to his *William Dunbar*, see Ross's "Dunbar's Vision of the 'Four Last Things,'" in Aitken et al., *Bards and Makars*, pp. 88-106, where he argues that Dunbar "has a part in the collective eschatological scheme as the witness and recorder of evil in high places."

34. Hay, "William Dunbar's Flying Abbot: Apocalypse Made to Order," *Studies in Scottish Literature* 11 (1973): 217-25; Milner, "Some Aspects

of Satire in the Poetry of Dunbar," *Casopis pro moderní filologii* 38 (1956): 32–41. See also Joseph B. Jacobi, "William Dunbar—An Appreciation," *American Catholic Quarterly Review* 44 (1919): 303–15, who found Dunbar memorable for sage advice and pious meditations, and classified his poetry as world-wise songs, a monk's nature poems, and expressions of spiritual longing and aspiration bordering on those of a mystic; Rowland Smith, "The Poetry of William Dunbar," *Theoria* 22 (1964): 75–84, who attempts to refute apologists for Dunbar's superficiality and his colloquial satires, though this critic actually demonstrates excellence of technique rather than weightiness of content; and R. J. Lyall, "Some Observations on The Dregy of Dunbar," *Parergon* 9 (1974): 40–43, who detects a serious moral purpose in the parody: to remind the King that spiritual purgatorial intent keeps him from court.

35. Walter Scheps, "'The Goldyn Targe': Dunbar's Comic Psychomachia," *Papers on Language and Literature* 11 (1975): 339–56. R. J. Lyall, who seeks a serious statement in the poem, also discusses commentary upon it, in "Moral Allegory in Dunbar's 'Goldyn Targe,'" *Studies in Scottish Literature* 11 (1973): 47–65.

36. Lewis, *Allegory of Love*, pp. 251–52. In addition to the Speirs reference cited in the text, see also Speirs, "William Dunbar," *Scrutiny* 7 (1938): 56–68, where he condemns aureate diction as "rootless, without activity"; Patrick Cruttwell, "Two Scots Poets," in *The Age of Chaucer*, ed. Boris Ford (Harmondsworth: Penguin Books, 1954), pp. 175–76, who asserts "In such diction, fixed and prefabricated, living poetry can hardly be made"; H. Harvey Wood, *Two Scots Chaucerians: Robert Henryson, William Dunbar* (London: Longmans, 1967), who finds both "The Goldyn Targe" and "The Thrissill and the Rois" "brilliant set pieces," the former the more lifeless example of dream-garden allegory; and Wittig, *Scottish Tradition*, pp. 56–67, who notes that in "The Goldyn Targe" meaning is relatively insignificant, the allegory perfunctory, conventional, merely an adjunct to the description, which is important for its own sake.

37. Fox, "Dunbar's "The Golden Targe,'" *Chaucer Review* 7 (1972): 147–59. Earlier Wittig, *Scottish Tradition*, p. 63, had noted the resemblance to tactile art: Dunbar "aims at the harder and more brilliant colour-contrasts of a miniature or a piece of enamelling—'anamyllit' indeed is one of his favourite words." See also Derek Pearsall and Elizabeth Salter, *Landscapes and Seasons of the Medieval World* (Toronto and Buffalo: University of Toronto Press, 1973), p. 194: "The master of this painted style is Dunbar, whose bejewelled landscapes are the most extravagant literary manifestation of decorated Gothic." Scheps, "'Goldyn Targe,'" pp. 339–40, claims

that Tom Scott's discussion of the poem as "almost a parody" of the poetry of *amour courtois* (in *William Dunbar*, p. 41) is "The most forceful and persuasive articulation" of the view that it is about poetry. Others agree on the theme: E. Allen Tilley, "The Meaning of Dunbar's 'The Golden Targe,'" *Studies in Scottish Literature* 9–10 (1973): 220–31; Gerald B. Kinneavy, "Metaphors of the Poet and His Craft in William Dunbar," in *Essays in Literature in Honor of Maurice Browing Cramer*, ed. Donna G. Fricke and Douglas C. Fricke (Bowling Green, Ohio: Bowling Green University Press, 1976), pp. 57–64, who believes that Dunbar is consistently concerned with the act of poetic creativity.

38. In order, such views are held by Ross, *William Dunbar*, pp. 258–68; Lyall, "Moral Allegory"; Kratzmann, *Anglo-Scottish Relations*, p. 149 ("the fear of irrational sensual love"); Tilley, "Meaning of 'The Golden Targe,'" p. 231; and Scheps, "'Goldyn Targe,'" pp. 339–56, who concludes that the poem is a parody of the love vision. Frank Shuffelton, "An Imperial Flower: Dunbar's 'The Goldyn Targe' and the Court Life of James IV of Scotland," *Studies in Philology* 72 (1975): 193–207, believes its complex aureation and lack of interest in the allegory result from its being written for a tournament welcoming Bernard Stewart in 1508.

39. See A. M. Kinghorn, "The Medieval Makars," *Texas Studies in Literature and Language*, 1 (1959): 80–81, who notes the influence of the pulpit in both Douglas and Dunbar; and "Dunbar and Villon," pp. 200–01, where he notes Dunbar's contrast with Villon, who does not insist upon the obvious.

40. As J. Swart says, Dunbar's "poetic ability is never in doubt. But on great questions such as justice or loyalty, or the power of evil he can say only minor things"; "On Re-Reading William Dunbar," in *Chaucer and Middle English Studies in Honour or Rossell Hope Robbins*, ed. Beryl Rowland (London: Allen and Unwin, 1974), p. 206. For further discussion of Dunbar's skillful handling of the commonplace, see Kratzmann, *Anglo-Scottish Relations*, pp. 140–44; and J. V. Cunningham, "Logic and Lyric: Marvell, Dunbar, and Nashe," *Modern Philology* 51 (1953): 40–41, 50–53.

41. "Dunbar and the Language of Poetry," p. 141. In this all-too-brief essay Morgan demonstrates much of the what, why, and how of Dunbar's poetic effects. Other excellent studies of his technique and results are those of Priscilla Bawcutt, "Aspects of Dunbar's Imagery," in Rowland, *Chaucer and Middle English Studies*, pp. 190–200, on the comic poems; Isabel Hyde, "Primary Sources and Associations of Dunbar's Aureate Imagery, *Modern Language Review* 51 (1956): 481–92, and "Poetic Imagery: a Point of Comparison between Henryson and Dunbar," *Studies in Scottish Literature* 2 (1965): 183–97, on the aureate; and Wilhelm F. Nicolaisen, "Line and Sentence in Dunbar's

Poetry," in Aitken et al., *Bards and Makars*, pp. 61-71, on metrics. Among others, David Daiches notes Dunbar's coupling of European and Latin traditions with narrative material, imagery, attitudes, and alliteration from the Scottish scene; "The Writing of Scottish Literary History," in *Literary Essays*, p. 142. Dunbar's most striking exploitation of contrast is in "The Tretis of the Tua Mariit Wemen and the Wedo," which has been variously interpreted. For an excellent survey of commentary, see Elizabeth Roth, "Criticism and Taste: Readings of Dunbar's *Tretis*," *Scottish Literary Journal* suppl. no. 15 (1981): 57-90; as well as Singh, "Alliterative Ancestry," pp. 22-54; and Lois Ebin, "Dunbar's Bawdy," *Chaucer Review*, 14 (1980): 282-85. For an approach as novel as that of A. D. Hope, see K. M. Abenheimer and J. L. Halliday, "The Treatise of the Two Married Women and the Widow," *The Psycho-analytic Review* 31 (1944): 233-52: the women are witches, escaped from their daily round to a secret conventicle.

42. See, for example, Speirs, *Scots Literary Tradition* pp. 54-68, whose survey indicates something of the variety. See also John Leyerle, "The Two Voices of William Dunbar," *University of Toronto Quarterly* 31 (1962): 316-38: and Patrick Cruttwell, "Two Scots Poets," in *The Age of Chaucer*, ed. Boris Ford (Harmondsworth: Penguin, 1954), p. 175, both of whom detect in the poetry differences so great as almost to suggest different poets; Douglas Young, review of Kinsley, *William Dunbar: Poems* in *Scottish Historical Review* 38 (1959), who notes the extremes in subjects and the heterogeneous vocabulary. But see also Dorsch, "Of Discretioun in Asking," pp. 285-86, who is concerned to limit the claim of versatility to tone and technique, finding the poet's range of interest narrow.

43. "Dunbar and the Language of Poetry." p. 156.

44. On the effect of restrained emotion see Kinsley, *William Dunbar: Poems*, p. xix: "his demon is leashed"; and Kinghorn, "Dunbar and Villon," p. 208: his emotions "are always kept under tight rein." On the dislike Dunbar arouses, see Dorsch, "Of Discretioun in Asking," p. 288: his verse suggests "that Dunbar was not always easy to get on with"; Kinghorn, "Dunbar and Villon," p. 200: he was a "self-centered unhappy moralist," who "can generally be relied upon to pick out the worst qualities of man in society"; and Young, review of Kinsley, *William Dunbar: Poems*, p. 19: he often discloses a "warped personality that leaves a nasty taste for a moment."

45. *Allegory of Love*, p. 290; *English Literature in the Sixteenth Century*, pp. 77-80.

46. Kinneavy, "Gavin Douglas," pp. 52-68; and review of Bawcutt, *Shorter Poems of Gavin Douglas*, in *Medium Aevum* 37 (1968): 356. Kratzmann, *Anglo-Scottish Relations*, p. 106; and "The Poet in 'The Palice of Honor,'"

*Chaucer Review* 3 (1969): 280–303. But see Kinghorn, "Medieval Makars," p. 82: it is only a "trial run," a contrived experiment revealing command of language and classical learning; and Fox, "Scottish Chaucerians," p. 196: here Douglas "seems to make no effort to preserve any reasonable narrative coherence."

47. J. A. W. Bennett, "The Early Fame of Gavin Douglas's *Eneados*," *Modern Language Notes* 61 (1946): 83–88, traces commentary upon the translation; and Bruce Dearing, "Gavin Douglas' *Eneados*: a Reinterpretation," *PMLA* 67 (1952): 845–49, briefly discusses its reputation. See also, Lauchlan MacLean Watt, *Douglas's Aeneid* (Cambridge: Cambridge University Press, 1920. Reprint. New York: AMS Press, 1975), pp. 3–24, who cites a number of early references to Douglas and his work, pp. 3–24. Kinghorn, "Medieval Makars," p. 82, takes Douglas's immediate object to have been to stabilize and enrich the language, demonstrating that it was capable of bridging the gap between Roman and medieval Scots civilization.

48. See Louis Brewer Hall, "Caxton's 'Eneydos' and the Redactions of Vergil," *Medieval Studies* 22 (1960): 136–37, and "An Aspect of the Renaissance in Gavin Douglas' *Eneados*," *Studies in the Renaissance* 7 (1960): 184–92. On Douglas's faithfulness to his text, (which Wittig, *Scottish Tradition*, p. 77, notes as a new attitude toward translation) see Priscilla Bawcutt, "Douglas and Surrey: Translators of Virgil," *Essays and Studies* 27 (1974): 53–55; "Lexical Notes," pp. 48–55; and "Gavin Douglas and the Text of Virgil," *Transactions of the Edinburgh Bibliographical Society*, 4, pt. 6 (1973): 213–31, where she argues that Douglas probably used the Badius Ascensius edition of Vergil, and from that derived some of his apparent errors. But Dearing, "Gavin Douglas' *Eneados*," p. 847, speaks of "the persistent error of praising the *Eneados* as a strict line-for-line rendering of the *Aeneid*"; Lewis, *English Literature in the Sixteenth Century*, p. 86, of his errors, and with disapproval of his explanations. R. W. B. Lewis, "On Translating the *Aeneid*: Yif that I Can," *Yearbook of Comparative and General Literature* 10 (1961): 10–12, is as concerned with Douglas's faithfulness to Vergil's effect as to his literal statement.

49. See Hall, "An Aspect of the Renaissance"; Thalia Phillies Howe, "The Zeitgeist as Translator: *Aeneid* IV.1–5," *The Classical Journal*, 50 (1955): 244, who see Douglas reflecting enthusiasm for new humanistic studies. To both Kinghorn, "Medieval Makars," p. 84, and Speirs, *Scots Literary Tradition*, pp. 69–70, 76, Douglas apparently as a translator, responding to humanistic scholarship and the classics, was of the Renaissance; as a poet, of the Middle Ages. But see Lewis, *English Literature in the Sixteenth Century*, p. 234, who finds Douglas to be more medieval than Surrey, and the faults of his

translation to arise from "the general medievalization to which he subjects the *Aeneid*," p. 86.

50. This is Dearing's thesis, "Gavin Douglas' *Eneados*," pp. 845-62, with which W. I. McLachlan, "Translation and Critical Judgement: a Comparative Study of Ezra Pound and Gavin Douglas," *Diliman Review* 14 (1966): 188, agrees completely, finding "the motive behind Douglas's translation . . . an awareness of its immense moral significance for the chaotic times." Morgan disagrees: Douglas was "unwilling to restrict the impact of his poem to princes and nobles," hoping rather for a wider audience, "so that readers from princes to school-boys would understand it and imbibe its message of high duty and heroic action," ("Gavin Douglas and William Drummond as Translators," in Aitken et al., *Bards and Makars*, pp. 194-98).

51. Lewis Brewer Hall, "Caxton's 'Eneydos,'" p. 147.

52. See McLachlan, "Translation and Critical Judgment," p. 189: his view "had to be adapted to his own time if its relevance were to carry real conviction"; and Speirs, *Scots Literary Tradition*, p. 70: Douglas's task "implied nothing less than an attempt to . . . assimilate in Scots—a civilization." Speirs's discussion should be read in full, pp. 69-76, 165-97.

53. See, for example, Bawcutt, "Douglas and Surrey," pp. 52-67, who stresses primarily the greater diffuseness of Douglas, occasioned partially by his didactic intent; Kratzmann, *Anglo-Scottish Relations*, pp. 169-89, who notes the resemblances between the translators, compares them to Douglas's advantage, offering some interesting observations, on, among other things, Douglas's sensitivity to rhythm and sound and his ability to balance "the demands of prosody against a feeling for the rhythms and the idiom of speech"; and Ridley, ed., *The 'Aeneid' of Henry Howard, Earl of Surrey* (Berkeley and Los Angeles: University of California Press, 1963), who describes the differences between them and indicates Surrey's borrowings from Douglas by italicizing them in the text.

54. Letter VII, *The Polite Correspondence*, or *Rational Amusement*, c. 1741, quoted by Bennett, "The Early Fame of Gavin Douglas's *Eneados*," p. 85; Robin Fulton, "Notes and Documents: Douglas and Virgil," *Studies in Scottish Literature* 2 (1964), 125-29.

55. See Wittig, *Scottish Tradition*, p. 23.

56. Ezra Pound, *How to Read* (London: D. Harmsworth, 1931), p. 45; *ABC of Reading* (London: Faber and Faber, 1951), p. 118; as well as *Literary Essays of Ezra Pound*, ed. T. S. Eliot (Norfolk, Conn.: New Directions, 1954), p. 245. In addition, see particularly Morgan, "Douglas and Drummond," p. 197, and Speirs, *Scots Literary Tradition*, pp. 190-92.

57. Charles R. Blyth, "Gavin Douglas' Prologues of Natural

Description," *Philological Quarterly* 49 (1970): 164–77, traces the shift of attention from the translation to the prologues, as does Bennett, "The Early Fame of Gavin Douglas's *Eneados*," and discusses some criticism of them by Cruttwell, Speirs, and C. S. Lewis.

58. See Bawcutt's discussion, in *Gavin Douglas*, pp. 164–91, especially p. 172; Lois Ebin, "The Role of the Narrator in the Prologues to Gavin Douglas's *Eneados*," *Chaucer Review* 14 (1979): 353–65. Penelope Schott Starkey, "Gavin Douglas's *Eneados*: Dilemmas in the Nature Prologues," *Studies in Scottish Literature* 11 (1973): 82–89, finds the three nature prologues (7, 12, 13) important as indicators of the narrator's presence, and as reflections of Douglas's moods.

59. See Coldwell's summary of the prologues' content, in *Virgil's Aeneid*, 1.87–88.

60. Mackenzie, *An Historical Survey of Scottish Literature to 1714* (London: Alexander Maclehose, 1933), p. 102. See also Hugh MacDiarmid, "Gavin Douglas," *Agenda* 14, no. 2 (1976): 89–92; Wittig, *Scottish Tradition*, p. 85; Pearsall and Salter, *Landscapes and Seasons*, p. 204. But see also Blyth, "Gavin Douglas' Prologues," p. 174; Starkey, "Gavin Douglas's *Eneados*," pp. 82–83; Bawcutt, *Gavin Douglas*, p. 190, who disagree with the opinion that the landscape description is an end in itself and thus an innovation. On the evocative effect of the description, see particularly C. S. Lewis, *English Literature in the Sixteenth Centrury*, pp. 87–90, and Wittig, *Scottish Tradition*, pp. 85–90; on the winter prologue, no. 7, see particularly Speirs, *Scots Literary Tradition*, pp. 72–75, and Blyth, "Gavin Douglas' Prologues," pp. 171–73, 177, who also praises no. 13, pp. 173–77.

61. *Landscapes and Seasons*, p. 200–03.

62. Fulton, "Notes and Documents," pp. 125–28; Speirs, *Scots Literary Tradition*, pp. 165–97, especially pp. 169–75.

63. For suggestions about genre study see Allan H. Maclaine, "The Christis Kirk Tradition: Its Evolution in Scots Poetry to Burns," *Studies in Scottish Literature* 11 (1964): 3–18, especially pp. 16–17, who argues that several of Dunbar's satires are part of an established genre, the mock tournament; R. J. Lyall, "William Dunbar's Beast Fable," *Scottish Literary Journal* 1 (1974): 17–28, on "The Wowing of the King quhen he was in Dunfermline"; Roy J. Pearcy, "The Genre of William Dunbar's 'Tretis of the Tua Mariit Wemen and the Wedo,' " *Speculum* 55 (1980): 58–74, who defines the poem as an example of a subgenre, the "jugement"; Ebin, "Dunbar's Bawdy," pp. 278–86, who shows how Dunbar satirizes the traditional genre of praise of woman and the pastourelle. Wittig (*Scottish Tradition*) points to similarities between Gaelic and Scots traditions,

especially pp. 70–75, 185–98, and has scattered references to the relation between Dunbar's poetry and court pageants. See also Douglas Young, review of Kinsley, *William Dunbar: Poems*, *Scottish Historical Review* 38 (1959): 16–19; and on the part a poem by Dunbar might have played in a court celebration, W. S. Ramson, "The nynt morow of fresch temperit May," *Parergon* 1 (1971): 23–24, and Helena Mennie Shire, ed., *The Ninth of May* (Cambridge: Shire, 1962), pp. 25–27. As Kratzmann, *Anglo-Scottish Relations*, p. 31, says, much Scots poetry has a performance quality.

There were early suggestions of the relation between Dunbar's poetry and Flemish art: see quotations by Kinsely, *William Dunbar: Poems*, pp. 128, xxvi; and W. L. Renwick: Dunbar was "painter by turns in the school of Hieronymus Bosch and Holbein." See also Douglas Young, review of Kinsley, pp. 17–18, who thinks too little has been made of the Flemish influence; David Murison, "The Dutch Element in the Vocabulary of Scots," in Aitken et al., *Edinburgh Studies*, pp. 159–76, who gives historical background, an applicable bibliography, and lists Dutch words in medieval Scots, a first source for a number of them being Gawin Douglas; and Ian Ross, who in "Dunbar's Vision of 'The Four Last Things,'" pp. 97, 102–06, makes illuminating comments about the relevance of Flemish painting to Dunbar. Both here and in his *William Dunbar* Ross provides a wealth of references to art and music. Wilhelm F. H. Nicolaisen, "Line and Sentence in Dunbar's Poetry," in Aitken et al., *Bards and Makars*, pp. 60–71, studies the varying relation between line of poetry and syntactical unit, by which Dunbar gives a sense of ease and tension as grammar reinforces meter (see especially p. 66). Then, too, Bawcutt, "'Library' of Douglas," pp. 124–25, is probably right in suggesting that the learned Latin context of the poetry should be investigated more.

64. As to the music, Thea Musgrave has provided a score for mixed voices, *Rorate coeli: For Unaccompanied Chorus* (Borough Green: Novello, ca. 1977). On the suitability of the poetry for musical setting, see Ross, *William Dunbar*, pp. 249, 205–06. On meter and irony, see Morgan, "Dunbar and the Language of Poetry," p. 149: he can reflect contempt through meter and sound; and Ridley, "Scottish Transformations of Courtly Literature," in *The Expansion and Transformations of Courtly Literature*, ed. Nathaniel B. Smith and Joseph T. Snow (Athens, Ga.: University of Georgia Press, 1980), pp. 178–80.

# Part II
# Language and Paleography

# Texts, Textual Criticism, and Fifteenth Century Manuscript Production

## Derek Pearsall

There has been, in recent years, an increasing recognition of the need to reevaluate our understanding of Middle English literature—and of Old English literature, too—in the light of a renewed assessment of all the information provided by the manuscripts in which that literature survives. They are, though it may seem superfluous to remind ourselves of the fact, the primary and in most cases the sole source of information that we have, and it is clear that the way in which that information has been extracted and used, especially by modern editors, and the extent to which it has been subjected to acts of interpretation need to be exposed and constantly reexplored. There is need to be conscious, always, of how behind every text presented in a modern edition, with all the reassuring apparatus of titles and text divisions, capital letters and full stops, paragraphs and line numbers, there lies the spoil heap of the manuscripts from which it has been drawn. That spoil heap needs to be examined with all the care that an archaeologist would devote to a midden, so that all the information the manuscripts have to yield, through contents and contexts, make-up and layout, decoration and illustration, as well as texts and textual affiliations, is made available for assessment. A valuable contribution to this kind of study has been made of late by the publication of a considerable number of facsimiles of important fifteenth-century manuscripts, particularly complex manuscripts of varied content.[1] There have also been some challenging reexaminations of the textual traditions of certain major works and writers, including Chaucer and Langland, which have made it clear that the answers that satisfy one generation of scholars may well provoke a later generation to further questions.[2] And one should mention too an important essay by two of the most distinguished paleographers of the day, which has emphasized yet again the necessary and integral part that modern codicology and paleography have to play in the study of literature.[3] The time may therefore seem right for a brief survey of some of the ways in which modern editors may have tended to ignore or misrepresent certain kinds of evidence provided by manuscripts, and to suggest some of the aspects of manuscript study which may yet have a richer harvest to yield for our understanding of literature.

Historically, the role of the paleographer in Middle-English literary studies has not been an elevated one: for the most part he has been summoned by an editor to approve a technical description of a manuscript and provide a date for the handwriting, and has then been dismissed to go about his grubby and mysterious business. Manuscripts themselves have been treated in a rather similar way: having been tested for error by the editors of critical texts, those that have failed have been dismissed to a kind of codicological limbo, labeled "worthless," "corrupt," or "degenerate" to mark their inferior status (it is interesting to see how the language of moral approbation and disapprobation hangs around textual criticism, and to speculate on how it may affect thinking on the subject), while the manuscripts favored by the editor have been ushered into the antiseptic operating theatre of "the critical edition." That this procedure involves some neglect of important kinds of information that may be gleaned from "inferior" manuscripts is clear, and I will deal with this later, but it may be useful to dwell for a moment on the procedure itself, and the doubts to which it gives rise.

It is very difficult, in the first place, to construct reliable or useful genealogical "trees" for the manuscripts of the chief vernacular texts of the period, by means of which they can be classified according to their value as witnesses to what the author, or his copyist, may originally have written. The traditional method of constructing such trees, or stemmata, was to group manuscripts according to their agreement in common error, but the editors of the Athlone text of *Piers Plowman* have shown that coincidental error is so common among scribes of this poem that agreement in error is a very insecure guide to textual affiliation.[4] Their method, therefore, having chosen as their base manuscript a text as near as possible in date to the time when the author was writing and with consistent spelling and grammar, has been to emend that text, where necessary, in accord with what they conceive to be the author's *modus scribendi*. The "critical edition" thus becomes an extended exercise in literary taste, whereby the editor sees himself not as the practitioner of a science, but as a literary critic, making a multitude of minute judgments about the value of particular readings, his opinion being based on a larger judgment of his author which is derived from an accumulation of judgments of the kind he himself has been making. Any manuscript may preserve an authentic reading, and none can be automatically discarded.

It might be argued that *Piers Plowman*, with the high degree of participation it elicited from scribes because of its subject matter, is a special case, but there are problems of other kinds in the way of the traditional critical edition. The editors of the Chicago edition of the *Canterbury Tales* have to recognize constantly, for instance, that their classification of manuscripts is disturbed by shifts in affiliation.[5] Their method of discussing such shifts as part of their tale-by-tale analysis obscures the way in which they are likely to have arisen, that is, through mechanical defect in the exemplar. (It must be acknowledged too that the amount of information they are dealing with is beyond comprehension complex.) For instance, the departure of the Helmingham manuscript from Manly-Rickert group *b* around *Cant. Tales* B 4155 is well demonstrated in their analysis, but they do not specifically observe the temporary adherence of the Helmingham manuscript and an aberrant group of manuscripts, including Cambridge MS. Gg.iv.27, at this point.[6] It lasts for some 140 lines and could well represent the supply of text made necessary by the loss of a bifolium at the centre of a gathering, presumably in an ancestor of Helmingham.[7] The manuscripts of the *Confessio Amantis* provide us with a clear and nonhypothetical example of the same phenomenon. Macaulay points out that MS. Harley 7184, which has habitually a very close affiliation with the Keswick Hall manuscript, shares the readings of a completely different group of manuscripts for a section of about 600 lines in Book III.[8] This section corresponds exactly with the section of text lost by loss of leaves in the Keswick Hall manuscript. Macaulay makes the further point about the latter manuscript that the affiliation with the Fairfax manuscript varies very considerably, depending upon the particular scribe at work of the six who are represented in the manuscript.[9] This may be attributable to differences in the habits of the scribes in relation to care in transcription, but Macaulay raises the possibility, and it certainly cannot be dismissed, that the stints of the different scribes may have been set from portions of different exemplars. Such complexities in the transmission of texts make the task of the textual critic much more daunting; they also oblige him to recognize the value of the evidence provided by the whole surviving body of manuscript evidence.

If the habits of scribes were predictable, the editor's task would no doubt be easier, and it is true that in so far as scribes were careless, the consequences of their carelessness can be adequately predicted. But the editorial work that goes into the preparation of exemplars for scribes to copy is often careful, scrupulous, and intelligent, and the activity of mind has as its intention the production of just such smooth, correct, and regular texts as the modern editor aims at. To recognize this characteristic kind of contemporary or near-contemporary editorial activity, and to acknowledge the intelligence behind it, it is necessary for the editor to be familiar with the whole range of manuscript evidence so that he is not deluded by that which he favors. It is clear, for instance, that the meter of Chaucer's *Canterbury Tales* in the standard modern edition, that of Robinson, is the meter of the Ellesmere manuscript, a manuscript which is now recognized to have been subjected to extensive editing.[10] This editing was carried on in a highly intelligent and responsible manner and was designed to systematize grammar and inflexions, to clear up apparent irregularities and inconsistencies, and to regularize Chaucer's meter according to a ten-syllable pattern. This is what modern editors tend to want as well, and when Ellesmere fails them they have to resort to other manuscripts, equally conscientiously edited, such as MS. Harley 7334 or Corpus Christi College, Oxford, MS. 198, or to their own ingenuity, in order to present a text that conforms to their ideas of what Chaucer should have written.[11] In this way, certain characteristic metrical practices of Chaucer, in particular a very flexible and idiomatic use of the five-stress line, are obscured, and a pedantic anesthetized version substituted. Only in his second edition, for instance, does Robinson remove the final *-e* from *Aprille* in the first line of the General Prologue,

> Whan that Aprill with his shoures soote,

and so restore the "headless" line which is a characteristic Chaucerian variation on the decasyllable. The final *-e* has no manuscript support whatsoever. Likewise, in their efforts to avoid the 'Lydgate' line of *Cant. Tales* B 4608 (as represented in both the Hengwrt and Ellesmere manuscripts),

> And whan the fox saw that he was gon,

modern editors have seized on one or other of the expedients offered by other manuscripts, Robinson for instance on Cambridge MS. Dd.iv.24,

> And whan the fox saw that the cok was gon.

The "Lydgate" line is properly infamous because of Lydgate's jaw-breaking use of it, but in Chaucer's hands, as can be seen, it is a legitimate and euphonious variant on the normal decasyllable, with the consonant cluster of *fox* + *saw* acting to prolong the effect of the stress on *fox* and to bridge the gap created by the missing unstressed syllable. The line as it stands in Hengwrt and Ellesmere is certainly preferable to the "ten low words" of Chaucer's improvers.

Editors, of course, feel the need of some kind of help in the determination of original readings, some set of guidelines that they can appeal to as apparently objective, especially if they have abandoned recension, and a metrical theory may sometimes provide a tempting substitute for the exercise of subjective judgment. It is no accident that the editors of the Athlone B-text of *Piers Plowman* produce a set of systematic metrical criteria for their poet, from which they allow him no deviation, and which they use as the means to detect unoriginal readings. Few would accept that such rigidity of practice is necessary to a poet for him to be well thought of, though all would recognize the heavy constraint placed upon the editor to find something that promises certainty in an uncertain world. The point to stress again is that the whole weight of manuscript evidence, and in particular the evidence of intelligent editorial or scribal activity operating to precisely the same objectives as those of the modern editor, needs to be borne in mind.[12] Huntington Library MS. HM 137, the manuscript of the C-text of *Piers Plowman* used by Skeat,[13] is an excellent example of this principle of convergent editorialization, for what Skeat wanted—a clean, full, careful text, purged of gross error, as of awkwardness and obscurity, systematic in metrical practice (even to the extent of splitting excessively long lines into two and padding them out with inert material)—was what the editor or scribe of MS. HM 137 provided.[14] The care taken to remove every blur is still a monument to editorship.[15]

In such a situation, with the more intelligent fifteenth-century editors preventing the modern editor in all his doings, it becomes more and more difficult to be certain about the jurisdiction of the modern editor in determining original readings. An intelligent contemporary editor, with an intimate knowledge of his poet's language and idiom, may hit upon readings that seem preferable not only to him and his modern counterpart, but which might even have been preferred by the poet himself if he had thought of them. The distinction between original readings and skillfully editorialized readings is not always easy to make, and a "better" reading may as well be the product of improvement as a "worse" reading may be the result of scribal carelessness. The editor who accepts the principle of *lectio difficilior*, and who accepts also the associated principle of economy in the hypothesis of the generation of variants,[16] will sometimes find himself constrained to adopt "worse" readings simply because they are harder to explain as scribal given the ubiquity of editorializing improvement. When the fox, in the *Nun's Priest's Tale*, having made off with Chauntecleer to the woods, lets him escape up into the tree, he tries to explain his conduct in the following manner:

> 'Allas!' quod he, 'O Chauntecleer, allas!
> I have to yow', quod he, 'ydoon trespas,
> In as muche as I maked yow aferd
> Whan I yow hente and broghte out of the yerd'
> (*Nun's Priest's Tale* B 4609–12)

For *out of the*, in the last line, the Hengwrt manuscript, generally assumed to be the closest of all surviving copies to what Chaucer wrote, reads *into this*. The reading hardly seems to make sense, yet it cannot readily be explained except as an act of prodigious carelessness on the part of an exceptionally careful scribe. On the other hand, it is very easy to understand how the reading *into this*, evidently "wrong," would have generated the reading *out of the*. Even the most modest improver would have seen this as an obviously necessary change to make. Perhaps, therefore, *into this*, as the harder reading, needs to be considered as possible Chaucerian, and some speculation needs to be entertained concerning the fox's motives in pretending to Chauntecleer that he should really feel quite reassured and at home, among friends, in *this yerd*.

Such are the problems of the editor and the manner in which the traditional machinery of the critical edition is made to groan by the circumstances of vernacular manuscript production. It is even worse when one descends to the level of the more pedestrian and routine verse, where there can be no certainty, no act of faith, that the level of poetic and intellectual activity of the author is superior to that of the scribal editor, and no certainty, therefore, that a "better" reading is necessarily the responsibility of the author. It is here, too, particularly in the case of the popular verse romances, that the problem of what constitutes "the text" is most acute. The modern critical editor must needs have as his goal the restoration of a text that represents a single moment in its existence as a composition, preferably that at which the author "released it for publication," or that at which the scribe of the first copy from the author's papers laid down his pen with a "Deo gracias. And þanne ho no more."[17] Such a moment, if it ever existed for the popular romances, is of little importance, for the surviving manuscripts of a poem like *Beves of Hamtoun* make it clear that each act of copying was to a large extent an act of recomposition, and not an episode in a process of decomposition from an ideal form. The standard edition of *Beves*, that of Kölbing, where the material in the textual notes threatens to swallow the supposed 'text,' quite obscures this fact;[18] any future edition of *Beves* that wishes to represent the manuscript evidence accurately must treat every manuscript on its merits as a witness to a different state in the poem's existence.[19]

Chaucer, it may be thought, is different, and we may be persuaded that the author who prayed for the text of his *Troilus* has a sense of the sanctity of artistic form which the modern editor can approve and be reassured by.[20] As to the integrity of the text of *Troilus*, Windeatt has made an interesting distinction between a prolonged but integrated act of composition, stages of which may have leaked into the manuscript tradition, and successive deliberate acts of revision upon a poem previously 'released for publication.'[21] Whatever the case with *Troilus*, the *Canterbury Tales* are certainly a problem for the modern editor, since the poem was never released or even prepared for publication, and the stages of recomposition are manifest in the surviving manuscripts. The usual procedure in modern editions is to print everything that can be found in the manuscripts that is plausibly Chaucerian, with or without indication of its manuscript status. This is useful, if sometimes misleading,[22] but even this expedient is not possible with variant passages such as the short and long forms of the Nun's Priest's Prologue, which clearly represent different stages in the evolution of the *Tales* and should be edited as parts of the A-text, B-text, etc., of the poem. As to the order of the *Tales*, Chaucer left only a half-assembled kit with no directions.

But whatever the problems for the editor of the *Canterbury Tales*, they pale into insignificance beside those of the editor of *Piers Plowman*. Langland certainly had no notion of finished form, and his whole life was spent in a perpetual and unfinished act of composition. He himself does not seem to have been clear about what he had written, and the revision of his poem represented in the C-text was done with a scribal copy of the B-text in a fairly advanced state of corruption, toward the original of which he constantly gropes in his revisions.[23] The editors of the Athlone B-text have made a vehement defense of the exclusive integrity of the three texts of Langland's poem, and probably they needed to if they were to retain their sanity, since the problems of editing a text in a continuous state of flux are no doubt considerable.[24] The possibility remains, though, that the surviving manuscripts include representatives or parts of versions intermediate between, preceding, or following what we have come to regard as the three versions of the poem. It is wholly reasonable, given what we know of Langland's manner of working, that this should be so.

It may seem, then, that the modern editor's veneration of the critical text, and his methods of extracting such a text from the body of surviving manuscript evidence, may be something less than completely faithful in their representation of that evidence. Without wishing to question further the value of trying to establish "what an author wrote," or offering to debate the difference between establishing what an author wrote and conjecturing what he should have written, I should like to pass on now to mention some of the ways in which fifteenth-century manuscripts have, in addition to trip-wires for the modern editor, more positive kinds of information to yield.

It is clear, at the outset, that the manuscripts discarded in the process of setting up a critical edition often deserve far more than the total neglect they are subsequently accorded, since they contain very rich materials for the literary historian. Manuscripts dismissed as worthless by editors of critical texts are often the very ones where scribal editors have participated most fully in the activity of a poem. Such editors, as Windeatt has remarked recently, are the first literary critics, even though they may not realize it.[25] Highly eccentric manuscripts, like Bodleian MS. Arch. Selden B.14 and the Delamere manuscript (now Takamiya MS. 32) of the *Canterbury Tales*, or the Sion College manuscript, Bodley MS. 851, and Huntington Library MS. HM 114 of *Piers Plowman*, provide fascinating insight into the methods of scribes and the expectations of their readers, yet they tend to be lost to scholarship once they have been declared inauthentic. There is much to be done on the uses of bad manuscripts, and not all of it would merely demonstrate how stupid everyone but the author was. On the contrary, the canons of taste according to which an author was received are an important part of our understanding of that author. The very widespread antipathy among scribal editors to enjambement in Chaucer and Gower is an example of the operation of such taste, and may be considered to be an "English" reaction to the versification of these writers, though doubtless it was a reaction not discouraged by the habit of copying line by line.[26] Similarly, the processes of amplification, emphasis, and censorship undergone by the *Piers Plowman* manuscripts demonstrate in the liveliest way the reactions of readers and prospective readers to the poem, and provide a sort of history of popular religious ideas in the fifteenth century, as we see the changes that are made in the text of what is still a living poem.

Likewise, late manuscripts of the popular metrical romances (and early printed editions as well) are part of the literary existence and literary history of those romances in a very real sense, evidence not only of editorial recomposition which is often little different in character or quality from original composition, but also of the literary circles and reading habits within which such poems continued their vigorous life. What might be seen, from the point of view of the textual purist, as debased texts of little value, may be seen from this point of view in a more fruitful way as part of a process of literary transformation and metamorphosis of which we in the end are the inheritors, not the resurrectors.

Another valuable kind of understanding to be gained from the study of manuscripts is that derived from seeing poems in their authentic manuscript context. Here the facsimiles that I mentioned earlier provide a most immediate access to the realities of fifteenth-century poetic culture:[27] the gluttonous appetite for didactic and instructional verse of all kinds, for instance; the ease with which our notions of the division between the secular and religious are violated; the irrelevance of many of our modern generic categories—romance, religious lyric, secular lyric—to the discussion of the production and readership of poetry in the fifteenth century. This is a healthy countermand to the habits encouraged by modern editors, who, having decided what constitutes a poetic genre, extract poems from their authentic contexts in the manuscripts and group them together so as to make them fit in with modern ways of understanding literature. T. A. Shippey has put the matter most engagingly in a review of the facsimile of Bodleian MS. Fairfax 16:

> Medieval literature as it appears in printed texts is often in a sense domesticated. Across its expanses editors have strung the barbed wire of "canonicity"; from the fields so created, herds of literary, intellectual and iconographic "traditions" moo gently to each other; in the learned journals prize milch texts are deftly milked of meanings and ironies, to be lorried off to the great consumers in university literature departments. One of the functions of facsimiles is, if not to shatter this idyllic state, at least to allow in a whiff of the (relatively speaking) dunghills in which the flowers of medieval poetry grew and seeded.[28]

It must be added, of course, that one would not want Shippey's mooing herds to trample undifferentiated over the plain. The claims that one makes for the value of the recovery of historical context are not absolute: the material so recovered must be subjected to the proper processes of analysis. What the compilers of these manuscripts did in bringing together poetic texts in their collections is usually interesting and often revealing of the assumptions about poetry that they consciously or unconsciously made. But sometimes it is revealing of no more than their ignorance or stupidity or confusion of mind, or, above all, of the practical limitations placed upon them by the availability or nonavailability of exemplars. The physical make-up of the manuscript needs also to be kept in mind. The texts of Lydgate's *Life of Our Lady,* Gower's *Confessio Amantis,* Hoccleve's *Regement of Princes,* and John Walton's verse translation of Boethius in The Royal Society of Antiquaries MS. 134 are copied continuously in the same hand,[29] and there is no doubt that the modern reader is well advised to take account of the serious moral and religious context here provided for Gower's poem, a context which is reinforced by almost every aspect of the poem's manuscript existence. On the other hand, the presence of Saint Edmund's *Speculum Religiosorum* in the company of the *Confessio* in MS. Harley 3490 may be of no significance whatsoever, since, although it is copied in the same hand, it constitutes a separate quire and may have been put together with Gower's poem merely for convenience.[30] Given these provisoes, however, there can be no doubt of the value of studying fifteenth-century poems in their fifteenth-century manuscript context.

Manuscripts have a further use for those who have a generous conception of the historical context needed to understand poetry. Over fifty years ago, Brusendorff wrote a book in which he attempted, through the study of the manuscripts, to show how profoundly our reception of Chaucer is influenced by the fifteenth century and how the fifteenth century itself can be understood through the extraordinary domination exercised over it by Chaucer.[31] His account of the provenance of the manuscripts opened up a particularly rich field of enquiry for those who wish to understand how and by whom Chaucer was read in the fifteenth century, and his book has been superseded only in part by the information presented for the *Canterbury Tales* manuscripts by Manly and Rickert.[32] More needs to be done, and more is likely to be achieved through meticulous study of particular manuscripts, on the model of the introduction by M. B. Parkes and Elizabeth Salter to the facsimile of Corpus Christi College, Cambridge, MS. 61 of *Troilus.*[33] Special interest attaches to manuscripts of known provenance, such as MS. Harley 7333, made and kept at the Austin priory of Leicester, in which some poems have been subjected to a process of censorship, sometimes aimed at removing the element of obscenity, but sometimes, as in the *Reeve's Tale,* at removing the suggestion of anticlericalism.[34] Another interesting manuscript is Bibliothèque Nationale MS. fonds anglais 39, a manuscript of the *Canterbury Tales* made for Jean d'Angoulême, brother of Charles d'Orléans, who like his brother spent most of his mature years as a prisoner in England. The manuscript contains marginalia in his own hand, and the selection and treatment of the *Tales* presumably reflect his own literary judgment:[35] particularly noteworthy are the references to Geoffrey Chaucer as the "compiler" of the work, which may allude to the activities of the medieval *compilator* as they have been described in an important recent article.[36] Jean shows no interest in the structure or framework of the *Tales*, and rearranges tales to suit himself; he cuts away most of the *Squire's Tale*, which he calls *valde absurda*, and also cuts the *Monk's Tale* to a bare three tragedies, as being *valde dolorosa*. Such comments are important, especially in the absence of other kinds of information, for the evidence they provide of a reader's critical response to Chaucer in the fifteenth century. Indeed, all manuscript marginalia have their interest, even though they may be of much later date than the manuscript itself. There is evidence, for instance, in marginal comment in British Library MS. Add. 35157 of the C-text of *Piers Plowman*, of a seventeenth-century reader continuing to take a lively interest in the matter of the poem. Beside C.V. 168 he writes, 'A prophecye trulye fulfilled by Kinge Henrye the viii$^{th}$.'[37] Occasionally, though, the understanding we gain is only of how easy it is to go wrong, as when another annotator, this time of the sixteenth century, writes beside C.V. 1–2, 'Pers dwelled in Cornewell with his frind Christopher or his wyf Cath . . . in there beds had a vision."

There are many other ways in which the study of fifteenth-century manuscripts, engaged in in a properly discriminating way, helps to enlarge our understanding of the literature of the period. The excerpting of passages from long major poems, such as the *Canterbury Tales* or Lydgate's *Fall of Princes*, provides valuable insight into fundamental assumptions about the nature and function of poetry on the part of scribal editors and the readers they served.[38] It is not only the nature of the excerpts chosen that is important here, but also the further manuscript context in which they make their appearance. Choices made in the decoration of manuscripts are also worth remarking for the evidence they provide of the status and dignity allotted to particular works. And as a final specialized aspect of the study of manuscripts, one might mention the potential importance to the student of literature of a proper evaluation of the illustrations that accompany texts of Chaucer, Gower, Lydgate, and a few other writers. It is true, and needs to be constantly recognized, that such illustrations must be interpreted in the light of the art-historical conventions and workshop contexts within which they were produced, but they do nevertheless provide tantalizing glimpses of an authentic primary response to a text which we shall rarely get from other sources, especially where an illustrator, or his supervisor, is put in the position of choosing themes or scenes to suit a previously unillustrated work. The illustrations of the pilgrims in the Ellesmere and Gg.iv.27 copies of the *Canterbury Tales*, inserted at the point where the pilgrim begins his tale, are evidence, for instance, that the "dramatic" reading of the *Tales* was alive and flourishing very early in the poem's career, while the choice of the statue of Nebuchadnezzar's dream as the subject of one of the two regular illustrations of Gower's *Confessio Amantis* provides a further confirmation, especially if it was done at Gower's instigation, of the moral and didactic intent of the poem.[39] The frontispiece to the *Troilus* text in Corpus Christi MS. 61, meanwhile, is a study in itself.[40]

I have made no mention, in what I have said, of the value of manuscript study for what it tells us about the techniques of book production or other matters related to the more specialized business of the codicologist or historian. I have concentrated rather on the central importance of manuscripts, in all the aspects of their existence, to the student of literature. In just the same way that we should not be content to look at medieval paintings in the sterile context of the modern art gallery or listen to medieval music played on modern instruments, so we should not rest content to confine our view of medieval poetry within the scholarly intensive-care unit provided by the modern critical edition. The poetry should be allowed to live and breathe more within its own natural environment, and every clue to the recovery and understanding of that environment that may be gained from the manuscripts is worth following up. And if it be argued that all this is a matter for the mere historian of taste, and of no great importance to the literary critic's consideration of the intentions that he presumes to exist in the act of composition, then one would have to retort that no work of literature exists in a state of such pure being, and that reading is always an act in which we share with the writer in the making of meaning. Our knowledge of the activities of the scribes, compilers, editors, decorators, and illustrators of our fifteenth-century manuscripts helps us to ensure that the reader's share is fairly apportioned.

# Notes

1. Among these may be mentioned the facsimile presentations of *The Thornton Manuscript* (Lincoln Cathedral MS. 91), with Introductions by D. S.

Brewer and A. E. B. Owen (London: Scolar Press, 1975; with revisions, 1977); of *The Findern Manuscript* (Cambridge Univ. Lib. MS. Ff.1.6), with introduction by Richard Beadle and A. E. B. Owen (London: Scolar Press, 1977); of *Cambridge University Library MS. Ff.2.38*, with introduction by P. R. Robinson and Frances McSparran (London: Scolar Press, 1978); and of *Bodleian Library MS. Fairfax 16*, with introduction by John Norton-Smith (London: Scolar Press, 1979). From the previous century there is, in addition, *The Auchinleck Manuscript* (Nat. Lib. of Scotland, Advocates' MS. 19.2.1), with introduction by Derek Pearsall and I. C. Cunningham (London: Scolar Press, 1977).

2. For Chaucer, see the essay by N. F. Blake, "The Relationship between the Hengwrt and the Ellesmere Manuscripts of the *Canterbury Tales*," *Essays and Studies* 32 (1979): 1–18; for Langland, see the introduction to *Piers Plowman: The B Version*, ed. George Kane and E. Talbot Donaldson (London: Athlone Press, 1975), and the lively debate occasioned thereby, both in reviews and also in the subsequent edition of the B-text by A. V. C. Schmidt (London and New York: Everyman's Library, Dent and Dutton, 1978).

3. A. I. Doyle and M. B. Parkes, "The Production of Copies of the *Canterbury Tales* and the *Confessio Amantis* in the Early Fifteenth Century," in *Medieval Scribes, Manuscripts and Libraries: Essays Presented to N. R. Ker*, ed. M. B. Parkes and Andrew G. Watson (London: Scolar Press, 1978), pp. 163–210.

4. For the edition of the B Version, see note 2, above; the A Version was edited by George Kane, *Piers Plowman: The A Version* (London: Athlone Press, 1960), with an introduction of great importance to textual criticism.

5. *The Text of the Canterbury Tales, Studied on the Basis of All Known Manuscripts*, ed. John Matthews Manly and Edith M. Rickert, 8 vols. (Chicago: University of Chicago Press, 1940).

6. Manly and Rickert, *Canterbury Tales* 1: 259–60; 2: 57, 416–18.

7. The evidence is contained in the Corpus of Variants for the *Nun's Priest's Tale* printed by Manly and Rickert in vol. 7 of their edition, but is more prominently displayed in the forthcoming edition of the *Tale* for the *Variorum Chaucer* (to be published by the University of Oklahoma Press under the general editorship of Paul Ruggiers) prepared by the present author. This edition has supplied some of the other illustrations in this paper.

8. *The English Works of John Gower*, ed. G. C. Macaulay, Early English Text Society, ES 81–82, 2 vols. (London, 1968), 1: clxiii.

9. Ibid., 1: clxii.

10. *The Poetical Works of Chaucer*, ed. F. N. Robinson (Boston: Houghton Mifflin; London: Oxford University Press, 1933; rev. edn. 1957).

11. Robinson follows Skeat (*The Complete Works of Geoffrey Chaucer*, ed. W. W. Skeat, 6 vols. [Oxford: Clarendon Press, 1894]) in using the Corpus group (Corpus 198 with British Library MS. Lansdowne 851 and the Petworth MS.) and MS. Harley 7334 for metrical emendation in *Nun's Priest's Tale* B 4091, and in using the Corpus group with the addition of the less extensively edited Cambridge Univ. Lib. MSS. Dd. 4.24 or Gg.4.27 in 4232, 4274, and 4618. Manly and Rickert provide the MS. evidence.

12. It is not always possible to tell whether a scribe worked from an already edited exemplar or whether he sometimes did his own editing as he went along. I therefore use the terms "editor," "scribe," and "scribal editor" rather interchangeably.

13. *The Vision of William Concerning Piers the Plowman, in Three Parallel Texts*, ed. W. W. Skeat, 2 vols. (London: Oxford University Press, 1886).

14. For further detail, see *Piers Plowman, by William Langland, an Edition of the C-text*, (ed.) Derek Pearsall (London: Edward Arnold, 1978), p. 21.

15. "Every blur is a challenge," said Kenneth Sisam (*Fourteenth Century Verse and Prose* [Oxford: 1921], p. xliii), speaking of the understanding of Middle English texts.

16. That is, given two readings, the editor should accept as original that which is less readily explained as arising, by any process, from the other.

17. As does the scribe of British Library MS. Egerton 1991 at the end of the concluding matter of Gower's *Confessio Amantis* (*English Works*, ed. Macaulay, I: cxlvii).

18. *Sir Beves of Hamtoun*, ed. E. Kölbing, Early English Text Society, ES 46, 48, 65 (London, 1885–94).

19. Such an edition is being prepared by Jenny Fellowes, and has already been submitted as a Cambridge Ph.D. in the form of an edition with four MSS. in parallel, and a further two texts from another MS. and from the early printed editions.

20. *Troilus and Criseyde*, Book V, lines 1793–96.

21. Barry Windeatt, "The Text of the *Troilus*," in *Essays on Troilus and Criseyde*, ed. Mary Salu, Chaucer Studies, 3 (Woodbridge, Suffolk: D. S. Brewer; Totowa, N.J.: Rowman and Littlefield, 1979), pp. 1–22. It may be interesting to observe that Windeatt, as a reintegrator of the text, is also a prospective editor of the poem.

22. As for instance in Robinson's edition, where the Nun's Priest's Endlink is left intact, in position, with only the smallest of square brackets to warn readers that he is seeing a ghost of text past.

23. See *Piers Plowman: The B Version*, ed. Kane and Donaldson, pp. 98–127.

24. Ibid, pp. 16–17, 70–74.

25. Barry Windeatt, "The Scribes as Chaucer's Early Critics," *Studies in the Age of Chaucer* 1 (1979): 119–41.

26. For Chaucer, see the treatment of *Cant. Tales* B 4305, 4308, as recorded in Manly and Rickert; for Gower, the treatment of *Conf. Am.* I. 3396, as recorded in Macaulay. For examples in *Troilus*, see Windeatt, "Scribes as Critics," pp. 134–135. Kate D. Harris, of New Hall, Cambridge, reports a systematic resistance to enjambement in the Gower excerpts contained in the Delamere manuscript (now Takamiya MS. 32).

27. See above, note 1. Other fifteenth-century MSS of similar kind, that would well repay presentation in facsimile, are British Library MSS. Add. 16165, 31042, 34360, Cotton Caligula A.ii, Egerton 1995, and Harley 2251; Lambeth Palace Library MSS. 306 and 853; Bodleian MSS. Ashmole 61 and Rawlinson C.86; Trinity College, Cambridge, MSS. R.3.19, R.3.20 and R.3.21; Nat. Lib. of Wales MS. Porkington 10; and Chetham's Library (Manchester) MS. 8009.

28. A review of the Fairfax 16 facsimile (see above, n. 1) in *TLS*, 7 March 1980, p. 272.

29. *English Works of John Gower*, ed. Macaulay, I: cxliii.

30. Ibid., I:cxlii.

31. Aage Brusendorff, *The Chaucer Tradition* (London: H. Milford, 1925; reprint, Gloucester, Mass.: P. Smith, 1965).

32. In volume 1 of their 8-volume edition of the *Canterbury Tales* (see above, n. 5).

33. Published by D. S. Brewer (Cambridge, 1978).

34. See *Canterbury Tales*, ed. Manly and Rickert, I:212.

35. See Paul Strohm, "Jean of Angoulême: A Fifteenth-Century Reader of Chaucer," *Neuphilologische Mitteilungen* 72 (1971): 69–76.

36. M. B. Parkes, "The Influence of the Concepts of *Ordinatio* and *Compilatio* on the Development of the Book," in *Medieval Learning and Literature: Essays Presented to R. W. Hunt*, ed. J. J. G. Alexander and M. T. Gibson (Oxford: Clarendon Press, 1976), pp. 115–41.

37. Line-numbers are from my edition of the C-text, as cited above, note 14.

38. See D. S. Silvia, "Some Fifteenth-Century Manuscripts of the *Canterbury Tales*," in *Chaucer and Middle English Studies in Honour of R. H. Robbins*, ed. Beryl Rowland (Kent, Ohio: Kent State University Press, 1974), pp. 153–63; A. S. G. Edwards, "Selections from Lydgate's *Fall of Princes*: A Check-list," *The Library*, 5th ser., 26 (1971): 377–42. See also Ethel Seaton's remarks on "the habit of making excerpts or centos from long poems," *Sir*

*Richard Roos: Lancastrian Poet* (London: Hart-Davis, 1961), p. 458.

39. For illustration of the *Canterbury Tales*, see the chapter on illuminations by Margaret Rickert, in Manly's and Rickert's edition, 1:561–605; for illustration of Gower's *Confessio*, see Macaulay's account of the manuscripts of the poem, *English Works* I: cxxxviii–clxvii. See further, Elizabeth Salter and Derek Pearsall, "Pictorial Illustration of Late Medieval Poetic Texts: The Role of the Frontispiece or Prefatory Picture," in *Medieval Iconography and Narrative: A Symposium*, ed. Flemming G. Anderson, Esther Nyholm, Marianne Powell, and Flemming Talbo Stubkjaer (Odense: Odense University Press, 1980), pp. 100–23.

40. See the introduction to the facsimile, cited in n. 33 above.

# Taboo-Words in Fifteenth-Century English

## Thomas W. Ross

When Chaucer wrote "pisse" would his audience have been shocked or titillated? or would they have considered the word innocent enough? Was it in fact a neutral term? Or was it the kind of locution, albeit reprehensible, that one would expect from the Wife of Bath, rather than the pompous, Latinate "purgacioun of uryne" which she uses at one point?

The present study attempts to throw some light upon this matter, focusing upon hitherto unpublished manuscript sources. My concern is not prurient nor are the purposes trivial. Everyone knows that Chaucer and his Scottish followers Dunbar and Henryson used blunt words for comic effects— less often for their shock value.[1] The manuscript materials employed here were composed in the fifteenth century. They therefore fall between Chaucer's death and the *floruits* of the Scottish Chaucerians. Admittedly they would be better evidence if they were more nearly contemporaneous with the English poet, but so far as I know there are no analogous materials from the late fourteenth century. Between 1400 and 1500 there were shifts in Englishmen's attitudes toward taboo-words. Indeed Chaucer himself may well have been responsible for an emergent acceptance of such words in polite literature. But if "pisse" loses its comic or shock effect, it is no longer of use to a writer who wants to make us laugh or gasp. The change in the fifteenth century was slow, and it is, of course, still in progress. Terms, blunt or clinical, for copulation, excretion, and the middle anatomical parts are still not acceptable in all situations. Many English and American families do not speak of bellies or belches but employ euphemisms like "tum(my)" and "burp" or avoid mentioning such things altogether.

In assessing the effects produced by hearing or reading "pisse" in the fifteenth century, I have begun not with a preconception of the emotional impact of the term in the late Middle Ages but with its reputation today. That is, the direction of inquiry is from the known to the unknown in good experimental fashion. The words chosen for inclusion in this study are therefore those that are still taboo today, or at least those that the present writer thinks are probably still taboo and may have been taboo five hundred years ago. There are of course no absolute calibrations for such notions. Therefore these pages are to be regarded as tentative and exploratory.

Charles Muscatine and E. Talbot Donaldson have shown us that it is possible to describe shades of tonal color in the poetic diction used in medieval literature. But, as both these giants of Chaucer criticism are quick to point out, it is a delicate task. Naturally both Muscatine and Donaldson focus upon Chaucer: so far as I know, there has been no parallel investigation of the poet's contemporaries, such as Lydgate or Hoccleve. I too have excluded them from this study since neither is notable for his comic powers or for his ability to shock us.

On the other hand, the Scottish Chaucerians not only imitated their master in form and style but went beyond him in their use of blunt language. Therefore I have included Henryson, Dunbar, and occasionally Sir David Lindsay as comparisons with Chaucer. I have also referred to two poems that are nearly contemporaneous with Chaucer, *Piers Plowman* and *Sir Gawain and the Green Knight*. There are admittedly problems with my analytical method. Ideally one would include all Latin-English glosses and all the late medieval poets. A more serious objection is that Middle Scots has its own store of Northern English terms that were perhaps unknown or at least uncommon in the South. I may be accused, therefore, of comparing apples and pears. However, the Middle Scots words have their own charm and vigor. It would be a shame to exclude them—which is perhaps all the justification that is necessary. Dunbar's "quhillelillie" alone is worth three or four Middle English "manhys thyngis."

The conclusions that I suggest must, as I have said, be regarded as tentative, but I am confident that they are sufficient to provoke further investigation. When the compiler of British Library Additional MS. 37075 refuses to provide an English equivalent for his Latin, it is likely that he felt the native term to be objectionable. That is, there must have been a taboo against setting it down on paper or parchment. It is of course possible that there were other reasons for the omissions: scribal lassitude (a familiar complaint) of the absence of the English term from the scribe's copy text, and the scribes were not consistent. On one folio they readily provide the

English word, with synonyms; on another folio they seem to develop a sudden primness. In any event, the omission of a term, for whatever reason, is taken as evidence that it was taboo.

The sources I have used are listed below, along with the abbreviations by which they are cited in the sections that follow. The first word list catalogues unglossed Latin terms. The second treats the English terms and indicates, with specimen passages, those words that the English and Scottish poets employed. Manuscripts are cited by folio, printed sources by column number.

## Sources

*Brit. Lib. Add. MS. 37075 (A).* Dated last quarter of the fifteenth century; 385 folios of paper (outer leaves vellum). The British Library notes that a few scattered passages from the manuscript have been published, but the material in the present essay has not appeared in print.[2] The bulk of the manuscript is a series of lessons in Latin, evidently intended for young students but not beginners. Some are arranged according to logical category: parts of the body, words associated with the fishing trade, terms for professions. Others are designed to instruct the student in Latin grammatical categories—deponent verbs, for instance. Therefore some terms appear more than once. Along with the Latin-English glosses are some proverbs and various (schoolboy?) scribbles such as "I haue fownd a snakys skyne" (fol. 275b). The manuscript was presumably the master's property. Perhaps he loaned it to one of his pupils who proudly recorded the marvelous snake's skin discovery, and who perhaps was also guilty of the naughty interlinear gloss "ars lyke" (see below). There is also a good deal of Latin poetry: pseudo-Ovid, doggerel, and macaronic verse. One of the largest sections in the collection is known as "Os, facies, mentum" ("mouth, face, chin") which obviously deals with parts of the body. Other versions of "Os . . ." are to be found in the collections of the same type (e.g., the Harley MS. described below).

*Brit. Lib. Harley MS. 1277 (H).* Paper, not dated, but probably also from the late fifteenth century. Included is item 13, "Tractatulus dictus, Os, Facies, Mentum," fols. 221a-243b.

*Brit. Lib. Royal MS. 17.C.XVII (R).* Another late fifteenth-century collection. Only the material on fol. 39, which is not printed by Wright or Wülcker, is included here.

My major manuscript source then, is Add. 37075. I have also consulted the editions of Wright (*W*) and Wülcker (*Wu*), whose sources are also fifteenth-century manuscripts (Harley 12002; Royal 17.C.CVII; Trinity College, Cambridge, 0.5.4), and the *Promptorium Parvulorum* (*P*). The latter prints the Sylkestede manuscript from the Chapter Library of Winchester Cathedral, dated 1440 by the *Middle English Dictionary*.[3]

## Unglossed Latin Terms

The scribes sometimes refuse to gloss certain Latin words in English, perhaps indicating their sense of decorum or shame. As stated above, however, they are inconsistent in this practice, since the same Latin words are occasionally given perfectly straightforward English translations. The following are some for which they provide only Latin equivalents:

adulterior: luxuriare *A* 144a; caricia: fallax ancilla *W* 217;[4] coeo: luxurior *A* 158a;[5] confedero: ligare in amore *A* 344b;[6] copulare: sacrare *A* 160a; crissor: luxu[r]are *A* 144a;[7] defloro: virginitatem auferre *A* 346b; deuergino: virginitatem auferre *A* 342b; extercoro: stercora auferre *A* 344b; incesto: adulterari *A* 349a; lecor: luxuriare *A* 145b;[8] lenocinor: luxuriare *A* 145b;[9] luo: luxuriare *A* 170a; lupanar: fornix *A* 170a;[10] matrix: est pellis in qua concipitur infans (stera, idem est) *A* 310a; mecor: luxuriare *A* 145b; mentula: uirga virilis *H* 238a;[11] merdula: parua merda *A* 310a;[12] meretricor: luxuriare *A* 145b;[13] nequam: luxuriosus *A* 172b;[14] peculari: luxuriare *A* 145b;[15] pelico: luxuriare *A* 331b;[16] pelignus: proplus, homo natus de pelice, id est meretrice *A* 176a;[17] presto: perpeccato stare velut meretrix *A* 349b;[18] scortor: meretricor *A* 146b;[19] stupror: luxuriare *A* 146a; tentigo: signum mulieris *H* 221a;[20] vrino: vrinam facere, mingere *A* 308a[21].

Most of the foregoing glosses pertain to the act of sex, which suggests that although the scribe felt free enough to gloss Latin names for parts of the body and for excretion, he felt some delicacy about certain words that pertain to lechery and fornication. As we shall see below, the commonest English word for the sex act, "swyve," does not occur at all in the long compilation that is MS. A, though Wülcker records a variation. Similarly, "fukke(n)" does not exist in any of the compilations, though Dunbar uses it later. Words for excretion or excretory matter were evidently not taboo; or at least the taboo feeling was not strong. Solid excrement was a familiar sight (and odor) in the fourteenth and fifteenth centuries, not only in the barnyard but probably also in the streets.

## English Terms

The scribes who composed MS. A and the others written at about the same time were ready enough to gloss a great many words that today are considered taboo.

**ars(e) arce, hars, narse, ners:**   anus, culus, podex, vino *A* 8b, 310a, *H* 221a, 238b, *P*14, *R* 39a.

   The Latin shows that the word had the same ambiguity in the fifteenth century as it does today. It can mean either the buttocks or the anus. The common form in the Chaucer manuscripts seems to be "ers," rhyming for example with "wers."[22] Two arse themes emerge in Chaucer's works: it is something to kiss and it is that part of Satan in which friars dwell. When one is tricked or forced into kissing another's arse, one is of course humiliated, as is Absolon in the *Miller's Tale*: "But with his mouth he kiste hir naked ers" (A 3734). Since his lips encounter long hair, we must imagine that Alison is unusually hirsute between the buttocks, for he kisses her there, on her nether eye, full savorly. When he gets his revenge, he thrusts the hot coulter into Nicholas's anus: "And Nicholas in the ers he smoot" (A 3810).[23] In the Middle English *Romaunt of the Rose*, the Old French "cul d'enfer" is translated "devels ers of helle." And of course in the *Summoner's Tale* Chaucer specifies that the friars live in the "develes ers." A complete set of arse references in Chaucer is A 3734, 3755, 3700, 3810, D 1690, 1694, 1698, 1705, RR 7576. One gets the impression that the word was mildly shocking but appropriate both to tale and teller in the passages from the *Canterbury Tales*.[24]

   Henryson uses the word in a blunt but comic fashion at the end of the rollicking "Sum Practysis of Medecyne," lines 89-90: "It is ane mirk mirrour,/ Ane uthir manis erss."[25] Like Chaucer, Dunbar finds it comic to kiss another's arse in "The Flyting of Dunbar and Kennedie," line 131.[26] Twice the word occurs in the boisterous "Sowtar and the Tailyouris War," lines 83 and 99, both times associated with the befouling of the arse with excrement ("beschittin" is Dunbar's word) and once also associated, as in Chaucer, with the devil: "Belliallis ers unblist." Henryson, "Practysis," line 30, has the repellent line "The crud of my culome [arse] with your teith crakit." Dunbar also associates evacuation with the fundament, as in "Flyting," line 467: "thou was louse [loose] and redy of thy bune [arse]"; and he speaks of the "tone," another synonym for arse, in the same light in lines 502 and 520. He uses an endearing diminutive (equivalent to Chaucer's "toute," A 3812, 3853) in "In Secreit Place," line 48: "My stang ['sting,' penis] dois storkyn [stiffen] with your towdie [arse]." Henryson and Dunbar are thus seen as somewhat cruder or perhaps more naturalistic than Chaucer in their use of "arse."

**ars(e) hole, arce h., narse h., anarse h., aars h.:**   intestinum, lingeo, penitorium, podex *A* 8b, 294b, *H* 221a, *P* 14, *R* 39a, *W* 184. None of the poets uses this

**ars(e) hole, arce h., narse h., anarse h., aars h.** *continued*
   term, perhaps because it was too crude. Still today, one can perhaps say, "She fell on her arse," but one would hesitate to use "her arsehole" as freely.

**ars holere:**   pirtomen *W* 186. Evidently a word for a sodomite; however, the meaning of the Latin gloss is not clear. The English phrase is not used by the poets, for reasons similar to those for "ars hole." Also, sodomy inspired horror in the medieval mind.[27] Nonetheless, Dunbar, in "Flyting," line 526, has "bugrist abhominabile."

**ars lyke:**   societas *A* 323b. The English interlinear gloss is in a hand different from that of the scribe. It may well be a naughty schoolboy's graffiti, not intended to gloss "societas" at all, though it is placed above it. See "pyntyl" below, where the same hand has entered the word above "suspirium." The act of licking another's arse is still distasteful and taboo today. Not used by the poets.

**ars wysp(e):**   anitergium, menpirium, -perium *P* 14, *W* 179. "Anitergium" means anus cleaner. Bunches of straw or hay are still used for this purpose in certain parts of the world. The phrase is not used by the poets.

**balloc poc:**   mentula *H* 221a. Not in the *MED*. *OED*, "poke" bag; but the spelling "poc" is not recorded. The phrase is synonymous with "baloke cod," q.v. Not used by the poets.

**ballok(k)e, -kys:**   genitale, piga, testiculus, -i *A* 294a, 310a, *H* 221a, 238a, *R* 39a. "Piga" is a vague word. DuCange glosses it "nates, bursa, mentula" (buttocks, "purse" or scrotum, penis). It was also glossed "ballok ston(e)," q.v. Chaucer does not employ "ballok," but the Scots were not so prudent. Henryson, in "Practysis," line 75, prescribes as an ingredient for medicine "the bellox of ane brok" (ballocks of a badger). Dunbar uses it in his invective in the "Flyting," line 119: "Thow hes na breik [breeches] to latt thy ballokis gyngill." Both Scottish instances are vulgarly comic.[28] Chaucer does, of course, speak of the Pardoner's (missing?) "coillons," C 952. See Ross, *Chaucer's Bawdy*, p. 57.

**ballok(e) ston(e):**   genitale, testiculus, piga(r) *H* 238a, *R*39a, *W* 208, 246. The phrase is a pleonasm since both "ballock" and "stone" mean testicle. Chaucer does not employ the term, but there are a couple of occurrences of "stones" that might have a latent or secondary sense of testicles: Nicholas's "augrym stones layen faire apart" (A 3210); and the Pardoner's "Thanne shewe I forth my longe cristal stones" (C 347). But one should be careful about seeing such a meaning in Pandarus's swearing to Criseyde "yis, by stokkes and by stones" (*Troilus and Criseyde*, III.589). In the *Romaunt* there are repeated references to "cristall stonys" (e.g., line 1568)—usually, and properly, interpreted as eyes.[29]

**ballukod:**   menticulosus *Wu* 595. The Latin shows that the last syllable is not to be equated with "cod" but indicates a participial adjective: ballocked, well

**ballukod** *continued*
    endowed. "Menticula, -tula" is the common word for penis. "Ballockode," glossed "menticula," occurs in *R* 39a; I am not sure whether it belongs here or with "ballock cod," above. Not used by the poets.

**bal(l)oke cod(e), balluc c., ballokkod:** omembrana, piga *A* 310a, *W* 208, 246, *Wu* 599. "Cod" is the generic Middle English word for a bag. Although Chaucer uses it, he does not refer to "ballok cod." Henryson, "Practysis," line 49, does: he prescribes a salve "for to bath your ba cod." The term is in tune with the boisterous men's-room tone of the poem. See "balloc poc."

**baud, bawde:** lena, -o, meretrix, pronuba, -o *A* 168a, 320a, *P* 26, *Wu* 605. As the Latin indicates, the word can be either masculine or feminine. It could mean simply a low-life person, but the Latin glosses also show that more commonly the sense was a procurer, procuress, or whore. Evidently the word was undergoing pejoration in the fourteenth and fifteenth centuries. *Piers*, C-text, IX.72, speaks, among other low-lifers, of "Denote the baude" and Conscience tells the king that Mede is a "baude," IV. 165. In the first of these two passages, the relatively innocent sense (a low-life person) is intended. Chaucer uses the word frequently: in the first sense, D 1354, "A theef, and eek a somnour, and a baude" in the second (procurer), *Troilus and Criseyde*, II. 352-53, Pandarus speaking to Criseyde, "For me were levere thow and I and he / Were hanged, than I sholde ben his baude." The first sense is present again in the Pardoner's "Syngeres with harpes, baudes, wafereres" (C 479), but the Parson is clearly using the second when he says that "putours . . . constreyne wommen to yelden hem a certeyn rente of hir bodily puterie, ye, somtyme of his owene wyf or his child, as doon thise bawdes" (I 885). The *Romaunt* translates Old French "baus" (an adjective) as "many a ribaud is mery and baud" (line 5674) and "maquereaus" as "bawdes." The Friar speaks of the archdeacon who punishes "wicchecraft, and eek . . . bawderye" (D 1305). Thus the word is ambiguous in a passage (D 1339) like that later on in the same tale, where it is said that the summoner "hadde alwey bawdes redy to his hond" (rascals? procurers?). In the Temple of Venus in the *Knight's Tale* one sees "Beautee and Youthe, Bauderie, Richesse . . ." (A 1926). But the meaning is simply "dirty" in the *Canon's Yeoman's Tale*, G 635, where the Canon's "overslope" is described as "al baudy and totore also." See Ross, *Chaucer's Bawdy*, p. 42.

**bawd(e)strot(t):** pronuba *H* 235b, *W* 217, *Wu* 605. The Latin glosses are always feminine; however, the *MED* defines the English "baudestrot" as "procurer, procuress, pander." The word is not in the *OED*. It is perhaps a more blunt and less equivocal word than "bawd" and hence is not used by the poets.

**beschittin:** see "schit."

**bobrelle:** caturda *W* 246. *MED*, "bobrelle (presumably OF; ? cp. *bobbe*, = a cluster of fruit), the clitoris or the lips of the vulva." Evidently a very naughty word, not used by the poets. See "kekyre," below.

LANGUAGE AND PALEOGRAPHY

**bordyl hows(e), bordel h., bordelle h.:** fornix, lupanar, prostibulum, scortorium, stuprum, suarium *A* 136a, 318a, *H* 232b, *W* 235. The Latin words are euphemisms: a "fornix" is a furnace, a "suarium" is a pig pasture or sty. In MS. *A*, fol. 218a, "lupanar" (glossed "bordelhowse") immediately follows "fornix" (glossed "furnace"). Evidently the scribe permitted his association of words to dictate the sequence. Chaucer does not use "-house" but simply "bordel": *Parson's Tale*, I 975, 885, "commune bordel wommen . . . thilke harlotes that haunten bordels." See Ross, *Chaucer's Bawdy*, p. 46.

**breke or sownde:** crepo *A* 128b, 129b. The Latin suggests that anal wind emission is probably understood. Chaucer does not use the word in this sense (but see "fart"). Dunbar has "Ane blast of wind son fra hir slippis," line 41 of "A Dance in the Quenis Chalmer," where a beldame commits this indiscretion.

**broke ballockyd:** hernia *W* 176. There is not much potential for comedy in a hernia, which is probably why the poets eschew the phrase.

**buttok(e), -ys, bicttockys (scribal error); natis, -es:** *A* 8a, 294a, 309b, *H* 221a, 238b, *P* 53, *W* 183, 207. The word can be neutral, simply a term for the posterior; and it can also be used in a passage that expresses admiration for a woman's buttocks (or appears to do so), as in Chaucer's description of the miller's snub-nosed daughter, Malyn, *Reeve's Tale*, A 3975, "with bottokes brode." Compare the Lady of the Green Chapel in *Sir Gawain*, lines 996–97, "Hir body watz schort and þik,/ Hir buttokez balȝ and brode."[30] But more often it is a body part to inspire our laughter or (less often) disgust. The particularity of Nicholas's exact position in the shot window is comical: "And out his ers he putteth pryvely,/ Over the buttok, to the haunche bon" (*Miller's Tale*, A 3802–03). Old Thomas's lean and smelly bottom eventually disgusts the friar in the *Summoner's Tale*, D 2142, "Bynethe my bottok there shaltow fynde/ A thyng that I have hyd in pryvettee." The Parson finds men's buttocks repellent, especially if exposed by immodest dress: "the bottokes of hem faren as it were the hyndre part of a she-ape in the fulle of the moone," and "of the hyndre part of hir buttokes, it is full horrible for to see" (I 420, 425). Lindsay speaks of "buttock-mail," a comic expression which means ecclesiastical fines for fornication.[31] See Ross, *Chaucer's Bawdy*, pp. 50–51.

**codde:** coputa; c., of a mannys pryuyte: fiscus, mentula, piga *P* 89, *W* 575. See "baloke cod," above. The poets do not employ "cod" for the scrotum.

**cokkupyntel:** see "pyntyl."

**cok(e)walde, -wolde, cokold:** ninarius, ninerus *P* 90, *W* 194, *Wu* 597. There appears to have been no taboo involved, but cuckoldry was a shameful and (to the noncuckold) a comic matter. *Piers*, C-text, V.159, says that he who weds Mede will "be knowe for cokewold"; and speaks of Wrath, who gossips in the kitchen: "dame Clarice a knyghtes doughter . a cokewold was hure syre" (VII.134) Chaucer uses the word frequently, always ridiculing the hoodwinked

144

**cok(e)walde, -wolde, cokold** *continued*
husband—e.g., the Miller taunts the Reeve with "Who hath no wyf he is no cokewold" (*Miller's Tale*, A 3152); and John the carpenter "demed hymself been lyk a cokewold" (A 3226). See also C 382, D 1214, D 1616, E 1306, E 2256; and Ross, *Chaucer's Bawdy*, pp. 58-60.

**cun(c)t(te):** cunnus, lanugo, vulva *R* 39a, *W* 186, 208, 246. In *Chaucer's Bawdy*, pp. 175-84, I made the mistake of associating "cunt" etymologically with "queynte." The former is a common Germanic word; the latter is from Old French and is derived from the sense of "hidden secret." Chaucer never uses "cunt," though he mentions the female pudendum under the guise of such euphemisms as "bele chose" or "quoniam" (q.v. in *Chaucer's Bawdy*). Henryson, on the other hand, in "Practysis," line 37, offers as some of his more practical medical advice "the count of ane sow kiss." Dunbar, "The Wowing of the King Quhen He Was in Dunfermline," line 39, produces an amusing euphemism: the wooer promises "that he suld nocht tuich hir prenecod": literally a pincushion (the *mons veneris*). But he also has the blunter old word: in "The Manere of Crying of Ane Play," lines 78-79, he speaks of a giantess who "pyschit fyf quhalis [whales] in the Firth,/That cropyn war in hir count for girth [refuge]"; and twice in the "Flyting" (lines 50, 239) he attacks his enemy by calling him "cuntbittin crawdoun [coward]" and by referring to his "countbittin, beschittin, barkit hyd." Clearly the Scots had no hesitation about using the word, which years ago Henley and Farmer in *Slang and Its Analogues* coyly referred to as "the monosyllable." Cf. "manhys thyng," below.

**donge:** inder deris [?], fimus, letamen, lutum, -o *A* 63a, 107b, *P* 129, *Wu* 577. See also "muke" which is a synonym. Chaucer clearly did not consider the word taboo: it was simply a fact of farmyard life, and his references are usually to animal dung—e.g., the Plowman "that hadde ylad of dong ful many a fother" (A 530). The alchemist Canon uses it in his noxious concoctions: "poudres diverse, asshes, donge, pisse, and cley" (G 807); and the Parson uses it to express his revulsion from sin and extravagant clothing (I 135, 415). The other Chaucer occurrences are similar (B 4208, 4225, 4238, C 535); see Ross, *Chaucer's Bawdy*, pp. 79-80. *Piers*, C-text, V.144, IX.184, also employs it in the sense of manure for fields. Again the Scots are more daring: they use the word for human excrement. Henryson, "Practysis," line 72, advises that one anoint oneself with "nurice [nurse's] doung, for it is rycht nyce" and Dunbar, "Flyting," line 395, threatens thus: "Duerch [dwarf], I sall ding the, quhill [until] thow dryte [excrete] and dong."

**donge carte:** titubatorium *P* 129. I think that the Latin is probably a coinage intended to be comic; there is no trace of the word in the dictionaries. Chaucer uses the English twice, B 4208, 4226, as an innocent, accurate term.

**donghepe:** sterquilinium *Wu* 613. Chaucer does not employ the term. *Piers*, C-text, XVII.265, uses it as the equivalent of something loathsome: "lothliche dounghep."

**dong hylle:** fimarium, forica, sterquilinium *P* 295. See also "muckelle." in Chaucer's *Parlement of Foules*, line 597, the tercelet sneers at the duck: "Out of the donghil cam that word ful right." Again the association is with the barnyard. It is the same in Henryson, "The Taill of the Cok and the Jasp," line 66, where the cock "flew furth upon ane dunghill sone be day."

**dongyn or mukkyn londe:** fimo, pastino *P* 139. Another barnyard association: Chaucer, B 4226, mentions "a dong-carte, wente as it were to donge lond."

**fart(e), ferte:** bumbus, -a, -um, petigo, trulla; fart(e), v.: pedo; fartyng: bombizacio, peditura *A* 130a, 134a, *P* 154, *R* 39b, *W* 209. See also "breke," "fyse," "pinge," "trulle." Chaucer viewed the word (and the physiological event) as comic. Farts fly freely throughout his works, as everyone knows. Perhaps the most noteworthy fart is in the *Miller's Tale*, A 3806, "This Nicholas anoon leet fle a fart." But the fart-division in the *Summoner's Tale* is also an effective narreme. For evidence that some present-day readers find this particular occurrence offensive, see Ross, *Chaucer's Bawdy*, pp. 85–86. Chaucer also creates a pun on the word (D 1967): "What is a ferthying worth parted in twelve?" Further occurrences (fart, farting, farts) are in A 3337-38, D 2149, 2155, 2226, 2233, 2249, 2270, 2284. *Piers*, C-text, XVI.205-06, sneers at vain entertainers who include farting amongst their bag of tricks; Peers prentys the Plouhman says, "Ich can nat tabre ne trompe . ne telle faire gestes,/ Farten, ne fithelen . at festes, ne harpen." Henryson has a comic ingredient in "Practysis," line 69: "ane grit gowpene of the gowk fart" (a great doublehandful of cuckoo-fart). Like *Piers*, Dunbar associates farting with the lower classes: in "The Sowtar and Tailyouris War," the combatants fart more than they fight. There is "ane rak of fartis, lyk ony thunner" (line 35) and one jouster knocks down another with his farting (lines 86–87): "Baith hors and man he straik till eird,/ He fartit with sic ane feir [manner]." I also think that it is probable that in "A Generale Satyre," line 71, Dunbar may intend a pun in "fartingaillis [fart(h)ingales]." In the fourteenth and fifteenth centuries, there seems to have been no taboo associated with the word.

**fylth of the nose:** polipus *P* 419. See also "snot." As one might expect, no poet finds a use for the phrase.

**fyse:** lirida *W* 209. *MED*, "fyse; cp. *fist* (2) and OI *fisa*, break wind; (a) a fart." I suspect that "fyste" ("suspeticio") from MS. R, fol. 39b, also belongs here, but the Latin is no help. So far as I know, the word survives only in "feisty" and in "feist" (or "fice") an American regional term for a noisy and nervous terrier. The medieval poets do not employ the word.

**geldydmen:** enucos *A* 106a. As is frequently true in MS. *A*, the Latin is illiterate. A closely associated word occurs in Chaucer, where the poet utters his contemptuous authorial aside about the Pardoner (A 691): "I trowe he were a geldyng or a mare." I suspect that "geld-" was normally a barnyard word, like "donge," which makes its application to the Pardoner particularly powerful. See Ross, *Chaucer's Bawdy*, p. 94.

**gett, -in:** gestio *A* 166a, *P* 205. Additional glosses in MS. *A* show that the word had unpleasant sexual connotations in the fifteenth century; the scribe adds "cupio, proprie cum motu corporis." We still speak today of a lazy, irresponsible hillbilly's too-numerous offspring as his "git." *Piers*, B-text, I.33, tells of Lot, who "gat in glotonye . gerlis that were cherlis"; and C-text, XXIII.157-58, speaks contemptuously of Life and Fortune who "geten [preterite] in here glorie . a gadelyng atte laste, / On that much wo wroughte . Sleuthe was hus name." Elsewhere (B-text, IX.192) the poet warns that a man and his wife should be clean of soul and in perfect charity when they engender offspring, "And thei that othergatis ben geten . for gedelynges ben holden" (A-text, "i-geten"; C-text, "gete"). In Chaucer the term is usually neutral. However, when old January says that he will take no old wife, "ne children sholde I none upon hire geten" (E 1437), the crude and soiled word seems to have been carefully chosen to fit the character. Dunbar, "Flyting," line 244, speaks of "feyindis gett," where there is no question but that there is an evil connotation.

**gong(e):** cloaca, feterna, gumphus, ipidromium, latrinam *H* 239b, *P*347. See also "prevy," "wardrope." Chaucer's Parson (I 885) speaks with horror of "thilke harlotes that haunten bordels of thise fool wommen, that mowe be likned to a commune gong, where as men purgen hire ordure." But surely the Latin terms "gumphus" and "ipodromium" suggest that the word had a comic aura, too. See "prevy" for further evidence, including the Latin term "catacumba." And see Ross, *Chaucer's Bawdy*, p. 95.

**harlat:** scurrus: harlattry: scurrilitas; to do harlattry: scurror *A* 146a, 285b, *P* 214. For the association of the word with sex, see under "hore," below. As I argued in *Chaucer's Bawdy*, p. 102, "harlot," though usually equivalent to "rogue," was taking on sexual senses. In his edition of *Piers*, Skeat glosses "harlot" as "scurrilous person, ribald, buffoon, teller of ribald stories (used, apparently, of men only)." C-text, VIII.94-95, paraphrases Ps. 100: 7 (Vulgate) "Non habitabit in medio domus mee qui facit superbiam, qui loquitur iniqua" thus: "Sholde non harlot haue audience . in halle ne in chaumbre/ Ther that wise men were." In C-text, VIII.22, Sloth says that he does no charitable deeds: "Ich hadde leuere huyre of harlotrye," where again we have the association of "harlot, -try" with ribald talk or stories. This is Chaucer's sense in several passages, e.g., A 3184, where the poet says of the Miller and the Reeve, "And harlotrye they tolden bothe two." But there is a

**harlat** *continued*

hint (or more than that) of sexual misconduct and roguery when the Parson (I 625) equates two terms of abuse, "thou holour [lecher, adulterer]" and "thou dronkelewe harlot." The same is to be found in the *Merchant's Tale* (E 2262) when Pluto tells Proserpine that he will reveal May's adultery to January: "Thanne shal he knowen all hire harlotrye." In the *Romaunt*, "ribaus, ribaudiaus" are translated "harlotes," illustrations of the less pungent sense. But the Parson (I 885) speaks of "thilke harlotes that haunten bordels," where, though speaking of men, he gives the word an unmistakable taint of sexual misconduct. For Henryson's use of "harlot," see "hore," below.

**hars-tharme:** cirbus *W* 186. Wright was unable to determine the meaning. OED defines "tharm" as intestine, and "hars" is a variant of "ars" (q.v.). The Latin "cirbus" exists in no dictionary (s.v. c-, s-) and may be an error for "viscus." The term may refer to the lower bowel. None of the poets uses it.

**horcoppe:** pelignus, -a *A* 289b. *MED*, "horcop: bastard." Not even the Scots will touch this word. It was either uncommon or powerfully taboo. Cf. the Latin "pelignus," in the list of unglossed Latin terms above, which the scribe refuses to gloss. Also cf. Henryson's "hureson" under "hore," below.

**hore:** amasia, bipa, meretrix *H* 235b, *P* 226. Chaucer does not speak of whores except in one doubtful passage (see Ross, *Chaucer's Bawdy*, p. 110). *Piers*, C-text, V.161, says of Mede, "the comune called hure . queynte comune hore," where there is a wickedly clever repetition of "comune" in different senses, a jingle in "hure, hore," and probably a pun in "queynte." See *Chaucer's Bawdy*, pp. 175–84. Twice in *Piers*, C-text, VIII.76; B-text, XIII.353–54, the poet links harlotry and whoredom. They make an effective alliterative pair. Henryson, "The Trial of the Fox," line 1071, does the same: "This harlet hureson, and this hound of hell."

**horehowse:** fornix, lupanar, prostibulum *P* 226, *Wu* 804. See also "strumpettis howse." The poets do not employ the word. It seems to have carried a powerful taboo.

**iordeyn, iurdon:** iurdanus, madella, -dulla, vrna *A* 8b, *P* 242. Chaucer speaks only once of the jordan or chamberpot. It appears to be a crude word (it is put into the mouth of Harry Bailly), but not one with a strong taboo. The Host congratulates the Physician on his pious tale with a remark about "thyne urynals and thy jurdones" (C 305). In *Piers*, C-text, XVI.92, a glutton is called a "iordan," where the term is insulting but also comic. Dunbar also uses the word in invective. In the "Complaint to the King," line 15, he speaks of "fowll, jow-jowrdane-hedit jevellis" (foul Jew-jordan-headed low-fellows); and in "Sir Thomas Norny," line 38, he says that someone "callit him ane full plum Jurdane." This is mildly funny scatological humor. See "pispot," below.

**kekyre, kykyr: tentigo** R 39a, W 246, Wu 616. The word is from "keken," to look (up). *MED*, "kekir," reflects an uncertainty about its sense: "(a) the clitoris; (b)? the penis; ? an erection." It is not used by the poets, but there is perhaps a suggestion of tumescence when Nicholas in the *Miller's Tale*, A 3445, stares up into the air, "as he hadde kiked on the new moone." The complete gloss in Wülcker is "tentigo, id est extensio vel arrectio virilis membri." See also "tentigo" in the list of unglossed Latin words, above. "Kekyre" is an amusing word, but one that evidently bore a taboo strong enough to keep it out of polite literature. It is not in the *OED*, Partridge, Henley and Farmer, or Wright's *Dialect Dictionary*.

**kyttchene:** prostibulum A 109a. For "prostibulum," see "horehowse." MS. A also glosses it "strumpettis howse," q.v. The connection with "kitchen" is clear: a euphemism for a whorehouse was "fornix" (furnace) and later "stew." The idea behind the euphemisms is, of course, heat. The furnace, the stew, the kitchen, and the whorehouse all generate it. Chaucer does not use "kitchen," but "stew" meant a heated room in his time—or a brothel ("styves" in the *Friar's Tale*, D 1332). Surely there is a suggestion of the brothel in the "stewe" (*Troilus and Criseyde*, III.601, 698) in which Pandarus hides Troilus until Criseyde is ready to receive him in her bed.

**laske:** vnguem H 238a. The Latin gloss throws no light on the sense; but *MED* glosses "laske" as "loose in the bowels." The poets avoid the word.

**lech(ch)ery:** fornicacio, luxus, luxuria, mechia, venus; do lechery: fornicor, liueo, luxuriare, -ior, patro A 123b, 178b, 287a, P 139, 258. "Luxuriare" is the Latin word most commonly used by the scribes to gloss a term they felt to be taboo (see unglossed Latin terms, above), but "lechery" was in common use. *Piers* makes him an allegorical figure, Lecherie. He says (C-text, VII.193-95), "Whenne ich was old and hor . and hadde lore that kynde [lost that nature],/Ich had lykynge to lauhe . of lecherous tales./Now, lord, for thy leaute . of lechours haue mercy." Previously he had been active, though callous, in his lovemaking—kissing, groping, even kissing "by-nythe" (180). The word was associated with "likerous," which could carry the connotation of fondness for drink (see Ross, *Chaucer's Bawdy*, pp. 132-34). Chaucer uses the word freely, always with a sense of the forbidden and the sinful. For instance, in the *Monk's Tale*, B 3483, Zenobia has intercourse but once, in order to conceive; for others "it was to wyves lecherie and shame . . . if that men with hem pleyde." The same powerful emotional aura surrounds the word elsewhere: C 150, 206, 481; D 737; E 1451, H 259. The *Parson's Tale* has twenty-five passages in which the word occurs. It is also common in the Scots poets.

**lem(m)an:** amasia, -ius, concubina H 226b, P 259, W 217, Wu 563. "Leman" could be used in a neutral and in a benign sense. In *Sir Gawain*, line 1782, occurs "a

**lem(m)an** *continued*
lemman, a leuer," which is glossed "loved one, mistress." *Piers*, C-text, XXI.186, includes a passage where Pees says, "Loue ... is my lemman." But in the same work it is equated with concubine (C-text, IV.188): "lemmanes and lotebyes." In his note Skeat says (II.47), "The word *loteby*, meaning paramour or concubine, was used of both sexes," as was "lemman." In Chaucer's *Miller's Tale* and *Reeve's Tale* (A 3278, 3280, 3700, 3705, 3719, 3726, 4240, 4247), it always carries the sense of the forbidden (Ross, *Chaucer's Bawdy*, pp. 134–35). In the *Romaunt* it translates "amie" or "amis" six times, "drue" once. Dunbar uses the word freely. In the edition of Henryson I have used, the glossary has "lemanrye = adultery," but I cannot find the word in Henryson's works.

**lemanesse:** lupa *H* 235b. Toward the end of the fifteenth century, there was some confusion about the gender of "leman" (see above); hence the addition of "-esse" to indicate a female. "Lupa" is a whore, something far removed from a genteel lover or mistress, which demonstrates the changes that were taking place in the sense of the word. The poets do not use "lemanesse."

**letchour, -owre:** amasius, fornicator, -trix, lecator, -trix, leno, -a, luxuriosus, meca *H* 235b, *P* 258. Like "leman," "letchour" could apply to either sex. There is no taboo feeling about the word, but in Chaucer it is charged with a strong sense of revulsion, especially by the Wife of Bath, who says to one of her husbands, "sire olde lecchour," and speaks of a loose woman who "lete hir lecchour dight hire al the nyght" (D 242, 767); see also B 1935, D 1371, E 2257, 2298. The Scots use the word in the same way. See Ross, *Chaucer's Bawdy*, pp. 131–32.

**lye:** locium *Wu* 592. Also glossed "pysse" in this manuscript. As the Latin indicates, the word, perhaps properly "chamber-lye," meant a detergent. Urine was used for washing. "Lye" does not occur in the poets in this sense, but everyone will recall the boisterous reference to "chamber-lye" in Shakespeare's *1 Henry IV*.

**lykerows: ambroninus; lykorow[s]nesse:** delectacio; to do lycoruse delyte: oblecto *P* 263, *Wu* 598. This complex word was associated (1) with gourmandizing—with food, drink, and licking; and (2) with lechery. *Sir Gawain*, lines 968–69, says that the lady "more lykkerwys on to lyk/Watz þat scho hade on lode": a note (p. 103) translates (clumsily) "sweeter to taste was she whom she was leading" and continues, "*lyk* is not the modern sense 'lick' but rather 'taste.'" *Piers*, A-text, XI.120, speaks of "lykerous-drinke," which Skeat glosses "luxurious, dainty, lecherous." Chaucer exploits the pun in the *Wife of Bath's Prologue*, D 466: "A likerous mouth moste han a likerous tayl." See also the *Parlement of Foules*, lines 79–80, the *Canterbury Tales*, A 626, 549, I 1085; *Romaunt*, 7028. The association with licking naturally suggests oral sex, but anything like an explicit description of such

**lykerows** *continued*
  acts was naturally taboo among the poets—even the Scots. See Ross, *Chaucer's Bawdy*, pp. 132-33.

**lykyng:** innamen *A* 324b. The Latin is correctly transcribed, but it may be a scribal error. It is to be found in no dictionary. "Liking" could mean sexual pleasure (*MED*, 1. b). There are some passages in Chaucer where this meaning may be intended: Thopas's retainers sing to him of "love-likynge" (B 2040). The Wife of Bath speaks of Pasipha's "horrible lust and hir lykyng" (D 736), and in her tale the knight's wife says that she will do anything "that myghte doon hym plesance and likyng" (D 1256). The word occurs frequently in the *Romaunt*, translating "pleisent, plessant" (868, 1416), "ioie" (76, 2041), "voloir" (1975), "honor" (2607). "plesir" (6343), and "plesans mestier" (6980). See Ross, *Chaucer's Bawdy*, p. 138.

**manhys thyng:** menticula *W* 184. "Menticula" is the diminutive form of the word for penis. The manuscript adds some more, rather confusing glosses: "testiculi, idem est stentigo, idem est." See "balloke" and "kekyre" above. "Thyng" for the genitals, male or female, was (and is) a common euphemism. Chaucer's most familiar use of the word is in the *Wife of Bath's Prologue* (D 120ff.): "That they were maked for purgacioun/Of uryne, and oure bothe thynges smale/Were eek to knowe a femele from a male . . . they maked ben for both,/This is to seye, for office, and for ese/Of engendrure." Dunbar's "Tua Mariit Wemen" twice uses the term: "Na leit never enter in my thought that he my thing persit" (line 389); "And a stif standand thing staiffis [stuffs] in my neiff [fist]" (line 486). See Ross, *Chaucer's Bawdy*, p. 222, together with "cunt," above and "pyntyl," below, which were the commonest taboo-words for which "thyng" was substituted.

**muckelle, mukhylle:** fimarium, forica, sterculinium, sterquilinium *P* 295, *W* 270. See "dong hylle," a synonym, where the uses of the term are discussed.

**muk(k)e:** fimus, -um, letamen, luto; for to moke: fimare, stercoro *A* 107b, 339b, 345b, *P* 295. *Piers*, C-text, XI.96, speaks of lords who are concerned only with "here mok and here meeble." Skeat glosses as "filthy lucre (lit. muck)." *MED*, "muk: animal or human excrement." In the fifteenth century, the word had begun to assume its modern sense of anything filthy and slimy, but the idea of excrement was still the central sense. Henryson, "The Taill of the Cok and the Jasp," line 83, uses it in relation to the barnyard, "buryit thus amang this muke on mold," as does Dunbar, "Complaint to the King," line 52, where a courtier "Sa far above him set at tabell/That wont was for to muk the stabell." "Muk" is a mild word, primarily referring to animal excrement. Chaucer does not choose to use it, but we probably should not conclude that it was taboo with him.

**pap(pe), -pys:** mamma, mamilla, uber *A* 8a, 294a, 310a, *H* 221a, *P* 327, 477, *W* 186, 208, 246 (twice). See also "tete" and "wret" below. The manuscript

## Language and Paleography

**pap(pe), -pys** *continued*
transcribed by Wright (246) makes distinctions: "lytyl pap: mamilla; pap of a woman: mamma; pap of a best: uber." Like "muk," "pap" is a relatively inoffensive word which Chaucer finds no occasion to use. It was certainly not taboo among the Scots. Indeed, in most of the following examples it seems to be associated with the descriptions of gentle ladies, as in Henryson, "The Thre Deid Pollis," line 27, "O ladeis quhyt . . . / With palpis quhyt"; "The Wolf and the Lamb," line 2653, "my lippis . . . sowkit milk ffrom Pappis off my dam"; and "Orpheus and Eurydice," line 69, "scho [Calliope, mother of Orpheus] gart him souk of her twa paupis quhyte." In Lindsay's "Satire," line 228, Sensuality says, "Behauld my paps, of portrature perfite."

**penis:** The Latin term was evidently not in common English or Scottish use. However, MS. *A* (fol 305a) has an amusing note that deserves to be recorded: "de malo in penis: þe lenger þe wors." In the "Flyting," line 157, Dunbar has what may be a pun, "Thow plukkis the pultre, and scho pullis off the penis," where the last word is glossed "feathers." There is no doubt about the meaning in the same poet's "Tua Mariit Wemen," line 135: "Thoght [though] his pene [glossed 'penis'] purly me payis in bed."

**pinge:** crepo *A* 157a. Perhaps this unique manuscript entry is a scribal error (there are plenty of them in MS. *A*). "Pinge(n)" does not occur in the *OED*, but it may have been a synonym for "fart." Dunbar perhaps uses the word in the "Flyting," line 114: "Bettir thow ganis [suits] to leid ane doig to skomer [defecate] . . . than with thy maister pingill," where "pingill" is given the tentative gloss "quarrel."

**pispot:** iurdanus, madella, -dula, vrna, idem quod pissing vessel *P* 242, 338. Not used by the poets. See "iordeyn," above.

**prevy, prewy, prive, -y:** cat(h)acumba, cloaca, feterna, forica, -ruca, galfabie, gumphus, ipodromium *A* 103b, 318a, 322a, *P* 347, *W* 179, 235, 270, 274. See "gong," above. Surely the Latin "catacumba" and "ipodromium" are intended to be comical. "Gumphus" may have been comical, too: it *sounds* funny. The scribe of MS. *A* associates the word with "sorbeo" and explains that the privy "sorbet feces" (absorbs feces). The term occurs so frequently in the manus
tion with the house of easement. Chaucer makes frequent use of "pryve, -vetee" in the sense of "private, secret(s)," but sometimes with the suggestions of the privy or the privates: see Ross, *Chaucer's Bawdy*, pp. 169–72. Twice it occurs in an unequivocal sense: the Pardoner says that a glutton "of his throte he maketh his pryvee" (C 527) and the "fresshe" May in the *Merchant's Tale* disposes of her lover's note in the "gumphus": "in the pryvee softely it caste" (E 1954), an appropriate prelude to the coupling in the pear tree. As these two passages indicate, the word had unpleasant associations for the poet.

**pyntyl:** priapus, putibunda, vala-, vere-, veratrum; þe cuttyng of þe pyntyl hende [end]: prepucium; cokkupyntyl: jarus [a plant; also glossed "calvysfote"] *A* 310a, 323b, *H* 221a, 238a, *R* 39a, *W* 184, 186, 208, *Wu* 588. There was a strong taboo against the word in Chaucer's time. At least he does not use it. The same seems to be true of the Scots, but they find plenty of synonyms. Henryson speaks of a "drekterss" (drake's penis), in "Practysis," line 42 (see *OED*, "tarse[1]"). Dunbar uses the terms "lume" (as does Lindsay), "pene," "penis," "quhillelillie," "stang," "tersis," and "yerd." Lindsay, "Satire," line 1929, also speaks of priests who "like ramis rudely in their rage/Unpizzlet rins among the silly ewes." Clearly "unpizzlet" does not mean "un-penised" but rather with penises out and erect. For Dunbar's "pene" and "penis" see "penis," above. Of the other occurrences in Dunbar, one line should be recorded for its silly naughtiness. The country lover in the poem "In Secreit Place," line 34, says that his lady's beauty "garris ryis on loft [makes rise aloft] my quhillelillie." There is no silliness, however, in the "Tua Mariit Wemen," line 96; instead, one of the women expresses petulant resentment when she complains of her husband, "bot soft and soupill as the silk is his sary lume," and again (line 175), "his lume is waxit larbar [impotent] and lyis in to swonne." See "manhys thyng," above, for Chaucer's euphemism for "pyntyl."

**pys(se), pysch:** locium, mictura, urina, venia [error for urina?]; pyssyng: vrina; pisse, v.: facit mictum *A* 127b, *H* 238a, *P* 337, *R* 39b, *W* 209, *Wu* 592. See also "pispot," above. Clearly "piss" did not suffer from the taboo that affects it today. All the poets use it freely. *Piers*, B-text XX.217-18, speaks of proud priests with "pisseres longe knyues."[32] Chaucer employs the word in two of the fabliaux to explain why a character rises in the night: "This Nicholas was risen for to pisse" (A 3798), and "[She] gan awake, and went hire out to pisse" (A 4215). The Parson speaks of old lechers that "been lyk to houndes; for an hound, whan he comth by the roser or by othere [bushes], though he may nat pisse, yet wole he heve up his leg amd make a contenaunce to pisse" (I 855). There are three other Chaucerian occurrences, two of them spoken by the Wife of Bath: D 534, 729, G 807. See Ross, *Chaucer's Bawdy*, pp. 155-57. Dunbar, "Manere," line 63, has the speaker describe his own grandmother: "Scho pischit the mekle watter of Forth." For another Dunbar passage, see the entry under "cunt." Dunbar has other terms. He perhaps echoes Chaucer in the "Tretis," line 186, with "He dois as dotit [foolish] dog that damys [urinates] on all bussis." And again in the "Manere," line 62, he says, "Scho . . . stalit [urinated] Cragorth."

**pyssyng place:** oletum *P* 337. Not used by the poets.

**pyssying vessel:** madellum, -dula, mamadella *P*337-38. Not used by the poets. See "iordeyn" and "pispot" above.

**quene:** carisia; sturdy qwene: virago *P* 362, *W* 268. Also glossed "woman of lytyl price." "Quean" was a near homophone with "queen," and the poets exploit the similarity. *Piers*, C-text, IX.46, says that it is hard to know "a knyght fro a knaue . other a queyne fro a queene." Chaucer's Host says to the Cook (H 18), "Or hastow with some quene al nyght yswonke," and the *Romaunt*, line 7032, speaks of a "priest that halt his quene hym by," where the word translates Old French "amie." See Ross, *Chaucer's Bawdy*, pp. 174–75. In the "Flyting," line 146, Dunbar speaks of "thow and thy quene," and in Lindsay's "Satire," line 753, Flattery, reading Deceit's palm, says, "I see ye will have fifteen queens." "Quean" was not a common term, but it had no taboo attached.

**rawns:** picten, pubes *R* 39a. Not in the *OED*, nor is it used by the poets. It is evidently a rare term, perhaps the basis for Modern English "raunchy," which is listed "of uncertain origin" in modern dictionaries.

**schare, schere:** lanugo, pecten, prima barba, pubes *A* 8b, 176a, 178a, 310a, *H* 221a, 238a, *R* 39b, *W* 183, 246. *OED*, "share, sb.$^2$: the division or fork of the body; the pubic region, groin." In the fifteenth century, "share" was evidently a common term, though it is in desuetude today. The only occurrence of "share" in Chaucer is when the smith prepares Absolon's weapon, with which he will take his revenge upon Nicholas (*Miller's Tale*, A 3763): "He sharpeth shaar and cultour bisily," where the central meaning is of course "plowshare." The word may, however, carry the secondary meaning of the pubic area and thus in some way foreshadow the terrible fate that awaits the "hende" clerk.

**schit:** The word does not occur in the manuscript sources, suggesting that the schoolmaster-scribes found it objectionable. It is included here because the reader will probably expect to find it. Chaucer uses the word only in a barnyard context, where it refers to animal excrement, in his description of the Parson (A 504): he speaks of "a shiten shepherde and a clene sheep." The Scots used it and its derivatives in relation to human beings—and applied it much more freely: "beschittin," "schit," "schot," "schute," "scutard," "skyttand," together with synonyms like "cuk" and "skomer." Cf. "donge," above.

**scrate, sk-:** armifodrita, armifraudita *W* 217, 268. *OED*, "skrat: hermaphrodite." The Latin glosses reveal ignorance of the origin of the term. Clearly the blunt, ugly word carried a powerful taboo: none of the poets uses it, though it would have been useful in the alliterative invective of which Dunbar was so fond.

**sinner:** fornicatrix *W* 217. The sexual focus and the sexism are striking: the scribe equates the neutral word with female fornicators. Naturally "sinner" is employed by all the poets, but without this kind of equation; however, it is

**sinner** *continued*
obvious that there was a powerful sexual association with sin. See "vykkydnesse," below.

**snot:** polipus *H* 237b, *P* 419. Also glossed "fylth of the nose," q.v. "Snot" probably carried no taboo, though it is a crude term today. The poets simply do not find an occasion to use the word, though Dunbar, "Flyting," line 550, writes, "Out! Out! I schout, apon that snowt that snevillis."

**spows brekere:** adulteria *W* 217. "Spouse" was in common use in the fifteenth century, but "-breaker" does not occur in the poets considered here. The scribe's equation of an agentive and an abstract noun indicates that he misunderstood either the English or the Latin.

**strumpett, -ytt; elea, meretrix, pronuba, tabernaria; strumpet(t)is howse:** fornix, prostibulum *A* 69b, 109a, 168a, 320a, *W* 217. "Strumpet" bore no taboo, at least not a strong one. However, Chaucer uses it but once, in his *Boece*, I. pr. l. 48: " 'Who,' quod sche, 'hath suffred aprochen to this sike man thise comune strumpettis of swich a place that men clepen the theatre.'" Loose women were thought to haunt the tavern (see the Latin gloss) and the theater. The phrase "strumpettis howse" is also glossed "kyttchene," q.v.

**swyver:** flabellum *Wu* 583. The Latin literally means weathervane or fly-whisk, which suggest a comic metaphor. "Swyve" is used commonly enough; it carried a less powerful stigma than did "fukken." Chaucer uses "swyve" without reservation, especially in the *Reeve's Tale*. It seems to carry a connotation of violence or at least of boisterousness. Says one of the clerks, "If that I may, yon wenche wil I swyve" (A 4178), and the word is repeated in A 3850 and 4266. The Cook's fragment concludes with "and swyved for hir sustenance" (A 4422). The cuckold January cries out to the "fresshe" May, his wife, "He swyved thee, I saugh it with myne yen" (D 2378). See Ross, *Chaucer's Bawdy*, pp. 216–17. Dunbar has a variation in the "Flyting," line 246, "yadswyvar," where "yad" is an old mare, "In Secreit Place," line 13, has the blunter term: "Yit be his feirris [manners] he wald have fukkit." The "Flyting," line 38, also has an amusing variant: Kennedy says that Dunbar is so pale that he is "wan-fukkit," the meaning of which is termed "obscure" by the editor, but surely the sense is evident.

**tete:** mamma, mamilla, vber *A* 186a, *H* 238a, *P* 477, *W* 179. Also glossed "pap" q.v. The scribe of MS. *A* attempts to differentiate "mamma" and "uber": "Mammam fertile fertilitatem denotat vber. Hec ponit differentiam inter hoc vber, -ris, idem que mamma: a tete, vt in euangelia beata vbera que suxisti . . . vber, fertilis, fertile: plentuys . . . fertilitas: plentuysnesse." The scribe of MS. *H* adds, "tete of a best: vber," but the two Latin words

**tete** *continued*
nevertheless seem to have been used interchangeably. Chaucer's only use of "tete" occurs in the *Miller's Tale*, A 3704, where Absolon whimpers to Alison, "I moorne as dooth a lamb after the tete." See Ross, *Chaucer's Bawdy*, p. 220. Evidently the word was not taboo, but perhaps slightly embarrassing—certainly in the mouth of the absurd Absolon.

**thees:** nates *W* 186. "Thighs" most frequently refers to the upper leg, but evidently the word could be used in the sense of buttocks, as the Latin indicates. The poets do not employ the word in the latter sense.

**thoste:** stercus *P* 486. *OED*, "thost(e): dung, excrement." It would seem likely that the word was unusual even in the fifteenth century. The poets do not employ it.

**torde:** merda, stercus *A* 310a, 325a, *P* 486, *R* 39b, *W* 208, 247. The word occurs in Chaucer a couple of times, both in contexts that indicate that it is a disgusting term. The Host is the speaker on both occasions: "Thy drasty rymyng is nat worth a toord!" (B 2120) and "They [the Pardoner's (missing?) testicles] shul be shryned in an hogges toord!" (C 955). Henryson does not use the word in his verse but there is an amusing tale told of the poet's death. A witch-woman offers to cure him of the flux that is sapping his strength and enjoins him to repeat certain incantations. Henryson asks if it wouldn't be just as efficacious if he spoke to the oaken table in the room: "oken burd, oken burd garre [make] me shit a hard turde."[33] Though "turd" was used freely by the poets, there was something of a lingering taboo, as the scribe's refusal to gloss "merdula" indicates (see list of unglossed Latin terms, above). See also "turdyll," below.

**trulle:** trulla *Wu* 617. "Trulla" means fart. "Trulle" seems to be a (Latinate) English term, but it is not recorded in the dictionaries. For "trulla," see "fart," above. Not in the poets.

**turdyll:** merda *A* 310a. Unhappily, this diminutive does not occur in the poets' works.

**vykkydnesse:** luxuria *A* 172b. Also glossed "nequam, facinus." The equation of wickedness and sexual misbehavior is revealing: see "sinner," above. Naturally "wickedness" occurs often in the poet's works. It is probable that it carries a sexual aura in Chaucer's *Merchant's Tale*, E 2249, where Pluto berates Proserpine and all women for their corruptive habits.

**wardrope:** cloaca *A* 318a. See "prevy." The euphemism indicates some hesitation about using the more direct word. Chaucer gives the daintier term to the Prioress (B 1762): "I seye that in a wardrobe they hym threwe," where the throwers are the Jews, the throwee the "litel clergeoun." See Ross, *Chaucer's Bawdy*, p. 235.

**wolde [i.e., old] woman:** anus *W* 179. The identity of "anus" (old woman) and "anus" (anus) caused considerable merriment among those learned in the Latin tongue, though not the poets considered here. The scribe (*W* 180) adds these comic verses, which he also glosses: "Dum dormitat [nappyt] anus, velud ancer sibulat [hyssyt] anus" (while the old woman naps, her anus hisses like a goose).

**woman of lytyl price:** carisia *P* 362. Also glossed "quene," q.v. "Carisia" (or "caricia") evidently caused the scribe some discomfort, since it is one of the Latin terms that elsewhere he refuses to gloss (see the list of unglossed Latin terms, above). The blunt word "(w)hore" would naturally come to mind, but not to the scribe's pen-hand.

**wret of a pap or tete:** papilla *P* 535. "Wret" is "wart" metathesized; see *OED*, "wart, 2.: nipple." The only occurrence of "werte" in Chaucer is in the description of the hairy wart on the Miller's nose (A 555), where the coincidence of meanings may have provoked a titter from some listeners.

**ȝong hore:** pubes *W* 208. "Hore" means hair. The scribe perhaps had in mind "prima barba" (see "share," above). There was some ambiguity about "pubes": it meant the pubic area generally or the pubic hair more specifically. Not used by the poets.

The foregoing list can only suggest a few guidelines for readers of late Middle English literature. I hope that some of these readers will be able to investigate for themselves the large areas untouched in this paper, notably the anonymous lyrics and the drama.*

# Notes

*I am grateful to Professor Robert F. Yeager for his enthusiastic criticism and for his many learned comments that led to the improvement of this essay. The English glosses from MS. Add. 37075 will be published by Edward Brooks, Jr., and myself (Norman, Oklahoma: Pilgrim Books, 1984).

1. In a recent essay, "Dunbar's Bawdy," *Chaucer Review* 14 (1979–80): 278–86, Lois Ebin points out that Dunbar uses his bawdy diction for humorous purposes and also to revaluate the forms, styles, and traditions in which he worked. He employs not only puns but also shifts in levels of diction, as, for

example, in "In Secreit Place," where the shock value is analogous to that provided by Chaucer when he moves from the *Knight's Tale* to the *Miller's*. Bawdry may indeed be more central to Dunbar's poetry than it is to Chaucer's, Ebin claims. For a discussion of the comic effect of bawdry in a sylvan setting, see my "William Dunbar's *Dialogus Obscoenus* in *Locus Amoenus*," *University of Mississippi Studies in English*, n.s., 1 (1980): 32–49.

2. The bibliographical note in the British Library is: "L. Morawski, *Le Facet en Françays*, Poznan, 1923, pp. 3–15 (fols. 52b, 58a); J. W. Bartlett [*sic*: see below], *Medieval and Linguistic Studies in Honor of Francis Peabody Magoun, Jr.*, ed. J. B. Bessinger, Jr., and R. P. Creed, London, 1965, pp. 274–289 (fols. 70a–71a); S. Gieben, O. F. M., Cap., *Vivarium*, v. 1967, pp. 47–74 (fols. 20a, b)." The reference to "Bartlett" is an error for B[artlett]. J. Whiting; the Magoun Festschrift was published in New York by the New York University Press. Whiting's essay is a transcription of some of the English proverbs in the MS.

3. Thomas Wright, ed., *A Volume of Vocabularies* (London, 1857; privately printed); R. P. Wülcker, ed., *A Volume of Vocabularies*, 2nd ed. (London: Trübner, 1884); *Promptorium Parvulorum*, ed. A. L. Mayhew, Early English Text Society, ES 102 (London: Kegan Paul and Trübner, 1908). I am grateful to the Trustees of the British Library for permission to publish the material derived from the MSS. in that library. In all the transcriptions below, brevigraphs have been expanded silently.

4. *P* 362 has "carisia: quene, woman of lytyl price." C. DuFresne DuCange, *Glossarium Mediae et Infimae Latinitatis* (Paris: Didot, 1840), "carisa," cites *Gloss. Isid.*, "Lena vetus et litigiosa, ancilla dolosa, fallax" (old and contentious bawd; false, deceitful maid).

5. "Coeo" means to accompany; the scribe equates it with sex; see also "confedero," "nequam," "peculari," below.

6. "Confedero" means simply to ally; the scribe takes it in a narrow sexual sense.

7. "Cris(s)o" means to move the haunches. It was apparently also used to indicate orgasm: DuCange, *Glossarium*, "crissare: cevere, clunem movere" (move the buttocks): "Juvenal and Martial: cevere est canum more caudam clunesque movere" (to wag the tail and buttocks like a dog); s.v. "clunagitare": "Clunagitant homines; sed crisantur mulieres; opus venereum consummare" (men move their buttocks; women wag; to consummate the act of love).

8. See "letchour" below. "Lecor" is associated with licking and eating.

9. "Lenocinor" is not in the standard dictionaries; it is derived from "leno, -a," pimp, bawd, lecher.

10. "Fornix" (furnace), along with "kitchen" and (later in the history of English) "stew," is a common euphemism for a bordello. See "bordyl hows," "horehowse," "kyttchene," and "strumpett," below.

11. Earlier the scribe glosses "mentula" as "balloc poc"; P glosses it "codde, of a mannys pryuite."

12. "Merda," of which "merdula" is the diminutive, is glossed readily enough elsewhere.

13. "Meretrix," from which the verb "meretricor" is formed, is glossed by this scribe and others.

14. "Nequam" is a general term for wicked; the scribe takes it in a particularized sense to mean lecherous.

15. "Peculari" simply means to sin.

16. "Pelico" is not to be found in the dictionaries; however, "pelix" ("paelix") means concubine. See DuCange, *Glossarium*; R. E. Latham, *Revised Medieval Latin Word List: From British and Irish Sources* (London: Oxford University Press, 1965); J. F. Niermeyer, *Mediae Latinitatis Lexicon Minus* (Leiden: E. J. Brill, 1976).

17. "Pelignus" is not listed by DuCange, Latham, or Niermeyer; see "pelico" and its accompanying note, above. Also compare "horcoppe," in the section below.

18. "Presto" means simply to perform or to show; again the scribe takes it in a sexual sense.

19. Although "scortor" does not appear in the dictionaries, DuCange, *Glossarium*, has "scortatorium = lupanar; scortum, per puero meretricio"; Latham has "scorta, -atrix = whore; -atio: fornication; -orium: brothel."

20. Charlton T. Lewis and Charles Short, *A New Latin Dictionary* (New York: American Book, 1907), define "tentigo" as lust. See "manhys thyng" and "kekyre," below.

21. P glosses "vrina" as "pys, pysche" (337).

22. Eight of the ten MSS. employed by the Variorum Chaucer spell it "ers" in A 3734; one has "ars," one "hers." See my *Miller's Tale*, Variorum Chaucer (Norman: University of Oklahoma Press, 1983).

23. This is the reading of the Hengwrt MS., used as the base-text for my edition of the *Miller's Tale* (see previous note). "Amydde" for "in" is probably a scribal sophistication. The analogues to the tale make it clear that the injured lover traditionally thrust his hot coulter (poker, or whatnot) into the enemy's anus. See "schare" below. Other quotations are from F. N. Robinson, ed., *The Works of Geoffrey Chaucer*, 2nd ed. (Boston: Houghton Mifflin, 1957).

24. For a full treatment of the poet's use of the word, see my *Chaucer's Bawdy* (New York: Dutton, 1972), pp. 82–84.

25. *The Poems and Fables of Robert Henryson*, ed. H. Harvey Wood, 2nd ed. (Edinburgh: Oliver and Boyd, 1958).

26. *The Poems of William Dunbar*, ed. W. Mackay Mackenzie (Edinburgh: Porpoise Press, 1932).

27. See my edition of *A Satire of Edward II's England* (Colorado Springs: Colorado College Studies, 1966) pp. 23, 43–44, for evidence from the fourteenth century that the order of Knights Templar was suppressed in part because of members' reputations as sodomites: when they met one another "deosculabantur se in ore, in umbilico, seu ventre nudo, et in ano, seu in spina dorsi" (they kissed one another on the mouth, the navel, the bare belly, the anus, or the backbone). See also Arno Karlen, "The Homosexual Heresy, *Chaucer Review* 6 (1971): 44–63.

28. A "ballokknyf" is one of the ostentatious adornments of corrupt priests in *Piers the Plowman*, ed. W. W. Skeat, 2 vols. (London: Oxford University Press, 1886), B-text, XV.120–21: "Sire Iohan and sire Geffray . hath a gerdel of syluer, / A basellarde, or a ballokknyf . with botones ouergylte." The term refers to its shape, not to its use as a castrating device; Skeat (II. 219) cites the *Paston Letters*, ed. Gairdner, I.478, for an inventory of goods of Sir John Fastolf (dated 1459) which includes "Item, j. bollok-hafted dager."

29. For an example of latent bawdy meaning in Chaucer's long romance, see my "*Troilus and Criseyde*, II. 585–87," *Chaucer Review* 5 (1971): 137–39.

30. *Sir Gawain and the Green Knight*, ed. J. R. R. Tolkien and E. V. Gordon; 2nd ed. rev. Norman Davis (Oxford: Clarendon Press, 1967).

31. Sir David Lindsay, *A Satire of the Three Estates*, ed. Matthew McDiarmuid (London: Heinemann, 1967), line 2138.

32. Skeat's note (II.281) expresses his impatience with those who conjecture that the word means "baker" (from the Latin "pistor") or "fisherman" (from Old French "pischer," to fish): "Surely the word expresses exactly what the sound tells us, and is equivalent to a familiar Biblical expression for 'every male.'" The biblical reference is to 1 Kings 14:10 and 6:11, which speak of him "that pisseth against the wall," i.e., a male.

33. Henryson, *Poems and Fables*, p. xiii; the editor says that the story comes from the introduction to Sir Francis Kynaston's Latin translation (1635) of the first two books of *Troilus and Criseyde*.

# Caxton and Chancery English

## John H. Fisher

I have discussed elsewhere the part played by the English civil service in helping to create and to disseminate a standard written English in the fifteenth century.[1] From 1066 to 1417, all official writing in England was in Latin and French. Writing in English, always unofficial and intended for local audiences, was essentially the phonetic transcription of various regional dialects. The characteristic which sets a "standard language" apart from a "dialect" is the degree of its uniformity throughout a society. This uniformity is more nearly achieved in written than in spoken language. M. L. Samuels has indicated that the first movement toward the creation of an English written standard was in the sermons and tracts written by Wyclif and his followers in the North Midlands in the last quarter of the fourteenth century.[2] This Wycliffite standard was spread throughout England by the Lollard preachers. Eventually it came to be used for secular works, and it continued to be used throughout the fifteenth century.

Concurrently with the Wycliffite writers, the government and merchant classes in London began to turn to English. Their writings are not as uniform as the Wycliffite. The court poetry and the text printed by Chambers and Daunt reveal no metropolitan "standard," but rather a bundle of related dialects reflecting in different ratios the Southern substratum of London speech and the overlays of Midland and Western dialects imposed by immigrant clerks.[3]

An official written standard came into existence in August 1417 when Henry V embarked upon his second invasion of France. Until that time, all of his correspondence had been in Latin and French, but from August 1417 until his death in August 1422 Henry communicated in English with the officers of his government, the London municipal corporation and other municipalities, guilds, abbeys, individuals, and institutions. Although written by more than a dozen different scribes, his Signet letters are remarkably uniform in style and language, without any trace of regional dialect, and in orthography and syntax which point the way toward Modern English. Two extant holograph letters indicate that this Signet usage was based on Henry's personal style. As Malcolm Richardson has shown, the English of Henry's Signet letters served as the model for the English of documents written in the other offices of government, which together were designated as "Chancery."[4] Although few in number and diverse in style before 1422, from 1422 onward documents in English in the files of the Privy Seal, Parliament, and Chancery increase in number, and by 1430 had evolved the fairly standardized forms and expression M. L. Samuels designated "Chancery Standard." Malcolm Richardson, Jane Fisher, and I have prepared an anthology of the 103 original Signet letters of Henry V and 138 other documents from the Privy Seal and Chancery collections in the Public Record Office in London illustrating the evolution of Chancery Standard to 1455. This essay will make some comparisons between Caxton's language and the language of these Chancery documents.

The spread of Chancery Standard outside of government is only now beginning to be studied. Its influence is acknowledged in the frequently quoted statement of 1422 explaining why the Brewer's Guild was changing its record keeping from Latin and French to English:

> Whereas our mother-tongue, to wit the English tongue, hath in modern days begun to be honorably enlarged and adorned, for that our most excellent lord, King Henry V, hath in his letters missive and divers affairs touching his own person, more willingly chosen to declare the secrets of his will, and for the better understanding of his people, hath with a diligent mind procured the common idiom (setting aside others) to be commended by the exercise of writing; and there are many of our craft of Brewers who have the knowledge of writing and reading in the said English idiom, but in others, to wit, the Latin and French, before these times used, they do not in any wise understand. For which causes with many others, it being considered how the greater part of the Lords and trusty Commons have begun to make their matters to be noted down in our mother tongue, so we also in our craft, following in some manner their steps, have decreed to commit to memory the needful things which concern us . . .[5]

The original of this statement, by William Porland, clerk of the Brewers' Guild, is in Latin; the translation is from the Brewers' abstract book. The passage nicely illustrates the complementary roles of Signet and Chancery. "Letters missive" are the Signet letters of Henry V; the "matters" of the "Lords and trusty Commons" are the proceedings of Commons and of the Court of Chancery, which were in the hands of the Chancery clerks. Susan Hughes has compared the English of the London Guildhall records with Chancery English before 1422.[6] She concluded that the Guildhall clerks assimilated the Signet usage more rapidly than did the Chancery clerks themselves. We know that Henry wrote directly to the London corporation because eight of his English letters are preserved in the Guildhall letter books, and it is noteworthy that the language of the letter books and other documents originating in the Guildhall more closely resembles Chancery Standard than does the language of the returns from the guilds and the Parliamentary and Chancery proceedings before 1422.

Mary Relihan has studied the English of the Stonor Letters 1420–83. She finds that although nonstandard and dialectal forms persist throughout the correspondence, "there is no letter in any classification which does not have several of the characteristics of Chancery Standard," and, not surprisingly, the most standard usage appears in letters written by professional scribes who might be presumed to have had formal training.[7]

Although he was not studying it in the light of Chancery Standard, Norman Davis has shown how the language of John Paston II and III began to move in the direction of Chancery Standard after 1360.[8] Many years ago, H. C. Wyld in *A History of Modern Colloquial English* remarked that the letters of John Shillingford (1447–50) and the writings of Reginald Pekok and John Fortescue (ca. 1450) reveal a movement in the second half of the fifteenth century toward a common form of English.[9] Most recently Ian Doyle and Malcolm Parkes have shown that Hoccleve, himself a clerk in Privy Seal, joined four other clerks writing in Chancery script in copying a manuscript of the *Confessio Amantis*.[10] One of these four scribes was the copyist of the Hengwrt and Ellesmere manuscripts of Chaucer's *Canterbury Tales*. This evidence that Chancery clerks, or clerks with Chancery training, took part in the London book trade shows how Chancery usage could influence more general writing.

It should be made explicit that what I describe as a movement beginning in the Signet of Henry V and moving outward from Chancery to the municipalities, guilds, and bookshops, Wyld, Davis, A. C. Baugh, E. J. Dobson, and other historians of the English language regard simply as a linguistic consensus emerging among the literate classes in the London metropolis.[11] "Chancery Standard" was introduced by Samuels as a descriptive term without any implication as to the direction of influence. Like Wyld and Dobson, Samuels sees the uniformity of the written language reflecting a growing uniformity in speech. I argue, on the other hand, that since a principal characteristic of any standard language is its divorce from regional pronunciation, lexicon, and syntax (a Scot and an Englishman write the same, no matter how they speak), the most important development in the writing of English in the fifteenth century was the beginning of its emancipation from speech—the beginning of an ideographic rather than a phonetic code (as in the spellings of *rite* and *right, rowed* and *rode, bow* and *bough*; the signals of capitalization and punctuation; and so forth).[12] This development has never been absolute, and some of the orthographic changes in the seventeenth and eighteenth centuries continue to reflect developments in pronunciation (such as the distinction between *ee* and *ea*). To a large extent, however, the vocabulary, syntax, and orthography fixed upon in the fifteenth century have come down as a system independent of developments in speech (for example, the *r*'s in *here* and *there* have been preserved in the writing of those who have lost them in pronunciation, and writing is full of locutions like "have not" and "it is I" that are no longer characteristic of speech).

The part played by Caxton in the creation of the written standard is still subject to debate. No one denies the eventual influence of printing upon standardizing of the language. Marshall McLuhan made a profession of the typographic fracture between head and heart.[13] Margaret Shaklee (1980) speaks for what Caxton ought to have done for the standardizing of the language:

> Caxton may have influenced the direction in which the language grew more than any other man, for he set himself up as the editor of the texts he printed and tried to settle the variant forms both of spelling and grammar that came across his desk. . . . Caxton probably adopted the current Chancery standard when he began to print in 1476, since he set up his press in Westminster instead of London and since Chancery standard had become the written language in which most businessmen (Caxton included) were schooled.[14]

But Norman Blake in *Caxton and His World* (1969) categorically denies that Caxton had any direct influence upon modernizing or standardizing the language.[15] He allows that various groups of scribes before Caxton had begun to develop standardized "house styles" (what I would describe as the usage of Chancery and Chancery-related offices). But Caxton himself was not a professional scribe, says Blake, and had no interest in the development of uniform usage. In an earlier study of the printed editions of *Reynard the Fox*, Blake discerns an unsystematic and unselfconscious drift toward a standard orthography,[16] but he would place the influence of printing much later, after the emergence of handbooks and dictionaries.

Helmut Wiencke in *Die Sprache Caxtons* (1930) is more affirmative than Blake about the development of Caxton's language.[17] In a study of four of Caxton's editions, *Recuyell of the Histories of Troye* (ca. 1474), *History of Jason* (ca. 1477), *Fables of Aesop* (ca. 1484), and *Eneydos* (ca. 1490), he discerns a drift toward normalization and modernization. However, both Blake and Wiencke base their discussions upon the recurrence of isolated words—mostly nouns and verbs—in various parts of the text. Although this method makes possible Blake's valid generalizations about the influence of his sources on Caxton's spelling and about the poverty of the vocabulary of his prefaces in comparison with his translations, it fails to convey the texture of Caxton's writing.[18] This texture is created by the form words—articles, prepositions, auxiliary verbs, and pronouns—even more than it is by the substance words—nouns, verbs, and adjectives.

In order to examine the similarity between Caxton's usage and Chancery English, I have chosen the four passages, each about two hundred words, printed in appendix 2:[19] the prologue to the *Recuyell of the Histories of Troye*, ca. 1474; a paragraph from the *Mirour of the World*, translated in 1480; the end of Caxton's prologue to *Eneydos*, ca. 1490; and a paragraph from *Eneydos*, translated in 1490. These passages yielded 264 different words, omitting proper nouns, listed in the table of forms in Appendix 1, along with the parallel forms from our Chancery glossary, now in the process of completion. Of these 264, 48 are not found in the Chancery documents, which leaves 216 for comparison. The same poverty of vocabulary that Blake has noted in Caxton's prefaces and epilogues can be seen in connection with our Chancery documents, whose 70,000 words yielded only some 4,000 different items.

This limitation of vocabulary can be interpreted as evidence of the paucity of content in these administrative missives, but it can also be recognized as evidence of the legalistic urge to confine the vocabulary to terms and formulas that mean as nearly as possible the same thing on every occasion. Linguistic variation may be the soul of poetry; it is anathema to a law or contract, where words have exact denotations established by precedent and legal decisions.[20] Blake's description of Caxton's personal vocabulary as "limited and generally of a prosaic, practical nature"[21] is an accurate characterization of the vocabulary of the Chancery documents (one of which I print, as an example, at the end of Appendix 2).

The number of occurrences in the Caxton selections and the Chancery documents is noted in the table of forms. Chancery never achieved anything like absolute uniformity in its orthography. What can be documented from 1422 to 1455 is a gradual drift toward normalization and modernization. In most cases, the form that has passed into Modern English (MnE) was the majority form in Chancery. The orthographic variations which Blake found persisting longest in the fifteenth-century printed editions of *Reynard the Fox* are likewise characteristic of Chancery. The interchanges between *i/y, i/j, u/v, u/w,* and *ʒ/y/gh* were essentially graphemic, just as we today use different shapes for *s, t, f,* or other letters in our handwriting. Interchanges between voiceless *c* and *s* were products of the conflict between French and English usage. Interchange between *a/o* and *a/au* before nasals, *er/ar,* and *o/ou* and the inconsistent doubling of vowels and consonants may have originated in different pronunciations, but were in the process of becoming conventionalized.

In the face of these variations, the remarkable thing is the extent of similarity between the forms in the Caxton selections and the favorite forms in the Chancery glossary. Of the 216 parallels, 186 (86 percent) are identical or nearly identical in Caxton and Chancery (Appendix 1, tables B–I). Only 42 (19 percent) are different (tables J–L). (These and other totals add up to more than 100 percent because some forms are listed more than once, as in tables C and D). Of the 186 equivalents, 76 (41 percent) are MnE forms; 24 (13 percent) are MnE forms except for final *e*; 26 (14 percent) are MnE forms except for *i/y*; nine (5 percent) are MnE forms except for *u/v*. If these essentially graphemic distinctions are ignored, 135 of the 186 (73 percent) parallels are close to MnE. This 73 percent may be taken as an index of the degree of modernity of Chancery Standard as it appears in these Caxton selections. Even more significant as evidence of the influence of Chancery Standard upon Caxton and his compositors are the 51 parallels (27 percent, tables F–I) that do not represent MnE forms. Of these, 43 (23 percent, table F) are exact parallels; five are the same except for *i/y*; two are the same except for final *e*. These parallels suggest that we are not dealing merely with a generalized drift toward modernity but with similar ME spellings that persisted in Chancery and in Caxton.

Not surprisingly, 59 of the 186 parallel items are form words (table M), since it is in syntax and accidence that standardization occurs first. Only five of Caxton's form words are not favorite Chancery forms (table N): *ony* (no. 152), *than* (adv. no. 208), *therin* (no. 212), *them* (no. 213), and *thise* (no. 218). All of these are variant forms in the Chancery documents. Caxton's *them,* where the Chancery favorite is *theym,* is the one instance where Caxton's form is more modern that the Chancery favorite. Among the 42 instances where Caxton's forms are different from the Chancery favorites (tables J–L), Caxton's forms are more modern in 11 instances (table L) and Chancery's more modern in 15 instances (table K). This ratio of 11:15 provides an index to the conservatism of Caxton's orthography.

This comparison does not support Helmut Wiencke's conclusion about the movement of Caxton's language:

> Die Caxtonsche Drucksprache—Sprache in orthographischer, phonetischer und morphologischer Hinsicht—repräsentiert nicht ein starres, "zuständisches" Gebilde; sei is in dauerndem Wandel begriffen. Welcher Art dieser klar erkennbare Umbildungsprozess sei, is mit dem einen Satz gesagt:
> Die Caxtonsche Drucksprache schlägt gleichsam die Brücke von der mittel-zur neuenglischen Sprachwelt—anders formuliert: aus anfänglichem Polymorphismus, wie er fürs Mittelalter charakteristisch ist, erwächst allmählich die sprachlich Einheit.[22]

He gives lists showing how nonstandard forms in the *History of Troye* and the *History of Jason* appear in more standard forms in *Aesop* and *Eneydos*. The problem is that these lists are eclectic. As it turns out, there are only 50 overlapping words in the four passages I have chosen for comparison. In 36 instances (table O), there is no difference between the early and later texts, In eight instances (table P) there is movement forward, of the sort indicated by Wiencke. But set against these, there are the same number of instances of movement backward (table Q).

In sum, the orthography and morphology of these selections would appear to indicate that Caxton employed, and therefore transmitted, essentially Chancery forms from the time that he began to publish until the end of his career, with no perceptible drift toward more modern or more regular forms. A more complete analysis might alter this conclusion, but not eclectic studies like those of Blake and Wiencke. It would be surprising if Caxton's practice shifted much through the sixteen years of his publishing career. He was some fifty-three years of age in 1474. For thirty-seven years, since being apprenticed to the Mercers' Guild in 1437, he had been exposed to Chancery Standard as it was employed in English government and business. There is every reason to suppose that his own writing habits were well established. It is likely, as Norman Blake has indicated, that he was inclined to preserve some spellings and locutions from his originals, but even here the evidence is clouded. Arthur Sandved in *Studies in the Language of Caxton's Malory* concludes that there are many forms in the Winchester manuscript and are different from Caxton's own forms as recorded by Wiencke.[23] Among the ten verbs treated by Sandved that are found in my table of forms, Caxton's *Malory* parallels the Winchester usage in five instances (Appendix 3, A). In three instances, the manuscript has Chancery forms not found in Caxton's *Malory* (Appendix 3, B). In two instances Caxton's *Malory* uses Chancery forms not found in the manuscript. This evidence does not disprove Sandved's conclusion, but it is too slight to warrant any independent judgment.

Analysis of this kind could be carried on ad inifinitum, but it would, I believe, lead to essentially the same conclusion. From the beginning of his printing career until the end, Caxton and his compositors used a preponderance of Chancery forms and spellings. He was influenced by his sources in the spellings of substance words, but his form words and inflections are essentially Chancery. He shows in my examples as much variation in 1490 as in 1474, and very nearly the same sort and same amount of variation as in the Chancery documents themselves.

Caxton's place in the history of the development of standard written English must be regarded as that of a transmitter rather than an innovator. He should be thanked for supporting the foundation of a written standard by employing, 86 percent of the time, the favorite forms of Chancery Standard, but he is also responsible for perpetuating the variations and archaisms of Chancery Standard to which much of the irregularity and irrationality of MnE spelling must be attributed. Some of these variations have been ironed out by printers, lexicographers, and grammarians in succeeding centuries, but modern written Standard English continues to bear the imprint of Caxton's heterogeneous practice.

# Appendix 1

# Table of Forms

A: Caxton's prologue to *The Recuyell of the Historyes of Troye*, 1475
B: From Caxton's translation of the *Mirrour of the World*, 1480
C: From Caxton's prologue to *Eneydos*, 1490
D: From Caxton's translation of *Eneydos*, 1490

|  | Caxton's Forms | Chancery Forms |
|---|---|---|

Numbers represent the number of occurrences.

| | Caxton's Forms | Chancery Forms |
|---|---|---|
| 1. | a 2A 4D | The usual form before consonants |
| 2. | abreggyng (abridging) 1B | |
| 3. | after 1C | after 126, aftir 31, aftur 10, aftre 9 |
| 4. | alle 1B 2C | all 207, alle 120, al 94 |
| 5. | alayaunce (alliance) 1D | alliaunces 1 |
| 6. | almyghty 1C | almyghty 4, almighty 1 |
| 7. | also 1 D | also 163, alsoo 4, al soe 2 |
| 8. | am (1st sing.) 1C | Usual form |
| 9. | and 13A 11B 8C 7D 7 5C 1D | and usual form 7 never used; & common |
| 10. | arryued 1D | arriued 1, arived 1, aryved 1 |
| 11. | as 1B | as 811, als 17 |
| 12. | assayed 1D | |
| 13. | at 1A 1B, att 1B | at 352, atte 86, att 7 |
| 14. | away 1B | away(e) 6, awey 4 |
| 15. | be (inf.) 1B 1C, (3rd subj. sing.) 1C | be 814, bee 23 |
| 16. | ben (3rd pl. = are) 2B | ben = are 46, ben = past part. 20 |
| 17a. | bere (bear) 1B | bere 8, beer 1 |
| 17b. | bare (past t. = bore) 1D | bare 1, bere 1 |
| 17c. | born (born) 1C | born 4, boryn 1, bore 1 |
| 18a. | begynneth 1A | begynn + 4 |
| 18b. | begonne 1A 2D | begonne 1, bigonne 1, bygonnen 1 |
| 19. | begoten 1C | |
| 20. | besoughte 1D | |
| 21. | body 1B | |
| 22. | bookes 1A, boke 2C | bokes 4, bok 1, buke 1 |
| 23. | braunches 1D | braunches 1 |

169

LANGUAGE AND PALEOGRAPHY

| | Caxton's Forms | Chancery Forms |
|---|---|---|
| 24. | but 2B 1D | but 121, bot 1, buth 1 |
| 25. | by 4A 1B 2C 1D | by 792, bi 11 |
| 26. | byseching 1C | *bi* forms 16, *be* forms 5, *by* forms 3 |
| 27. | chapelayn 1A | chapeleyn 3, chapellain 2, chaplein 1, chapelyn 1 |
| 28. | called 1D | called 29, callid 7, callidde 1, callyd 1 |
| 29. | can 1B | can 25, kan 10 |
| 30. | castell 1D | castel(l) 62, castil 1, chastel 1 |
| 31. | cause 1B | cause 38 |
| 32. | coffres 1B | coffors 2, coffres 1 |
| 33. | comaundement 1A, commaundemente 1D | commaundement 17, comaundement 13, com(m)andement 11 |
| 34a. | come 1B 1C | come 31, com 3 |
| 34b. | cometh 1B | comeþ 1, commeth 1 |
| 34c. | came 1D | com(e) 14, c(k)am 6 |
| 35. | composed 1A | |
| 36. | correctyon 1C | coreccione 1, correcte 1 |
| 37. | counseilled 1B | counseilled 1, conseled 1 |
| 38. | countre 1A, contrey 1D | contre(e) 12, cuntre(e) 7, contray 6, countre 1 |
| 39. | creatour (creator) 1B | creature (creature) 2 |
| 40. | crysten 1C | cristen(e) 5, crysten 1, cristian 1 |
| 41. | cyte 2A 2D | citee 38, cite 28, cyte 5 |
| 42. | dampned 1B | |
| 43. | day 2A, dayes 2B | day 292, daie 6, daye 2 |
| 44. | deed (dead) 1B | ded 2, dede 2, deed 1 |
| 45. | delyte 1B | |
| 46. | deth (death) 1B | deth(e) 14, ded(e) 4, deþ 1 |
| 47. | disordinat 1B | |
| 48. | doctrynes 1B | doctrine 1 |
| 49. | dommage 1D | damage 3 |
| 50. | doo 2D | doo 6, do 2, doe 2 |
| 51. | dradde 1C | dradde 1, dred 1 |
| 52. | drawen (past part.) 2A | drawen 1, draw 1 |
| 53. | duc 1C | duc 33, duke 9 |
| 54. | duchesse 1A | |

| Caxton's Forms | Chancery Forms |
|---|---|
| 55. dye (die) 2B | deyde 5, died 2 |
| 56. dyuerce 1A, dyuerse 1D | diuers(e) 39, dyuers(e) 16, diuerce 1 |
| 57. dwelle 1D | *dw* forms 15, *du* forms 5 |
| 58. egal 1C | egalli 1 |
| 59. encreasyng 1C | encresyng 12, encreses 1, encresced 1 |
| 60. ended 1A | end(e) (noun) 30, eend 1 |
| 61. englisshe 1A | englyssh 1, Englissman 1 |
| 62. enleuen (eleven) 1A | |
| 63. enterprysed 1D | enterprise 1 |
| 64. erle 1C | erle 31, erl 13 |
| 65. euerlastynge 1C | *eu* forms 36, *ev* forms 3 |
| 66. eyghte 1A | |
| 67. feest 1D | fest(e) 53, feest 1 |
| 68. folke 1D | folk(e) 14 |
| 69. fonde 1D | |
| 70. for 1B 1C 6D | for 821, ffor 33, fore 8 |
| 71. fortresse 1D | forteresses 1 |
| 72. foure (four) 5A | four(e) 3 |
| 73. frenshe 1A, frensshe 1A | |
| 74. fro 2C, from 1D | fro 70, from 29, froo 2 |
| 75. fynysshid 1A | finisshed 7 |
| 76. fyrst 1A 1C | first(e) 17, furst 9, ferst(e) 4, fyrst 1 |
| 77. garlandes 1D | |
| 78. glad 1C, gladly 1C | gladde 2, gladly 1, gladnesse 1 |
| 79. gloryous 1A | glorious 2 |
| 80. god (God) 4A 3C, goddes (pl.) 1D | god 241, godde 6, gode 1 |
| 81. grace 1A 3C | grace 78 |
| 82. grete (great) 2B 1D | grete 211, greet 37, gret 19 |
| 83. greue (grieve) 1B | greved 2 |
| 84. greuaunce 1D | greuaunce 1 |
| 85. grounde 1D | ground 3, grounde 2, grond 4 |
| 86. handes 1D | handes 31, hondes 6 |
| 87a. haue 3B | haue 428, haf(e) 6, han 2 |
| 87b. had 2D | hadd(e) 59, had(e) 48, hed 1 |

## Language and Paleography

| Caxton's Forms | Chancery Forms |
|---|---|
| 88. he 2C 4D | he 382 |
| 89a. his 1A 4C, hys 1A | his 553, hus 15, hys 5 |
| 89b. hym 1D | hym 287, him 113 |
| 90. hedes (heads) 1D | hed 1, hede 1 |
| 91. helpe 1B | help 2, helpe 1 |
| 92. here (here) 1A | here 57, her 15, heere 4 |
| 93. herte 1B | hert(e) 10 |
| 94. heuen 1C | |
| 95. heyer (heir) 1C | heir(e) 5, heyr 1, eyres 3 |
| 96. historyes 1A | |
| 97. holy 1A | holy 23, holi 1, hooly 1 |
| 98. honderd 3A, hondred 1D | |
| 99. humble 1C | humble 21 |
| 100. hurte 1D | hurt 18, hurte 9 |
| 101. hye 1A 1C | high 30, total *gh* forms 47, hye 9, heye 5, hie 4 |
| 102. I 4C | I 154, y 5 |
| 103. yf 1B 2C | if 77, yf 26, yif 18, other $y/z$ forms 12 |
| 104. in 7A 4B 4C 5D | in 1683, yn 199 |
| 105. Incarnacion 2A | |
| 106. intituled 1A | |
| 107. is 1C | is 347, ys 42 |
| 108. it 1C | it 213, hit 161 |
| 109. kepe 1B | kepe 16, keep 1 |
| 110. kynge 2C, kyng 2D | kyng(e) 307, king(e) 68 |
| 111. lady 1A | lady 19 |
| 112. latyn 1A | |
| 113. lette 1D | lette 3 |
| 114. londe 1D | land(e) 30, lond(e) 27 |
| 115. longe 1D | long 22, longe 17, lang(e) 2 |
| 116. lord 3A 2C, lorde 1C | lord 301, lorde 72 |
| 117. loste 1C | lost 6, loste 1 |
| 118. loue 1D | loue 18, love 11, luf 1 |
| 119. lyf 2B 2C, lyfe 1C | lif 8, lyf 7, lyfe 7, life 1 |
| 120. lyke 1C | like 29, lyk(e) 21, liche 3 |
| 121. lyue 1B 1C | |
| 122. lyttyl 1D | litil(l) 4, litel 1, lytyll 1, lytle 1 |

|       | Caxton's Forms | Chancery Forms |
|---|---|---|

| 123. | made 2D | made 6 |
| 124. | make 1D | make 47, maake 6 |
| 125. | maker 1B | makers 1 |
| 126. | man 1A, men 2D | man 49, manne 1, men 65, mene 1 |
| 127. | manere 1B | maner 90, manere 51, maniere 3 |
| 128. | mangeries (managements) 1C | |
| 129. | many 1C | many 32, meny 3 |
| 130. | march (March) 1A | March 12 |
| 131. | may 2B 2C | may 152, maye 3 |
| 132. | me 1C | me 55 |
| 133. | mercer 1A | mercer 4 |
| 134. | messagers (messengers) 1D | |
| 135. | more 1C | more 90, mo(o) 7, moore 5, mor 4 |
| 136. | moste 1B 1C, most 3C | most 60, moste 15 |
| 137. | mouth 1B | |
| 138. | muste 2B | most(e) 2, must 1 |
| 139. | my 2C | my 158 |
| 140. | myghty 2A | myghty 5, mighty 1, myghti 1 |
| 141. | named 1A | named 3, nempned 1 |
| 142. | nature 1B | nature 1 |
| 143. | naturall 1C, naturell 1C | naturell 1 |
| 144a. | ne 2B | ne 77 |
| 144b. | nor 2D | nor 43, ner 21 |
| 145a. | nede (noun) 2B | nede 14 |
| 145b. | nedes (adv.) 3B | nedes 1 |
| 146. | noble 1A 2C | noble 61, nobill 3 |
| 147. | not 4C 2D | not 158, nat 28, noght 1 |
| 148. | noye (annoy) 1B | |
| 149. | of 22A 5B 9C 10D | of 4416 |
| 150. | olyue (olive) 1D | |
| 151. | ones (once) 1C | ones 1, onys 1 |
| 152. | ony 1C 2D | any 130, eny 104, ony 16 |
| 153. | or 1B | or 376, vre 1 |
| 154. | ooste (host) 1D | hoost 28, oost 5, ost 1 |
| 155. | other 1B | other 155, oþer 59, othir 33 |
| 156. | otherwyse 1C | oþerwise 2, otherwyse 1, otherwise 1 |

## Language and Paleography

| Caxton's Forms | Chancery Forms |
|---|---|
| 157. ouermoche 1B | |
| 158. our 3A 1B 1C | oure 893, our 263, owr 21, owre 4 |
| 159. out 2A | oute 49, out 31, owte 11, owt 3 |
| 160. peas 2D | pees 39, peas(e) 6 |
| 161. persone 1A | persone 49, person 15, personne 4 |
| 162. peryllis 1B | periles 1 |
| 163. possyble 1C | possible 4 |
| 164. praye 1C | pray 17, praye 5, prey 3 |
| 165. preest 1A | prest 7, preest 6, priestes 1 |
| 166. present 1C, presente 1D | present 76 |
| 167. prynce 1A 1C | prince 17, prynce 5 |
| 168. pryncesse 1A | princesse 1, princes 1 |
| 169. procede 1B | procede 10 |
| 170. progenytours 1C | progenitours 6, progenitoures 2 |
| 171. prosperous 1C | |
| 172. proued 1D | proued 3, provid 1, preued 1 |
| 173. receyue 1C | resceyve 6, receyue 3, receiue 3 |
| 174. recuyell (collection) 1A | |
| 175. redoubtyd (respected) 1A | redoubted 1 |
| 176. rendre 1B | |
| 177. rentes 2B | rentes 14, rentis 2 |
| 178. requyre 1D | requere 3, requir 1 |
| 179. rest 1D | reste 6, rest 3, reest 1 |
| 180. reteyne (retain) 1B | |
| 181. renommed (renowned) 1C | |
| 182. right 1A, ryght 2A | right 124, ryght 18 |
| 183. royame 1D | reaume 25, roialme 3, royaume 5 |
| 184. ryche 1D | riche 2 |
| 185. same 1D | same 329 |
| 186. said 1A, sayd 2A 3C | seid 710, said 695, sayd 42 |
| 187. sciences 1B | science(s) 3 |
| 188. self 1B | self 15, selfe 6, selue 1 |
| 189. sende 1D | sende 5, send 3 |
| 190. septembre 1A | |
| 191. seruaunt 1C | seruant 40, seruaunt 4 |
| 192. shall 1C | shall 89, shal 89 |
| 193. shortyng 1B | |
| 194. sixty 3A | |

## Caxton and Chancery English

| | Caxton's Forms | Chancery Forms |
|---|---|---|
| 195. | so 1B 1C, soo 1D | so 220, soo 18 |
| 196. | sonner (sooner) 1B | sonner 3, soner 1, souner 1 |
| 197. | sone (son) 1A | sonne 6, sone 2, son 1 |
| 198. | souerayn 2C | soueraigne 41, souerayn(e) 30, souuerain 2 |
| 199. | soule 1B | soule 9, sowle 4 |
| 200. | streyngthes 1D | *streng* forms 5, *streyng* forms 1, *stren* forms 1 |
| 201. | studyed 1B | |
| 202. | subget 1C | subgit 4, subget 1 |
| 203. | submytte 1C | |
| 204. | suche 2B | suche 113, such 72, *sw* forms 9, *si/y* forms 7 |
| 205. | susteyne 2B | |
| 206. | sygnyfieth 1D | signifie 3 |
| 207. | take 1B | take 40, taake 1 |
| 208. | than (adv. then) 1B | then(ne) 60, than(ne) 29 |
| 209. | thank 1C | thanke 3, thankke 1, þank(k)e 3 |
| 210. | that 6B 2C 9D | that 799, þat 842 |
| 211. | the 17A 6B 5C 8D, ye 1A | the 3512, þe 1988, ye 156 |
| 212. | therin 1C | þerinne 4, therin 3, therein 2 |
| 213. | them 5B, theym 1D | theym(e) 32, them 21, þaim 13 |
| 214. | they 7B 3C, theye 1B | they 132, thei 48, *ai/ay* forms 44 |
| 215. | their 11B, theyr 1B 1C 4D | their 45, þeire 19, theyre 2 |
| 216. | thinge (pl.) 1B | *ing* forms 30, *yng* forms 24 |
| 217. | this 1B 2C 1D | this 251, þis 154, thys 19 |
| 218. | thise (pl.) 1B | thes(e) 39, this(e) 10, thees(e) 37 |
| 219. | thousand 3A | |
| 220. | thus 1B | thus 10 |
| 221. | to 2A 1B 4C 12D | to 2520, too 7 |
| 222. | tocomynge (future) 1C | |
| 223. | towarde 1D | toward 11 |
| 224. | towne 1D | towne 65, town 33, towen 1 *ou* forms 69 |
| 225. | transitorye 1C | |
| 226. | translacion 1A | translacion 3 |
| 227. | translated 1A | |
| 228. | tree 1D | tree 2 |

LANGUAGE AND PALEOGRAPHY

Caxton's Forms | Chancery Forms

229. tresours 1B
230. tyme 1A — tyme 301, time 19
231. vnderstode 1B — vnderstande 16, vnderstanden 7, vnderstonden 1
232. vnderstondyng 1B — vnderstondyng 1, vundrestondyng 1, vnderstandyng 1
233. vnto 1A 3C — vnto 338, unto 1
234. vpon 2D — vpon 94, vppon 45, opon 6, upon 4
235. vsed 1B — vsed 18, vsyd 1
236. venerable 1A
237. vertue 1C — vertue 9, virtue 3
238. vertuouse 1A
239. volume 1A — volumes 1
240. was 1A 2D — was 197, wos 1
241. we 1C — we 462, wee 3
242. wel 2B, well 1C — wel 114, well 22
243. wente 1D — went 1, wentte 1, wende 1
244. were 1D — were 106, wer 17
245. werke 1A — *er* forms 5, *ir* forms 2, *or* forms 1
246. whan 2B 1D — whan 12, whanne 7, when 9, whenne 3
247. where 1D — where 65, wher 29, whar 1
248. wherin 1B
249. wherof 1B — wherof 10, whereof 6
250. whiche 1A 1B 1C — whiche 206, which 149, wiche 13
251. whom 1B — whom 22, whome 5, whoom(e) 3, wham 1
252. wolde 1B 1D, wold 1B — wolde 36, wold 20, would 1, wuld 1
253. worde 1B 1C — worde 7, word 3, woord 2
254. worshipfull 1A — worshipful 94, worshipfull 8
255. wyse 1B — wyse 53, wise 15
256. wyses (ways) 1D
257. wysest 1D — wysest 2
258. wysedom 1D — *is* forms 9, *ys* forms 2
259. wyth 1C 2D — with 346, wyth 24
260. wythin 1D — *wi* forms 55, *wy* forms 28
261. wythoute 2D — *wi* forms 50, *wy* forms 5

176

| Caxton's Forms | Chancery Forms |
|---|---|
| 262. wytte 2C | wittes 1 |
| 263. yere 3A | yere 99, yer 25 |
| 264. yonge 1D | yonge 2 |

### Table A
### Forms Not in the Chancery Glossary

2B 12D 19C 20D 21B 35A 42B 45B 47B 54A 62A 66A 69D 73A 77D 94C 96A 98AD 105A 106A 112A 121BC 128C 134D 137B 148B 150D 157B 171C 174A 176B 180B 181C 190A 193B 194A 201B 203C 205B 219A 222C 225C 227A 229B 236A 238A 248B 256D (Total: 48)

### Table B
### MnE Forms in Both Caxton and Chancery

1AD 3C 7D 8C 9ABDC 11B 13AB 14B 15BC 17cC 24BD 25ABCD 28D 29B 31B 34aBC 34bB 43A 60A 70BCD 78C 80AC 81AC 88CD 89aAC 92A 97A 99C 102C 104ABCD 107C 108C 111A 116AC 123D 124D 125B 126A 129C 130A 131BC 132C 133A 135C 136C 139C 141A 142B 144bD 146AC 147CD 149ABCD 153B 155B 166C 182A 185D 187B 188B 192C 195BC 207B 210BCD 211ABCD 214BC 215B 217BCD 220B 221ABCD 228D 239A 240AD 241C 244D 247D 251B (Total: 76)

### Table C
### MnE Forms except Final *e*

4BC 57D 68D 72A 85D 91B 100D 115D 117C 158ABC 159A 161A 164C 179D 189D 199B 204B 209C 216B 223D 224D 243D 250ABC 253BC (Total: 24)

### Table D
### MnE Forms except *i/y*

6C 10D 18aA 48B 56D 63D 76AC 79A 89bD 103BC 110CD 120C 140A 156C 163C 167AC 168A 173C 184C 206D 230A 255B 257D 259CD 260D 261D (Total: 26)

### Table E
### MnE Forms except *u/v*

10D 56D 65C 87aB 118D 172D 233AC 234D 235B (Total: 9)

## Table F
### Non-MnE Parallel Forms in Caxton and Chancery

16B 17aB 17bD 18bAD 23D 27A 30D 33A 37B 46B 50D 51C 52A 53C
58C 64C 74C 82BD 84D 86D 90D 93B 109B 113D 143C 144aB 145aB
145bB 151C 154D 169B 177B 196B 226A 232B 237C 242B 245A 246BD
249B 252BD 263A 264D (Total: 43)

## Table G
### Non-MnE Parallels except Final *e*

61A 127B (Total: 2)

## Table H
### Non-MnE Parallels except *i/y*

26C 61A 119BC 170C 262C (Total: 5)

## Table I
### Non-MnE Parallels except *u/v*

83B (Total: 1)

## Table J
### Differences between Caxton and Chancery

5D alayaunce/alliaunces   32B coffres/coffors   34CD came/com(e)
36C correctyon/correccione   38AD countre, contrey/contre, cuntre
41D cyte/citee   44B deed/ded(e)   55B dye/deyde 67D feest/fest(e)
75A fynysshid/finisshed   122D lyttyl/litil   160D peas/pees
165A preest/prest 183D royame/reaume   186 AC said/seid
202C subget/subgit (Total: 16)

## Table K
### Chancery Form nearest to MnE

40C crysten/cristen(e), cristian   49D dommage/damage
95C heyer/heir(e)   101AC hye/high   114D londe/lande
152CD ony/any   162B peryllis/periles   175A redoubtyd/redoubted
191C seruaunt/seruant   198C souerayn/soueraigne
200D stryngthes/strengthes   208B than/then   218B thise/these
254A worshipfull/worshipful   258D wysedom/wisdom (Total: 15)

## Table L
### Caxton Form nearest to MnE

22AC bookes/bokes   59C encreasyng/encresyng
71D fortresse/forteresses   78C glad/gladde   87bD had/hadd(e)
138B muste/moste   178D requyre/requere   197A sone/sonne
212C therin/þerinne   213A them/theym
231B vunderstode/vnderstande (Total: 11)

## Table M
### Form Words the Same in Caxton and Chancery
### (Those Underlined Not in the MnE Form)

1 3 4 7 8 9 11 13 14 15 <u>16</u> 24 25 29 70 <u>74</u> 87a 88 89a <u>89b</u> <u>103</u> 104 107 108 131 132 139 <u>144a</u> 144b 147 149 <u>158</u> <u>159</u> 185 188 192 195 <u>204</u> 210 211 214 215 217 220 221 <u>233</u> <u>234</u> 240 241 244 <u>246</u> 247 <u>249</u> <u>250</u> 251 <u>252</u> <u>259</u> <u>260</u> <u>261</u> (Total: 59)

## Table N
### Form Words Different in Caxton and Chancery

152 208 212 213 218 (Total: 5)

## Table O
### No Change between Early and Late Texts

1 a   4 alle   9 and   15 be   18b begonne   24 but   25 by   34a come
41 cyte   70 for   76 fyrst   80 god   81 grace   82 grete   88 he   89a his
101 hye   103 yf   104 in   119 lyf/lyfe   131 may   146 noble   147 not
149 of   152 ony   158 our   210 that   211 the   217 this   221 to   233 vnto
240 was   246 whan   250 whiche   253 worde   259 wyth (Total: 36)

## Table P
### Movement Forward

33AD comaundement/commaundement   56AD dyuerce/dyuerse
74CD fro/from   98AD honderd/hondred   110CD kynge/kyng
136BC moste/most   144BD ne/nor   242BC wel/well (Total: 8)

## Table Q
### Movement Backward

13AB at/att 22AC bookes/bokes   116AC lord/lorde   186AC said/sayd
195BCD so/soo   213BD them/theym   215BCD their/theyr
252BD wold/wolde (Total: 8)

## Appendix 2

**Selection A.** Caxton's prologue to *The Recuyell of the Historyes of Troye*, printed 1475, ed. W. J. B. Crotch, Early English Text Society, OS 176 (London, 1928), p. 2

Here begynneth the volume intituled and named the recuyell of the historyes of Troye / composed and drawen out of dyuerce bookes of latyn in to frensshe by the ryght venerable persone and worshipfull man. Raoul le ffeure. preest and chapelayn vnto the ryght noble gloryous and myghty prynce in his tyme Phelip duc of Bourgoyne of Braband etc In the yere of the Incarnacion of our lord god a thousand foure honderd sixty and foure / and translated and drawen out of frenshe in to englisshe by Willyam Caxton mercer of ye cyte of London / at the commaundement of the righht hye and myghty and vertuouse Pryncesse hys redoubtyd lady. Margarete by the grace of god. Duchesse of Bourgoyne of Lotryk of Braband etc / Whiche sayd translacion and werke was begonne in Brugis in the Countre of Flaundres the fyrst day of marche the yere in the Incarnacion of our said lord god a thousand foure honderd sixty and eyghte / And ended and fynysshid in the holy cyte of Colen the .xix. day of septembre the yere of our sayd lord god a thousand foure honderd and sixty and eneleuen etc

**Selection B.** From Caxton's *Mirrour of the World*, translated 1480, ed. Oliver H. Prior, Early English Text Society, ES 110 (London, 1913), p. 21

Yf the men in thise dayes vnderstode wel this worde, they wolde reteyne more gladly the doctrynes that procede and come fro the mouth of our creatour and maker. But the grete rentes that they haue, and the grete tresours of their coffres be cause of shortyng and abreggyng of their dayes, by their disordinat mangeries that ouermoche noye and greue them, so that nature may not wel bere ne susteyne, wherof they muste nedes the sonner rendre their soule and dye. Thus their Rentes, their tresours or other thinge wherin they delyte them, take a waye theyr lyf, their herte and their wytte alle att ones, in suche wyse than whan deth cometh and muste nedes dye, they haue loste wytte and vnderstondyng; of whom many been deed and dampned, whiche at their nede may not be counseilled ne can not helpe them self whan they haue most nede.

They lyue not lyke them that, for to kepe them fro peryllis, studyed in sciences and vsed their lyf in suche manere that they wold but systeyne their body only as . . .

**Selection C.** From Caxton's prologue to *Eneydos*, printed 1490, ed. W. J. B. Crotch, Early English Text Society, OS 176 (London, 1928), p. 110

[For I haue but folowed my copye in frenshe as nygh as me] is possyble / And yf ony worde be sayd therin well / I am glad. and yf otherwyse I submytte my sayd boke to theyr correctyon / Whiche boke I presente vnto the hye born. my tocomynge naturell 7 souerayn lord Arthur by the grace of god Prynce of Walys Duc of Cornewayll. 7 Erle of Chestre fyrst bygoten sone and heyer vnto our most dradde naturall 7 souerayn lorde 7 most crysten kynge/ Henry the vij. by the grace of god kynge of Englonde and of Fraunce 7 lord of Jrelonde / byseching his noble grace to receyue it in thanke of me his moste humble subget 7 seruaunt / And I shall praye vnto almyghty god for his prosperous encreasyng in vertue / wysedom / and humanyte that he may be egal wyth the most renommed of alle his noble progenytours. And so to lyue in this present lyf / that after this transitorye lyfe he and we alle may come to euerlastynge lyf in heuen / Amen:

**Selection D.** From Caxton's *Eneydos*, translated 1490, ed. W. T. Culley and F. J. Furnivall, Early English Text Society, ES 57 (London, 1890). p. 123

Whan Eneas had begonne his fortresse / he called to hym a hondred of the wysest men that were in his ooste / for to sende theym towarde kyng Latynus, in his cyte of Laurence, for to requyre hym of peas 7 alayaunce; and that he was not arryued in his londe for to doo to hym, nor to the contrey, ony dommage / but besoughte hym that he wolde not lette hym of that he had enterprysed to make a castell vpon his grounde that was begonne / For he made this for to rest hym and his folke / and for to dwell wythin his royame, by the commaundemente of the goddes, wythoute to doo hym ony hurte nor greuaunce. The messagers wente soo longe wyth theyr ryche presente that they bare from Eneas / to kyng Latynus, and wyth garlandes vpon theyr hedes, made of olyue tree / and also in theyr handes, braunches of the same / that peas and loue sygnyfieth / that they came to the cyte of Laurence, where they fonde, a lityll wythoute the towne, a grete feest of yonge men / that proued and assayed theyr stryngthes in dyuerse wyses/ ...

**Selection E.** Example from a petition to the Chancellor by Thomas Bodyn, PRO Ancient Proceedings C1/19/492, 1450–54 (no. 220 in the forthcoming Fisher-Richardson *Anthology of Chancery English*)

And often tymes in the bigynnyng of the same terme and mony tymes sithon:

the said Thomas with his frendes hath prayed and required the said Robert to putt and fynd hym to scole in fourme aforsaid after the effecte of the said covenaunt and accorde. the which to doo the said Robert wolnot. but that to doo at all tymes vtturly hath refused to the grete hurte harme and losse of the said Thomas. Please hit your good and graciouce lordship to consider the premisses and that the said Thomas therof may haue no remedy by the course of the comen lawe of this lande / And theruppon to graunt a write to be direct to the said Robert to appere by fore the kyng in his Chauncerie at a certeyn day and vppon a notable payne by your gracious lordship to be lymyted there to answere and to doo resceyve of and in thise premisses as by the Courte of the same Chauncerye thenne shall be ordeigned and he shall pray to god for you

# Appendix 3

Numbers refer to the Table of Forms, Appendix 1.

A. Forms in Caxton's *Malory* possibly influenced by the Winchester MS.

16. ben. Sandved finds the 3rd pl. "are" in the majority in Winchester and the Caxton *Malory*. Wiencke finds "ben" the usual form in the early texts, "are" increasing in frequency in text D. Caxton may have been influenced by Winchester (Sandved, p. 371).

17a. bere. Wiencke finds "bere" Caxton's usual form. Winchester and *Malory* have "beare" (Sandved, p. 364).

28. called. The usual ending is "-ed" but Winchester and *Malory* sometimes have "-yd" (Sandved, p. 335).

51. dradde. The 8 *a* forms in *Malory* correspond to 8 of the 16 *a* forms in Winchester, and 9 *e* forms correspond to *e*'s in Winchester. But 6 times *Malory* changes Winchester *e* to *a* (Sandved, p. 349).

175. redoubtyd. Winchester has only "doute." *Malory* folows this three times. Wiencke finds *bt* the usual form (Sandved, p. 322).

B. Chancery forms in Winchester not found in Caxton's *Malory*

34c. came. Winchester usually has "com"; *Malory* tends to change this to "cam(e)" (Sandved, p. 353).

59. encresyng. Winchester regularly us *es*. Wiencke finds *es* in early Caxton, *eas* in late (Sandved, p. 335).

186. said/seid. Winchester regularly has *ei/ey*, Caxton *ai/ay* (Sandved, p. 351).

C. Chancery forms in Caxton's *Malory* not found in Winchester

10. arryued. Winchester regularly uses *r*, Caxton *rr* (Sandved, p. 337).

50. doo. Winchester regularly has *do*. Wiencke finds *do* in early Caxton, *doo* in late (Sandved, p. 373).

## Notes

1. John H. Fisher, "Chancery and the Emergence of Standard Written English in the Fifteenth Century, *Speculum* 52 (1977): 870-99.
2. M. L. Samuels, "Some Applications of Middle English Dialectology," *English Studies* 44 (1960): 81-94.
3. R. W. Chambers and Marjorie Daunt, eds., *A Book of London English*, (Oxford: Clarendon Press, 1931).
4. Malcolm Richardson, "Henry V, the English Chancery, and Chancery English," *Speculum* 55 (1980): 726-50.
5. Quoted in Chambers and Daunt, *Book of London English*, p. 139.
6. Susan E. Hughes, "Guildhall and Chancery English, 1377-1422," *Guildhall Studies in London History* 4 (1980): 53-62.
7. Mary Patricia Relihan, "The Language of the English Stonor Letters, 1420-1483" (Ph.D. diss., University of Tennessee, 1977), p. 279; see also pp. 284ff.
8. Norman Davis, "The Language of the Pastons," *Proceedings of the British Academy* 40 (1955 for 1954): 119-44, especially pp. 130-31.
9. Henry Cecil Wyld, *A History of Modern Colloquial English* (London: Unwin, 1920), pp. 70-98.
10. A. I. Doyle and M. B. Parkes, "The Production of Copies of the *Canterbury Tales* and *Confessio Amantis* in the Early Fifteenth Century," in *Essays Presented to N. R. Ker*, ed. M. B. Parkes and A. G. Watson (London: Scolar Press, 1978), pp. 163-212.
11. For Wyld and Davis, see nn. 8 and 9, above. Albert C. Baugh, ed., *A History of the English Language*, 3rd. ed., rev. Thomas Cable (Englewood Cliffs, N.J.: Prentice-Hall, 1978), pp. 194, 250; E. J. Dobson, "Early Modern Standard English," *Transactions of the Philological Society* (Oxford: Blackwell, for the Society, 1955), pp. 25-54.
12. The ideographic nature of standard written English is discussed by Henry Bradley, *On the Relation of Spoken and Written English*, pamphlet published by the Oxford University Press, 1919.
13. Marshall McLuhan, *The Guttenberg Galaxy* (Toronto: University of Toronto Press). 1962.
14. Margaret Shaklee, "The Rise of the Standard English," in *Standards and Dialects in English*, ed. Timothy Shopen and Joseph M. Williams (Cambridge, Mass.: Winthrop, 1980), p. 48.
15. N. F. Blake, *Caxton and His World* (London: Deutsch, 1969), pp. 173ff. See also his "Caxton's Language," *Neuphilologische Mitteilungen* 67 (1966): 122-32.

16. N. F. Blake, "English Versions of *Reynard the Fox* in the Fifteenth and Sixteenth Centuries," *Studies in Philology* 62 (1965): 63–77.

17. Helmut Wiencke, *Die Sprache Caxtons*, Kölner Anglistische Arbeiten, no. 11 (Leipzig: Tauchnitz, 1930).

18. W. J. B. Crotch, ed., *The Prologues and Epilogues of William Caxton*, Early English Text Society, OS 176 (London, 1928); Oliver H. Prior, ed., *Caxton's "Mirrour of the World,"* Early English Text Society, ES 110 (London, 1913); W. T. Culley and F. J. Furnivall, eds., *Caxton's "Eneydos,"* Early English Text Society, ES 57 (London, 1890).

19. Blake, "Caxton's Language," and *Caxton and His World*, p. 177. The four passages are quoted from Crotch, *Prologues and Epilogues of Caxton*, p. 2; Prior, *Caxton's "Mirrour,"* p. 21; Crotch, *Prologues and Epilogues of Caxton*, p. 110; and Culley and Furnivall, *Caxton's "Eneydos,"* p. 123.

20. Margaret Bryant, *English and the Law Courts: The Part that Articles, Prepositions, and Conjunctions Play in Legal Decisions* (New York: Columbia University Press, 1930), illustrates the importance of precedent, uniformity, and form words in modern legal proceedings.

21. Blake, "Caxton's Language," p. 128

22. Wiencke, *Die Sprache Caxtons*, p. 315.

23. Arthur O. Sandved, *Studies in the Language of Caxton's Malory and That of the Winchester Manuscript* (Oslo: Norwegian University Presses, 1968).

# Part III
# Literary Criticism

# The Drama:

## Learning and Unlearning

### Donald C. Baker

Of the genres of literature in the late Middle Ages, the English religious drama, which developed in the fourteenth century, flourished in the fifteenth, and died a somewhat mysterious death in the sixteenth, is perhaps most particularly a popular genre. It is also the genre in which, with due respect to continuing interest in the writers of romance, lyric, and ballad, the most feverish scholarly and critical rethinking is going on today. All fields have seen a burgeoning of interest in the past three decades, but that in the English religious drama is truly remarkable. Scholarly knowledge and theory generally had seemed more or less embodied and preserved in E. K. Chambers' two volumes of the *Medieval English Stage* (1903), the continental and liturgical origins in Karl Young's two mighty volumes *The Drama of the Medieval Church* (1933), and all was capped in 1955 with the appearance of Hardin Craig's *English Religious Drama*. These works, reflecting and summarizing the studies of their times, now seem to have been informed by certain ideas about the origins, development, and functions of drama that no longer appear very germane.

It is not an exaggeration to say that nearly all theories about the medieval drama in England until thirty-five or forty years ago were based upon quite specific premises: (1) that the drama had a liturgical origin, as illustrated by Young, Chambers, and Craig, and was derived from something like the *quem quaeritis* trope; (2) that the drama developed by a gradual accretion of the liturgical "plays" and changed its function and purpose; (3) that the drama was gradually removed from the churches for varying reasons and placed in the hands of the secular civic groups, principally guilds; (4) that the drama changed linguistically by translation of the Latin into the vernacular; (5) that it flourished as processional civic religious drama and entertainment following the establishment of Corpus Christi Day in 1311; and (6) that the religious drama died a natural death because it was replaced by the vibrant professional secular drama which was the precursor of Shakespeare. As a part of this theory, it was assumed that the cycles were all acted in the processional fashion recorded by the antiquarian David Rogers at Chester in the first half of the seventeenth century. All of these assumptions have now been seriously challenged by one or another scholar; the whole neo-Darwinian view of the organic growth and development of the drama was severely questioned by O. B. Hardison, Jr., Glynne Wickham, and V. A. Kolve, within a few years of one another, and all within ten years of the publication of Craig's life's work, which enshrined each of the above explanations of how the religious drama came to be, what it was, and why and how it disappeared.[1] It will not do, however, to be dismissive of such scholars as Chambers, Young, and Craig, and indeed much of what we still accept as valid is owing to their labors. They were the products of their age and its assumptions about the world (as we are, we shouldn't forget!), according to which everything had to "develop," "accrete," "flourish," and "die," giving way to superior species.

It must be immediately observed that recent study is most effective when it is dismantling previous theories; it is less convincing when it seeks to propound its own explanations. Father Harold Gardiner's *Mysteries' End*, published soon after the Second World War, proposed a new theory about the drama's death: it had not died of lack of interest; rather, it died because of too much interest.[2] He proposed that the drama was killed by the reformed church because, however much the civic groups attempted to make the drama conform to new political and theological realities, it preserved its patent idolatry. That this is correct in a number of cases is clear, but it is much too sweeping an explanation. Hardison, Wickham, and Kolve are likewise better on the attack than on the defense. To argue that there was no translation from Latin into the vernacular conveniently if uncomfortably dismisses the Shrewsbury Fragments (though what they are evidence of is unclear) and the written tradition of translation in the case of the *Chester Cycle*.[3] That this tradition is confused and unreliable there is no doubt; that it is totally wrong is too strong to maintain. Kolve's explanation, received with much enthusiasm and deserved respect at the time, that the cycle plays all evolved at about the same time as a systematic representation of God's providence in honor of the new feast of Corpus Christi, and thus were not developments of liturgical drama, has since been much more skeptically treated. As for the theory of presentation, Alan Nelson has more recently argued that the largest of the plays, the *York Cycle*, was not in fact acted processionally on wagons at all, as has been nearly always assumed: he points with cogency to the logistical difficulties and to the seemingly insuperable obstacle of the time involved.[4] But his own explanation, that the plays were acted indoors after a day or days of "pageants" merely representing the plays in *tableaux vivants*, seems equally unbelievable. And, as he admits, there is incontrovertible evidence that the *Chester Cycle* was acted processionally on wagons, if in a "free processional" manner, and the evidence for similar performance at Coventry is much too circumstantial to be dismissed. Other attendant "development" theories, treating the morality as a later offshoot of the cycle drama and dealing with the relation of the folk drama to the religious drama, which had held sway for so long, now seem much more questionable. The exact relation of the morality to the cycle drama will probably always be shrouded in mystery; but it is fairly clear that the old explanation that it was a late outgrowth of the religious drama cannot really hold water, particularly in view of the fact that our earliest morality manuscripts antedate most of the manuscripts and even the records of much of the civic religious drama. The relation of the folk drama to the religious plays, assumed even by F. M. Salter, is now highly debatable—how old is the folk drama?[5]

The relation of the religious drama to other forms of literature and art has received much attention in the past three decades. Eleanor Prosser and others have given us admirable insight into the aesthetics and theology of the drama, and Rosemary Woolf has usefully linked the drama to the traditions of the lyric and of artistic representation.[6] But even here, as the earlier work of M. D. Anderson shows, we are often not sure of the ground upon which we stand: which came first, for example, in particular cases, iconographical or dramatic representation?[7] In short, we now think that a lot of what we once knew is wrong or debatable; we are not at all certain that much of what is currently being thought and taught is correct. Too many questions remain, some of which will be further discussed in the course of this essay.

The heartening aspect of current study is not in the field of theory; it is rather in the enormous energy now being directed to the records and to the thorough reediting of the principal texts. Particularly noteworthy is the work of the Records of Early English Drama project at Toronto, which has begun to publish the dramatic records of counties and cities, complementing the work already done or in progress by the Malone Society.[8] The *Macro Plays*, the *Chester Cycle*, the *Non-Cycle Plays and Fragments*, and the *Digby Plays* have all been reedited, and these efforts will reach fruition in the work underway by Stevens and Cawley (following the latter's valuable edition of the "Wakefield" plays in the *Towneley Cycle*) of the whole *Towneley Cycle*, the completion of Arthur Brown's life work of reediting the *York Cycle*, as well as the appearance of the new edition of that cycle by Richard Beadle, and Stephen Spector's reediting of the *N-Town Plays*. Together with this work, the Leeds Texts and Monographs Series of facsimiles, which has already produced two of the Chester manuscripts, the *Towneley Cycle* manuscript, the *Non-Cycle Plays and Fragments*, and the *Digby Plays*, with more forthcoming, has been enormously useful, as has the Folger Shakespeare Library's facsimile of the *Macro* manuscript. To this list we add the project at the Medieval Institute at Western Michigan, which is attempting a survey of the iconography and art in its possible relation to the drama.[9]

Along with these achievements and plans, one must not forget to mention the enthusiastic and learned performances of the drama, particularly during the past forty years.[10] It is quite possible that we may learn a great deal more about the staging of the plays, although here, as always, we run the risks of extrapolation and analogy: we will be on much firmer ground if we speak carefully and specifically of a particular cycle or group of plays, or a single play, at a particular time in its history, and not attempt sweeping judgments. In another ten years, the time will perhaps be propitious for a new history, one less directed by assumptions based upon biological and geological analogies and more committed to a recording of the facts as they have become known. That the spirit that informed the religious drama was a single spirit we have really no reason to doubt; that the methods for selecting subjects, writing the plays, and ordering and performing them were similar from town to town, and that they were performed under similar conditions by similar people or groups of people, we now have every reason to doubt. We need fewer theories and more simple information, which we are fortunately now receiving.

After this survey of the problems, I shall proceed to a brief discussion of the principal cycles of plays—Chester, York, Wakefield (Towneley), and N-Town (and, in connection with the latter, some of the East Anglian drama)—in which I will examine, as far as is now known, their form, themes, styles, and relationships; the manner of their maintenance, governance, and production; and the people who were involved in their production. In summary, what can be tentatively and cautiously assumed about the nature of the medieval English religious drama will be concluded.

*The Drama*

## The Cycles: Their Origin and Development

Traditionally, the *Chester Cycle* has been considered the oldest of the cycles. Whether this is true or not is very debatable, but it is a bibliograpically Whether this is true or not is very debatable, but it is a bibliographically convenient starting-point.[11] It is a group of plays of relatively homogeneous style, it exists in whole or in part in eight manuscripts, and it is at least as thoroughly described in contemporary records and accounts as any of the others. It will be used here as a peg upon which to hang discussion of some of the many characteristics and problems of all the cycles.

The *Chester Cycle* consists, in the five more or less complete late sixteenth-century and early seventeenth-century manuscripts that survive, of twenty-four (or twenty-five) plays, and is thus the smallest of the four great cycles in number of distinct plays. It should be noted, however, that the material in a single play in one cycle might be covered in two or more plays in another cycle, and that therefore the number of plays is not a reliable indicator of the amount of material covered or of the total "length" of a cycle in number of lines and time required to play, under whatever conditions.

The individual subjects with pageant numbers are: (1) the Fall of Lucifer; (2) Adam, including Cain and Abel; (3) Noah; (4) Abraham, including Lot and "Melchysedeck," Abraham and Isaac; (5) Moses, including Balaak and Balaam; (6) the Annunciation and Nativity; (7) the Shepherds; (8) the Three Kings; (9) the Offering of the Three Kings; (10) the Slaughter of Innocents; (11) the Purification, with Christ and the Doctors; (12) the Temptation, with the Woman Taken in Adultery; (13) the Blind Chelidonian, with the Raising of Lazarus; (14) Christ at the House of Simon the Leper, with Christ and the Money-Lenders and Judas's Plot; (15) the Last Supper, with the Betrayal of Christ; (16) the Trial and Flagellation; (16A) the Passion; (17) the Harrowing of Hell; (18) the Resurrection; (19) the Road to Emmaus, with Doubting Thomas; (20) the Ascension; (21) Pentecost; (22) the Prophets of Antichrist; (23) Antichrist; (24) the Last Judgment. The plays are, with some exceptions, written in the famous "Chester eights," either *aaabaaab* or *aaabcccb*. They vary in length from just over three hundred to just over seven hundred lines. Certain things become clear by looking at the list of plays as it appears in the edition by R. M. Lumiansky and David Mills.[12] If the plays restricted themselves to a single subject, each play running to between three hundred and four hundred lines, the *Chester Cycle* would appear very much larger, physically, than we are accustomed to thinking it to be. The amalgamation of subject matter reveals the cycle to be a very flexible arrangement; the plays are frequently duples as far as the essential illustrative points are concerned. We do not know how to interpret this, whether the combination of episodes represents a compression of an earlier, larger group of separate plays or whether the compounding of parallel exempla was always a part of the scheme. We find here the usual puzzling medieval qualities of expansion and compression and a frequently confused story (the normal confusion of Christ at the house of Simon the Leper, for instance; it was, of course, Simon the Pharisee; see Luke 7:36–50). Dramatic propriety and decorum are essentially post-Renaissance concerns and have little to do with medieval drama, except insofar as they influence our own reaction to the drama. But at the same time, we note a curious duplication of plays in numbers 8 and 9, the first dedicated to the Three Kings and the second to the Offering of the Three Kings. We should look for explanation of such curiosities, not to a specific grand design, but more probably to the subjects, within a generally accepted iconographical and exemplary scheme, that individual sponsoring groups wished to present and that ecclesiastical authorities approved. We need not create for ourselves a romantic historical drama in which the Vintners and Mercers quarreled over who was to "do" the Three Kings, the question being decided by dividing the episode, the Vintners doing the arrival and the Mercers handling the offering, but clearly such a pragmatic explanation is at least possible. Much has been written about the episodes of the Corpus Christi play being parceled out to the guilds on the basis of their economic interests, and there is much to give rise to such theories—Noah being done by the Waterleaders and Drawers, the Last Supper by the Bakers, the Harrowing of Hell by the Cooks, and so forth—but such explanations are limited and circumstantial, however tempting and amusing they may be.

    The subjects of the plays have occupied all who have attempted to explain the origins of the cycles. It is true that the Old Testament is "covered" from Genesis through part of Exodus, whereas the New Testament is treated much more fully, and that within the New Testament the Book of Revelations is given proportionately more coverage than the Gospels themselves, the last five plays at Chester being derived from Revelations, with one, the Prophets of Antichrist, deriving much of its material from the Old Testament prophets. And, of course, the New Testament's apocryphal material and tradition makes an important contribution. A great deal of learning has been directed to determining why particular subjects were chosen. Certain are obvious: if the play is to represent the providence of God in honor of Corpus Christi, from Alpha to Omega, then a Fall of Lucifer, Creation, Expulsion from Paradise, Birth of Christ, Death of Christ, and some treatment of the Last Judgment are presumably essential. But it is obvious that a mere "covering" of the subject

## The Drama

was never intended in such a limited sense by those who, in whatever order of time, in whatever relation to one another, and under whatever instructions or suggestions from the church, designed the cycle and altered it as the years passed. It is clear, from the work of Kolve and Woolf (it has always been generally clear, but their work has given much more specific point to the subject) that the subjects were chosen for their typological significance generally, and were subjects particularly popular in sermon and iconography, used to inculcate in the medieval mind the spiritual security derived from the truth of the parallelism and foreshadowing of the New Testament by the Old, that the word of God proved a magnanimous and beneficent continuity which offered them parallels for their own lives and confidence in the ultimate completion of God's design for the world and for the individual.

Although all episodes of the Old Testament had been interpreted by one *auctoritas* or another as anticipating an episode of the New, as well as having inherent typological significance, certain ones were singled out for sermons and for the popular versions of the Bible in the fourteenth and fifteenth centuries. This resulted in a highly foreshortened treatment of the Old Testament. As Woolf remarks, "The four extant cycles have a sequence of Genesis i–xxii and part of Exodus; but the Beverley cycle did not proceed beyond Genesis xxii, a stopping point which is perhaps confirmed by the Holkham Bible Picture Book."[13] Kolve had earlier argued that the principle of selection for the English cycles was that of assigning a play or part of a play to each of the figures traditionally representing one of the Seven Ages of the World.[14] The first five ages would have been represented by Adam, Noah, Abraham, Moses, and David, and the last two by episodes from the New Testament. Kolve points to the *N-Town Plays*, in which Noah explicitly says "In me Noe the secund age/in dede begynnyth."[15] That this general idea was influential is suggested by the existence of a David play in the no longer extant Norwich cycle. There is, of course, a problem here for an all-encompassing theory, for a David play exists in no other cycle. Kolve's argument that a Prophet's play was equivalent to a David is interesting but not quite convincing, in that our surviving text of York does not have one, nor does the play-list of the nonextant Beverley cycle. In any case, the Prophet's play, derived as it probably was from the Augustinian *Sermo contra paganos*, particularly emphasized Augustus, the Roman Sibyl, and Vergil, as well as Old Testament prophets otherwise untreated in the cycles, with David as merely one of them.[16] The *Wakefield* (or *Towneley*) *Cycle* has a Caesar Augustus play performing a similar function of anticipating the birth of Christ.

195

Woolf's examination of possible origins of pattern is interesting in that she provides two possible sources. One is an equation with "various stages at which the labourers entered the vineyard with Old Testament figures. This produced a series of five: Adam to Noah, Noah to Abraham, Abraham to Moses, Moses to the birth of Christ, and the birth of Christ to the Last Judgment."[17] This, as she points out, was set forth in a homily of Gregory the Great. The other series, she argues, might have consisted in the allegorisation of the seven office hours. This was a list of those "who praise God: Adam and Eve, Abel, Noah, Abraham, the prophets, the apostles, and the just on the last day."[18] As she admits, none of these lists reflects very well the actual content of the cycles, and, of course, much of the "New Testament" material comes from apocryphal sources. It seems evident that no single theory accounts for the known states of the plays, But the suggestions of Kolve and Woolf are particularly useful in that they point to the impulses of a didactic and reassuring kind which provided the intellectual and theological bases of the cycles. We would appear to be dealing with a set of attitudes toward the continuity of God's grand design rather than with a carefullly worked out and agreed upon method of representing that design. If there had once been a fully worked-out theory of selection of episodes, it is clear that it became rather formless in the actual development and practical year-to-year functioning of the drama: the curious "appendices" to the cycles—for example, the Wakefield play of "*Suspencio Jude*," the York "Coronation of Our Lady," the N-Town "Last Judgment"—added to the ends of those manuscripts are plays that fall beyond the formal structures of the cycles. The above overall theoretical explanations, taken in a very general way, may be a useful starting point for assumptions. Any more specific and internally coherent explanation fails to convince, for the evidence simply does not support it. It is altogether probable that the particular design of each cycle arose, within the larger framework of the festal purpose, from local interests, and the reasons for particular plays taking the form that they did, some subjects being treated in one cycle and not in another, some important subjects being ignored completely (Samson and Jonah, for instance, which are powerfully represented in both sermon and iconography), may have derived from those local interests. It is likely that local records, as they are further studied and assimilated, may provide as much of an answer to certain of the puzzling matters as do the larger preaching, teaching, and iconographical traditions.

The York and Wakefield cycles pose the same general questions as the Chester, but are rather more complex in some ways. The York, which is and apparently was the largest of the cycles in number of plays, survives in a

## The Drama

single manuscript register, but the earlier records and the extant text together show the many alterations made during the life of this great play.[19] The play at York is known to date from at least 1376, but nothing of its earliest form is certainly known.[20] It can, however, be guessed at from a list of the plays made by the town clerk Roger Burton in 1415; this is quite similar to the contents of the late fifteenth-century text. Interestingly, Burton made a second list a few years later which reveals that some changes occurred during the interval of about six years between the two lists. The second records fifty-seven plays, or nine more than the number of plays actually found in the text of the register.[21] Such fluctuations over a period of only about thirty or forty years would suggest endless possibilities: certainly, among them, that not all plays were acted, in whatever form, each year; the great duplication of Biblical events (from a typological point of view) would suggest that no didactic purpose would have been served by their all being acted each year, except for the key symbolic and narrative elements. The state of the lists and text would indicate that the individual sponsoring groups had a considerable range of materials allowed outside those key symbolic and narrative elements, and that this selection was in turn affected by the rise and fall of the guilds themselves, for some were replaced by others in the register of the York cycle. Also indicated is the possibility, even the probability, that some of the plays offered by various groups may have been found wanting in entertainment value and dropped, or that ecclesiastical authorities may from time to time have objected to certain plays. It also becomes evident that in a number of cases two or more plays may in effect have been acted together (for example, "Trial before Herod," "Remorse of Judas," and the "Second Trial," numbers 31–33 in the L. T. Smith edition of 1885). The way in which such continuous or simultaneous acting may have been done is suggested by the Digby "Killing of the Children," in which Herod's knights walk about the place, looking for the children, while Mary, Joseph, and Jesus make their escape to Egypt.

Many more plays are in the York register than are found in the Chester manuscripts, but the York plays are on the average much shorter (250–75 lines each, with none reaching more than 546 lines) than those of Chester. The Chester records indicate that the plays were acted at four stations, whereas York records suggest at least twelve, and on occasion more.[22] The York register has no banns; their absence could possibly be owing to the rearrangement of the manuscript of the register, for the compiler clearly received texts of some plays after the register had been begun, but the whole question of the relation of the banns to the cycle plays needs to be given more consideration.

The *Wakefield* (or *Towneley*) *Cycle* has, of course, by reason of its modern popularity as drama, received by far the greater part of scholarly and critical attention.[23] The presence of a number of plays that were apparently derived directly from the *York Cycle* has given "source" scholars an always-ready field, and the dramatic brilliance in modern terms of a group of five plays attributed to the "Wakefield Master" has given critics an equally rich field to till. The manuscript has thirty-two plays, several incomplete at beginning or end because of *lacunae* in the manuscript; a quire is missing at the beginning which may have contained banns. The tradition in the Towneley family, in whose library the manuscript was found, that the plays may have been written by Augustinian canons at Widkirk or Woodkirk may have some substance; it is usually assumed that clerical figures were chiefly involved in the writing of the plays, at least in the earlier period. The plays, however, were almost certainly those of Wakefield town, and the cycle should therefore be called the *Wakefield Cycle*, rather than the *Towneley Cycle* after the family that owned the manuscript.[24] The part of the "Wakefield Master" in the cycle has ranged, according to various critics, from just the five plays assigned to him on the basis of his curious nine-line tail-rhyming stanza (*aaaabcccb*) to a variety of other work, revisions of individual plays, and in at least one theory, the overall revision and rearrangement of the entire cycle.[25] The mysterious figure of the "Wakefield Master" and his work have given a particular prominence to this cycle, so much so that for very many students of English Literature, medieval English drama means "The Second Shepherd's Play" (with the later morality *Everyman* added). This is, of course, quite unfair to the other great cycles.

Having said this, however, one must admit that the plays of the "Wakefield Master" do have for the modern reader and audience the capacity for individuated existence not quite reached by other cycle plays. The perfection of symmetry of the "Second Shepherd's Play," in which the ancient pun on the *agnus dei* informs the farce of the first part and provides the metamorphosis that results in the stasis of the second—as Christ stilled the waters so the storm of farce is stilled through the quiet of the very lamb that had precipitated the blanket-tossing earlier—is visible to the atheist and the unknowledgeable believer alike. Other single plays from this and other cycles have been enacted in modern times to good effect, but the "Second Shepherd's Play" seems to answer most fully the expectations of "drama" of its original audiences in its iconographical and doctrinal symmetry, and its concluding tableau, which might almost have been adapted from a bit of stained glass, all seasoned with the riotous farce of purely human concerns.

Although the *York Cycle* has sustained power, as anyone who has seen productions of it can attest, the *Wakefield Cycle* with its longer, more self-contained plays (averaging 384 lines, thus amounting in total lines to a larger play than the present text of the *York Cycle* if the lines of obviously missing parts of plays are counted in, it must have at one time extended to well over 15,000 lines) provides units which are more individually satisfying to us. This apparent self-containedness in itself has led to the suggestion that, whereas the *York Cycle* may have been presented in a processional style, the *Wakefield Cycle* was presented at one "station," in the round.[26] And, of course, the presence of two Shepherds' plays, both evidently by the same writer, has given much grist for the mills of scholars and critics: the second is, both by modern and medieval standards—as far as we can determine the latter—better entertainment and celebration, but the first is no mean play, confessed by most to be superior to plays on the subject in the other cycles. Martial Rose has suggested that both were played, the first at the end of the first day's play, the second at the beginning of the second.[27] This seems, however, to take the presence of the plays side-by-side too seriously; presumably the text is a register of extant and recent plays which had been acted, not the record of an actual performance series.

The *Beverley Cycle*, though not extant, lives in the records which the town provides us. The list of plays (thirty-six, thirty-seven, or thirty-eight in number) suggests that, like the *Wakefield Cycle*, the Beverley plays were influenced to some degree by the great play of York, but any attempt at closer definition must be futile because, lacking a statement in the records to this effect, we must treat the titles of the plays as ambivalent evidence, considering, as we have seen, the multiplicity of subject matter which might be concealed behind a single, simple title.[28] Craig argues that the order of plays was "virtually the same as in York" but mere order cannot be given a great deal of weight.[29] The records are rich, revealing as few others do the seriousness and pride with which the guilds, under the supervision of the Beverley Guild of Corpus Christi, approached their responsibilities, and human weaknesses are indicated by the fines levied for poor performances or failure to perform. The Beverley plays are first recorded in 1377, making them of perhaps about the same antiquity as the York, and as always, in records they are described as "ancient."

The Newcastle and Norwich cycles, never apparently of a size comparable with the others, are very useful in our continuing efforts to reconstruct English cycle drama, for, in addition to records, one play from each survives. From the *Newcastle Cycle*, the play of Noah's Ark survives in a mutilated form, included curiously enough in O. Waterhouse's edition of

*Non-Cycle Plays*.[30] That this was certainly a member of a flourishing cycle is clearly indicated by documentary evidence; Norman Davis works out a scheme of twelve plays from guild and local records and postulates that there may have been as many as twenty-five, though this may stretch the evidence a bit.[31] But interestingly enough, one guild, the Merchant Adventurers, was responsible for five plays not named in the records, and six other companies are mentioned as being responsible for unnamed plays.[32] It is too bad that the guild that was responsible for the Noah play, the Shipwrights, has left few records to illuminate the surviving text. We are more fortunate in the case of Norwich, for the Grocers have left rich records which help us to understand the preparation and production of their play of Adam and Eve. These records have played an important part for most of a century in our attempts to understand what happened before and during the playing of a cycle: amounts paid to named actors for their parts, a description of materials used and their cost, rent for storage of the pageant wagon, and the only detailed contemporary description of the pageant wagon that has come down to us.[33] The pertinent records are printed in full by Davis. Since neither play exists in a contemporary text, but in much later, imperfect copies, we have been well served by Davis's painstaking editorial work. He prints again the Norwich minute of 1527 which discloses a list of twelve pageants, all but the Smiths' and Worstedweavers' being presented by a combination of at least two guilds, and, in one case, pageant number 10, the Baptism of Christ, by a total of seventeen guilds![34]

One of the famous cycles, the Coventry (the "true" Coventry, not the so-called *Ludus Coventriae*), exists in only two plays, but these plays are extremely instructive in revealing how various the cycle drama could be. Craig, in his edition, reconstructs a cycle of only ten plays (originally he thought that no Old Testament plays were included, but changed his mind in a postscript [p. xl] to the later edition), which he argues were presented at ten stations in the ten wards of the city.[35] (This would seem too many stations given the evidence; a more likely number, three, is suggested by Nelson.[36]) Craig's evidence for the number of plays is by no means convincing, but the surviving texts (again not in a satisfactorily contemporary form) are certainly unusual, and make very plausible the assumption that fewer plays than normal were included in the cycle, for the two plays are extensive amalgamations which, taken together, run to well over 2,000 lines, by far the largest of the surviving cycle plays. The two plays, though complex, are essentially the Annunciation, the Birth, the Shepherds, the Flight into Egypt, Herod (of the Sheremen's and Taylors' pageant), the presentation in the Temple, and the Disputation with the Doctors (of the Weavers' pageant).

There is some overlapping in that both plays involve prophet scenes. Craig, with his view of the development of cycle drama, was naturally led by this amalgamation—together with the considerable variety of verse and stanzaic forms, including Chester "eights," tail-rhyming stanzas, and quatrains—to assume that the plays are late, representing gradual accretion, and that, because of stanza forms and themes, they were probably imported from the north.[37] This conclusion is by no means a foolish one, and Craig argues strongly that the Christ before the Doctors scene in the Coventry Weavers' pageant was borrowed imperfectly and modified from the same text in the *York Cycle* from which the Chester play on the subject was also borrowed; the evidence, however, is not sufficiently substantial to support such a thesis. The plays were first published by Thomas Sharp in 1817 (the manuscript of the Sheremen's and Taylors' pageant was later destroyed by fire, but the 1539 manuscript of the Weavers' pageant in the hand of Robert Croo is in the Muniment Room of St. Mary's Hall, Coventry).[38] We owe a great deal to Sharp for the preservation of Coventry records relating to the pageants, for a fire in Birmingham destroyed most of the originals, and, together with those of Norwich, the Coventry records provide the most circumstantial descriptions of the activities: payments to players and to named persons for copying the plays or for "berying the playe-boke" and the costs of costumes are among the details that are noted. They also provide incontrovertible evidence that at Coventry, at least, the pageants were in fact played in succession at various stations. The pageants at Coventry seem also to have been among the most persistent, for as late as 1584 a new pageant, the "Destruction of Jerusalem," was performed,[39] though the last regular performance of the cycle was apparently in 1579. The Coventry Corpus Christi play may have not been among the oldest, but Sharp records a date of 1392–93 for the first mention in the records.[40]

The Coventry records in particular are interesting in that they reveal the dominant role that one person could play in the pageants; in this case, that person was Robert Croo (Crowe), who not only "corrected" the Sheremen's and Taylors' pageant in 1577, but was paid twenty shillings for "makyng of the boke" for the Drapers' Company in the same year. He also mended the "devells cottes" in 1560, played God for the Drapers' Company in 1561, provided a hat for the "Pharysye" in 1562, and copied two leaves of the play-book for the Smiths' Company in 1563.[41] Earlier, the records of the Weavers' Guild in 1535 record payment of five shillings for the "makyng of the playe-boke," but do not note to whom the payment was made; this was almost certainly, however, to Croo, whose manuscript of 1534 is probably a revision of an earlier play. We are not, of course, certain that the

Robert Croo or Crowe is in every case the same man; the family seems to have been active, for John Croo was paid two shillings for "mendyng of Herodes hed" in 1547.[42] These references cast some light (or darkness) upon the use of terms that puzzle us, such as "writing" or "making" a play, or in the case of the 1534 manuscript, "translating" a play. It is difficult to pin down in records whether original composition, revision, or copying is intended; clearly, however, "translation" in a modern sense is not intended. The Coventry records do provide definite evidence that one man, John Green, composed a pageant, the late "Destruction of Jerusalem," for the Mercers' Company, which paid him five shillings for it.[43] Though Green may have been merely a copier, the contemporary making of the play and its performance for the first time would suggest that Green was indeed the author.

In spite of Craig's criticisms of the plays as decadent, the two surviving pageants of Coventry, however altered over the years, are by no means mere shoddy stuff; they make effective, amusing, exciting, and touching drama when played today or simply read aloud.

## The N-Town Cycle and East Anglian Drama

The final cycle to be considered is the greatest puzzle of all, the *N-Town*. (Let us have done with other traditional names: *Ludus Coventriae*, given erroneously—or by generic analogy with the famous Coventry plays—in a note on the fly leaf of MS. Vespasian D. viii; or "Hegge," because a family of that name once owned the manuscript. Both cause confusion to the student. "N-Town" comes, of course, from the "In N. town wherfore we pray" of line 527 of the proclamation of the cycle, and seems by far the best title.) That it is a cycle of sorts cannot be doubted. Its origins, and almost everything else about it, are dark apparently beyond present illumination.

Beginning with the study of W. W. Greg, scholars of the early drama have made repeated attempts at analysis.[44] It is not dismissive to say that we have had nothing so far that in many respects convinces, in spite of the really excellent edition by K. S. Block, which was far ahead of other Early English Text Society volumes of her time in bibliographical detail and subtlety of interpretation;[45] the excellent bibliographical analysis of Meredith and Kahrl in their facsimile edition;[46] and the work of Spector, whose edition replacing Block's is eagerly awaited.[47] What is the *N-Town Play?* That it is an amalgam, all are agreed. What it is an amalgam *of* is not agreed upon. Spector's essay, which analyzes the layers of the cycle and concludes that it is, at bottom, a cycle written fairly uniformly in varieties of thirteen-line stanzas, headed by banns (the proclamation) in the same stanzaic form; that to this basic cycle the *Contemplacio* Marian group of plays in *abababab* stanzas was added, for which the date 1468 written on folio 100$^v$ may provide an indication of the time at which the addition was made; and that a group of passion plays was incorporated into the cycle, probably replacing some other plays, is the most satisfactory so far.[48] Spector argues that Passion Play 2 was transcribed as it was actually being added to the cycle. We are left, however, with many questions. Was the present cycle, probably of the late fifteenth century, though transcribed over a period of time, ever acted? That parts of it had been performed at various times can scarcely be doubted, given the fulsome English and Latin stage directions, but there is little to indicate, to consider only a certain lack of correspondence between the proclamation and the actual content of the whole cycle as it stands, that this particular and discrete body of plays was ever acted.[49] This is not to argue that it was not, but only to point out the essential differences between this text and those of the other cycles. (No one argues that the registers and texts of the Chester, York, and Wakefield cycles represent, *in toto*, what was played every year, for they do not; but these do represent a body of material which, taken together, forms the bulk of the play of Corpus Christi Day or Whitsunday or whatever, which was played, more or less consistently, over a period of years.)

Since they were first recognized to be no part of the real Coventry cycle, the *N-Town Plays* have posed a peculiar problem. We have lots of town records that indicate clearly that those towns had regular cycles of Corpus Christi plays, but in this case we have an elaborate cycle with no town. Craig made a determined effort to locate the plays in Lincoln, an argument that has continued to have some support, particularly from Kahrl and Gauvin.[50] That there was drama at Lincoln cannot be doubted, particularly in view of Kahrl's fine edition of the records for the Malone Society.[51] Kahrl also worked out an elaborate theory for the performance of the *N-Town Plays* at Lincoln.[52] The difficulty, of course, as E. J. Dobson long ago pointed out, is that the language of the *N-Town Plays* is not that of Lincolnshire; it is clearly East Anglian, and more probably that of Norfolk.[53] It is remotely possible, of course, that a Norfolk scribe copied texts that were derived from Lincolnshire ones, and one must recognize that, though modern knowledge of late medieval English dialects is far superior to that of a century ago, we have scarcely reached the state at which we can pinpoint exactly the language of a particular town or parish. Late Middle English of the East and Southeast was becoming far too eclectic and contaminated for such certainty. But it remains that the language of the *N-Town Plays* is far closer to the East Anglian of the *Macro* and *Digby Plays* than it is to Lincolnshire texts. It would appear also from the proclamation and the "N. town" reference that the basic cycle, at least, had been a production which travelled from town to town, "N. town" usually being taken from "Nomen-" or "fill-in-the-name-town." If this assumption is valid, it would also square with the bulk of surviving East Anglian drama, all of which that exists in sizeable texts is, except for the Norwich cycle play and the Brome Abraham and Isaac play, pretty evidently drama which was played by traveling groups. That this extant drama is largely of the traveling, single-play type, whereas the *N-Town Plays* are a cycle, is not really an argument against the generic description of the *N-Town* as a traveling play, insofar as each of the other East Anglian plays of this sort is essentially unique in its form, and one, the Digby "Killing of the Children," may well have been a little play (two little plays, actually, the second part being the Candlemas play) picked up from a small town cycle by a traveling group. The elaborateness of the *N-Town Plays* cannot be a strong argument against their being the principal plays of a traveling group, for though the cycle is very long, it is in its theatrical requirements no more demanding than the *Castle of Perseverance* or *Mary Magdalen*.

To return for a moment to the case for Lincoln's having been at least the original home of the *N-Town Plays*, it is unfortunate that the earliest reference to the Corpus Christi play in Lincoln is from 1471–72; although the Cotton Vespasian manuscript was probably transcribed a bit later than this, there is nothing to suggest in record and chronology that the *N-Town Plays* originated at Lincoln and then were set wandering elsewhere to be transmuted into another dialect. The Saint Anne's Day play discussed in detail by Craig, and which is richly illustrated in Lincoln documents, does not seem to bear any very close relation to the *N-Town Plays* as we have them, and the Saint Anne's Day play continued to be acted well into the sixteenth century. It is unlikely that such a play would have existed in a Norfolk dialect in a manuscript transcribed in the late fifteenth century. (Several copies of the whole cycle could have existed, of course, but this was apparently not the normal case, certainly not with the others—the Chester case being an exception having little to do with the actual performance of that cycle.) There is, in the argument for Lincoln's being the home of the cycle, no explanation of what the "N. town" reference is doing in the proclamation of a play which, it is argued, had a clear and traditional place of playing such as Lincoln.

All of this is not, of course, to be taken to mean that there is no possibility that the *N-Town Plays* were ever acted at Lincoln. Indeed, it would be improbable that a group with such an elaborate cycle to play would have avoided such a center as Lincoln, in spite of the relatively great distance from Norfolk-Suffolk. I am saying simply that the concrete evidence for the *N-Town Plays* having been the Corpus Christi or Saint Anne's Day play of Lincoln is very slight in spite of Craig's near certainty.[54] I think that the growing argument for a strong dramatic center or group of centers in East Anglia, focused upon one or more great religious house, is a more likely solution of the problem than the location of *N-Town Plays* in a particular town. Religious or secular groups may have travelled from them, some to small towns (with plays like the *Digby* "Conversion of Saint Paul" and the "Killing of the Children" or the *Macro* "Mankind"), others to larger towns with plays like *Mary Magdalen*, the *Castle of Perseverance*, and the *N-Town Plays*. Gail Gibson has recently argued in great detail that the *N-Town Plays* likely had their home at such a religious center and suggests that Bury St. Edmunds is a good candidate for that center.[55] However, in the absence of more convincing records, this can be taken only as an interesting speculation.

The evidence seems to suggest that East Anglian drama in general, with the exception of the drama of Norwich and perhaps of Lynn, was quite different from that of the towns which had great cycles; the East Anglian drama is probably as old, in spite of the lack of records supporting the antiquity of the surviving plays, for the manuscript of the *Castle of Perseverance* is probably from the first part of the fifteenth century. This essential difference of form and perhaps of purpose, the lack of temporal or festal continuity evident in the surviving East Anglian drama (excepting the *Digby* "Killing of the Children," which apparently was once intended for Saint Anne's Day), must be remarked.[56] But, as the evidence seems also to suggest, the civic religious cycles themselves varied greatly from one another, in spite of an occasional borrowing and influence. They all changed their times of performance at one year or another, ranging from Whitsunday in Chester to Saint Anne's Day in Lincoln, from the day before Corpus Christi through the day itself to the succeeding days, for a variety of reasons. The cycles were in the overall control of various groups, ranging from a religious house to a religious guild to the town corporation, all instances showing some indication of change over the century-and-a-half to two centuries of the life of these plays. The broad difference that one should point out between the East Anglian drama and that of the town cycles is to some extent geographic and demographic. There can be no question of original design or intent, but in fact the existing East Anglian drama is a country drama, largely a traveling drama, under whosoever's auspices: it is the drama of a larger, more diversified community than the city drama.

And by its very nature, it is therefore to a greater extent the product of persons who spend much time in solving logistical problems of traveling with considerable baggage, advertising, and locating suitable playing areas (one assumes that such areas became more or less permanently established: the notion of the players of *The Castle* digging a huge ditch, filling it with water, throwing up a dike of dirt, and constructing a palisade every time they played is patently ridiculous);[57] in short, they must have been people who, whatever other religious or secular functions they may have had, became to some degree professional theater people in a way that apparently did not happen so frequently in the great cycle towns. Even in the great towns, professionalism entered whether banned or not, at least in later times. And at Coventry as elsewhere, one individual is from time to time singled out as "shewyng the playe."[58] One takes this phrase to mean being responsible for its production, in short, assuming the jobs of producer and director.

## Production of the Drama

I have left until the end the specific problem of staging the plays because of its complexity, because discussion of each of the cycles has provided some implications relevant to the topic, and because the East Anglian drama has demanded separate treatment. None of the cycles lends itself very easily to modern reconstruction of the way in which it was acted, so far as that can be determined. One must concede from evidence, first of all, that the method of presentation of all of the town cycles was altered to some degree during the course of their lives, as the festival day or days on which they were presented and the pageants themselves were changed. It is clear that the old, appealing, and simple idea of the pageant wagon's rolling through the streets from station to station, performing its play and moving on, followed by its successor, will not do as a paradigm for the whole. But then, an acquaintance with the diversity of surviving records should not have allowed such a simple idea to take hold in any case. That pageant wagons existed is beyond a doubt;[59] that the plays were actually performed on the pageant wagons (and in the streets) is true beyond doubt in certain cases, notably Coventry, and almost certainly true in the case of Chester. Strong arguments have been recently made by Nelson, as we have seen, that in the case of York the wagons were merely *tableaux vivants* and that the plays were not acted in the street-station method at all, but were all acted at one place subsequent to the great procession. Martial Rose, as I noted earlier, urged that the *Wakefield Cycle* was actually presented in something akin to an "in-the-round" method not very different from continental styles and styles which seem to have prevailed in East Anglia. Nelson's arguments about the *York Cycle* derive from the problems presented by the great number of plays, playing stations, the presumed time of travel, waiting, and so forth. He raises a number of important questions about York, but errs, I think, in extrapolating from York to other cycles, though he attempts to avoid this trap. The *N-Town Plays*, rife with manuscript references to "scaffolds," was almost certainly designed to be performed at a fixed locality, though the method has never been satisfactorily described. Southern's *Medieval Theatre in the Round* solves some problems but creates others, some of them posed by Schmitt.[60] It is not likely that we shall ever have more explicit evidence than the drawing in the *Macro* manuscript, and if even this is doubtful in its implications, then we are almost driven to despair. We must conclude that here, as in everything, the English religious drama was, beneath superficial similarity, extremely various.

Modern attempts at production under a variety of circumstances may well be as enlightening as our gleaning of documents. Wickham, as I have observed, has a useful chronological listing of modern productions of this drama from 1901 through 1973. This list is supplemented by annual reports in *Research Opportunities in Renaissance Drama* which give detailed accounts of the methods of production. Emphasis upon production as well as records is also found in the publications of the *Records of Early English Drama*, such traditional journals as *Theatre Notebook* and *Theater Survey*, joined by the new journal from Lancaster, *Medieval English Theatre*. That the theater-in-the-round works well for *Mary Magdalen*, at least, I can attest from our production at the University of Colorado in 1976. Nearly all English religious drama has been performed in recent years, and study of the reports of these productions may be very illuminating. It is altogether appropriate that practical stage experience should go hand-in-hand with documentary study, economics, theology, iconography, editing, and criticism—all our scholarly and critical tools—to advance our understanding of this drama, for this drama required all the talents and resources of its community to create it.

## Conclusions

Of the English religious cycle drama, and of the religious drama as a whole, one can make certain observations of a critical and analytical nature. It was, as was no other form of literary expression of the age, the reflection and work of the community that produced it. It was immediately responsive to that community, both to the secular, economic community and to the religious community, inevitably combined. It was created by both in a manner unique in English literary history: written, at least in the beginning, by the religious, produced and directed, at least later, by the secular, representing the economic power of the community, ranging from what we even today might call "big business" to the poorer sort of artisan group banded together for self-protection. At least until the dissolution of the monasteries, the religious community represented considerable economic power as well. The drama expressed religious devotion and hope of salvation, but it also expressed pride, pride of the economic group and pride for and of the town. That it was not only the creation, by and large, of the whole, but that it was responsive to public reaction is obvious by the many changes of plays during the course of a cycle's life, by the records of fines imposed for poor performing and production. Influenced by traditional preaching analogies, with impressions drawn from ancient iconographical representation of the biblical (and Apocryphal) scenes rich in awesome symbol, comforting in reassurance of the continuity of the whole, incorporating the present with the Creation, Fall, Crucifixion, and Last Judgment— but at the same time endowing those scenes with a rich humor involving a human response to mystery that paralleled on a secular, communal level the austere theological subtleties of interpretation in the religious community— the drama distilled medieval life and belief and employed literary talent of varying degrees of quality in the service of a community in a quite unparalleled way. It apparently died a lingering death, a victim of the attempt, as old as Christendom and its iconoclastic controversies, to resolve the problem of dealing with the visible church. Much has been written about medieval concepts of structure, alleging that overall design and structure are lacking, but this is far from the mark. The drama was always changing, but the design is the play, and it was always complete, like Noah's rainbow.

Contemporary scholarship and criticism, as I observed earlier, has not so much provided understanding as it has made us reconsider old assumptions, and, more important, examine each play and cycle anew. The path forward is clear: further intensive study of records, which seem always to continue turning up if one looks hard enough, and reexamination of those which have been too carelessly considered in the past; continuation and expansion of the almost always happy resurrection of the cycle and religious drama as plays, in every sense of that word; and study of the language—more than just the dialect, but the dramatic language—of English medieval drama. The phrase, alliteration, and tag should tell us a great deal about the relation of the cycles to one another and give us some clearer glimpse into the writers' stock of received ideas, their awareness of one another, and the degree to which the plays attuned themselves to one another.[61] We have for far too long analyzed with appreciation of the work of the "York Realist" or the "Wakefield Master" without providing this appreciation with a context: that context must be the whole cycle, which lived and breathed as a whole. The individual plays caught reflections from one another both deliberate and contextual, contained sermon and satire, and were parts of a continuing celebration, a living Mass, with its powerful sense of awe, despair at sin, and joy in hope, seasoned with a certain satisfaction with the earth in man that made Corpus Christi necessary. Too much concern with the "Wakefield Master" is rather like praising the structure of one part of a religious service over another. He was, and must have considered himself, for all his individualism, a part of the whole as did the builders and decorators of cathedrals. And surely, part of the appreciation of an individual play must be as it fulfills its function within the greater play. No field of literary study is better suited to combining scholarship, editing, and study of language with criticism than that of the English religious drama. We must not study the text, the play as "poem," as is often done with Shakespeare, in isolation from the great pageant itself.

# Notes

1. O. B. Hardison, Jr., *Christian Rite and Christian Drama in the Middle Ages* (Baltimore, Md.: Johns Hopkins University Press, 1965); Glynne Wickham, *Early English Stages, 1300 to 1600* (London: Routledge, 1959; rev. ed., 1980); V. A. Kolve, *The Play Called Corpus Christi* (Stanford, Calif.: Stanford University Press, 1966).

2. *Yale Studies in English*, 103 (New Haven, Conn., 1946).

3. Norman Davis, ed., *Non-Cycle Plays and Fragments*, Early English Text Society, SS 1 (London: 1970), pp. xiv-xxii.

4. Alan H. Nelson, *The Medieval English Stage: Corpus Christi Pageants and Plays* (Chicago: University of Chicago Press, 1974), especially pp. 38–81. See my review in *English Language Notes* 14 (1976): 57–61.

5. F. M. Salter, *Medieval Drama in Chester* (Toronto: University of Toronto Press, 1955), suggests a considerable contribution from the folk drama (pp. 11–12), though the matter of the age of the folk drama, once considered primeval, is now in question, particularly in a work in progress by Michael Preston of the University of Colorado.

6. Eleanor Prosser, *Drama and Religion in the English Mystery Plays*

(Stanford, Calif.: Stanford University Press, 1961), and the good criticism in Arnold Williams, *The Drama of Medieval England* (East Lansing: Michigan State University Press, 1961) in particular; Rosemary Woolf, *The English Mystery Plays* (Berkeley and Los Angeles: University of California Press, 1972).

7. Mary D. Anderson, *Drama and Imagery in English Medieval Churches* (Cambridge: Cambridge University Press, 1963), and Clifford Davidson, *Drama and Art: An Introduction to the Use of Evidence from the Visual Arts for the Study of Early Drama* (Kalamazoo: Medieval Institute, Western Michigan University, 1977) are good points of departure.

8. Under the general editorship of A. F. Johnson: the first three, York, Chester, and Coventry, have proven extremely useful. The Malone Society continues its good work with D. Galloway and J. Wasson's *Records of Plays and Players of Norfolk and Suffolk* (excluding Norwich) in Collections XI, to add to G. E. Dawson's volume on Kent (Collections VII) and Stanley J. Kahrl's on Lincolnshire (Collections VIII). J. Coldewey's volume on Essex was announced as Collections XIII of the series, but will now appear in the Records of Early English Drama program.

9. Under the general editorship of Clifford Davidson, whose volume *York Art: A Subject List of Extant and Lost Art* (Kalamazoo: Medieval Institute, Western Michigan University, 1978) with David O'Connor sets a good example for the series.

10. See Glynne Wickham, *The Medieval Theatre* (London: Weidenfeld and Nicolson, 1974) for a partial list of performances since the beginning of the century, pp. 221-26.

11. See the discussion of this by Salter, *Medieval Drama in Chester*, pp. 41-42, and Hardin Craig, *English Religious Drama in the Middle Ages* (Oxford: Clarendon Press, 1955; hereafter cited as *ERD*), pp. 166-70.

12. Only the first volume of two has appeared (1974); the second volume with notes, glossary and commentary is eagerly awaited. Another volume, *The Chester Mystery Cycle: Essays and Documents* (Chapel Hill, N.C.: University of North Carolina Press, 1983), has just appeared by the same editors.

13. Woolf, *English Mystery Plays*, p. 64.

14. Kolve, *The Play Called Corpus Christi*, pp. 57-100.

15. Ibid., p. 96.

16. Craig, *ERD*, pp. 66-70, summarizing the theory of Marius Sepet in *Les prophètes du Christ: ètude sur les origines du théâtre au moyen âge* (Paris: Didier, 1878).

17. Woolf, *English Mystery Plays*, pp. 64-66.

18. Ibid., p. 65. Lucy Toulmin Smith in her edition of the *York Plays* (Oxford: Clarendon Press, 1885), pp. xlii-l, has suggested the

*Cursor Mundi* as an impulse behind the creation of the cycle, and northern devotional treatises, particularly the translation of the pseudo-Bonaventura *Meditationes vitae Christi*, for some of the "New Testament" material.

19. British Library Add. MS. 35290, formerly in the Ashburnham Library.

20. Though Smith, *York Plays*, had suggested (p. xlv) that the age of the cycle "may safely be set as far back as 1340 or 1350," she knew of no documentary evidence before 1378. The 1376 date is from a record of the rental of a storage space for three pageants; see A. C. Cawley, ed., *Everyman and Medieval Miracle Plays* (London: Dent; New York: Dutton, 1956), p. x.

21. Burton's lists are reprinted by Smith, in *York Plays*, pp. xviii–xxvii. See also Johnston and Rogerson, eds., *York*, Records of Early English Drama, vol. 2, appendix 6, Toronto: University of Toronto Press, 1980, pp. 657–85; and Richard Beadle's edition of the *York Plays* (London: Arnold, 1982), pp. 23–27.

22. Salter, *Drama in Chester*, pp. 55–56, from Rogers's description; and Smith, *York Plays*, pp. xxxii–xxxiii.

23. So much has been written on these plays that one is best referred simply to A. J. Mill's bibliography, part 12 of the fifth volume of *A Manual of Writings in Middle English*, ed. Albert E. Hartung (Hamden, Conn.: Archon Books/Shoe String Press for the Connecticut Academy of Arts and Sciences, 1975), pp. 1315–56, 1557–98. It is easy to point out, however, that the general trend of criticism has been much more appreciative since A. P. Rossiter's dismissal of many as crude in *English Drama from Early Times to the Elizabethans: Its Backgrounds, Origins, and Developments* (New York and London: Barnes and Noble, 1950); one might particularly cite recent studies such as Stanley J. Kahrl's general *Traditions of Medieval English Drama* (London: Hutchinson, 1974); Martial Rose's introduction to his *The Wakefield Mystery Plays* (London: Evan Bros., 1961); John Gardner's *The Construction of the Wakefield Cycle* (Carbondale and Edwardsville: Southern Illinois University Press, 1974); and the several essays of M. Stevens which will undoubtedly be reflected in his forthcoming edition with A. C. Cawley, of the *Towneley Plays* for the Early English Text Society. Particularly to be noted, however, is his explanation of the lacunae in the Towneley manuscript, including loss of banns and two or three plays, as owing to Reformation censorship; "The Missing Parts of the Towneley Cycle," *Speculum* 45 (1970): 254–65. The manuscript is now in the Huntington Library, MS. HM1.

24. See Cawley, *Everyman*, pp. xvi–xvii.

25. Gardner, *Construction*, pp. 133–40.

26. Rose, *Wakefield Mystery Plays*, pp. 29–46, and Nelson, *Medieval English Stage*, pp. 82–87, argue for the single fixed station, but Cawley, *Everyman* p. xxv,

assumes a processional performance.

27. Rose, *Wakefield Mystery Plays*, pp. 23-37.

28. A. F. Leach's *Beverley Town Documents*, Selden Society (London, 1900), pp. lviii-lix, lists plays. Also see his "Some English Plays and Players," in *An English Miscellany Presented to Dr. Furnivall in Honour of His Seventy-Fifth Birthday* (Oxford: Clarendon Press, 1901), pp. 205-34.

29. Hardin Craig, ed., *Two Coventry Corpus Christi Plays*, Early English Text Society, ES 87 (Oxford, 1902), p. xxxiv.

30. O. Waterhouse, ed., *The Non-Cycle Mystery Plays Together with the Croxton Play of the Sacrament and the Pride of Life*, Early English Text Society, ES 104 (London, 1909).

31. Davis, *Non-Cycle Plays*, pp. xl-xliv.

32. Ibid., p. xliii:

33. Ibid., pp. xxii-xxxvi.

34. See Alan H. Nelson, "Recovering the Lost Norwich Corpus Christi Cycle," *Comparative Drama* 4 (1970): 241-52, and J. Dutka, "Mystery Plays at Norwich: Their Formation and Development," *Leeds Studies in English* 10 (1979): 107-20, for two efforts to reconstruct the cycle.

35. Craig, *Two Coventry Corpus Christi Plays*, p. xi.

36. Alan H. Nelson, "Configuration of Stages in Medieval English Drama," in *Medieval English Drama: Essays Critical and Contextual*, ed. Jerome Taylor and Alan H. Nelson (Chicago: University of Chicago Press, 1972), p. 28.

37. Craig, *Two Coventry Corpus Christi Plays*, pp. xxvi-xxxiv.

38. Thomas Sharp, *The Pageant of the Sheremen and Taylors, in Coventry* (Coventry, 1817).

39. Craig, *Two Coventry Corpus Christi Plays*, p. 90. See also R. W. Ingram, ed., *Coventry*, Records of Early English Drama (Toronto: University of Toronto Press, 1981), p. xix.

40. Ingram, *Coventry*, p. 98.

41. Taken from the records printed by Craig in *Two Coventry Corpus Christi Plays*, passim. Craig, *ERD*, p. 295, uses the prominence of Croo, "ignorant, inept, and pompous..." to explain the shoddy aspects of both the Sheremen's and Taylors' and the Weavers' pageants; since Craig could have known nothing of what Croo actually did to the plays, this seems excessive. Croo represented to Craig the later degeneration of the plays in their natural life cycle; for all we know, Croo may have vastly improved them. His pomposity can be inferred only from his activity, which seems a presumptuous inference. Croo would seem merely to have been one of those enthusiastic persons who make any sort of civic activity "go," and to whom the companies looked for work of all sorts (writing, acting, costuming)—a semi-

professional, in short.

42. Craig, *Two Coventry Corpus Christi Plays*, p. 86.

43. Ibid., pp. 98, 103.

44. W. W. Greg, "Bibliographical and Textual Problems of the English Miracle Plays," *The Library*, 3rd ser., 5 (1914): 365–99 (part 4 is the *Ludus Coventriae*.

45. K. S. Block, *Ludus Coventriae, or The Plaie Called Corpus Christi, Cotton MS. Vespasian D. viii*, Early English Text Society, ES 120 (London, 1922 for 1917). The reference after the title is to the British Library classification.

46. P. Meredith and Stanley J. Kahrl, eds., *The N-Town Plays*, Leeds Texts and Monographs, Medieval Drama Facsimiles, general editors, A. C. Cawley and S. Ellis, University of Leeds School of English, 1977.

47. S. Spector, "The Composition and Development of an Eclectic Manuscript: Cotton Vespasian D. VIII," *Leeds Studies in English* 9 (1977 for 1976 and 1977): 62–83.

48. Ibid., p. 77.

49. See Block, *Ludus Coventriae*, pp. xxxiv–xxxv, and Spector, "Composition and Development," passim.

50. See Craig, *ERD*, pp. 267–80; Stanley J. Kahrl and K. Cameron, "The N-Town Plays at Lincoln," *Theatre Notebook* 20 (1965–66): 61–69; C. Gauvin, *Un cycle du théatre religieux anglais au moyen âge: Le jeu de la ville de "N."* (Paris: Centre national de la recherche scientifique, 1973), pp. 63–92.

51. Stanley J. Kahrl, *Records of Plays and Players in Lincolnshire, 1300–1585*, Collections, VIII, The Malone Society (Oxford, 1969 [1974]).

52. Stanley J. Kahrl and K. Cameron, "Staging the N-Town Cycle," *Theatre Notebook* 21 (1967): 122–38.

53. E. J. Dobson, "The Etymology and Meaning of *Boy*," *Medium Aevum* 9 (1940); 146; and also M. Eccles, "*Ludus Coventriae*: Lincoln or Norfolk?" *Medium Aevum* 40 (1971): 135–41.

54. Craig, *ERD*, 267–80.

55. Gail Gibson, "Bury St. Edmunds, Lydgate, and the *N-Town Cycle*," *Speculum* 56 (1981): 56–90.

56. On this point see my introduction to the Early English Text Society edition of *The Digby Plays*, OS 283 (Oxford, 1982), pp. lx–lxi.

57. Richard Southern, *The Medieval Theatre in the Round: A Study of the Staging of "The Castle of Perseverance" and Related Matters* (London: Faber and Faber, 1957), pp. 20–27. For evidence of permanent village and town "game-places" see K. M. Dodd, "Another Elizabethan Theater in the Round," *Shakespeare Quarterly* 21 (1970): 125–56; R. Wright, "Community Theater in Late Medieval East Anglia," *Theatre Notebook* 28 (1974): 24–39;

H. R. L. Beadle's doctoral thesis, "The Medieval Drama of East Anglia" (University of York, 1977), I: 166–240, and his article, "The East Anglian 'Game-Place': A Possibility for Further Research," *Records of Early English Drama* 1 (1978): 2–4.

58. Craig, *Two Coventry Corpus Christi Plays*, p. 103; and J. Coldeway, "The Digby Plays and the Chelmsford Records," *Research Opportunities in Renaissance Drama* 18 (1975): 104.

59. The two issues of volume 1 (1979) of *Medieval English Theatre* are devoted to a series of papers on the evidence of the wagons given at a conference on the subject held at the University of Lancaster on 7 April 1979.

60. R. Hosley, "Three Kinds of Outdoor Theatre Before Shakespeare," *Theater Survey* 12 (1971): 1–33; and N. C. Schmitt, "Was There a Medieval Theatre in the Round?" *Theatre Notebook* 23, 24 (1969): 1–15, 14–21.

61. In this connection the series of concordances being undertaken by M. J. Preston and J. Pfleiderer at the University of Colorado is of particular importance. The *Chester Cycle* has now been published, as have the "Wakefield Plays" of the *Towneley Cycle* (New York, 1981, 1982). *The Macro Plays* and the *Digby Plays* had earlier been concorded (Ann Arbor, Mich., 1977). The other cycles and groups are in progress, and eventually the entire English medieval drama will be melded in a KWIC (Key Word in Context) concordance. It will then be possible to compare any words or phrases, any stage directions, any speakers, with those of any other plays; much should be learned about "borrowing" and the community of language in the drama. I described some of these possibilities in a paper, "A Report on Applications Possible of the Material in the 'Archives' of the Center for Research in Early English Drama at Boulder, Colorado," read at the Medieval Institute at Kalamazoo, Mich., May 8, 1981.

# O Moral Henryson

## C. David Benson

### I

Both the time and place of Robert Henryson's birth were unfortunate for his modern critical reputation. As a Scotsman, he is still sometimes seen as a provincial author whose subjects are *wee beasties* and local social conditions, instead of being recognized as probably the last great medieval poet of Europe. As a fifteenth-century author, he is automatically labeled a "Chaucerian," with the result that he is usually compared exclusively with this single predecessor and only rarely with the other Ricardian poets: John Gower, the *Gawain*-poet, and William Langland. Henryson does owe much to Chaucer, but his verse is not saturated with the older poet's tag phrases as is the work of many English Chaucerians like John Lydgate; the influence is instead deeper and more subtle. Henryson's handling of dialogue, characterization, and word choice, in addition to the complex narrators of the *Testament of Cresseid* and some of the *Fables*, are certainly indebted to Chaucer, as are his playful stance toward his material and his sense of what need *not* be said. But despite these similarities, Henryson also reveals an equally deep poetic kinship with the other great fourteenth-century English poets.

To call Henryson the last of the Ricardian poets is, of course, only a metaphor and not a historical fact, but it is astonishing how much his work resembles those characteristics of the Ricardians defined by John Burrow. Space does not permit a detailed analysis of each, but some of the qualities central to both Henryson and the Ricardians are a "pervasively ironic mode of address," an "authentic story-telling style," use of old stories (all three of Henryson's major works are traditional stories), "a strongly literary sense of form and structure in their handling of text-divisions," effective use of detail, an "elusive way of working within the exemplary mode" (which will be the principal subject herein), an "unheroic image of man," "a sense of humour" (as opposed to wit), and the use of " 'proverbial' similes."[1] Henryson is also like the Ricardians in more specific ways. When he declares that Aesopian *Fables* were intended to appeal to both high and low estate, he recalls Gower's claim in *Confessio Amantis* to "go the middel weie," writing "somewhat of lust, somewhat of lore."[2] Similarly, he is like the *Gawain*-poet in his combination of alliteration and rhyme and in his precise, concrete descriptions, especially of nature.[3]

The Ricardian poet that Henryson resembles most closely, however, is William Langland.[4] Their most obvious similarities are the ability to mix strong allegory with detailed, energetic narrative and a real feeling for ordinary life expressed in their compassion for the poor and their indignation at social corruption. The more profound similarities between the two poets, principally their ability to explore serious moral questions in poetry of the highest quality, will be noted throughout these pages.

## II

That Henryson, like Langland, is explicitly and essentially a didactic and moral poet, and not a court, love, or occasional poet, has long been recognized; but the skill and originality of his achievement have not always been sufficiently appreciated.[5] The most obvious manifestation of his desire to instruct and improve is also his longest work: the *Morall Fabillis of Esope the Phrygian*, as the early printed editions call it. Henryson's *Fables*, which are generally considered the greatest medieval example of this continually popular genre, comprise a prologue and thirteen narratives (the fables proper), each of which is followed by a clearly labeled *moralitas*.[6]

Because the appropriateness of the individual *moralitas* to the events of its narrative is not always clear, the division of each fable has caused problems for commentators. As Richard J. Schrader states, "No critical problem in Henryson is more important than the relationship of his tales to their *moralitates*."[7] Three solutions to this problem have been proposed, each of which has the unfortunate effect of simplifying the moral thought of the *Fables*. The older view, which is not entirely extinguished today, regards the *moralitates* as conventional, tedious, and irrelevant to Henryson's poetic genius, whose virtues are humor, narrative skill, and human sympathy. This very limited conception of Henryson, which is something like seeing Langland as primarily a poet of medieval English rural life, results in an almost total disregard for the second part of each fable.[8] More recently, other critics have gone almost to the opposite extreme in insisting upon the absolute thematic unity between *moralitas* and narrative, despite superficial dissonance.[9] These critics sometimes become overly ingenious in their attempts to harmonize both parts of each fable and run the risk of presenting Henryson as no more than a mechanical versifier, however skillful, of medieval orthodoxies. Nevertheless, they are right to stress both the poet's moral seriousness and the need to include the *moralitates* in any full interpretation of the *Fables*.[10] A third group of resolutely modern critics, reacting against the view of Henryson as either kindly or traditional, claims that the gap between story and morality indicates a deep pessimism in Henryson that questions the very order of the universe.[11] This argument, while of real interest, is almost impossible historically and is finally as reductive as the other two. In seeing only a modern despair in the *Fables*, these critics rob Henryson of his own serious, complex, and thoroughly medieval moral vision.

All three groups of critics recognize at least some discord, however superficial, between Henryson's narratives and *moralitates*, but none has adequately explained the purpose of these differences. James Kinsley, for example, declares that the "moral applications" are "often too ingenious for modern taste."[12] The ingenuity is there, but it is a reason for congratulation, not complaint. I suggest that what readers like Kinsley take to be a blemish in Henryson's art is the key to the correct understanding of the *Fables*. The frequent gaps between story and moral are deliberate and serve to make the reader aware of other tensions and conflicts in the work. Although Henryson is a Christian philosophical poet, he does not offer simple, reductive lessons, as has sometimes been assumed.[13] The *moralitates* alert us to the moral seriousness of the *Fables*, but they do not themselves entirely contain it, for Henryson is no dispensor of easy platitudes. Like the Ricardian poets he offers no pat answers, and so his lessons are more difficult and more exhilarating than they seem at first. By exploiting the dissonance between story and moral to lead the reader into the deeper complexities of his work, he teaches us not what to think, but how to think.[14] The result is a justification of the art of the fable and a demonstration that it can be a more entertaining, more demanding, and ultimately more successful teacher than conventional, straightforward moral instruction.

In his prologue to the *Fables*, Henryson makes clear that his moral art is not simple. Two images insist that while his *sentences* are delightful, they are only to be discovered with difficulty.[15]

> In lyke manner as throw a bustious eird,
> Swa it be laubourit with grit diligence,

> Springis the flouris and the corne abreird,
> Hailsum and gude to mannis sustenence;
> Sa springis thair ane morall sweit sentence
> Oute of the subtell dyte of poetry,
> To gude purpose, quha culd it weill apply.
>
> The nuttis schell, thocht it be hard and teuch,
> Haldis the kirnell, sueit and delectabill;
> Sa lyis thair ane doctrine wyse aneuch
> And full of frute, vnder ane fenʒeit fabill.
>
> (lines 8–18)

The image of cultivation, developed from a simpler simile in Gualterus Anglicus, emphasizes the great effort needed to bring forth the desired moral product.[16] This effort is one that, as Denton Fox suggests, is probably demanded of the reader: it is he who must struggle with poetry whose complexity is insisted upon ("subtell dyte") in order to make it yield the flower and corn of "ane morall sweit sentence."[17] And that is not the end of his contribution; Henryson declares that the *sentence* will have a good effect only as long as the reader fully participates in the application: "quha culd it weill apply." The second, even more traditional image, that of the nut, emphasizes the pleasant reward for such moral effort. Again Henryson insists on the difficulty of his hard, tough poetry (line 15), but, in contrast to those who find him pessimistic, the poet also promises that the result of his moral poetry will be "delectabill," just as in the previous image it was associated with life and rebirth. Henryson's is not a harsh, dry teaching but one that is "hailsum and gude to mannis sustenence."[18]

After instructing us in the difficulty of reading the *Fables*, Henryson significantly begins the collection with his most flagrant and most frequently commented on example of disunity between narrative and morality, "The Cock and the Jasp." It becomes the model by which we are taught to read all the fables that follow. In the story, the cock finds a jasper swept into the dirt by careless girls but rejects it as too precious for him and useless in his pursuit of food. His conclusion would seem reasonable enough, but the *moralitas* condemns him for choosing material pleasure over wisdom. Those who say that such a conclusion goes against the tone of the narrative are certainly correct in one sense, but they ignore Henryson's purpose in creating such a conflict.[19]

The tension between the two parts of this fable is itself the most important lesson and shows us by example the difficulty of accomplishing genuine moral instruction. In the *moralitas* to "The Cock and the Jasp," Henryson builds on the apology for fables found in his sources and confronts the wider questions of discovering, recognizing, and using wisdom.[20] "Perfite prudence and cunning" (line 128), symbolized by the jasper, is easy to overlook, as the "damisellis wantoun and insolent" (line 71) do when they sweep it out of the house, but it is also possible to ignore even when seen directly, as by the cock or by an inattentive audience. The first fable demonstrates that real moral teaching is not as simple as it sometimes seems. It is one thing for a preacher or poet to provide a moral lesson, another to have it understood and accepted. Yet unless that is done, all instruction, however true and useful, is merely dust to lazy housekeepers, jasps to cocks, or pearls to swine (line 147). The gap between tale and lesson in the first fable initiates the reader into the difficulty of achieving true wisdom, which is always "tynt and hid" (line 155). To be truly possessed, wisdom must not be merely passively accepted but actively and continually striven for (line 153), as rarely happens: "We seik it nocht, nor preis it for to find" (line 156). The active verbs suggest the same effort and personal involvement demanded in the prologue: a labor of discrimination and judgment that Henryson's indirect method of teaching both advocates and trains.[21]

Another and even more revealing way in which Henryson indicates that the reader needs to go beyond automatic acceptance of the *moralitas* to discover the full wisdom of the *Fables* is his practice of including moral instruction within the narratives themselves.[22] This additional level of *sententia* once again stresses the complexity of moral choice and warns us against conclusions that are too facile. Some of these passages, like the warning in "The Two Mice" that "efter ioy oftymes cummis cair, / And troubill efter grit prosperitie" (lines 290–91), serve primarily to emphasize or deepen the concluding *moralitas*. Others, however, are in conflict with the end, such as the quite impassioned stanza in "The Trial of the Fox" on the foolishness of risking one's soul for wealth that will be enjoyed by an ungrateful heir (lines 831–37), a lesson that is more worldly than the one in the *moralitas* on the temptations that beset men of religion.[23] Although many such moral passages within the narrative are brief, "The Preaching of the Swallow" begins with an elaborate discussion of God's wisdom and the order of the seasons (lines 1622–1712) that is more powerful in itself, and seems to have a more profound relation to the fable, than the concluding *moralitas*.[24]

The most important example of a fable with moral comment within the narrative is "The Cock and the Fox." This wonderful tale, which plays with, responds to, and is almost the equal of Chaucer's *Nun's Priest's Tale* (while remaining quite independent), illustrates much about the complexity and wit of Henryson's moral teaching.[25] His most important addition, the speeches of Chantecleir's three wives after they believe he has been killed by the fox (which are for Henryson what the long speeches on dreams are for Chaucer), is not reflected in the *moralitas* at all. These speeches have almost no narrative function (the death they are discussing has not really happened, and all takes place during the stasis of the widow's "swoun"), but they are one of Henryson's most brilliant demonstrations of the difficulties of moral judgment.

The first speech is by Pertok, whose words are undercut before they even begin with an inappropriately human detail that is perhaps better than any in the *Nun's Priest's Tale*: we are told that as she makes her mourning "teiris grit attour hir cheikis fell" (line 496). Her words, highly rhetorical and including "a parody of the formal lament for the dead,"[26] regret the loss of one who was for his wives a reliable time piece, an entertainer, a breaker of bread, and as good a lover as nature allowed (lines 495–508). All this is conventional enough, but now Chantecleir's second wife, Sprutok, has her say, in words that are more colloquial in style and very different in content. She dismisses Pertok's sentiments and asserts that she intends to be a gay widow since their husband was not only harsh but a poor lover: "Let quik to quik, and deid ga to the deid" (line 522). That Pertok and Sprutok respond so differently to the same situation already suggests the difficulty any commentator has in interpreting events.

The problem is then further complicated when Pertok responds with a second speech that totally contradicts her first. She now declares that a score of such as Chantecleir could not entirely satisfy his wives (this is especially funny when we remember how cocksure is Chaucer's bird), and she vows to find them a lover within a week who "suld better claw oure breik" (line 529). Now that Henryson has made us begin to doubt the whole procedure of drawing reliable conclusions from events, the third henwife, Coppok (or Toppok), utters "lyke ane curate" (line 530) a sermon which in its simple-minded self-righteousness and haste to draw moral lessons is almost a parody of a conventional *moralitas*.[27] She asserts that Chantecleir was punished by God because he would not repent of his lecherous adultery. In this last speech especially, Henryson the moralist, like Chaucer in his parallel beast fable, suggests the dangers of automatically accepting easy moral certainties. Coppok is a chicken who condemns a sin (adultery) in which she also participates and who sees "the verray hand off God" (line 542) in a death which has not, in fact, even happened. Henryson even goes so far as to make Coppok's moral conclusions ("Prydefull he was, and ioyit off his sin" [line 537]) somewhat resemble his own *moralitas* ("Fy, puft vp pryde, thow is full poysonabill" [line 593]). Likewise, the conclusion to this same *moralitas* ("Thir twa sinnis, flatterie and vaneglore, / Ar vennomous" [line 612–13]) must raise a smile in the reader who remembers that what is venomous in the *Nun's Priest's Tale* is far less serious, if more unpleasant—laxatives.

Henryson's playing with moral instruction here does not mean that he is cynical or a bitter pessimist, only that he wishes to illustrate the difficulty of attaining true wisdom. Lessons are easy enough to come by (even hens provide them!), but the problem as shown in these four speeches is deciding which lessons apply to which situations ("quha cleirlie vnderstude" [line 610]). The reader must finally teach himself.

The moral complexity of these tales is equalled by the artistic complexity of the *moralitates,* which are variously long, short, satirical, angry, or pleading. Much less detailed critical comment has been expended on this part of each fable than on the narratives (and almost none on their artistry), yet they are not merely mechanical, reductive lessons. They often contain as much wit and art as the fables proper and are as "sueit" and "delectabill" as the prologue promises.[28] For example, in the *moralitas* to the first fable, Henryson compares the cock to one who feeds precious stones to swine (lines 141–47). This is clever use of the human/animal confusion, which is one of the hallmarks of the genre (a rooster feeding pigs?), with a profoundly serious biblical echo (Matthew 7:6). The *moralitas* to the second fable contains an illustration of Henryson's talent for establishing an intimate narrative relationship with the reader: "Thy awin fyre, freind, thocht it be bot ane gleid, / It warmis weill, and is worth gold to the" (lines 389–90). More dramatic, but equally effective appeals to the reader can be found in the description of death and damnation at lines 1930–36 and in the touching prayer to Mary that concludes the abstract allegory of "The Trial of the Fox" (lines 1139–45). Henryson frequently demonstrates that he has lavished as much poetic skill on his moralities as on his stories. The *moralitas* to "The Preaching of the Swallow," for example, cleverly develops the image of a seed from the story (lines 1902–08). Likewise, the *moralitas* to "The Fox, the Wolf, and the Husbandman" contains two fine allegorical passages: the woods, which play almost no part in the narrative, are carefully presented as a symbol of the dangers of riches (lines 2441–47), and the wolf's desire for the cheese is described as covetousness, which tempts man into a well of vices leading straight to hell (lines 2448–54). The latter passage is not only a witty expansion of the incident in the fable but is even more dramatically narrated: "Dryuand ilk man to leip in the buttrie / That dounwart drawis vnto the pane of hell" (lines 2452–53).[29]

Some of the often neglected *moralitates* contain even better and more powerful poetry than their narratives. For example, the moralities to "The Sheep and the Dog" and "The Wolf and the Lamb," both of which are quite lengthy and whose numerical sequence (fables VI and XII) may be significant,[30] are passionate denunciations of injustice that reveal an unsentimental but deeply sympathetic compassion for the poor that is reminiscent of Langland.[31] The *moralitas* to the first of this pair contains such sophisticated literary devices as the active involvement of the narrator (lines 1276-85) and speeches and actions that are presented dramatically and without allegorization (for example, lines 1286-92).[32] The sheep's lament to God, which begins, "O lord, quhy sleipis thow sa lang?" (line 1295), is justly famous and makes the reader feel close to the sufferer for the first time in the entire fable.[33] The second *moralitas* (fable XII) contains several direct addresses to the various oppressors of the poor and much precise, emotionally charged poetry whose specific details do not obscure the general application (see for example, lines 2749-55).

Henryson presents his moral teaching with such indirection, complexity, and art because, like the other great Ricardian poets, he knows that it is one thing to state a truth, another to have it accepted, understood, and acted upon.[34] Standard moral lessons, while not wrong, may be too facile or limited to offer real guidance. Such mechanical lessons are like the often contradictory proverbs that Henryson scatters so freely throughout the *Fables*: they are of limited use because they demand that the reader exercise his own judgment in choosing and applying the correct lesson to a specific situation.[35] To be truly understood a moral question must be explored and experienced, and poetry offers a way of doing that by engaging fully our minds and emotions. The country mouse in "The Two Mice" is aware from the first of the tale's *moralitas*—"Ane modicum is mair for till allow,/ Swa that gude will be keruer at the dais,/ Than thrawin vult and mony spycit mais" (lines 236-38)—yet at this point she is unable to convince her city sister or even herself to follow this truth. Although her terrifying experiences as a bourgeois beast only bring the mouse to her original conclusion (lines 343-52, which is further developed in the *moralitas*), having actually gone through these events so skillfully told by Henryson, she now understands the same lesson in a more profound way—and so do we as readers. Henryson, like the other Ricardians, knows that real moral knowledge comes only after effort, struggle, and questioning, and this knowledge is finally his justification for the *Fables*. They are not merely a pleasant diversion, but, as his images of cultivation and the tough nut in the prologue indicate, something both more organic and more difficult.[36] The poet uses the pleasures of poetry to lead the reader into the complex moral questioning and affirmation that is possible only in the greatest art. As Henryson declares in the prologue, the "subtell dyte" of his poetry leads the reader to a "morall sweit sentence."

How hard it is to make moral teaching truly effective is demonstrated in the fable that is generally recognized as one of Henryson's best and that is often discussed as the key to his collection: "The Preaching of the Swallow."[37] The fable opens with a discussion of the "hie prudence" and "profound wit" (lines 1622-23) of God in contrast to the ignorance of man, which suggests the folly of any attempts to rely on our own knowledge. This realization is closely related to what seems to me the most important theme in the tale, although it has largely gone unnoticed: the demonstration of the ineffectuality of standard orthodox moral preaching, even when its message is absolutely correct and of vital importance to its audience.[38] The swallow, who thrice warns the other birds of mortal danger from the fowler, is identified in the *moralitas* as a "halie preichour" (line 1924), and yet Henryson has constructed his tale so that we are forced to question, if not the truth of the swallow's words, at least the manner of their presentation. Unquestionably the birds are foolish to disregard his dire warnings, as events make clear, but some of the responsibility for the deadly outcome rests with the swallow's method of teaching. The swallow's first warning that a farmer is sowing flax seeds which will ultimately become the material for nets (lines 1736-61) may appear unduly alarmist even to the reader because the danger is so remote and the warning is actually sounded (lines 1736-40) before the problem itself (the flax sowing) is even identified (lines 1743-47). The lark's objection that the swallow is only imagining the worst has some truth, even though the proverbs he uses to prove this indicate his own blindness (lines 1762-67).[39] The swallow's second warning is a further example of ineffective preaching (lines 1789-1800). Once more we may assume that his words are literally delivered from on high (see line 1735). Because they are so pompous and insulting ("O blind birds, and full of negligence" [line 1790]), they again fail to reach their audience, even though a truth that is not heard is useless. The birds' concern for their stomachs (lines 1804-06) is certainly unwise, but the preacher himself is not without blame.

The swallow's third warning, which begs the birds not to go into the trap, is the crucial one (lines 1853-59). If they heed him now, they will be safe, but he is no more successful than before. In their hunger, the birds prefer the literal chaff of the fowler to the symbolic fruit of the swallow's preaching. In fact, they totally ignore him (line 1869) and do not even answer as they go to their pitiful deaths, which the narrator describes with great emotion (lines 1874-80). The swallow is left in sorrowful and solitary self-righteousness, uttering a sigh that is like Troilus's at the end of the *Testament of Cresseid*: "Now ar thay deid, and wo is me thairfoir!" (line 1886). The swallow may blame the birds for ignoring his advice (lines 1882-84), but Henryson has shown that moral teaching, however sound, must reach and involve the audience to be of any use.[40] He elsewhere suggests that his *Fables*, which do just that, may, unlike conventional preaching, save us from Satan the Fowler, whose attack is so vividly described in the *moralitas* (lines 1930-36).

Henryson has already alerted us to his justification for fables at the beginning of his previous tale, "The Lion and the Mouse." There the poet dreams he meets Aesop, whom he asks for "ane prettie fabill/Concludand with ane gude moralitie" (lines 1386-87). The *auctorite* at first refuses to tell such a tale because of the sinfulness of men who lack devotion to God, "The eir is deif, the hart is hard as stane" (line 1393). He then asks in despair, "For quhat is it worth to tell ane fenȝeit taill, / Quhen haly preiching may na thing auaill?" (lines 1389-90). The answer that Henryson suggests with characteristic indirection is that feigned fables are useful precisely because the deaf ears and hard hearts of men often make direct preaching ineffective. The "Preaching of the Swallow" demonstrates that such explicit admonition, even when warning of genuine disaster, is often ignored. The solution, however, is not the despair to which Aesop momentarily gives in. Even though preaching, however holy, "may na thing auaill," a fable may avail, as Henryson the dreamer politely and delicately suggests, "Quha wait nor I may leir and beir away/Sum thing thairby heirefter may auaill?" (lines 1402-03). Although Henryson is a poet of moral truth, he also knows, as the fable of the "Cock and the Fox" demonstrates, that lies inspired by a "gude spirit" (line 558), just like feigned fables, may be the most efficacious words of all. If Henryson admires as well as disapproves of the clever fox, as Douglas Gray claims, perhaps it is because deceptive language and tricks played on an audience are not all that far from his own method.[41] Henryson is a poet who teaches us to value what is direct and true through poetry that is frequently neither.

# III

Once we recognize the intricacy of Henryson's moral thought and understand that it goes beyond the apparent lessons of the *moralitates*, it is possible to identify some of the deeper themes of the *Fables*, which are presented with his usual indirection. Like Langland, Henryson finds this a harsh world and continually emphasizes the limitations of man's power and his absolute need for God's mercy. The surprising good news of the work, however, is that the almost overwhelming pain of earthly existence is more than compensated for by the love of God.

No one who reads the *Fables* carefully can doubt that its world is terribly hard, with little peace, comfort, or companionship—the very opposite of many modern animal stories like *The Wind in the Willows*: "The transience of life and the sudden, unexpected coming of death is strongly felt."[42] Hunger is frequent in the *Fables*, as are sudden disasters and traps; mere survival is difficult, and images of the ups and downs of Fortune are common (for example, lines 303-33, 2418-19, 2891-92, 2939-40). If the creation is cruel in the *Fables*, its creatures are crueler still. The animals, who are the principal cause of their own misery and destruction because of "lust and appetyte" (line 53), present a frightening picture of sin and its consequence. With one notable exception, desire, will, and selfishness rule characters who are devoid of love or kindness and are frequently described as outlaws, thieves, and lovers of darkness (for example, lines 168, 203, 253-54, 618-20, 959, 2294).[43] Most of the animals seem locked into mechanical enmities and often act out the most primitive and brutal impulses, such as the bizarre, heartless treatment given his father's corpse by the aptly named "Father-war" in "The Trial of the Fox" (lines 796-830).[44]

The *Fables* are a powerful demonstration of the vanity of human pretensions, revealing again and again in the animal figures the limitations of human power and self-sufficiency. Perhaps the most terrifying example of this is the wether in "The Wolf and the Wether," who protects his flock disguised as a dog and even manages to make a hungry wolf run for his life. His success in only illusory, however, and once his false skin is stripped away his only defense against the indignant wolf is the lame one that he was not in earnest but only playing (lines 2558-59, 2578). For Henryson all practical effort by humans, every attempt to be self-reliant, is finally a joke and nothing but play. Nevertheless, the reward we can expect is deadly earnest indeed, as the fate of the wether proves: "Than be the crag-bane smertlie he [the wolf] him tuke,/Or euer he ceissit, and it in schunder schuke" (lines 2586-87). Men as purely natural beings, as animals, are isolated, unloved, and doomed—neither innocence, as several sheep discover, nor even cleverness, as father and son foxes learn in fables IV and V, can guarantee safety.

Like Langland throughout *Piers Plowman*, Henryson in his narratives and *moralitates* presents rational and practical solutions to the human condition only to show their inadequacy in such a world as this.[45] The apparently sensible *moralitas* of "The Two Mice," for instance, that small possessions bring "sickernes" and "blyithnes" (lines 373-96), is too smug and worldly a final answer.[46] As the narrative and the first stanza of the *moralitas* itself indicate, the deeper answer is the impossibility of real comfort or safety anywhere on this earth (lines 365-72). Although the country mouse may be wise to reject the city mouse's life, we should not overlook the real misery of her own situation (lines 169-70). The same fable continually exposes pretensions that are more human than mouselike. The urban sister is described as a solid bourgeois citizen with rights and privileges (lines 171-75), but, of course, she is really no more than a thief. Similarly, we almost believe in her great feast so lavishly described until the entrances of first the spenser and then the cat reveal how little and vulnerable the mice are. Later fables show even more clearly the inadequacy of the Horatian modesty of life advocated in "The Two Mice." The sheep in "The Sheep and the Dog" apparently lives humbly, but the law is so perverted—revealing the failure of another human institution—that the poor beast, far from being left with his small possessions, is forced to lose the very wool off his back.[47] Denton Fox notes that the second half of the *Fables* is bleaker than the first: "all virtuous persuasions are ineffective, and all evil ones obeyed."[48] The worldly advice of "The Two Mice," which is shown to be ineffective in "The Sheep and the Dog," is fatal in the next to last fable, "The Wolf and the Lamb." Neither the lamb's meekness and innocence, nor his appeals to logic and the law (for example, lines 2640-43), are of the slightest good against a foe determined to do evil. In this absolutely clear case of right versus wrong (lines 2624-25), wrong is triumphant to the apparent confusion of the narrator:

> Off his murther quhat sall we say, allace?
> Wes not this reuth, wes not this grit pietie,
> To gar this selie lamb but gilt thus de?
> (lines 2704-06)

Henryson's relentless presentation of the harshness of the world does not mean, as some have recently argued, that the poet is fundamentally a pessimist who sees all as meaningless. Throughout the *Fables* there are many indications that beyond the confusion of this world there is order in the universe. An elaborate example is the description of God's power and wisdom and the beneficent harmony of his creation in the opening lines of the "Preaching of the Swallow" (lines 1622-1712); a similar effect is created by the account of the heavens and the meaning they reveal in "The Fox and the Wolf" (lines 635–48). Furthermore, there is also some indication that those who live below, however steeped in sin, may occasionally possess the capacity to respond to the divine goodness. The one exception to the selfishness in the *Fables* is the mutual assistance between the lion and the mouse (and the cooperation of the mice among themselves) in fable VII, which occurs at the very center of the work, suggesting a potential for love in God's creation. Henryson is not given to modern despair; rather, he is what might be called a Northern Christian realist. Like many Anglo-Saxon poets, he recognizes that this life is indeed a brief and often painful passage. We are sinners in a fallen world and on our own are all doomed—but there is hope elsewhere.

Although Henryson's sympathy for human suffering and his anger at social abuses are genuine, he, like Langland, finds the only solution to the human condition to lie beyond this world in the love of God.[49] Henryson is not a simple moralistic poet giving rules for practical conduct, but one whose message is about God's astonishing mercy. His final optimism is real enough, and contains the sweetness promised in the prologue, but it is rarely presented directly. Instead, it is most powerfully seen in negative examples: the misery and self-destruction of beasts (and men acting like beasts) who cut themselves off from God's grace. Henryson forces us to look heavenward because of the absolute absence of justice or security on this earth. In addition, occasionally there are clear expressions of the ultimately hopeful lesson of the *Fables*, such as the moving prayer to Mary at the end of fable V (lines 1139–45), which has the same message as *The Prayer for the Pest*: although we are sinners deserving punishment, we beg for mercy. As in the *Testament of Cresseid*, Henryson in the *Fables* is neither a Scots puritan nor a modern pessimist. He sees the pain of this world but also the possibility of redemption.[50] The need for mercy and pity is emphasized throughout the central fable, "The Lion and the Mouse" (for example, lines 1461, 1537, 1595, 1597). It is even possible that the mysterious lord at whose request the poet says he undertakes the *Fables* (line 34) is the Christian Lord, whose redemptive power is cited at the very end of the poem (lines 2973–75).[51]

The first tale, "The Cock and the Jasp," not only demonstrates Henryson's method of moral instruction, as we have already seen, but also his ultimate message. The cock is a lively bird, "cant and crous" (line 65), but his views are too practical and worldly; he is a *coq moyen sensuel* who intends to live on bread alone. He rejects the precious jewel because it is too good for him: "Thow are ane iouell for ane lord or king. / It wer pietie thow suld in this mydding / Be buryit thus amang this muke and mold" (lines 81–83). In these words and others like them (see, for example, lines 106ff.), it is difficult not to see a parallel to the mystery of the Incarnation. Like the jasper of wisdom in the dungheap, God, confounding all logic and sense, lowered himself to share our humble state, and thus we are miraculously called to an inheritance equal to that of kings.[52]

Two fables already mentioned that seem extremely pessimistic on the surface actually begin to educate the reader about the poet's message of hope. Fable VI, "The Sheep and the Dog," is in the form of a negative exemplum. The sheep looks for justice (see line 1295 and the lines following), but in vain. Paradoxically, the injustice of the world demonstrates more forcefully than direct statement the need for God's salvation. Nothing else will avail. The last stanza of the *moralitas,* without providing a definite answer to the sheep's problem, suggests where that answer will have to come from: "sen that we ar opprest/In to this eirth, grant vs in heuin gude rest" (lines 1319-20).

Fable XII, "The Wolf and the Lamb," is more pessimistic still, for the tale shows that truth, reason, law, and innocence are no defense against pure evil. The lamb is almost comic as he tries to save himself with formal logic (see especially the *ergo* of line 2650), but his call for strict justice ("Off his awin deidis ilk man sall beir the pais,/As pyne for sin, reward for werkis rycht" [lines 1667-68]) is mistaken and too severe for humankind. The lamb's citation of this Old Testament text simply prompts another harsh precept from the Old Law by the wolf (lines 2672-75). As Saint Paul knew, because all men are carnal they are condemned under the law (Romans 7:14). The only answer is, not strict justice, which must whip us all, but a complete and unmerited mercy.[53] The pitiless world of the *Fables* demands the Atonement. Without denying the horror of its story or the seriousness of its call for social reform, I would argue that "The Wolf and the Lamb" also shows that the answer to the human condition is not what the lamb says, but what he represents. The lamb is a traditional symbol of Christ and the description of his death seems an undeniable reference to the Eucharist: "Syne drank his blude and off his flesche can eit" (line 2702). This identification is underlined by the oath with which the fox refuses the "reuth" that is the lamb's and our only salvation: "Be Goddis woundis" (line 2697). The hope Henryson expresses here is the familiar Christian paradox that God's mercy and grace, symbolized by the death of the lamb, can offer us the body and blood of salvation even when we act as wickedly as the wolf. Henryson's final lesson, then, is not an applicable moral but a mystery; God's complete goodness and his love of undeserving man confound logic and reason to redeem the terrible world of the *Fables* and its bestial creatures. In his excellent book on Henryson, Douglas Gray identifies the final attitude of the *Fables* as "wise, realistic, tolerant and religious at once."[54] Without denying this description absolutely, I would suggest it continues the tradition of defining our author in terms more applicable to Chaucer. Henryson is a different kind of poet, less detached and more passionate; like Langland, he is more tortured by the evil of the world and thirstier for God's grace.*

## Notes

*I wish to thank Carol McQuirk, who first suggested to me the complexities of Henryson's *Fables* in a graduate class at Columbia years ago, and Linda Georgianna, who much more recently helped to improve this piece.

1. This list includes the principal characteristics of the Ricardians as defined by John Burrow, *Ricardian Poetry* (London: Routledge and Kegan Paul, 1971), especially pp. 44, 46, 51, 58, 69, 90, 94, 111, and 137. After the completion of this essay, my attention was called to Robert L. Kindrick, *Robert Henryson* (Boston: Twayne, 1979), who also stresses Henryson's debt to the Ricardian poets in general (see especially pp. 29ff.).

2. All quotations from Henryson are from the excellent new edition of Denton Fox, *The Poems of Robert Henryson* (Oxford: Clarendon Press, 1981); the reference here is to lines 59-60 of the *Fables*. Gower, *The English Works of John Gower*, ed. G. C. Macaulay, Early English Text Society, ES 81 (1900: reprint, London: Oxford University Press, 1957), vol. 1, pro. 17-19.

3. For example, in his edition, Fox (*Poems*, pp. 279-80) compares lines 1692-1705 of the *Fables* to a passage in the alliterative *Destruction of Troy*.

4. Henryson has been compared with Langland by Marshall Stearns, *Robert Henryson* (1949; reprint, New York: AMS Press, 1966), especially p. 28, though Stearns is chiefly interested in their political similarities; by Kindrick, *Robert Henryson*, especially pp. 99-101; and briefly by Robert Pope, "Henryson's *The Sheep and the Dog*," *Essays in Criticism* 30 (1980): 205.

5. See, for example, David Irving, *The Lives of the Scotish Poets* (Edinburgh: David Brown, 1804), I: 377 ("The genius of Henryson seems to have been well adapted to didactic poetry"), and the more recent comment of John Block Friedman, "Henryson, the Friars, and the *Confessio Reynardi*," *Journal of English and Germanic Philology* 66 (1967): 550: "The very intensity of Henryson's religious views accounts for the quality of personal involvement which makes his *Morall Fabillis* the finest Aesop of the Middle Ages."

6. On the tradition of fables in the Middle Ages, see Stephen Manning, "The Nun's Priest's Morality and the Medieval Attitude toward Fables," *Journal of English and Germanic Philology* 59 (1960): 403–16; and Douglas Gray, *Robert Henryson* (Leiden: E. J. Brill, 1979), pp. 31–69. I wish to record my debt to Gray's superb study, which I found useful and stimulating throughout.

7. Schrader, "Some Backgrounds of Henryson," *Studies in Scottish Literature* 15 (1980): 132.

8. This view has been too frequently cited to need requotation, but see G. Gregory Smith, ed., *The Poems of Robert Henryson*, Scottish Text Society (Edinburgh and London: Blackwood, 1914), 1:xvi; H. Harvey Wood, ed., *The Poems and Fables of Robert Henryson*, 2nd rev. ed. (Edinburgh and London: Oliver and Boyd, 1965), p. xv; Richard Bauman, "The Folktale and Oral Tradition in the Fables of Robert Henryson," *Fabula* 6 (1964): 117; John Burrow, "Henryson, *The Preaching of the Swallow*," *Essays in Criticism* 25 (1975): 35; and A. M. Kinghorn, "The Mediaeval Makars," *Texas Studies in Literature and Language* 1 (1959–60): 77.

9. See especially Denton Fox, "Henryson's *Fables*," *English Literary History* 29 (1962): 337–56; and John MacQueen, *Robert Henryson* (Oxford: Clarendon Press, 1967), pp. 94–188.

10. See the correspondence in *TLS* (31 August 1967, p. 781; and 14 September 1967, p. 824) on the nature and importance of an allegorical reading of the *Fables*, especially the letters of Tom Scott. Often even very good critics of the *Fables* ignore the *moralitates:* for examples, Burrow, "Henryson"; and Daniel M. Murtaugh, "Henryson's Animals," *Texas Studies in Literature and Language* 14 (1972): 408–09. Douglas Gray (*Robert Henryson*) provides the best discussion to date of the relationship between narrative and *moralitas* in the *Fables*, but even he is apologetic for the latter: he declares that "no modern reader will ever be persuaded to prefer the *moralitas* to the fable—and there is no reason why he should" (p. 130); and that, though they should not be dismissed lightly, the *moralitates* "are obviously not as complex or as interesting as their fables" (p. 133).

11. See George Clark, "Henryson and Aesop: The Fable Transformed," *English Literary History* 43 (1976): 1–18; and Matthew P. McDiarmid, "Robert Henryson in His Poems," *Bards and Makars*, ed. by A. J. Aitken, M. P. McDiarmid, and D. S. Thomson (Glasgow: University of Glasgow Press, 1977), pp. 27–39. See also I. W. A. Jamieson, "The Beast Tale in Middle Scots: Some Thoughts on the History of a Genre," *Parergon* 2 (1972): 28–32, and his " 'To preue thare preching be a poesye': Some Thoughts on Henryson's Poetics," *Parergon* 8 (1974): 24–36, which argue that Henryson's views are experimental and relativistic. See also Murtaugh, "Henryson's Animals."

12. James Kinsley, "The Medieval Makars," *Scottish Poetry: A Critical Survey*, ed. James Kinsley (London: Cassell, 1955), p. 18. Even John MacQueen, one of the strongest proponents of thematic unity between the two parts of each fable, finds some of Henryson's allegorical explanations hard to accept (e.g., *Robert Henryson*, p. 175).

13. For example, Charles Elliott, ed., *Robert Henryson: Poems*, 2nd rev. ed. (Oxford: Clarendon Press, 1974), speaks of Henryson's "direct and blatant 'teaching' " (p. xi) and says that for the poet, "The paths of right and wrong, towards bliss or bale, are clear and distinct" (p. xii).

14. Harold E. Toliver, "Robert Henryson: From *Moralitas* to Irony," *English Studies* 46 (1965): 300–305, argues that the two parts of each fable suggest a double perspective, but ultimately he finds that in the most successful ones both are united; I. W. A. Jamieson, "Henryson's *Taill of the Wolf and the Wedder*," *Studies in Scottish Literature* 6 (1969): 248–57, sees the dissonance between narrative and *moralitas* as designed by Henryson to involve the reader, but his approach is different from that offered here; even Gray, who provides an exciting discussion of Henryson's "dark moralities" (*Robert Henryson*, pp. 121ff.), does not consider the discord between the two parts of each fable to be as central as I do. See also the interesting essay published too late to be fully considered here by Stephan Khinoy ("Tale-Moral Relationships in Henryson's *Moral Fables*," in *Studies in Scottish Literature* 17 [1982]: 99–115).

15. Gray, *Robert Henryson*, pp. 120–21; Toliver, "Robert Henryson," pp. 301–02; and Jamieson, "To preue thare preching," pp. 28–29, discuss these two images.

16. Fox, *Poems*, p. 189.

17. Ibid.

18. In a later discussion of his procedure in the *Fables*, Henryson uses the image of gold refined from lead (lines 1097–99), which again emphasizes not only the human ingenuity needed but also the beauty and value of the result.

19. Clark, "Henryson and Aesop," pp. 6–10, believes the conflict indicates Henryson's fundamental pessimism; Fox, "Henryson's *Fables*," pp. 341–46, argues that there is really not so great a dissonance as we first think (but see Clark, pp. 7–8).

20. The apology in Phaedrus and more faintly in Gualterus is that men should not disdain the wisdom of humble fables (Fox, *Poems*, p. 195).

21. The theme of wisdom runs throughout the *Fables* and has been discussed by Burrow, "Henryson"; Gray, *Robert Henryson*, pp. 156ff.; and Fox, *Poems*, p. lxxix. Wisdom is something that must be used correctly, however; the wolf in "The Fox and the Wolf" is "in science wonder sle" (line 667) but

also corrupt and evil. Similarly, one must be careful not simply to accept authority. The *moralitas* to "The Trial of the Fox" endorses the teaching of "doctouris of deuyne" (line 1101), yet in the preceding fable we have just seen a great deal of comedy at the expense of a supposedly learned wolf (e.g., lines 998, 1011, 1026) who is said to become a kind of Doctor of Divinity (line 1052) because he is stupid enough to be kicked in the head by a mare (i.e., he gets his red cap). Henryson implies that we need to use our own judgment, for, as the king notes, "The greitest clerkis ar not the wysest men" (line 1064).

22. Gray briefly notes the presence of moral comment within the narratives (*Robert Henryson*, p. 132).

23. This tale also includes a wordly and highly elaborate piece of rhetoric on the shame felt before royalty by those who are evil, which should teach us to flee falsity (lines 971–84). Fable IX contains a brief admonition to be content with enough (lines 2189–90), which is much less Christian a sentiment than the concern in the *moralitas* with a soul before death.

24. See Burrow, "Henryson," p. 30.

25. See Donald MacDonald, "Henryson and Chaucer: Cock and Fox," *Texas Studies in Literature and Language*, 8 (1967): 451–61.

26. Fox, *Poems*, p. 216, note to lines 495–508. See also Gray, *Robert Henryson*, p. 94.

27. Toliver, "Robert Henryson," p. 302, notes that Coppock's speech is limited and Henryson's sympathies wider, but I believe the effect goes beyond this.

28. Gray, *Robert Henryson*, pp. 121ff., discusses the enthusiasm with which Henryson moralizes and the delight and wit he produces; Toliver, "Robert Henryson," and Jamieson, in his several articles cited above, discuss the open-endedness of Henryson's lessons. There has been some praise of Henryson's *moralitates*. Edwin Muir, "Robert Henryson," *Essays on Literature and Society*, rev. ed. (London: Hogarth Press, 1965), p. 14, asserts that several of the *moralitates* "have sincerity that is far from dullness"; Geoffrey Tillotson, "The 'Fables' of Robert Henryson," *Essays in Criticism and Research* (1942; reprint, Archon Books, 1967), p. 4, says it is a marvel that the "*moralitas* can be so vigorous, its images so rampant"; and Fox, "Henryson's *Fables*," p. 353, finds the moral allegory of the "Preaching of the Swallow" to be "worked out with an extraordinary deftness."

29. Perhaps another example of Henryson's moral wit is the way he appears to play with some of his allegorical identifications. For example, the world and its pleasure are usually seen as false and deceptive in the *Fables* (e.g., lines 2217–20): in "The Lion and the Mouse" the "fair forest" with its songs of birds and "flouris ferlie sweit" is but the false pleasure of the world

"myngit with cair repleit" (lines 1580–83). In the next fable, however, the beauty in sight and smell of similar "iolie flouris" is not to be distrusted at all, but they are an exemplum that God is "gude, fair, wyis, and bening" (lines 1650–56). Delight in allegorical ingenuity is frequent in the Middle Ages, and here it may suggest the need for alertness and flexibility in the reader.

30. Fox, *Poems*, pp. lxxvii–viii, relying on H. H. Roerecke, and p. lxxxi, briefly mentions the possibility of such patterns in the order of *Fables*, but more work needs to be done on the subject.

31. See Elizabeth Salter and Derek Pearsall, eds., *Piers Plowman*, York Medieval Texts (Evanston: Northwestern University Press, 1969), p. 103, note to line 10.

32. For praise of the art of this *moralitas*, see Gray, *Robert Henryson*, p. 133, and Pope, "Henryson's *Sheep and Dog*," p. 209.

33. Gray, *Robert Henryson*, p. 148, compares the sheep's question to that posed by the story of Job.

34. The fox in "The Fox and the Wolf" knows that he is doomed if he does not repent (lines 649–53), but, like Coveitise in passus V of the B-text of *Piers Plowman*, he cannot.

35. Henryson's use of proverbs is as complicated as Chaucer's; see Donald MacDonald, "Chaucer's Influence on Henryson's *Fables*: The Use of Proverbs and *Sententiae*," *Medium Aevum* 39 (1970): 21–27, and his "Proverbs, *Sententiae*, and *Exempla* in Chaucer's Comic Tales: The Function of Comic Misapplication," *Speculum* 41 (1966): 453–65. Henryson, like Chaucer, undoubtedly shared some of the medieval affection for proverbial lore, but he also realizes that it is often too facile and adaptable to offer real wisdom. See the irony of the proverbs so confidently cited by the lark in "The Preaching of the Swallow" (lines 1763–67; see also note 39, below) and by the cadger in fable IX (lines 2063–69; Fox, *Poems*, p. 293).

36. In his defense of poetry in the *Genealogy of the Gods*, Boccaccio insists that the difficulty of poetry reinforces its teaching: see *Boccaccio on Poetry*, trans. Charles G. Osgood (1930; reprint, Indianapolis: Bobbs-Merrill, 1956), p. 51.

37. See especially Burrow, "Henryson: *The Preaching of the Swallow*"; along with "The Cock and the Jasp" and "The Two Mice," this is the most discussed of the *Fables*, especially in recent years.

38. Murtaugh, "Henryson's Animals," p. 411, briefly notes that the swallow's words, while eloquent, are useless.

39. The irony of the proverbs is mentioned by Burrow, "Henryson," p. 33; and Fox, *Poems*, p. 282, notes to lines 1763 and 1766–67.

40. See my discussion of the ineffective but wholly orthodox preaching

of Holy Church in *Piers Plowman*: "The Function of Lady Meed in *Piers Plowman*," *English Studies* 61 (1980): 195–97.

41. Gray, *Robert Henryson*, pp. 153–54. The themes of deception and appearance versus reality are important ones in the *Fables* and demand more study.

42. Gray, *Robert Henryson*, p. 136; in its unforgiving harshness, the world of the *Fables* is very much like the world of the *Testament*.

43. The love between the two mice at their reunion in the second fable soon gives way to scorn and mistrust; in the rest of the tales the most common relationship is that of victim and oppressor (in "The Wolf and the Wether" each character plays both roles). The wolf and the fox, who appear in several stories, are a parody of cooperation, and the collection ends with a tale of mutual destruction.

44. Materialism so dominates these creatures that spiritual values are utterly ignored. Confession and baptism are empty ceremonies in "The Fox and the Wolf," and in "The Two Mice" we are explicitly told that "God speid" (line 262) and grace (line 268) are not said and that Christian feasts are judged only by their caloric content. Twice creatures swear deceptive oaths by Jupiter (lines 2026 and 2869), another indication of the non-Christian values of the characters.

45. The most obvious attempted solution in *Piers* that is both rational and inadequate is the cooperative experiment of the half-acre, which fails because of human limitations; for other discussions of Langland's lack of faith in the sensible and rational, see Mary C. Schroeder, "The Character of Conscience in *Piers Plowman*," *Studies in Philology* 67 (1970): 13–30; and Benson, "Function of Lady Meed."

46. The *moralitas* to the second fable (be satisfied with what you have) almost seems an answer to the cock's problem in the first fable (indeed, this is the lesson Lydgate draws in his parallel fable of the cock), but it does not finally answer all the problems of either.

47. In "Henryson's *Sheep and Dog*," Pope argues (pp. 212–13), as I shall below, that for all his reformist zeal Henryson finally offers a Christian and other-worldly view. See also Khinoy, "Tale-Moral Relationships."

48. Fox, *Poems*, p. lxxxi.

49. Marshall Stearns, *Robert Henryson*; Robert L. Kindrick, "Lion or Cat? Henryson's Characterization of James III," *Studies in Scottish Literature* 14 (1979): 123–36; and Mary E. Rowlands, "Robert Henryson and the Scottish Courts of Law," *Aberdeen University Review* 39 (1961–62): 219–26, in particular, along with many others to a smaller degree, see Henryson's central concerns, in contrast to the argument presented here, as political.

50. For redemption in Henryson's *Testament of Cresseid*, see Elliott, *Robert Henryson: Poems*, p. xvi; Denton Fox, ed., *Testament of Cresseid* (London: Nelson, 1968), especially pp. 56–58; and C. David Benson, "Trolius and Cresseid in Henryson's *Testament*," *Chaucer Review* 13 (1978): 263–71.

51. Schrader, "Some Backgrounds," p. 130.

52. As the second stanza of the *moralitas* shows, the jasper does not symbolize merely practical wisdom but also the spiritual wisdom that brings eternal life (lines 134–40); see MacQueen *Robert Henryson* pp. 103–04.

53. Patrick Cruttwell, "Two Scots Poets: Dunbar and Henryson," *The Age of Chaucer,* ed. Boris Ford, rev. ed. (Baltimore and Harmondsworth: Penguin, 1969), p. 184, mentions briefly, but does not develop, the importance of the conflict between justice and mercy in the *Fables*.

54. Gray, *Robert Henryson*, p. 160.

# Courtly Love and Chivalry in the Later Middle Ages

## Larry D. Benson

My subject is courtly love, that strange doctrine of chivalric courtship that fixed the vocabulary and defined the experience of lovers in our culture from the latter Middle Ages until almost our own day. Some of its traces still survive—or at least they do in the old Andy Hardy movies. If you are old enough to have seen some of these films, or young enough to stay up for the really late, late movie, you will surely recall the obligatory scene, around reel two, when a despondent Andy (the younger Mickey Rooney), murmuring the name of the girl next door (Judy Garland), slowly leaves the table, his food untouched. Lewis Stone, stern but kindly Judge Hardy, frowns and turns to Mrs. Hardy: "What on earth's gotten into that boy? He doesn't eat. He doesn't sleep. He just moons around like a sick calf." And Mrs. Hardy—Fay Bainter—smiles with motherly understanding: "Pshaw! Can't you see the boy's in love?" And of course we can. Some, of an older generation than mine, may even have shared some of Andy's emotions, for the pangs of unrequited love and the suffering that necessarily accompanies it have been part of Western courtship for centuries.

Indeed, for many centuries—from the time of the Greeks through the seventeenth century—physicians regularly offered treatment for lovesickness, "the lovers maladye of heroes," which they regarded as both a physical and a mental affliction. It is true that William of Gaddesden, one of the authorities known to the Physician in Chaucer's General Prologue, treated it only briefly in his medical textbook, since, as he warned his students, "but little money can be made from this disease."[1] Moreover, Alain Chartier in the fifteenth century and Shakespeare in the sixteenth objected, "Men have died . . . and worms have eaten them, but not for love."[2]

Nevertheless, in the seventeenth century appeared the definitive medical study, *Eratomania*, which filled 336 large pages, and Robert Burton devoted over a quarter of his huge *Anatomy of Melancholy* to the problem of love sickness.[3] Even in the early nineteenth century some of John Keats's friends thought that the first symptoms of an illness from which he suffered were due to his languishing for unrequited love—though it now appears that he may not have been as unrequited as they thought, since he was actually suffering from syphilis.[4]

My subject, however, is not medicine nor even Andy Hardy. It is courtly love in the life of the chivalric classes in the later Middle Ages. I must begin by admitting that a good many scholars nowadays are convinced that my subject does not—indeed, never did—exist. E. T. Donaldson has announced that "courtly love" is only a critical myth, D. W. Robertson has even more vigorously dismissed it as a nineteenth-century invention, an impediment to the understanding of medieval literary texts.[5] You might think that if both Donaldson and Robertson, who agree on so little else, agree on this, there must be something to it. There is.

Most of what used to pass for fact about courtly love was simply wrong. I mean the idea that it was invented by the Arabs, Albigensians, or Primitive Germans, elegantly elaborated by the troubadours, diligently practiced in the court of Marie de Champagne, permanently codified by Andreas Capellanus, and defined for all time by C. S. Lewis as "Humility, Courtesy, Adultery, and the Religion of Love."[6] We can all remember when these supposed facts were adduced in article after dreary article in which it was proven that Chaucer or Gower or the *Gawain*-poet was being "ironical" whenever the work at hand failed to fit Andreas's rules or Lewis's definition—which was almost invariably the case.

The rejection of these ideas has been all to the good. Peter Dronke has shown that we need not turn to Araby or heresy for the sources of courtly love, which lay much closer to hand in the medieval Latin tradition.[7] John Benton has proven what we should have known all along—that the Countess Marie and her ladies did not carry on like so many Guineveres and Isoldes; if they had, the count would have locked them up in a nunnery.[8] Andreas Capellanus, it is now generally believed, was not trying to write a serious code of conduct; he was trying to be funny. I admit that the number of people who have laughed aloud while reading the *De arte honesti amandi* can be counted on one finger: he was a thirteenth-century Frenchman named Drouart la Vache.[9] Yet I think the current opinion is correct: Andreas was trying, and generally failing, to be funny. And clearly the assumption that there was a rigidly defined and widely accepted doctrine of love that required adultery is simply wrong. Insofar as "courtly love" is used as a label for a code of courtly adultery, the whole idea is indeed a critical myth that never had much real existence in life or literature.

However, it does not follow that, if a doctrine of courtly adultery did not exist, courtly love did not exist. The fact is that courtly love did exist, perhaps not in the twelfth century, but certainly in the fourteenth, fifteenth, and even sixteenth centuries. Indeed, as the recent book by Mark Girouard on chivalry and the English gentleman makes clear, it had a powerful influence not only on the realm of Romantic and Victorian fiction, but on Victorian life and manners as well.[10] Its power is to be explained by that fact that, as Kittredge said in his apt characterization, courtly love was part of "the settled language of the chivalric system."[11] That language echoes throughout the later Middle Ages, as in this stanza from Chaucer's "Complaint to his Lady":

> But I, my lyf and deeth, to yow obeye,
> And with right buxom herte, hooly I preye,
> As [is] your moste plesure, so doth by me;
> Wel lever is me liken yow and deye
> Than for to anythyng or thynk or seye
> That yow myghte offende in any tyme.
> And therfor, swete, rewe on my peynes smerte,
> And of your grace, graunteth me some drope;
> For elles may me laste no blis ne hope,
> Ne dwelle within my trouble careful herte.
> (Lines 118–27)

Even the most casual reader knows that late medieval literature simply swarms with characters like this. We need some term to describe what is going on, and we might as well use "courtly love." That phrase was not, as is sometimes said, invented in 1883 by Gaston Paris.[12] *Amor cortese*, courtly love, was in fairly common use in medieval Italian, and Chaucer might well have come upon the phrase *cortesi amanti*, courtly lovers, in his reading of Petrarch.[13] As for what he might have thought it meant, we need only note that the lover in Chaucer's complaint is so extravagantly humble that he will obey his lady in everything, so courteous he would rather die than offend her even in thought, and so religiously devoted to her that he prays for but one drop of grace, without which he can have neither bliss nor hope. The speaker is not, so far as we can tell, an adulterer, for the text tells us nothing of his or his lady's marital status. But if we omit adultery from C. S. Lewis's famous definition, I can think of no better description of the attitudes embodied in this stanza than "Humility, Courtesy, and the Religion of Love."

What distinguishes this style of love from the styles of other times and places is not only the theme of suffering, and certainly not the requirement of adultery, which is always with us and was never, except in Andreas's imagination, a necessary part of courtly love. The distinction lies rather in the conviction that this sort of love is admirable—that love is not only virtuous in itself but is the very source and cause of all the other virtues, that indeed one cannot be virtuous unless he is a lover. That idea, as might be expected, comes from Ovid. He used it in his *Amores*, where he playfully inverts the whole Roman value system, and one sees something of the same light-hearted use of the "world turned upside down" in Andreas and Chrétien.[14] No doubt Countess Marie of Champagne and the younger members of her court were delighted by the amusing, if unlikely, idea of a world ruled by women, in which all the handsome young men faithfully served their ladies for the sake of love, rather than their loutish feudal lords for the sake of plunder. One suspects that Marie's husband, Count Henry, was not amused. Marie was the patron of Chrétien's *Lancelot*: Henry patronized the composition of the *Vengeance Alexandre*, a good old-fashioned *chanson de geste*, in which religion, loyalty to one's lord, and the smashing of heads are the main concerns.[15] And, I need hardly add, there is no nonsense about love in the *Vengeance Alexandre*. Its author praises Count Henry for his piety, his prowess, and his riches, and he hails him as the new Alexander. That is the sort of thing a great nobleman of the twelfth century liked to hear. One can well imagine what the count would have thought if someone tried to compare him, not to Alexander, but to Lancelot—a knight who was neither pious nor rich, who was indeed an adulterer, guilty of sin with the wife of his own liege lord. Henry was liege lord of a good many knights, and the idea that Lancelot's way of carrying on was virtuous, was the very source of chivalric virtue, must have seemed to him downright pernicious.

Yet by Chaucer's time what two hundred years before would have seemed amusing to the countess and scandalous to the count was accepted by many as sober fact. The idea that love was the source of chivalric virtue becomes a commonplace not only in courtly romances and lyrics but even in the "nonfiction" of the time—in handbooks of conduct, such as the poem Edward III is said to have written for his son, the Black Prince:

> Love ladies and maidens
> And serve and honor them
> In thought, word, and deed . . .
> From ladies comes prowess,
> Honors, and dignities . . .

> For we hardly ever see a valiant man
> Who does not or has not loved.[16]

The proof of this, or so it was believed, was to be found in the old romances. The late fourteenth-century biographer of the great Marshal Boucicaut puts it this way:

> Thus one reads of Lancelot, of Tristan, and of many others whom Love made good and famous. Indeed, in our own time living now in France and elsewhere there are many such noble men.... Thus one speaks of Sir Otho de Graunson, of the good constable of Sancerre, and of many others whom it would be too long to name and whom love has made valiant and virtuous. O what a noble thing is love to him who knows how to use it![17]

Times had indeed changed since the twelfth century, and Chaucer's friend Otho de Graunson was doubtless delighted to be compared to Lancelot and Tristan. That is not to say that he was eager to be known as an adulterer. Lancelot's and Tristan's sins were not forgotten, but they were usually overlooked; that their ladies were married to others was their tragic misfortune, which enhanced the heroism of their devotion to love, since it added to the sufferings of these lovers. Moreover, as Malory explained, all this was far in the past, and "Love was not then as it is now."[18] To the aristocrats of the fourteenth and fifteenth centuries, what mattered was not these heroes' adulteries but their excellence as lovers and therefore as models of chivalric virtue.

The late Middle Ages was a time when many young aristocrats eagerly sought to emulate these models. This was the century that saw the first flowering of what Gervase Mathew calls the new "International Court Culture."[19] It brought a new elegance to court life, a new delight in elaborate ceremonialism, and a new and high degree of stylization to the manners of the aristocracy; indeed, if contemporary preachers are to be trusted, in many noble households the reading of romances was part of the ordinary education of aristocratic children.[20] When Chaucer in his ballad "To Rosamund" playfully claims "I am trewe Tristram the secounde," he echoes not only Froissart but many a young fourteenth-century gentleman who aspired to secular virtue and knightly renown.[21]

The new Tristans could most easily be recognized by the way they talked. The new courtly culture placed great emphasis on proper speech, what the author of *Sir Gawain and the Green Knight* called "the tecchles termes of talkynge noble."[22] In that poem, when Bercilak's provincial courtiers learn that their guest is Gawain they cluster about him, hoping to learn how to improve their speech. Likewise, when the French poet and chronicler Froissart first visited the English court, he was delighted to hear such polished talk "of love and arms."[23] The squires of the royal court, among whom Geoffrey Chaucer was later to number, were specifically charged in the Household Ordinances to entertain visitors with "noble conversation."[24]

To master the art of noble conversation was to a large extent to adopt the style of speech developed in courtly literature. None of Edward's or Richard's courtiers went so far as those sixteenth-century French gentlemen who tried to *amadiser* their speech by imitating the style of *Amadis of Gaul*.[25] Yet from what scattered evidence as we have it is apparent that the language of noble conversation, of talk of love and war, had a recognizable relation to courtly romances and lyrics.

The most obvious characteristic of this style of speech is its observance of verbal taboos. In recent years it has become so common to celebrate the jolly bawdiness of the later Middle Ages that it is not often recognized that, so far as our culture is concerned, this is the period in which the distinction between polite speech and vulgar, shocking words was first established. When the Pardoner in the *Canterbury Tales* is about to speak, the "gentles" object: "Nay, let hym tell us of no ribaudrye!" Ribaldry and the frank vocabulary in which it is expressed could be as offensive to the gently nurtured in the fourteenth century as in the nineteenth—and I am thinking here not only of that delightful girl in the fabliau who faints dead away every time she hears the word *foutre* but of the critical dispute that was then going on about the *Romance of the Rose*, which turned to a large degree on de Meun's use of frank and vulgar language.[26] Such words are now, as Chaucer says, "cherles termes."[27] Words used by churls, such as *foutre* in French and *swyven* in English, were at that time, for the first time in our culture, no longer used in polite company—not because of any religious objection, as the salty language of Chaucer's Parson shows, but because in polite, courtly speech they had been replaced by more elegant periphrases.

The difference between churlish and gentle words was a matter of decorum as well as decency. Chaucer's Manciple anticipated Rudyard Kipling by some five centuries in enunciating the principle that the Colonel's Lady and Judy O'Grady are sisters beneath the skin. But the Manciple, being a churl, put the matter more directly than his Victorian counterpart:

> And God it woot, myn owene deer brother,
> Men leyn that oon as lowe as lith that oother.

> ... the gentile, in estaat above,
> She shal be cleped his lady, as in love;
> And for that oother is a povre womman,
> She shal be cleped his wenche or his lemman.
> (lines IX 221–22; 217–20)

Words like "wenche" and "lemman" were not to courtly ears indecent; but they were completely inappropriate, misrepresenting entirely the relationship so precisely defined by "his lady, as in love." Courtly speech, that is, involved not only avoiding certain offensive words but the proper use of certain others: "lady," "servant," and such words as "love" itself.

The eloquent expression of love is, of course, one of the main concerns of courtly speech. The form of speech, as Chaucer reminds us in *Troilus* when he distinguishes love in his day from love in ancient Troy, is an essential part of any style of love. Courtly love, however, is especially dependent on the forms of speech, since not only is every lover a poet, but the main characteristics of the courtly lover—his courtesy, humility, and religion of love—are expressed in speech. To be adept at "luf talk" is therefore the first requirement of the courtly lover. He must not be too adept; it is best if in the actual presence of his lady he is so filled with religious awe that he is rendered speechless or even, like Troilus nearing Criseyde's bed, falls into a swoon. The rest of the time, however, he must be skilled in courtly talk. Criseyde's first question to Pandarus when she agrees to meet Troilus is "kan he speke wel of love?"

Criseyde in effect is asking, "Is he a gentleman?" since to speak well of love, to use what Kittredge called "the settled language of the chivalric system," is to use a class dialect, the first of which we have any clear indication in English. The gentle do not speak "in cherles termes"; the Knight of the General Prologue "nevere yet no vileynye ne sayde ... unto no maner wight." The churl, on the other hand, is incapable of speaking in "termes of talkynge noble." In the *Romance of the Rose*, when the Lover first speaks to the God of Love, the God responds:

> For thou answerid so curteisly
> For [that] now I wot wel uttirly
> That thou art gentyl by thi speche ...
> For sich a word ne myghte nought
> Isse out of a vilayns thought.
> (lines 1985–87, 1991–93)

Such a speech could not be produced by the mind of a *vileyn*, a churl, because a churl is incapable of love. This is one of the basic precepts of courtly love. Andreas Capellanus tells the young lover that if he should be attracted to a peasant girl he should waste no time on words, since such base creatures are incapable of understanding; he advises rape instead.[28] This idea that only the noble classes are capable of love persisted, and perhaps even grew stronger, in the later Middle Ages. Chaucer's Manciple uses the word "love" only in relation to the lady "of grete estate"; so does Chaucer himself. Though "love" is one of his favorite words, as narrator he rarely applies it to what goes on in his fabliaux.[29]

This attitude appears even in medical literature, which had dealt with the problems of "love sickness" since the time of Galen and before. None of the Greek, Arabic, or twelfth- and thirteenth-century Latin commentators ever connected this illness with any one social class. But now, at the end of the Middle Ages, an authority such as Giovanni Savanarola (not the later reformer, but his grandfather), in his *Practica major* specifies that the illness *ereos* (which earlier commentators had rightly derived from the Greek *Eros*) is so called because of its relation to the word *hero*. The malady, Savanarola says, is almost exclusively restricted to the aristocracy: "whence is it often called *ereos*, because it most often affects heroic and noble men."[30] As Kittredge said, "Love was the only life that became the gently nurtured, and they alone were capable of love."[31]

This cluster of ideas gave a powerful impetus to the use of the "settled language of the chivalric class" at a time when that class was still in the process of self-definition and the old idea that deeds rather than birth define gentility was still strong. If knights or ladies speak of love they must use the gentle language of courtly love; to do otherwise is to cease to be gentle, to become churls.

This must be emphasized, since we so often think of courtly love as a special, self-conscious form of love, as if it differed from what one critic calls "ordinary love." For the aristocracy of Chaucer's time courtly love was the ordinary form of love, because of the very nature of their language. Of course, there was wide variation. As Chaucer tells the audience of *Troilus*, "Scarsly ben ther in this place thre/That have in love said lik, or don, all." And scarcely are there three writers, or even three works of the same writer, in which the idea of love or the words and actions of the lovers are the same. Yet this wide range of variation occurs within the limits defined by the language of courtly love. If you were a late medieval gentleman, how did you tell a lady that you loved her? Certainly not in the way hende Nicholas declares his lust for Alison, grabbing her by the haunche-bone. Instead you spoke as Froissart reports Edward III did when he wooed the Countess of Salisbury:

> Ah fair lady . . . truly the sweet behaviour
> the perfect wisdom, the elegant grace, nobleness
> and surpassing beauty that I see in you, hath
> so enraptured my soul, that I cannot but love you;
> and without your return of love, I am but as dead.[32]

How do two gentle lovers converse? According to the *Disce Morum*, a book of religious instruction, they say:

> how she loveth him and he hir, and what he wol
> do and suffer for here and she for him, and what
> they wish and desire, each to other of wele and
> pleasaunce, it cannot her be expressed, for an
> hour suffiseth nat to hem, ne a day, ne dayes,
> ne no tyme to open þeire herte oon to other.[33]

Indeed, John of Trevisa, translating Bartholomeus Anglicus into English at the end of the fourteenth century, must use the language of courtly love even to describe the mating habits of birds:

> Males drawen to the companye of females and preyen
> iche oþir of loue and wowiþ by beckes and voys.[34]

For the gentle class of the time, or even for the gentlemanly scientific writer, there was no way to explain such feelings except in the language of courtly love.

This is nicely demonstrated in a series of letters written in the year 1398 by William Gold, an English mercenary captain who led the troop of Saint George then in the employ of Venice.[35] They were written to Luduvico Gonzaga, the Lord of Mantua, and they concern one Janet of France. In his first letter (July 30) Gold describes her as a "certain Janet" who has absconded with five hundred florins; he asks Gonzaga to arrest and detain her until he can send for her. We do not know Gonzaga's replies, but other letters follow quickly. On August 2 Gold repeats his request and pleads that "a diligent search be made for her in hostelries and that he be acquainted with the result, as nothing would give him greater pleasure." By August 4, poor Janet has been found and is evidently making counter-offers, for Gold writes, "that he has done, and will do, and is ready to do his lordship more honour than any French lady," and he pleads that she be held until his notary can arrive with legal proof of the five hundred florins with which she has absconded. August 6: I know nothing of her husband, Gold writes, and not only fails to mention the five hundred florins, but now says he will pay Gonzaga a thousand pounds if "though it be a trifle against the law . . . she may be placed in a nunnery and not allowed to depart" until he can fetch her. Finally, on August 9, Gold throws himself on Gonzaga's mercy, confessing that he is in love. The Lord of Mantua, he writes.

> should bear in mind that love overcometh all things—since it even prostrates the stout, making them impatient, taking all heart from them, even casting down into the depths the summits of tall towers, suggesting strife, so that it drags them into deadly duels, as hath happened to and befallen me for the sake of this Janet, my heart so yearning toward her that by no means can I be at rest or do otherwise; and consider that lovers ought to be succoured—therefore on my bended knee I devoutly beseech your lorship to put aside everything else and so ordain and command that the said Janet be detained until I send for her . . . for if I should have to follow her to Avignon I will obtain this woman. Now, my lord . . . [you] ought not to cross me in this, for someday I shall do for you more than a thousand united French women could effect; and if there be need for me in a matter of greater import, you shall have for the asking a thousand spears at my back.

This is the last of the series of letters preserved in the archives at Mantua, and we have no way of knowing whether poor Janet ever made it back to her husband in Avignon. I hope so. Gold was obviously a scoundrel. But, as his letters show, in the late fourteenth century even a scoundrel, if he had any pretensions to gentility, had to express himself in the language of courtly love. It was the emblem of aristocratic respectability.

This identification of courtly love with aristocratic virtue is why Chaucer represents John of Gaunt as a courtly lover, suffering from a dangerous case of *ereos* in the *Book of the Duchess*. Of course, the representation is not direct, for the idea is not to particularize John as the Black Knight but rather to generalize him, to show how much he resembles the great courtly lovers of the past and thus to imply how much of their virtue he embodies—to present him, that is, as a model of courtliness, speaking in the "settled language of the chivalric system."

The Black Knight has been accused by some critics of "immoderate grief," but if we want to consider his experience in relation to contemporary life, we would do no better than to turn to an autobiographical account of a similiar experience written by the Knight of La Tour Landry about the same time Chaucer was writing the *Book of the Duchess*. This is the prologue of the book that he wrote for the instruction of his daughter:

> In the year of the Incarnation of our Lord 1371, I was in a garden, all heavy and full of thought, in the shadow, about the end of April, but I little rejoiced me in the melody and sound of the wild birds. They sang there in their language, as the thrustle, the thrush, the titmouse and other birds, which were full of mirth and joy. And their sweet songs made my heart to lighten, and made me think of the time that is passed of my youth, how Love in great distress had held me, and how I was in her service many times full of sorrow and gladness, as many lovers are. But my sorrow was healed and my service well yset and quit, for she gave me a fair wife that was both fair and good, which had knowledge of all honour and all good and all fair maintaining, and of all good was she bell and flower. And I delighted me so much in her that I made for her songs, ballads, rondels, virelays, and diverse new things in the best wise that I could.
>
> But Death, which on all things maketh war, took her from me, that which hath made me have many a sorrowful thought and great heaviness. And so it is more than twenty year that I have been for her full of great sorrow. For a true lover's heart forgetteth never the woman that once he hath truly loved.[36]

Clearly the Knight does not regard his passion as sinful, for as readers of his book know, Geoffrey de la Tour Landry was somewhat puritanical, even priggish.

Of course, this is a literary reminiscence. We have no way of knowing what the Knight actually thought when his first wife died. The cynical may recall Fielding's *Tom Jones*, in which we learn that the death of a spouse is an infallible method of restoring lost affection. All we can know with certainty is that this is the way the Knight viewed his experience and wanted his daughters to view it, within the conventional mode of conduct appropriate to the chivalric class. It would not be surprising if in the year 1371 John of Gaunt thought of his loss in very similar terms.

That these terms were the language of the chivalric classes is shown by many other biographical episodes in the knight's book. For example, he tells us of his own courtship of a lady during his youth, when he was seeking a wife. On a visit the subject of the English treatment of prisoners of war came up. The courtly young man could not resist so obvious an opening:

> "Damsel, it were better to fall to be your prisoner than to many another, for I trow your prison should not be so hard to me as it should if I were taken by the English."
> And she answered, "I have seen some no long since that I would you were my prisoner."
> "Would you," I asked her, "put them in evil prison?"
> "Nay," she said, "I would keep them as I would my own body."
> I said, "Happy is he that might come into so noble a prison."[37]

Readers of *Sir Gawain and the Green Knight* will recognize the resemblance between this conversation and the "luf talkynge" of Gawain and Bercilak's lady, which also begins with the playful use of the common courtly metaphor of the prison.[38] Even the outcome is somewhat similar, for on reflection the knight decided, "She was so pert and light of manners that she caused me to be displeased with her." He left and never returned, "for which I have since after thanked God." He was, as I have noted, a bit of a prig, but his easy use of the conventional language of courtly love shows that in his time even chivalric prigs talked like courtly lovers.

The fact that prigs like Geoffrey de la Tour Landry and scoundrels like William Gold could so easily use the language of courtly love was one of its problems; the noble art of love talking was all too open to abuse by clever scoundrels, such as those clerks in the fabliaux, who realized the tactical advantages of love talking to impressionable young ladies. Perhaps that is why the most telling attacks on courtly love come from concerned mothers, such as Christine de Pisan or the wife of the Knight of la Tour Landry. His second wife listens carefully as he lectures his daughters on courtly love, and when he tells them that love is the source of all chivalric virtue, she breaks in:

> Ye say so, and so do all other men, that a lady or damsel is the better worth when she loveth paramours. And that she shall be the more gay and of fair manner and countenance, and how she shall do great almesse to make a good knight. These words are but sport and esbasement of lordes and of felawes in a language much common. For they say that all honour and worship which they have is coming to them by their paramours . . . but these words cost them but little to say for to get them the better and sooner the grace and good will of

their paramours. For such words and others much marvelous many one useth ful oft. . . . Therefore I charge you, my fair daughters, that in this matter you believe not your father.[39]

The lady then delivers an attack on courtly love that would have done credit to Chaucer's Parson. In the debate that follows, the Knight brings her around to admit that some of the forms and practices of courtly love may be acceptable, and she finally concedes that a lady may even reward a knight's services with a kiss. "But as for my daughters," she says, "I forbid it."[40] One kiss can lead to another. The Knight, priggish though he may be, meanwhile maintains a double standard that would have shocked a Victorian smoking car. It is a pity that the book that he says he wrote for his sons has not survived.

The Knight's wife had good reason for concern, for the use of the language of courtly love for the purpose of mere seduction was not restricted to the fabliaux. One of the contributors to Boucicaut's *Cent ballades* gleefully boasts in his refrain, "One can say one thing and mean another."[41]

The Marshal Boucicaut himself did not share that cynicism. Indeed, he was determined to protect the sely demoiseles of the time from such rascals, and he founded for this purpose a special order of chivalry, the Order of the Green Shield with the White Lady; some of Christine's other friends planned to do the same—to found an Order of the Rose.[42] In Paris in 1400 there was even a Court of Love to protect ladies from insincere lovers and slanderers of the fair sex.[43] You will recall that Chaucer is hailed before a court of love on the latter charge in the prologue to his *Legend of Good Women*. But that was fiction. This was a real court, presided over by the king of France, Charles VI, and his queen, Isabel. Charles, as it happened, suffered from recurrent fits of madness, and it may be thought that this court was founded during one of his spells. Yet the most sensible and influential men of the time, including even the Bishop of Paris, joined in this undertaking—or at least did not mind having it believed that they had done so (our records are all from at least seven years after the event). At the sessions of this court amatory poems were read, and the rules specified that they must be sincere: "Each must write about his own true love and none other."[44] And of course, the poems had to redound to the honor of the ladies. The court claimed jurisdiction even over nonmembers, and in later years it issued a solemn decree of banishment against Alain Chartier for having written *La belle dame sans merci*.[45]

The most astonishing thing about this astonishing court is that no one was much astonished by it. By 1400 courtly love had become for many not just a way of talking but a way of feeling and acting. Even in the 1340s, Bradwardine tells us, French knights were actually laboring strenuously in arms to earn the loves of their ladies, and Henry of Lancaster, so he confesses, actually jousted to win the favors of those whom he seduced. A few years later, Froissart reports, thirty English knights set off for the war in France, each with an eye covered by a patch which he had sworn not to remove until he had struck a blow for the love of his lady.[46] One of them may have been Sir Thomas Holland, whose lady was Joan, the Fair Maid of Kent, who later became mother of Richard II. The two secretly loved and secretly married—clandestine marriages of this sort, it now appears, were surprisingly common[47]—but Sir Thomas was absent for years, since after he fought for his lady in France he went on to fight for his faith in Prussia. In his absence Joan was forced into a second marriage, which, when Sir Thomas finally returned eight years later, was annulled on the grounds that, as the papal order specified, she was alone, fearful, "Voluntati parentum et amicorum suorum non audens contradicere."[48] Queen Joan must have listened to *Troilus and Criseyde* with special interest; perhaps, like Chaucer, she would have forgiven Criseyde, for in her own life she must have felt some of the same emotions and been in almost the same situation as poor Criseyde in the Trojan camp. Likewise, Joan's son, Richard II, would have heard with special sympathy the account of the Black Knight's grief in *The Book of the Duchess*. Richard sincerely loved Queen Anne, and when she died he was so stricken by grief that he ordered that the Manor of Sheen, where Anne had lived, be utterly destroyed, so that not a stone should remain to remind him of his loss.[49] This seems even to me a case of "immoderate grief," yet Lancastrian chroniclers, such as Walsingham, who criticize him for everything else they can think of, never criticize him for this.

The marriage of King James I of Scotland to Joan Beaufort was a purely diplomatic arrangement, yet James claimed—with what justice can not be known—that he fell hopelessly in love with Joan when he saw her from his prison tower, exactly as Palamoun and Arcite fell in love with Emelye in the *Knight's Tale*.[50] Lucia Visconti, daughter of the lord of Milan, seems to have had the same experience as Criseyde did when she first saw Troilus and asked, "Who yaf me drynk?" She saw the Earl of Derby, the future Henry IV, only once, when he visited Milan in 1392–93. But once was enough, and years later, in 1399, so the Venetian ambassador reported to his government, she refused a series of brilliant offers and swore to her father that if only she could have Henry for a husband she would wait the rest of her life, even though she were to die within three days after the marriage.[51]

Not only did aristocrats of the late Middle Ages fall in love in the ways prescribed in courtly literature, but they also earned their ladies' love in the manner of the old romances—in elaborate duels and grand tournaments of the sort that became increasingly fashionable in the fifteenth century. One of the most celebrated was held at Calais in 1419 by the Earl of Warwick, known to his contemporaries as "the father of courtesy."[52] Not only did he joust for his lady's sake, he seems to have realized in life the Franklin's ideal of marriage, writing his wife poems in which he swore:

> I shall howe sore pat me smert
> Right humbly with lowly herte
> Her ordenaunce
> Obeye, and in her governaunce
> Set al my welfare and pleasaunce.[53]

He so loved his wife that once, when it appeared that he and his lady would be drowned in a shipwreck, he lashed himself to a spar so that, their bodies being found together and recognized by his coat-armour, they might lie together in one grave, for he could not bear the thought of separation, even in death. John of Gaunt, we might note, provided in his last will—made thirty years after Blanche's death—that he was to be buried beside his "treschere jadys compaigne Blanch."[54]

Certainly not everyone was acting like courtly lovers in the late fourteenth and fifteenth centuries, and even those who were probably did so on rare occasions. Yet these few set the fashion that grew stronger and more widespread in the generations that followed. In Florence, Lorenzo the Magnificent, that patron of humanist learning and Renaissance art, fought for the love of Lucrezia Donati in a grand tournament, wrote poems to her, and composed a long treatise analyzing the sweet sufferings he endured for her sake.[55] About the same time Lorenzo was carrying on in this fashion, courtly love appears even in the usually prosaic Paston family. John Paston writes thus to Margery Brewer:

> And mistress, I beseech you, in easing of my poor
> heart that sometime was at my rule, which is now at
> yours, that in as short time as can be I will have
> knowledge of your intent.[56]

Margery replies with the declaration that she had fallen ill and will remain so "until I hear from you." She will follow the dictates of her heart whatever her friends say, and she lapses into verse to describe the pains of secret love:

> And there wotteth no creature what pain I endure;
> And, for to be dead, I dare it not discure.[57]

She ends by pleading that "this letter not be seen by none earthly creatures save yourself." While Margery and John were writing thus to one another—enjoying all the thrills of a secret passion—their parents were carrying on hard negotiations about the size of the dowry.

Margery and John were pretending. By the early years of the sixteenth century Henry VIII's courtiers were living the lives of courtly lovers, using stanzas from Chaucer's *Troilus* as love letters and carefully guarding their secret loves. Henry VIII himself was trying to use the style of courtly love. Trying, but not quite succeeding: his letter to Anne Boleyn starts out well enough, with protestations of love and service, but by the last line Henry is saying that he wants to "kiss her duckies."[58] I'm not sure I want to know what that means.

In France they did things better. The pages of Brantôme are rife with lovers, and famous soldiers such as the Sieur de Bussi proclaimed that "he fought not for his prince nor for glory but for the sole honour and glory of contenting his lady love."[59] By this time in Italy one is not too surprised to come upon a letter such as this, dated 3 August 1514:

> I have encountered a creature so gracious, so delicate, so noble that I cannot praise her so much nor love her so much that she would not deserve more. . . . [love put out her] nets of gold, spread among flowers, woven by Venus, so pleasant and easy that though a churlish heart might have broken them, I had no wish to do so, and for a bit I enjoyed myself in them until the tender threads became hard and secured with knots beyond untying. . . . And though I seem to have entered into great labor, I feel in it such sweetness . . . that, if I could free myself, I would not wish to do so for anything in the world. I have abandoned all thoughts and affairs that are grave and serious; I no longer delight in reading ancient things or discussing modern ones; they are all turned into soft conversations, for which I thank Venus and all Cyprus. . . . [as to greater things] I have never found anything in them but harm, and in those of love always good and pleasure. Farewell!
>
> Yours,
> Niccoló Machiavelli.[60]

That Machiavelli himself, that paragon of practicality, felt the sweet pangs of courtly love is not surprising in a time in which courtly love had become a force not only in the lives of the aristocracy but even in the fates of nations. At least that is what Castiglione says in his book *Book of the Courtier*:

> Many there be that hold the opinion that the victory of King Ferdinand and Isabella of Spain, against the King of Granada, was chiefly occasioned by women. For the most times when the army of Spain marched to encounter with the enemies, Queen Isabella set forth with all her damsels. And there were many noble gentlemen that were in love, who til they came within sight of their enemies, always went communing with their ladies. Afterward, each one taking leave of his [lady], in their presence [they] marched on to encounter with the enemies, with that fierceness of courage that Love, and the desire to show their ladies that they were served with valiant men, gave them. Whereupon it befell many times that a very few gentlemen of Spain put to flight and slew an infinite number of Moors, thanks be to the courteous and beloved women.[61]

The historians among you will recall that Columbus could not set out on his voyage of discovery until Ferdinand and Isabella had settled their war with the Moors. If Castiglione can be trusted—and why not?—we must conclude that had there been no courtly love that war never would have been won, Columbus would never have set sail, America would never have been discovered, and the present debate over whether or not courtly love actually existed would never have begun. As Chaucer's Theseus puts it,

> The god of love! a, *benedicite!*
> How myghty and how greet a lord is he! . . .
> He may be cleped a god for his myracles!
> (*The Knight's Tale* lines I 1785–86, 1788)

Not the least among his miracles is the fact that in the late Middle Ages, and for long thereafter, the God of Love actually did exist.

# Notes

*This paper was originally given as a lecture at the University of California at Berkeley and, in a revised form, at the University of New Mexico. It still bears the marks of oral delivery, but incorporates the helpful suggestions I received in discussions with faculty and students at both universities.

1. "Quia raro medicus lucratur pecuniam cum eis," quoted in John L. Lowes, "The Loveres Maladye of Hereos," *Modern Philology* 11 (1914): 503.

2. Alain Chartier, *Delectable Demaundes and Pleasant Questions, with Their Severall Answers, in Matters of Love*, trans. William Painter (London: Thomas Creede, 1596); William Shakespeare, *As You Like It*, IV.i.108.

3. Jacques Ferrand, *Erotomania or, A Treatise Discoursing of the Essence, Causes, Symptomes, Prognosticks, and Cure of Love or, Erotique Melancholy* (Oxford, 1645). Robert Burton, *The Anatomy of Melancholy* (1621; 6th rev. ed., 1651); on love-melancholy, see part 3, sec. 1–3.

4. See Aileen Ward, *John Keats: The Making of a Poet* (New York: Viking, 1963), p. 185.

5. E. Talbot Donaldson, "The Myth of Courtly Love," in *Speaking of Chaucer* (New York: Norton, 1970), pp. 154–63; D. W. Robertson, Jr., "Courtly Love as an Impediment to the Understanding of Medieval Literary Texts," in *The Meaning of Courtly Love*, ed. F. X. Newman (Albany: State University of New York Press, 1968), pp. 1–18. See also the interesting review by Jean Frappier, "Sur un procès fait à l'amour courtois," *Romania* 93 (1972): 145–93; and Francis Utley, "Must We Abandon the Concept of Courtly Love?" *Medievalia et Humanistica*, n.s. 3 (1972): 299–324.

6. C. S. Lewis, *The Allegory of Love: A Study in Medieval Tradition* (Oxford: Oxford University Press, 1936).

7. Peter Dronke, *Medieval Latin and the Rise of the European Love Lyric*, 2 vols. (Oxford: Clarendon Press, 1965).

8. John Benton, "Clio and Venus: An Historical View of Courtly Love," in *Meaning of Courtly Love*, ed. Newman, pp. 19–42.

9. Drouart La Vache, *Li Livres D'Amours*, ed. Robert Bossuat (Paris: Champion, 1926), lines 47–52.

10. Mark Girouard, *The Return to Camelot: Chivalry and the English Gentleman* (New Haven, Conn.: Yale University Press, 1981).

11. George Lyman Kittredge, *Chaucer and His Poetry* (Cambridge, Mass.: Harvard University Press, 1951), p. 63.

12. Gaston Paris, "Études sur les romans de la Table Ronde. Lancelot du Lac, II, *Le conte de la charette*," *Romania* 12 (1883): 459–534. For a useful survey of scholarship, see Edmund Reiss, "*Fin' Amours*: Its History and Meaning in Medieval Literature," *Medieval and Renaissance Studies* 8 (1979): 74–99.

13. Petrarch, canzone 9.75; cf. Chiaro Davanzati, rima I, lines 37–39:

"Ch'al primo quando amai/di folle amor mi prese;/or son d'amor cortese."; Cino da Pistoia, sonnet 80: "Lo fino Amor cortese, ch' ammaestra/ d'umil soffrenza ogni suo dritto servo." See Joan Ferrante, "*Cortes' Amor* in Medieval Texts," *Speculum* 55 (1980): 686–95.

14. Ovid, *Amores* 1.ix.

15. Jean le Névelon, *La Venjance Alixandre*, ed. Edward Billings Ham, Elliott Monographs, 27 (Princeton, N.J.: Princeton University Press; Paris: Presses Universitaires de France, 1931). Note especially Jean's direct address to Henry in the first lines of the prologue.

16. *Oeuvres de Froissart*, ed. Kervyn de Lettenhove, 25 vols. (Brussels: Devaux, 1867–77), 1:546.

17. *Livre des faits du Mareschal de Boucicault*, in *Collection complète des memoirs relatifs à l'histoire de France*, ed. Claude B. Petitot (Paris: Foucault, 1825), 6:393.

18. *The Works of Sir Thomas Malory*, ed. Eugène Vinaver, 3 vols. (London: Oxford University Press, 1967), 3: 1119–20.

19. Gervase Mathew, *The Court of Richard II* (New York: Norton, 1968), pp. 1–11.

20. On the reading of romances, see G. R. Owst, *Literature and the Pulpit in Medieval England: A Neglected Chapter in the History of English Letters and of the English People*, 2nd rev. ed. (Oxford: Blackwell; New York: Barnes and Noble, 1961), pp. 10–15. In *Amadís of Gaul*, Amadis's half-brother, Galeor, is inspired to the knightly life by the diligent reading of romances. See *Amadís of Gaul, Books I and II*, trans. Edwin B. Place and Herbert C. Behm (Lexington: University Press of Kentucky, 1974), p. 73.

21. Chaucer, "Merciles Beaute"; Froissart, "Nom ai Amans, et en surnom Tristrans." See F. N. Robinson's note to line 20 of "To Rosamounde," in *The Works of Geoffrey Chaucer*, 2nd ed. (Boston: Houghton Mifflin, 1957), p. 859. All references to Chaucer's poetry are taken from this edition.

22. *Sir Gawain and the Green Knight*, ed. J. R. R. Tolkien and E. V. Gordon, 2nd ed., rev. Norman Davis (Oxford: Clarendon Press, 1967), line 917.

23. See Frederick S. Shears, *Froissart: Chronicler and Poet* (London: Routledge, 1930), p. 16.

24. On the importance of speech see Richard Firth Green, *Poets and Princepleasers: Literature and the English Court in the Late Middle Ages* (Toronto: University of Toronto Press, 1980), pp. 73–84.

25. Cf. Edmond Huguet, *Dictionnaire de la langue francaise du seizieme siecle* (Paris, 1925), s.v. "amadigauliser, amadiser, amadiseur," for the last of which is cited "ces beaux Amadiseurs auroyent faveurs de dames."

26. *La Querelle de la Rose: Letters and Documents*, ed. Joseph L. Baird and John R. Kane, (Chapel Hill: University of North Carolina Press, 1978), 1:3197.

27. *Canterbury Tales*, line I 3169.

28. *De arte honesti amandi*, book 1, chap. 12.

29. It is used by the narrator six times in the *Miller's Tale* (lines 3200, 3278, 3290, 3349, 3715, 3754), but always in reference to the pretentious Absolon; it does not appear in the *Reeve's Tale* or the *Cook's Tale* and it is used but once, scornfully, in the *Manciple's Tale*, in the lines quoted above.

30. "Unde haec passio a multis dicta est hereoes. quia herois siue nobilis plus contigit." Quoted by Lowes, " 'Loveres Maladye,' " p. 43. Cf. Burton, *Anatomy*, part 3, sec. 2.

31. Kittredge, *Chaucer and His Poetry*, p. 63

32. Froissart, *Chronicle*, trans. Berners, 1:194.

33. Quoted by Lee W. Patterson, in "Ambiguity and Interpretation: A Fifteenth-Century Reading of *Troilus and Criseyde*," *Speculum* 54 (1979): 303.

34. *On the Properties of Things: John of Trevisa's Translation of Bartholomeus Anglicus De Proprietatibus Rerum*, ed. M. C. Seymour et al. (Oxford: Clarendon Press, 1975), 1:598.

35. *Calendar of State Papers: Venetian, 1202–1509*, ed. Rawdon Brown (London, 1864), 1:22–25.

36. *The Book of the Knight of La Tour-Landry*, ed. Thomas Wright, Early English Text Society, OS 33 (1868; reprint, Millwood, N.Y.: Kraus, 1973), pp. 1–2.

37. *La Tour-Landry*, p. 18.

38. *Sir Gawain and the Green Knight*, ed. Davis, lines 1208ff., especially line 1219.

39. *La Tour-Landry*, p. 172.

40. Ibid., p. 185.

41. *Les Cent ballades, par Jean le Seneschal*, ed. Gaston Raynand, Société des anciens textes français (Paris, 1905), p. 213: "On peut l'un dire, et l'autre doit onfere."

42. See Richard Barber, *The Knight and Chivalry* (London: Longmans, 1970), p. 149.

43. See Arthur Piaget, "La cours amoreuse dite de Charles VI," *Romania* 20 (1891): 417–54; Theodor Staub, "Die Gründung des Pariser Minnehofs von 1400," *Zeitschrift für romanische Philologie* 77 (1961): 1–14; and also my *Malory's Morte Darthur* (Cambridge, Mass: Harvard University Press, 1976), pp. 156 and 265, n. 70.

44. Charles Poitevin, "La charte de la Cour d'amour," *Bulletin de*

*l'Academie royale des sciences, des lettres, et des beaux-arts Belgique*, 3rd ser. 12 (1886): 210.

45. Arthur Piaget, "Un manuscrit de la cour amoreuse de Charles VI," *Romania* 31 (1902): 597–603.

46. Froissart, *Oeuvres*, ed. Lettenhove, 2:372.

47. Henry A. Kelly, *Love and Marriage in the Age of Chaucer*, (Ithaca, N.Y.: Cornell University Press, 1970), pp. 163ff. See also Michael M. Sheehan, "The Formation and Stability of Marriage in Fourteenth-Century England: Evidence of an Ely Register," *Medieval Studies* 3 (1971): 228–63.

48. See Margaret Galway, "Joan of Kent and the Order of the Garter," *Birmingham Historical Journal*, 1 (1947): 23.

49. See Mathew, *Court of Richard II*, p. 17.

50. James I of Scotland, *The Kingis Quair*, ed. John Norton-Smith (Oxford: Clarendon Press, 1971), lines 274–87.

51. *Calendar of State Papers and Manuscripts Existing in the Archives of Milan, (1385–1618)*, ed. Allen B. Hinds (London, 1912), 1:1–2. I owe this reference to Sumner Ferris, of California State College, California, Pa.

52. *Pageant of the Birth, Life, and Death of Richard Beauchamp, Earl of Warwick, K. G. (1389–1439)*, ed. Harold Arthur, Viscount Dillon, and W. H. St. John Hope (London: Longmans, Green, 1914), pl. 35.

53. Henry N. MacCracken, "The Earl of Warwick's Virelai," *PMLA* 22 (1907): 597–606.

54. See his testament of 3 February 1398, in Sir Sydney Armitage-Smith, *John of Gaunt, King of Castile and Leon, Duke of Aquitaine and Lancaster, Earl of Derby, Lincoln, and Leicester, Seneschal of England* (Westminster: A. Constable, 1904), p. 420.

55. See Cesare Carrocci, *La giostra di Lorenzo de' Medici* (Bologna: 1899); and André Pechon, *La jeunesse de Laurent de Médicis (1449–1478)* (Paris: G. de Bussac, 1963).

56. *Paston Letters and Papers of the Fifteenth Century*, ed. Norman Davis, 2 vols. (Oxford: Clarendon Press, 1971), 1:604.

57. *Paston Letters*, ed. Davis, 1:662.

58. *The Love Letters of Henry VIII*, ed. Henry Savage (London: Wingate, 1949), p. 47.

59. Pierre de Bourdeille, Seigneur de Brantôme, *Vies des hommes illustres et grands capitaines françois* (Paris: 1740), discours 85.

60. Niccoló Machiavelli, *Tutte le opere*, ed. Guido Mazzoni and Mario Cassella (Florence: G. Barbera, 1929), letter 15 (pp. 893–94).

61. *The Book of the Courtier, from the Italian of Count Baldassare Castiglione: Done into English by Sir Thomas Hoby, anno 1561*, introduction by Walter Raleigh (London: D. Nutt, 1900). p. 265.

# Hoccleve's *Series*

## Experience and Books

### John Burrow

Criticism has hardly begun to do justice to the poetry of Thomas Hoccleve. The names of Hoccleve and Lydgate are often coupled together, like Gray and Collins, or Moody and Sankey; but the two poets are different in many ways. Lydgate is, in my judgment, distinctly inferior to his contemporary as a writer—in his command, that is, of English idiom, syntax, and meter. Yet ever since the fifteenth century the massive bulk of Lydgate's work has overshadowed Hoccleve and obscured the qualities and merits of his work. To define his qualities and merits is not easy, for Hoccleve is in some ways an eccentric and peculiar writer—not at all the Chaucer clone of some literary histories—and he is also very uneven in the quality of his work. One moment the reader is startled by a sinewy felicity of phrase or a bold originality of conception; the next moment he is yawning over the "bore of the Privy Seal." But all Hoccleve's works—the shorter poems, the *Regement of Princes*, and the *Series*—merit more attention than they have so far received from editors, critics, and readers.[1] The present essay is devoted to the boldest and most interesting of them: the so-called *Series*.

The title *Series* was given by E. P. Hammond to a linked sequence of writings, mostly verse but including three short pieces of prose, composed by Hoccleve in the last years of his life (he died in 1426) and preserved complete or nearly so in six manuscripts.[2] It consists of the following parts: a prologue, the *Complaint*, the *Dialogue with a Friend*, an envoy, the *Tale of Jereslaus's Wife*, four linking stanzas, a prose *Moralization* of the preceding *Tale, Learn to Die*, three linking stanzas, a prose version of the ninth lesson for All Hallows' Day, a linking prologue, the *Tale of Jonathas*, a prose *Moralisation* of the tale, and (in one manuscript only) a single-stanza envoy.

Derek Pearsall draws attention to the chief peculiarity of the *Series* when he describes it, somewhat tartly, as "an attempt to make a longish poem out of nothing."³ At the core of the work, in the *Dialogue with a Friend*, Hoccleve does indeed represent himself as wishing to write but uncertain what to write about; and when after long discussion with his friendly advisor he finally settles on a story from the *Gesta Romanorum* (the story of Jereslaus's wife) and a moral discourse on holy dying, these decisions, though not random, are frankly advertised as secondary to that initial desire to "make a longish poem." Indeed, the *Series* as a whole is to an unusual degree preoccupied with the business of its own composition. It is a measure of the general neglect of Hoccleve that the current fashion for reading texts as "self-referential" or "reflexive" has not yet caught up with the *Series*, which is far and away the most reflexive of all medieval English writings.

Hoccleve, as I hope to show, understood quite well the tricks which could be played with self-reference. His conventional sections of narrative and moral discourse (the two tales, their moralisations, *Learn to Die*, and the version of the All Hallows lesson) are all "framed" by passages which purport to describe how they came to be written; and these passages of explanation, since they themselves form part of the work whose production they describe, enjoy a special double status, which Hoccleve from time to time exploits to produce that effect described by André Gide as "mise en abyme." The work turns in upon itself, as in the Escher drawing of a hand drawing itself. However, such reflexive tricks are neither so difficult of execution nor so profound in implication as some contemporary writers, artists, and filmmakers seem to suppose; and if Hoccleve's *Series* were chiefly a book concerned with its own production, it would indeed deserve to be dismissed as a longish poem "made out of nothing." A profoundly bookish work it certainly is—aware of its own existence as a book, of its derivation from other books, and of its destination in the hands of patrons and readers. But books are themselves a part of life, not least in the case of an author who was himself a professional scribe; and Hoccleve takes pains to represent the production of this particular book as an event of great importance in his own life.⁴ He has, he confesses, suffered a breakdown; and his friends and acquaintances still regard him with anxiety and suspicion, even though he has long since recovered. The *Series* is therefore designed both to affirm his recovery and also, by its very existence, to prove it by showing that he can indeed talk sense again. Both ways the book marks a stage in that social rehabilitation which has, he complains, been so slow to follow his medical recovery. The reflexiveness of the work is accordingly as far as could be from mere mandarin cleverness. With all its faults, the *Series* has deep roots in painful human experience.⁵

The prologue opens with an elaborate *chronographia* which invites comparison with Chaucer's *Canterbury Tales*:

> After that hervest Inned had his sheves
> And that the broune season of myhelmesse
> Was come and gan the trees robbe of ther leves
> That grene had bene / and in lusty fresshnesse
> And them into colowre / of yelownesse
> Hadd dyen / and doune throwne undar foote
> That chaunge sanke / into myne herte roote.
>   ( (*Complaint*, lines 1–7)

The plangent description of the "brown season of Michaelmas" seems designed, as Pryor suggests, to contrast pointedly with Chaucer's April opening; and this contrast is sustained in what follows. Whereas in the *Canterbury Tales* April inspires the poet to go out and join a company of pilgrims, November drives Hoccleve in upon himself in solitary meditation. He passes a sleepless night at the end of November, brooding on the unhappy aftermath of his illness:

> I see well sythen I with sycknes last
> Was scourged / clowdy hath bene the favoure
> That shone on me / full bright in tymes past
> The sonne abatid / and the derke showre
> Hildyd downe right on me.
>   (lines 22–26)

Hoccleve here develops Chaucer's image of Fortune "covering her bright face with a cloud" (*Monk's Tale, Canterbury Tales* VII 2766). The violent dark shower which pours straight down upon him represents the extreme distress which leads Hoccleve, next morning, to burst out in his complaint:

> I thowght I nolde it kepe cloos no more
> Ne lett it in me / for to olde and hore
> And for to pryve / I cam of a woman
> I braste oute on the morowe / and thus began.
>   (lines 32–35)

The rubric which follows these lines, "here endythe my prologe and folowythe my complaynt," may remind the reader that he is reading a book, in which a Prologue is followed by a Complaint; but the ensuing pages dispel this awareness for the time being. Hoccleve does indeed "braste oute" in his distress; and, apart from one Chaucerian reference to "my mater" (line 119), the 378 lines of the *Complaint* create an uninterrupted impression of direct and impassioned utterance. Hoccleve recalls his breakdown, the "wyld infirmytie" from which he claims to have recovered fully five years before on All Hallows' Day, and regrets that people do not even now believe that he is fully better:

> Chaungid had I my pas/some seiden eke
> For here and there/forthe stirte I as a Roo
> None abode/none arrest but all brain seke.
> (lines 127–29)

The more or less well-intentioned doubts of his acquaintances, so sharply etched in lines such as these (the choppy movement of 129 is particularly good), both depress and exasperate Hoccleve; and the exasperation and depression find convincing utterance in the rambling, repetitive progress of his complaint. At one point he reports "words of consolation" found recently in a book; but here, as in Chaucer's *Parliament of Fowls*, the record of reading serves only to confirm the actual reader's tendency to forget that what *he* is reading is also, in fact, a book.[6]

The opening of the *Dialogue with a Friend*, however, disturbs the illusion created by the preceding *Complaint*. With something of the impetuosity of Chaucer's Pandarus, a friend beats on the poet's door:

> And ended my complaynt/in this manere
> One knocked/at my chambre dore sore
> And cryed a lowde/howe hoccleve arte thow here.
> (*Dialogue*, lines 1–3)

Is "complaynt" in line 1 the title of a text, or does it simply refer to the utterance? The indecisive punctuation in Furnivall's edition, with inverted commas but no capital *C*, reflects a real uncertainty; but this is resolved once Hoccleve, in response to the friend's question "What dydist thow when I knocked?", reads the *Complaint* out to him (line 17; see also lines 39–42, 317). Hoccleve, in fact, has been writing. This is a new discovery, not prepared for in the previous section: indeed, the expression "braste out" distinctly suggested a spontaneous utterance, not a composition. If the *Complaint* can now be accepted as a piece of writing, this can only be because we have in fact been reading it. The logic of this response, it may be noted, would have been stronger in an age of manuscript that it is in the age of print. When the record of an act of writing is itself printed (in epistolary novels, for instance), no reader will ever be tempted actually to identify the two texts; but the reader of manuscript is in a rather different position. Hoccleve was himself a clerk and scribe; and Durham University Library still possesses a copy of the *Series* itself written in his own hand. It is not that any reader of the Durham *Series*, even if he had known the hand to be Hoccleve's, would have believed that the formal copy which lay before him, with its capital letters illuminated in red, blue, and gold, contained the actual leaves from which the poet read to his friend. The question is not one of real belief, but of suspended disbelief or literary illusion: the particular illusion which Hoccleve is here aiming at would have been easier for the author and stronger for the reader at a time when books were handwritten. It is surprising, in fact, that medieval writers did not more often employ this kind of reflexive device.[7]

After Hoccleve had read out his *Complaint* and discussed it with his friend (up to line 198 of the *Dialogue*), they go on to consider what he should write next. The *Dialogue*, in fact, acts as an extended "link" (in Canterbury terminology) between the *Complaint* and the two next parts of the *Series*: the *Tale of Jereslaus's Wife* and *Learn to Die*. This manner of construction implies that the *Dialogue* is itself not a composition, just as the Canterbury links are not tales; and Hoccleve sustains this pretense successfully, on the whole, with lively conversational effects. The main blemish—and it is a serious one—is the passage in which the poet harangues his friend on the evils of tampering with coin of the realm (*Dialogue*, lines 99–196). The impression of a written set-piece here is confirmed by an untimely reminder of its textual character in the shape of a clumsy postscript announcing that, since the passage was written, Parliament has made a new law to deal with the abuse (lines 134–40). In general, the *Dialogue* is certainly too long (826 lines); but it derives considerable interest from its relationship to the preceding and succeeding compositions.

The discussion of the *Complaint* turns on the question of whether this composition should be published ("made for the to goo amonge the people," lines 23–24). The friend advises against, on the principle of letting sleeping dogs lie:

> How it stode with the/leyde is all a slepe
> Men have forget it/it is owt of mynd.
> *(Dialogue*, lines 29–30)

He counsels a prudent silence, like the well-intentioned Arbuthnot in Pope's *Prologue to the Satires*: "Good friend, forbear! you deal in dangerous things."[8] But the friend's reasons for this advice exasperate Hoccleve, for he is displaying just that failure to understand which has been making life so difficult for the poet. How can he say that Hoccleve's history of mental illness is "owt of mynd"? Wasn't he listening when the poet, so very recently, read him his *Complaint*? The tragic theme of human isolation and misunderstanding is here given a comic twist, for the reader knows that the publication of the *Complaint* is a foregone conclusion. Also, Hoccleve seems to recognize in his own response something of that touchiness for which authors have always been notorious.

Discussion of the *Complaint* comes to an end with Hoccleve's harangue about the coinage. This display of public spirit evidently reassures the friend for the time being, and the conversation turns to future works. Now that the *Complaint* is finished, Hoccleve declares his intention of composing one last English piece: a translation of a little treatise in Latin called *Learn to Die* (lines 205–06). It seems an appropriate task for a poet who, at fifty-three years of age, realizes the vanity of life and the inevitability of death:

> Shee is the rogh besom/ which shal us alle
> Sweepe out of this world/ whan god list it falle.
> (lines 286–87)

At this, Hoccleve's friend begins to worry again. The poet's breakdown, he says, was caused by excessive study (musing, staring, and poring upon books, lines 404–05), and further bookwork may cause a relapse. With an effect of repetition which certainly does not lack point, the friend again gives expression to that mistrust from which Hoccleve seems unable to escape, in an image of great beauty and simplicity:

> Thogh a strong fyr/ that was in an herth late
> Withdrawen be/ and swept away ful cleene
> Yit aftirwarde/ bothe the herth ande plate
> Been of the fyr warm/ thogh no fyr be seene.
> (lines 309–12)

Hoccleve responds with appeals to friendship and protestations that his breakdown was caused not by study but by a physical illness, from which he is now fully recovered; and after he has promised not to overexert himself, the friend professes himself satisfied (lines 512–25).

The reader expects *Learn to Die* to follow on the next leaf, but it does not. Instead, three hundred more lines of the *Dialogue* serve as introduction to a composition which, in the event, precedes the moral discourse in the order of the *Series*: the *Tale of Jereslaus's Wife*. Courthope may have had this section in mind when he spoke of Hoccleve's "crude and inartistic conception";[9] but the unexpected developments in this last part of the *Dialogue* in fact confirm just the impression which the *Series* as a whole is seeking to create—the impression of a book whose contents are being inscribed, as it were, before the reader's very eyes. Despite all the thought and calculation of which we see so much, such a work will be a prey to present contingencies. On this occasion, the friend calls to mind that last September Hoccleve said he had promised a book to Humphrey, Duke of Gloucester. Is "this book" then meant for him (line 539)? Hoccleve answers this eminently reflexive question in the affirmative, but goes on to confess that he is not sure what will best please the Duke—a translation of Vegetius on the art of chivalry, perhaps, or a chronicle of Humphrey's own chivalrous deeds. The friend acknowledges the difficulty, and cites a well-known passage from Geoffrey of Vinsauf about the importance of planning or "avisament" in literary composition.[10] He proposes that Hoccleve should write something in praise of women, as an act of penance for the offense he gave them in an earlier work, the *Letter of Cupid*. The Duke himself will enjoy such a book, and also no doubt, being given to polite "daliance" with ladies, will show it to them and so restore Hoccleve to their favor. The friend leaves, and Hoccleve addresses a formal envoy of three stanzas to his female readers ("My ladyes alle . . .," line 806). He will translate a story of a good woman from the *Gesta Romanorum*:

> and that shal pourge I hope
> My guilt/as cleene/as keverchiefs dooth sope.
> (lines 825–26)

With this spirited, even faintly rebellious couplet Hoccleve concludes the *Dialogue* and introduces the *Tale of Jereslaus's Wife*.

The story of the virtuous wife of the Emperor of Rome is extravagant both in plot and character, much in the manner of Chaucer's *Man of Law's Tale*; but this very extravagance serves to mark the story off as existing on a different plane of reality from what has preceded it. In this case it seems entirely appropriate that Hoccleve should read it out to his friend, and that the friend should criticize it as a composition for lacking the *moralisatio*:

> Where is the moralizynge/y yow preye
> Bycome heere of/was ther noon in the booke
> Out of the which/that thow this tale tooke.
> (lines 12–14)

When the friend goes off home to get his own more complete copy, from which Hoccleve then obediently translates the allegorical moralization, the realism of these comings and goings is such that the reader is surprised when the prose text is followed immediately by the promised *Learn to Die*, with no link other than a rubric: "Explicit moralizatio & incipit ars utillissima sciendi mori."[11] In the *Canterbury Tales* the absence of a prologue or epilogue tears a hole in the fabric of the fiction; but the effect here is rather different, since the reader must by now understand the double nature of the book he is reading. It not only describes the making of a book, but also *is* that book—in which a simple rubric would be enough to link the most diverse items.

After translating part of the Latin *Learn to Die*, Hoccleve confesses that he has had enough and substitutes for the remainder his version of the ninth lesson for All Hallows' Day (the day on which, five years earlier, he had recovered from his breakdown, *Complaint*, lines 55–56). This describes the joys of the celestial Jerusalem, and its conclusion brings with it a strong sense of an ending: "to grete foles been we/but if we cheese the bettre part/which part god of his infynyt goodnesse graunte us alle to cheese/Amen." Hoccleve has produced the two works promised in the *Dialogue*; and the words just quoted suggest that, like Chaucer at the end of the *Canterbury Tales*, "the maker of this book here taketh his leave." But Hoccleve has one more surprise in store. The word *Amen* is followed immediately by another rubric: "Hic additur alia fabula ad instanciam amici mei predilecti assiduam." Hoccleve had indeed intended to end with the lesson ("This booke thus to han endid had y thoght," *Jonathas*, line 1); but his friend requests one more item: another *Gesta Romanorum* story to warn his unruly fifteen-year-old son against the wiles of women. He promises to let the poet use his own copy again; and Hoccleve, although afraid that such a tale may undo all his previous good work with women readers, agrees to make a version:

> He glad was ther withal/and wel content
> The copie on the morwe sente he me
> And thus y wroot as yee may heere see.
> (*Jonathas*, lines 82–84)

With that last characteristic direction to the reader, Hoccleve vanishes from the scene, leaving us, for what remains of the *Series*, face-to-face with a conventional book—first, the fantastic *Gesta* story of Jonathas and his unscrupulous mistress, then (without a link) a prose *moralisatio*, and finally, in the Durham copy, a single eight-line stanza directing the whole "smal booke" to the Countess of Westmorland.[12] The author's conjuring tricks are over.

As we have seen, Hoccleve presents himself throughout the *Series* as a reader of books engaged in producing, by translation from Isidore, Suso, and the *Gesta Romanorum*, a book of his own, and concerned that this book should meet a favorable reception from its readers. To appreciate the *Series* it is above all necessary to understand, and if possible sympathize with, the nature of this concern about the work's reception. From the start, Hoccleve displays an acute, even morbid, sensitivity to the possibilities of unfavorable response. First there is the question, discussed at length in the *Dialogue*, of whether his *Complaint* should be published at all. Hoccleve himself in the poem insists that it should, to set the record straight; but the friend's profound doubts and anxieties create a distinctly uneasy impression, preserved as they are in the text which Hoccleve in fact did publish. Then there is the question of what the poet should write for Humphrey of Gloucester. *Learn to Die* may please the "devout man" who first suggested it (*Dialogue*, lines 234–35), but is it not rather too heavy for the duke? And what about those ladies whom Hoccleve has unwittingly offended by an earlier act of translation? In the event, the friend persuades him to kill two birds with one stone by telling the story of Jereslaus's wife; but Hoccleve's worries are not over yet. The friend's innocent request for something to give his wayward son raises further problems, for a thoroughgoing exposure of female wiles, suitable for the boy, may once again alienate respectable lady readers. Even the conventional closing words of the *Series*, in the Durham autograph manuscript, seem to be tinged with anxiety. Hoccleve commands his "smal booke" to present itself to Joan, Countess of Westmorland (daughter of John of Gaunt and aunt of Humphrey of Gloucester):

> And byseeche hire / on my behalve and preye
> Thee to receyve / for hire owne right
> And looke thow / in al manere weye
> To plese hir wommanhede / do thy might
>  Humble servant
>  to your gracious
>  noblesse
>   : T: Hoccleve

267

Authors frequently express eagerness to please readers, not least wealthy and powerful patrons; but there is much more than mere convention or normal self-interest in Hoccleve's persistent expressions of concern about how his book will be received by his acquaintances, the Duke of Gloucester, the ladies, and the Countess of Westmorland. They are to be understood, in part, as manifestations of that "thowghtfull dissease and woo" (*Complaint*, line 388) of which he speaks at length in the *Complaint* and *Dialogue*—the same state of anxiety which drove him to practice sane faces in the mirror at home (*Complaint*, lines 155–68). His recovery from his breakdown (allowing him to have indeed recovered) has left him morbidly concerned about what people think of him and his work.

Hoccleve may have taken some hints for this self-portrait from Chaucer's dream poems; but no English writer had attempted such a full representation of anxiety before his time. He is our first chronicler of private worries—an ancestor, perhaps, of Charles Lamb and Philip Larkin. In his lowest moments, he seems simply to indulge his gloom: "This troubly lyfe/hathe all to longe enduryd//Not have I wyst/how in my skynne to turne." (*Complaint*, 302–03). But in the *Series* as a whole, he tries hard to "turn in his skin," and the work benefits morally and artistically from the effort. Hoccleve sees the writing and publication of his latest book as an important stage in the process by which he may finally be rehabilitated after his illness and its long aftermath. Furthermore, the book itself seems to trace the steps of such a rehabilitation. It is not tightly constructed, but the order of its parts is more significant than may at first appear. It begins in solitary alienation, and it ends with the reassumption (albeit hesitant) of a social role proper to a man of fifty-three. The structure of the work, though imperfect, does something to articulate the author's deepest concern.

The opening complaint is at first presented simply as a solitary outburst of unbearable misery; but, like Boethius's *planctus* at the beginning of *De Consolatione Philosophiae*, Hoccleve's marks the starting-point for a process of consolation.[13] In both works this process begins with the arrival of a second person: Lady Philosophy in the Latin, a friend in the English. The progress from one to two is itself significant; and in Hoccleve's discussion with his friend, as noted earlier, we for the first time see his complaint not as a mere solitary outburst but as a publishable writing.[14] Hoccleve's determination to publish it, against the advice of the friend (not, like Lady Philosophy, infallible), represents the first and decisive step in his rehabilitation. He is, he says, not ashamed of his affliction: it was "the stroke of god" (*Dialogue*, line 79). He is therefore ready to "make an open shryfte" (line 83) by publishing the *Complaint*, which both confesses his mental illness and affirms his recovery from it.

However, such a publication is itself too abnormal to mark a return to normality, and discussion of the three remaining publications (*Learn to Die* and the two *Gesta* stories) is colored by Hoccleve's still unsatisfied yearning for completely normal relations with his fellow men. *Learn to Die* is an entirely conventional moral treatise undertaken at the urging of a devout man, and there is nothing abnormal in the poet's desire to cleanse his soul by this act of translation (*Dialogue*, line 214–17); yet it is made clear in Hoccleve's discussion with his friend that the composition also has a private significance. It is the first true literary labor he has undertaken since his breakdown. He has waited for five years "al to preeve my selfe" (line 444); and now he is ready for the work which he has pondered so long. To perform it successfully will prove both to himself and to others that his mind really is, as he claims, "as sad and stable / As evere it was at any tyme or this" (lines 366–67).

Despite its impersonal and conventional nature, then, *Learn to Die* still plays a part in the private drama of Hoccleve's recovery. One might also see in Suso's descriptions of the dying man deserted by his friends (following lines 424 and 709) a reflection of the poet's own sense of isolation. By contrast, the two *Gesta* stories, of the virtuous wife of Jereslaus and the wicked Fellicula, have no direct bearing on Hoccleve's personal circumstances; and his account of their composition claims for them no diagnostic or therapeutic significance. Hoccleve, it seems, now takes for granted his ability to fulfill literary commissions. Yet there remains the question of how his writings will be received. Perhaps the discussion of Humphrey's literary tastes displays no more than a customary concern for the satisfaction of a patron; but when the friend speaks of Hoccleve's offense to women, we recognize the familiar, nagging personal note. The idea of making amends to women readers for an earlier literary offense is presumably borrowed from Hoccleve's master, Chaucer: the tale of Jereslaus's wife is a latter-day *Legend of Good Women*. Yet Hoccleve's tone is, in a very characteristic way, different from Chaucer's. When Chaucer has Alceste plead that he wrote about Criseyde "of innocence, and nyste what he seyde" (Prologue to the *Legend*, G 345), the unlikely claim coolly outstares the facts, with an effect of teasing comedy. By contrast, Hoccleve's defense of the *Letter of Cupid*, although conducted along similar lines, leaves an impression of real anxiety:

> Considereth / ther of / was I noon Auctour
> I nas in that cas / but a reportour
> Of folkes tales / as they seide I wroot
> I nat affermed it on hem / god woot . . .
> Who so that seith I am hire Adversarie

> And dispreise hir condicions and port
> For that I made of hem swich a report/
> He mis avysed is/and eek to blame.
> (*Dialogue*, lines 760–63, 768–71)

Such misunderstandings and mistaken gossip are no laughing matter, in the context of the *Series*, and the poet's attempt to set the record straight quite lacks Chaucer's *sang froid*. A note of pleading in Hoccleve's voice serves as a reminder that women formed an influential part of that society from which his illness alienated him.

Although Hoccleve's last conversation with his friend, in the prologue to *Jonathas*, still expresses some fear of being misunderstood, the main impression which he creates, in this final appearance, is one of confidence restored and status regained. To produce a moral tale for the benefit of his friend's erring son is a comfortable sort of commission. The poet, at last, has the advantage of his worried friend, and it is now Hoccleve who speaks for society, uttering the common wisdom of the elders of the tribe. It is a very different sort of utterance from the solitary grieving with which the *Series* began; and it seems intended to mark a happy ending to the poet's struggle to rehabilitate himself.

In the world of Hoccleve's *Series*, books are part of life—patrons commission them, readers borrow them, authors worry about them—and the *Series* itself strikes many readers as an almost painfully "real" book. One mark of this reality is the curious irritation which it seems to provoke. Like Lydgate, Hoccleve can be rambling and wordy; but his artistic defects do not fully account for the common response, which seems to have in it something of the herd's reaction to a wounded animal. Hoccleve's anxiety to be once more accepted puts backs up; and when he takes it upon himself to speak of the common good, as in the harangue on the coinage, readers are quick to detect a false note. We understand only too well, in short, why even his friend found it so hard to believe in him. But it is time that criticism began to do justice to a writer who had, besides his terrible frankness, a real literary talent.

# Notes

1. The Early English Text Society edition is still standard: *Minor Poems* I, ed. F. J. Furnivall, ES 61 (London, 1892); *Regement of Princes*, ed. Furnivall,

ES 72 (London, 1897); *Minor Poems* II, ed. Israel Gollancz, ES 73 (London, 1897). See also *Selections from Hoccleve*, ed. M. C. Seymour (Oxford: Clarendon Press, 1981). Further bibliography in the only book-length study, Jerome Mitchell, *Thomas Hoccleve: A Study in Early Fifteenth-Century English Poetic* (Urbana: University of Illinois Press, 1968) and in his essay in this present volume. The discussion of Hoccleve's metrical art in Ian Robinson, *Chaucer's Prosody* (Cambridge: Cambridge University Press, 1971), pp. 190–99, is a valuable recent addition.

2. Durham University Library Cosin MS. V.iii.9; Bodleian Library MS. Bodley 221; Bodleian Library MS. Laud Misc. 735; Bodleian Library MS. Arch. Selden Supra 53; Coventry City Record Office MS. Accession 325/1; Yale University Library MS. 493. The Durham copy is in the hand of Hoccleve himself from *Dialogue* line 253 to the end, and provides the basis of the text in *Minor Poems* I, and also in M. R. Pryor's doctoral thesis, "Thomas Hoccleve's *Series*: An Edition of MS. Durham Cosin V.iii.9," (University of California, Los Angeles, 1968), from which all quotations in this essay are taken. *Complaint* lines 1–308, is edited in J. A. Burrow's *English Verse 1300–1500* (London: Longman, 1977), *Dialogue*, lines 498–826, in E. P. Hammond's *English Verse between Chaucer and Surrey* (Durham, N.C.: Duke University Press, 1927). For the date of Hoccleve's death and other biographical matters, see A. L. Brown, "The Privy Seal Clerks in the Early Fifteenth Century," in *The Study of Medieval Records: Essays in Honour of Kathleen Major*, ed. D. A. Bullough and R. L. Storey (Oxford: Oxford University Press, 1971), pp. 260–81.

3. *Old English and Middle English Poetry* (London: Routledge and Kegan Paul, 1977), p. 237.

4. See H. C. Schulz, "Thomas Hoccleve, Scribe," *Speculum* 12 (1937): 71–81. Also A. I. Doyle and M. B. Parkes, "The Production of MSS. of the *Canterbury Tales* and the *Confessio Amantis* in the Early Fifteenth Century," in *Medieval Scribes, Manuscripts and Libraries: Essays Presented to N. R. Ker*, ed. M. B. Parkes and A. G. Watson (London: Scolar Press, 1978), pp. 164–210.

5. Penelope Doob, *Nebuchadnezzar's Children: Conventions of Madness in Middle English Literature* (New Haven, Conn.: Yale University Press, 1974), remarks that "many 'autobiographical' details in all [Hoccleve's] poems could easily be conventional or borrowed" (p. 228), stressing traditional elements in the poet's account of his breakdown in the *Series*. But it is not safe to assume that a real experience will not be described (or indeed experienced) in conventional terms; and A. L. Brown, "Privy Seal Clerks," gives grounds for supposing that Hoccleve was indeed ill at about the time indicated (*Complaint*, line 56): "He did not come to the Exchequer person-

ally between May 1414 and March 1417 to collect payments due to him" (p. 271). Pryor observes: "Comparing the records with events and personalities mentioned in the poems, there seems to be a remarkable coincidence between the autobiographical 'fictions' and the established facts" ("Hoccleve's *Series*," p. 28). See also J. A. Burrow, "Autobiographical Poetry in the Middle Ages: The Case of Thomas Hoccleve," *Proceedings of the British Academy* 68 (1982): 389-412.

6. The book has been identified by A. G. Rigg as Isidore of Seville's *Synonyma*, subtitled *De Lamentatione Animae Dolentis*: "Hoccleve's *Complaint* and Isidore of Seville,*"* see *Speculum* 45 (1970): 564-74. The sudden intrusion of the owner, who takes the Isidore back before Hoccleve can finish it, ingeniously marks the distinction, in the poem's fictive space, between Hoccleve's primary, foreground world and the secondary, recessed world in the books he reads. The commonplace critical term "three-dimensional" applies here with special force, since it is only in three dimensions that the edge of one thing can interrupt our view of another.

7. In his *Livre du Voir-Dit*, Guillaume de Machaut describes himself as compiling a book and invites the reader to identify the result with the volume in his hands ("ce livre"). He records the love poems and letters exchanged with Peronne d'Armentières, as they were written and received by him, in his "true-story book": see the edition of Paulin Paris (Paris: Société des Bibliophiles François, 1875; reprint, Geneva: Slatkine Reprints, pp. 17, 66, 76, 84-85, 134, 191, 202-03, 259, 261, 262, 263, 363. Hoccleve's younger contemporary, James I of Scotland, in his *Kingis Quair*, provides another example: "I set me doun,/ And furthwithall my pen in hand I tuke/ And maid a [cros], and thus begouth my buke" (ed. J. Norton-Smith [Oxford: Clarendon Press, 1971] lines 89-91). Where the editor's text reads "[cros]," the sole remaining manuscript has an actual cross.

8. A comparison suggested by W. J. Courthope in his interesting discussion of Hoccleve, *A History of English Poetry*, 6 vols. (London and New York: Macmillan, 1895), 1:333-40.

9. Ibid., p. 337.

10. *Poetria Nova*, ed. Edmond Faral, in *Les arts poétiques du XIIe et du XIIIe siècle* (Paris: Champion, 1924), pp 43-45. In the Durham MS. Hoccleve writes in the margin opposite *Dialogue*, lines 638ff., Geoffrey's words: "Si quis habet fundare domum non currit ad actum Impetuosa manus &c." The same sidenote appears in the three Bodleian MSS. I have not examined the Coventry or Yale MSS.

11. The source is Heinrich Suso's *Horologium Sapientiae*. See Benjamin P. Kurtz, "The Source of Occleve's *Lerne to Dye*." *Modern Language Notes* 38

(1923): 337–40, and his "The Relation of Occleve's *Lerne to Dye* to Its Source," *PMLA* 40 (1925): 252–75.

12. The Westmorland envoy and final signature can be seen in Hoccleve's own hand in Furnivall's facsimile opposite page 242 of his edition. Neither envoy nor signature is present in the other five MSS., in all of which the *Jonathas* moralisation is followed immediately by a separate item, Lydgate's *Dance Macabre*. Lydgate's poem is introduced by the peculiar rubric "Verba translatoris" in three of the MSS. (Coventry, Selden, and Laud; not so in Bodley 221; I have not seen Yale). Readers of these MSS. might well have taken the *Dance* to be part of the *Series*. I cannot explain the rubric.

13. Rigg, "Hoccleve's *Complaint*," assigns the *Series* to the genre *consolatio* or *Trostbuch*, comparing Boethius.

14. In the *De Consolatione*, similarly, the reader discovers that Boethius has been writing his *planctus* (book I, meter 1) only in retrospect, when Lady Philosophy enters: "Haec dum mecum tacitus ipse reputarem querimoniamque lacrimabilem stili officio signarem" ("In the mene while that I, stille, recordede these thynges with myself, and merkid my weply compleynte with office of poyntel, I saw, stondynge aboven the heghte of myn heved, a womman"; Chaucer's translation.)

# The Coherence of Henryson's Work

## Denton Fox

Henryson's three major works, the *Fables*, the *Testament of Cresseid*, and *Orpheus and Eurydice*, are poems which appear to be very dissimilar. I would like to argue here that they are more alike than has been recognized, and that they cast useful light on one another. While it would be possible to bring the dozen or so short poems that are usually attributed to Henryson into this comparison, since there are a number of parallels between them and the major works, it seems safer to leave them alone. This is partly because the attributions of the short poems are less secure, in some cases much less secure, than the attributions of the major poems, and partly because most of the short poems belong to quite specific genres, and are best considered in relation to other poems in these genres.[1]

While each of the three major works contains within itself a wide range of stylistic levels, it is plain that the *Fables* are predominantly in a lower style than the other two poems. But the same architectural methods are used in all three works. For a narrative poet, Henryson spends astonishingly little time in the narration of action: his habit is to relate action very laconically, even elliptically, and then leisurely to devote considerable space to speeches or to other set pieces. The opening fable of the cock and the jasp is a spectacular example: of the eight stanzas of the fable, five are given over to the cock's elaborate apostrophe to the jasp. But similar patterns can be found in most of the other fables. In the fable of the lion and the mouse, for instance, twelve stanzas, out of twenty-four, are given to the debate between the lion and the mouse; in the fable of the cock and the fox, seven of the twenty-seven stanzas are taken up by the debate between the cock and the fox, and, even more strikingly, just after the fox has run away with the cock, time apparently stops while the hens spend seven stanzas in discussing the cock and his dubious sexual prowess. Although the *Testament of Cresseid* is only 616 lines long, 203 of these lines are given over to the assembly of the gods—while 113 of these lines are spent in static descriptions of the gods—and Cresseid's formal complaint takes up another 63 lines.[2] *Orpheus* has only 414 lines, if one excludes the *moralitas*, but 63 lines are spent on Orpheus's genealogy and the nine muses and 50 lines on his lament. The 55-line passage describing Orpheus's trip to the planets (not in Henryson's source) and the musical theory he learned there might also be considered a set piece.

When one turns to the substance of the three works, the most obvious link, perhaps, is that they are all rather bookish. Aesopic fables were among the commonest of school texts and were frequently used as the raw material for rhetorical embellishment. The fable of Orpheus and Eurydice was among the most commonly rehandled of classical myths: Henryson's version is particularly bookish in that he follows very closely Nicholas Trivet's commentary on the Boethian meter which treats Orpheus. The *Testament of Cresseid* is bookish in a slightly different way, being based on, and in some sense a continuation of, Chaucer's *Troilus and Criseyde*.

All three works, too, are in some sense classicizing. *Orpheus and Eurydice* and the *Testament of Cresseid* are of course set in classical times, some of the *Fables* are genuinely of classical origin, and the whole collection purports to be "ane maner of translatioun" of "This nobill clerk, Esope."[3] Aesop's reputation now may be somewhat equivocal, but he was formerly thought of as one of the most central and important of classical authors.

The three works are consequently, in a certain limited sense, all non-Christian. Orpheus and Cresseid belong to the pre-Christian era: except in phrases like *God wait* ("God knows"), there is no reference to the Christian God in Henryson's version of either story, though there are some in the *moralitas* to *Orpheus*. The *Fables* are non-Christian in a slightly different way: animals do not have souls and cannot be Christians, though they can be made to parody Christian rituals, as in the parodies of confession and baptism in the *Fables*, and animal fables can be used to produce Christian morals. In the non-Christian world of these poems, tragedy is of course more possible than in a Christian world, where a virtuous man, or even a repentant sinner, must necessarily triumph, in heaven if not on earth.

To leave aside the *Testament* for a moment, *Orpheus* and the *Fables* are obviously similar in that they are both narrative poems with *moralitates* which, in the case of *Orpheus* and at least some of the *Fables*, allegorize the narratives. But there are other and more profound resemblances. One has to do with the figure of the poet and the function of poetry. In the prologue to the *Fables* Henryson makes very explicit the function of poetry. On the one hand it should entertain, "blyth the spreit," and contain both "sweit rhetore" and "sum merines" (lines 21, 3, 26). On the other hand, it should contain "ane morall sweit sentence," that is, a moral meaning, and "ane doctrine wyse," and should reprove man for his misliving (lines 12, 17, 6–7). This is all traditional enough, to be sure, but it still needs to be taken very seriously. It is obvious enough that the *Fables* contain plenty of morality and humor, and also that they are very subtle rhetorically, but it might be worth pointing out that they are centrally concerned with rhetoric in the other sense of that term: "the use of language to persuade." Almost every fable shows animals making speeches to persuade other animals to follow certain courses of action, whether good or ill. Henryson reinforces his remarks in the prologue by bringing into the *Fables*, at their midpoint, the figure of Aesop as the ideal poet. When the narrator asks him "to tell ane prettie fabill/Concludand with ane gude moralitie" (lines 1386–87), Aesop at first refuses, on the grounds that the world is now so corrupt that "my taillis may lytill succour mak" (line 1397). But the narrator finally succeeds in persuading him to tell a "morall fabill" by expressing the hope that "I may leir and beir away/Sum thing thairby heirefter may auaill" (lines 1402–03). Aesop tells the fable of the lion and the mouse, in which the mouse, by a long and eloquent speech, persuades the lion to virtuous action—action which later leads to the lion's preservation. This fable is the only one of the collection that is set firmly in the classical world: the implication is that rhetoric could once impel men to virtue, even if it is no longer so effective.

In *Orpheus*, a more symbolic work than the *Fables*, it is of course Orpheus himself who is the figure of the poet: he is shown not as just an instrumentalist, but as an inspired singer. And the persuasive power of his songs is the steady theme of the poem: they persuade the trees to dance, put Cerberus to sleep, let Ixion, Tantalus and Tityus be released from their torments, and, finally, move Pluto and Proserpina to release Eurydice. In the *moralitas* the power of wise and virtuous eloquence is made explicit over and over, especially with the repeated rhymes of *eloquence* and *sapience*:

> Bot quhen reson and perfyte sapience
> Playis apon the harp of eloquens,
> And persuadis our fleschly appetyte
> To leif the thocht of this warldly delyte . . .[4]

But at the end of the fable, when Orpheus loses Eurydice, it is clear that the power of even the supreme poet is severely limited. For all of his sapience and eloquence, Orpheus cannot restrain his own "fleschly appetyte."

The ends of the two poems are, indeed, worth comparing. The *Fables* end with a terrible picture of the human condition, with the mouse and the paddock struggling in the water, "The spreit vpwart, the body precis doun" (line 2959), and both about to be devoured by the kite, who is "deith, that cummis suddandlie / As dois ane theif" (lines 2962–63).[5] In *Orpheus* the image is not very different: Orpheus, the intellective part of man, struggles to bring upward Eurydice, the affective or passional part of man. But "the body precis doun": Henryson explains that "Orpheus has won Erudices, / Quhen oure desire wyth reson makis pes" (lines 616–17), but our desires and our reason cannot, the ending suggests, make any stable peace. And so, just as the mouse and the paddock cannot reach the sought-for bank, so Orpheus and Eurydice cannot, together, come up to light.

But we should return to the *Testament*. Where the *Fables* and *Orpheus* follow their sources in having separate *moralitates*, the *Testament* follows its source, Chaucer's *Troilus*, in having instead, first, some not altogether cogent moralizing comments made intermittently by the narrator, and, second, some slightly ambiguous morals drawn at the end. The mode of the *Testament*, then, is ironic, or to be more precise, it is a more consistently ironic work than either the *Fables* or *Orpheus*. Hence the figure of the poet is shown ironically, and we have almost a picture of the poet as liar. The loaded question is raised, "Quha wait git all that Chauceir wrait was trew?" (line 64), and Mercury is shown, "Lyke to ane poeit of the auld fassoun" (line 245), in clothes similar to Aesop's—but Mercury is the god of thieves and liars, as we are reminded by the line "Honest and gude, and not ane word culd lie" (line 252).

Apart from this, the *Testament* has some considerable resemblances to the other works. Cresseid is in many ways like Eurydice. They were both once queens of love, possessed of "myrth, blythnes, gret plesans, and gret play" (*Orpheus*, line 88). They both fled virtue, and hence were cast down to a place of torment. But Cresseid is also like many of the animals of the *Fables*, since she is a creature given over to her appetites, and a creature who takes refuge in self-deluding rhetoric.

The ending of the *Testament*, too, is not unlike the other works. In the fable of the mouse and the paddock, "The spreit vpwart, the body precis doun," and death comes to both. In the *Testament* Cresseid's body has been pressed down to that of a leprous beggar's, and to death, but there is the suggestion, when she bequeaths her spirit to Diana, that her soul presses upward. Orpheus and Eurydice are parted, and Orpheus, the survivor, says,

"I am expert, and wo is me thar-fore" (line 411); so Troilus, "Siching full sadlie, said, 'I can no moir;/Scho was vntrew and wo is me thairfoir'" (lines 601–02).

There has been much controversy about how Christian an interpretation we should place on the *Testament*, and, in particular, about whether Cresseid's final bequest, "My spreit I leif to Diane, quhair scho dwellis,/To walk with hir in waist woddis and wellis" (lines 587–88), signifies that she is redeemed. This last question seems to me now an unreal one, of the same order as such questions as "How many children had Lady Macbeth?" Cresseid is a fictional character, so we do not have to worry about where she will be after the Last Judgment; she is a pagan character, so Henryson could hardly have placed her in a Christian purgatory or heaven. Chaucer, of course, is similarly vague, and for the same reasons, about the fate of Troilus's soul: "And forth he wente, shortly for to telle,/Ther as Mercurye sorted hym to dwelle" (V. 1826–27). All one can say about Cresseid's end is that she has done more than ample penance, has come to full self-knowledge, has made a complete confession, and, if she were a Christian and a real person, would presumably be in a state of grace. The question as to whether the *Testament* is a Christian poem seems to me an ambiguous one. On the one hand, it is not a Christian poem in the sense that *Paradise Lost* is, since its machinery is all pagan. On the other hand, it is a serious moral poem written by a man who, from his other poems, was plainly a devout Christian; it was intended for a Christian audience; and, as far as I can see, there is nothing in the meaning of the poem that is not congruent with Christianity.

The ends of all three poems are, I think, ambiguous. In one sense, the ending of the *Fables* is the scene where the paddock and the mouse, struggling in the water, are caught up and devoured by the kite. In another sense, the ending of the *Fables* consists of the three last lines of the final *moralitas*:

> Now Christ for vs that deit on the rude,
> Of saull and lyfe as thow art Saluiour,
> Grant vs till pas in till ane blissit hour.

Similarly, the ending of *Orpheus*, on one level, is the final parting of Orpheus and Eurydice; on another level, it is the last lines of the *moralitas*: "Now pray we God . . . That he wald . . . geve vs grace to stand/In parfyte lufe, as he is glorius." Both the mouse, in the fable of the paddock and the mouse, and Eurydice are sympathetic enough, but they are not characters we are tempted to identify with: Eurydice is perhaps less human than the mouse. So Henryson is able to kill them off flatly and to balance this by introducing some slight hope in the *moralitas*. Our affections are more firmly fixed on Cresseid, so Henryson brings in some slight element of consolation in her death. What is important is not where her hypothetical soul goes, but that she has come to an understanding and acceptance of her fate, so that her death is not meaningless. Henryson was certainly following the Christian doctrine that the state of a person's soul at the time of death is all-important. But in literary terms, too, the meaning of a man's life is his final destination, what he has made of himself by the end of his life: ripeness is all.

If I am right, Henryson is not a stern moralist, as he has sometimes been called, but simply a man who looks very squarely at the world and sees that it is mostly thorns. In all three of his long poems, Henryson shows, ironically, wittily, but also seriously, a world in which there is very little justice, and a world in which apparently trivial faults can bring the harshest of punishments. But the world is not a meaningless world or a world without hope—though there may be very little hope for man on earth. Both sides are summed up in the fable of the preaching of the swallow: on the one hand,

> we may haif knawlegeing
> Off God almychtie be his creatouris,
> That he is gude, fair, wyis, and bening.
> (*Fables*, lines 1650–52)

On the other hand, God is distant and unknowable:

> our saull with sensualitie
> So fetterit is in presoun corporall,
> We may not cleirlie vnderstand nor se
> God as he is, nor thingis celestiall;
> Our mirk and deidlie corps materiale
> Blindis the spirituall operatioun,
> Lyke as ane man wer bundin in presoun.
> (lines 1629–35)

# Notes

1. This has been pointed out by Ian Jamieson, "The Minor Poems of Robert Henryson," *Studies in Scottish Literature* 9 (1971–72): 125–47.
2. This is commented on by A. C. Spearing, in "*The Testament of*

*Cresseid* and the 'High Concise Style,' " *Speculum* 37 (1962): 208–25.

3. Lines 32, 57. All quotations are from *The Poems of Robert Henryson*, ed. Denton Fox (Oxford: Clarendon Press, 1981). Since Henryson, like Lydgate, thought of Aesop as a Roman poet, the author of the versions in verse now attributed to Gualterus Anglicus, the title of the first prints, "The Morall Fabillis of Esope the Phrygian" is not likely to be authorial. But in the table of contents of the earlier Asloan MS. six of Henryson's fables are listed under the heading "þe fablis of Esope," which suggests that Henryson's attribution of his collection to Aesop was accepted.

4. Lines 507–10: see also lines 425–26, 469–70, and, for the rhyme *intelligence/eloquence*, 545–46. There are some variant readings in lines 469, 507, 508, and 546, but see my note to lines 469–70.

5. While it has sometimes been argued that the traditional order of the *Fables* is incorrect, H. H. Roerecke, in "The Integrity and Symmetry of Robert Henryson's *Moral Fables*" (Ph.D. diss., Pennsylvania State University, 1969), has proved conclusively, I think, that it can be trusted.

# Rhyme, Romance, Ballad, Burlesque, and the Confluence of Form

## Thomas J. Garbáty

In light of the dearth of textual evidence, it is a foolhardy venture to discuss once again the questions concerning the medievalism of the English and Scottish popular ballad: its origin, its creators, and its relationship to the romance and other contemporary genres. There is always the danger of restating what has often been said and perhaps expressed better. Indeed scholars have been involved in their own theories for so long that Holger Nygard's sober antitheory analysis of the issues came as a cathartic necessity.[1] Still, some answers may not be out of reach, because shreds of evidence before 1500 do exist, and the fifteenth century seems to have been a watershed of English literature. Let us start, therefore, by asking the following basic questions and noting some of the past responses.

The major question for our purpose here is not where the ballads originated, but when. Scholars seem to agree with Hodgart that the ballad was essentially a development of the later Middle Ages.[2] But within this time-scheme, literary historians start hedging. Vargyas chooses the twelfth (or eleventh) century through the fifteenth century, a wide range within which he at different times favors the fifteenth century, the sixteenth century, and the fourteenth century.[3] Generally, modern literary historians seem to accept the fifteenth century, as does Fowler, for the English and Scottish ballads, "when the metrical romance tradition of the later Middle Ages joined the mainstream of folksong to create a type of narrative song which we now call the ballad."[4] But in fact no specific time can be called the ballad age, writes Nygard, and his statement seems to be supported by the chronological wanderings seen above.[5]

Who were the original ballad makers? Vargyas identifies them as

French-Walloon peasants, the ballad being a "peasant genre."[6] Possibly the French peasants had greater creative powers than English or Scottish ones, but the hint of a Romantic, Rousseau-like noble and poetic illiterate, or of Grimm's *ex cathedra* "das Volk dichtet," seems to reflect a dated theory.[7] A separate category among the makers were the minstrels, who have been accused of debasing the grand topics and styles of the high Middle Ages, being themselves, in the fifteenth century, kings only of rags and patches. They were not wandering peasants, nor were they, according to scholarly dictum, "folk," a group to be discussed below.

Was there a link between romances and ballads, and which came first? We will examine some evidence of linkage and priority from a fifteenth-century romance, "The Weddynge of Sir Gawen and Dame Ragnell," and a fifteenth-century ballad, "The Marriage of Sir Gawaine," but Nygard has already given the only logical answer to this question: some romances (specifically of the Arthurian cycle, also *King Horn* and *Sir Orfeo*) are related to some ballads, but as to the matter of priority, no one can tell for sure.

The point we must never forget about this confusion existing in ballad scholarship is that only texts can help; they are the footprints of the past. Without these, all conjecture is useless, all theory a luxury. One thing seems certain: the idea of categorizing and defining popular verses was alien to the medieval mind. Such specifics were a product of the Age of Reason, and indeed William Shenstone, writing to Bishop Percy in 1761, first suggested the word "ballad" to separate songs of narrative "action" from those concerning only sentiment.[8]

What evidence then do we have for the medieval British ballad before 1500? Except for "Judas" (Child, no. 23), MS. Trinity College, Cambridge, 323 (B.14.39), ca. 1225-75, five ballads of Child's collection of 305 are found in manuscripts dated before 1500.[9] And indeed, all these five are from the fifteenth century. They are "Inter Diabolus et Virgo" (Child no. 1), MS. Bodleian Library, Oxford, 15444 (Rawlinson D.328), transcribed ca. 1444-45; "Robin Hood and the Monk" (Child no. 119), MS. Cambridge University Library Ff.5.48, from the second half of the fifteenth century; "Saint Stephen and Herod" (Child no. 22) and "Robin and Gandeleyn" (Child no. 115), MS. British Library Sloane 2593, ca. 1450; and "Robin Hood and the Potter" (Child no. 121), MS. Cambridge University Library Ee.4.35, ca. 1500. In addition there are one or two other texts, not in Child but often anthologized with ballads, which will be mentioned below. Finally, we have "A Gest of Robyn Hode" (Child no. 117), found in an incunabulum printed perhaps by Caxton somewhat before 1500, and "Adam Bell" (Child no. 116), another early printed text, which probably appeared contemporaneously. It is obvious from these references that the fifteenth century was indeed the age of literary deposition of ballads, few as they were compared with the hundreds collected in later centuries. In fact, some scholars have trouble accepting the fact that "Judas" should stand in splendid isolation in the thirteenth century, followed by total silence for two hundred years thereafter. "Judas," as we shall see, has been made into an "*un*ballad" in some quarters, by defining it away.

In a certain sense, there can be no question that the closest relatives to the ballads in the Middle Ages were the romances, with the branch groups of Breton lays and fabliaux. Their common blood was narrative verse. From the textual evidence, the romance can be seen as the big brother to the ballad, which expropriated romance vocabulary, tags, and clichés, until it finally supplanted its sibling in public taste by the end of the fifteenth century. Those few, scattered ballad manuscripts of the fifteenth century were harbingers of an ensuing change and should have been early warning signs for the romance makers. After 1500 the floodgates of balladry were opened, and the springs of romance ran dry. One has only to look at Helaine Newstead's chronology of romances after 1500.[10] There are a few printed editions of older stories, but barely anything new, and nothing after 1533. We can but conjecture as to why this transfer of literary favor away from romances occurred, but, whatever the reason, these poetic dinosaurs died in the fifteenth century. The idea of an "organic" evolution of oral literature, from epic to romance to ballad— commonly held and first suggested possibly by W. J. Courthope—is an enticing one, but in truth the only evolution we can vouch for is one of literary taste for a specific genre, not of the genre itself.[11]

The consanguinity of romance and ballad is evidenced by more than their common narrative style. A. C. Baugh has shown that romances have also undergone minstrel reproduction, of the same kind as that which produced different versions of a ballad: "I have elsewhere argued against the too easy acceptance of the view that the romances were written by minstrels, but in Professor Gerould's sense I believe they were rewritten by minstrels."[12] That is to say that romances would also have become part of an ongoing folk change, since that was Gerould's sense.[13] We can certainly not deny that some romances, like some ballads, show evidence of this.

Nor can we make a case for a general difference in presentation between romance and ballad. Both types were usually addressed to a listening audience, although the longer romances were also suited for silent reading. The beginning of *King Horn*, the preamble of *Partonope of Blois*, as well as other evidence, again attested by Baugh, show that romances were often sung, and indeed we have a long history of scops and minstrels singing or chanting narrative poems.[14] The singing could also be accompanied by music, as seen by the passage in *Sir Cleges*, "A harpor sange a gest be mowth," or the reference to melody in the opening prayer to *King Edward and the Shepherd*.

Of course, romances were also recited without musical accompaniment, and we have many references to "þis talkyng" in the texts themselves. It seems logical to suppose that all three processes of presentation depended on the audience and the occasion, and that they may even have occurred in separate stages for the same romance. Although Nygard uses the characteristics of song and melody in ballad to prove its separate genre from romance, it would seem from the above that the question is still open to debate.[15] There appears to be sufficient evidence that song and melody were indeed part of romance presentation.

On the other hand, we have no textual evidence that the ballads before 1500 were, indeed, sung. In fact, we know that some, at least, were recited, as Nygard himself admits, mentioning the "Geste of Robyn Hode" (Child no. 117).[16] He would agree with Friedman, who writes with conviction, "The longer, more elaborate minstrel ballads were patently meant to be recited rather than sung."[17] One scholar at least, in recognizing this fact, has reacted by wielding the all-powerful weapon of definition against these verses, making them into *un*ballads:

> What needs to be stressed, however, is that those early texts, such as "A Gest of Robyn Hode" (117), "Robin Hood and the Monk" (119), and "Robin Hood and the Potter" (121), to mention only a few, were not ballads at all, which is to say that they were recited and not sung.[18]

Like the romances, it seems that some of these shorter verses were recited and some may have been sung, but on this, prior to 1500, the texts are silent. Bronson, the champion of ballad music, agrees with Fowler without quite eliminating the type when he asks the riddling question at the beginning of his introduction:

> Question: When is a ballad not a ballad?
>
> Answer: When it has no tune.[19]

But not even Bronson can come up with tunes for the "Judas" and the fifteenth-century ballad texts. It does seem likely that "Saint Stephen and Herod" (Child no. 22) had a melody, since Bronson includes a version sung in Vermont in 1934.[20] And the beginning of "Robin Hood and the Monk" (Child no. 119) is similar to a song titled "Under the Greenwood Tree," which existed with a tune in the reign of Charles I. "No one, however, could seriously argue that there was a scintilla of likelihood that the tune and the ballad had any connection."[21]

A clear distinction, therefore, between medieval ballads and romances, based on presentation, vocabulary, narrative, or improvisation, cannot be made. Can we differentiate on the basis of audience, creative impulse, and authorship? As to the first and second, it may have been true, as Baugh asserts, that the romance was in its inception an aristocratic type, but I must question, as would Pearsall,[22] the absolutism of Baugh's remark that "English romances [after the decline of the French *roman d'aventure*], were still written with the more substantial classes, or the more serious among them, in mind and recited for the entertainment of those classes."[23] We do find very many of these "aristocratic" romances mixed in with homiletic material, saints' lives, short verses, and other catch-all material in manuscripts obviously meant as collections for the general entertainment of a middle-class household. MS. Rawlinson C.86 of the Bodleian, which includes the romance "The Weddynge of Sir Gawen and Dame Ragnell" examined below and also "Sir Landeval," is of such type, and so is the Thornton manuscript.[24] Certainly an aristocratic society could enjoy stories of Robin Hood as much as a bourgeois or even an agricultural society might take pleasure in listening to the exploits of Randolph, Earl of Chester. In fact, J. C. Holt strongly urges that the Robin Hood ballads were without class attachment but originally literature of the gentry. Yet they could not have developed without a mixed audience.[25]

No dictum, therefore, concerning romances and ballads or their makers, is acceptable, a fact certainly recognized by scholars. The opinion is that individual poets, some of them minstrels, created the romances, and that ballads were composed by individuals of the "folk." Both genres show evidence of "re-creation." And who were the "folk?" As MacEdward Leach describes them, they were people of the middle class, literate individuals familiar with tradition either because of long intimacy with their environment or through family association.[26] They were men and women with a gift for song or narrative lyric creation who liked to entertain others. The ballad folk of modern times are men like the owner of a general store on Cape Breton Island, or John Snead of the Smokies, known to be "soft on women," who gave "Barbara Allen" an unacceptable happy ending. The medieval ancestors of these "folk" were hardly French peasants, I would think. More likely some of them were medieval minstrels, for the only difference between the minstrel and the shoemaker ballad-singer was that the first used his talents for gain, and the second did not. Both had a gift for creation and presentation and a memory for song. The exigencies of the trade caused the minstrel to manipulate his audience, beg for attention, intrude into the story, and produce what some critics feel is "debased" work, but the ballad maker's sale of shoes did not necessarily depend on his singing. Friedman, in fact, sees the minstrel touch in some of the older Robin Hood ballads and in the later glorification of Scottish lairds in the border ballads.[27] Thus, we cannot distinguish with certainty between the originators of ballads and those of romances.

Why then are there no copies extant, at least of those ballads which were most closely connected with their "big brother" romances, *King Horn*, for instance, or *Sir Orfeo*? The gap of silence between *King Horn* (ca. 1225) and *Horn Child* (ca. 1320) is a hundred years, but between this latter date and "Hind Horn" (Child no. 17) in the 1827 Motherwell Manuscript is half a millenium. At least with *Sir Orfeo* (early fourteenth century) we have a late sixteenth-century version in a recently discovered Scottish *King Orphius* from a manuscript of 1585 which seems to be the ancestor of the nineteenth-century Scottish ballad.[28] Certainly the gaps are frustrating but understandable. After all, why preserve a shorter version of a poem when the longer, more complete text is known and can be verified in manuscript? Also, the vast preponderance of medieval religious lyrics extant, compared with secular ones, should have taught us not to expect many ballad-type poems to have been transcribed. For the most part, religious houses gathered the shorter verses in the thirteenth and fourteenth centuries, and, although some secular lyrics crept into the collections, perhaps for their possible allegorical or didactic potential, there was really no need for clerics to concern themselves with secular narratives even if minstrels brought them into their halls. The survival of MS. Harley 2253, the "Harley lyrics," must really be seen as a fortuitous anomaly. This manuscript is for the courtly lyric what the thin, paste strip of MS. Rawlinson D.193, the "Rawlinson Fragments," represents for truly popular song. Both are gifts of the past, all the more precious because there is no reason that they should have been forthcoming. Likewise, there is no reason to expect the transcription of medieval ballad texts, much as we may yearn for the unexpected.

It seems significant in this regard, however, to point out that, although religious ballads account for a very small fraction of the Child canon (only 5 or 6 of the 305 have religious or biblical themes), two of these ballads are among our six pre-1500 texts. Trinity College, Cambridge, MS. 323, which contains the "Judas" (Child no. 23), was either of Franciscan or Dominican provenance.[29] Surely we owe the survival of "Judas" and "Saint Stephen and Herod" (Child no. 22) to their affinity with saints' lives, apocryphal, and hagiographic literature. Nygard is certainly right when he says, "The ballad would seem to be a form which drew sporadically from the materials of romance as well as from other genres. . . . Ballads and romances may have existed together, not independent of one another, but each giving to the other."[30] Even the normal ballad stanza $4a3b4c3b$ would support this symbiosis, since it is a condensed tail-rhyme form of the romance stanza, either the romance six or its extension, $4aa3b4cc3b4dd3b4ee3b$. No other verse types in the Middle Ages bear this close relationship to each other.

Now if, as Nygard has remarked, ballads drew from romance and other genres, it would seem very likely that they might also become confused with other genres. Modern editors and anthologists appear confused, undoubtedly because the medieval singers did not themselves know what they were singing—that is, what specific genre or type of song—and the poets, unless they were copying French forms, did not know what they were composing. "Lyric" and "ballad," as mentioned, are modern terms; "carol" and "romance" were used by medieval authors—with largesse. Modern confusion is easy to document: the ballad "The Marriage of Sir Gawaine" (Child no. 31) is treated under the romance section of Severs's *A Manual of the Writings in Middle English* (vol. 1).[31] Old French "lyrics" when anthologized include twelfth-, and thirteenth-century *chansons de toile*, *chansons d'aventure*, and *pastourelles*, all of these being narrative poems, shorter than romances. They would, according to our definition, be ballads rather than lyrics. In fact, "The Knight and the Shepherd's Daughter" (Child no. 110) is a *pastourelle*. This ballad has strong affinities with the lyric "Now Springs the Spray" (no. 62 in Carleton Brown's *English Lyrics of the Thirteenth Century*), where a man rides out and meets a maid with the expectation on both sides of a sexual encounter.[32] R. L. Greene, however, includes this verse as no. 450 in his collection, *The Early English Carols*, because of the presence of a burden.[33] On the other hand, Greene's "Corpus Christi Carol" (No. 322) is today generally included in ballad anthologies.[34] Brown includes "The Ballad of Twelfth Day" as no. 26 of his lyrics, but this verse, in the same manuscript as "Judas," is in the ballad tradition.[35]

The reason for this confusion today is that we are tied into modern categories of definition. Medieval English short verse, as distinct from the contrived French, was really a free form, lacking the prescriptive idea of genre; it posits a confluence of "genre" in our sense, and it includes verses which we today label "ballads" and "lyrics," but which at the time may have been called by many names: carols, gestes, rhymes, or just songs.

Such a confluence of learned lyric, popular "folk" lyric, and ballad has been traced by Peter Dronke, who points out a very early example of the ballad "revenant" theme in a tenth-century Latin lyric, "Foebus abierat."[36] Also, a Cretan revenant ballad "Charos the Pedlar" leads back to Greek ballads of the tenth and eleventh centuries, perhaps originally to the fourth-century Syriac "Legend of Saint Euphemia." The end results of these generic adaptations are the revenant Child ballads, like "Sweet William's Ghost" (no. 77) and "The Suffolk Miracle" (no. 272). Dronke's evidence "suggests some of the bonds that unite learned and literary traditions with popular."[37] He also describes the eighth- and ninth-century Merovingian and Carolingian *rhythmi*, similar to the ballads in form with a content "that lent itself easily to telling in ballad fashion."[38] In light of these confluent free forms, one would have to agree with Dronke's statement that "the rise of the ballad in medieval Europe remains to be written afresh; when this is done, the evidence from the early Middle Ages can no longer be ignored."[39]

That the free form produces confusion is seen specifically in the unproductive argument over whether "Judas" is, or is not, a ballad, when there is no one who can dictate what a ballad should be. G. Gregory Smith arbitrarily pronounced that "Judas" was not a ballad, there being no ballads before the fifteenth century.[40] Vargyas calls it a transition form and worries about the ensuing "gap of three centuries," an overextended one and really insignificant in comparison with the long silence between the versions of *King Horn*.[41] Fowler would join the skeptics but admits, as does Nygard, that most modern scholars accept the piece into the ballad family.[42]

So it all comes down to definition after all. What can we consider to be a ballad before 1500, lacking, as we do, any evidence of music, any examples of folk recreation or "sea change," and having only the few manuscripts before us? We could start by asking, if "Judas," or "Saint Stephen and Herod," or "Robin Hood and the Monk," are not ballads, what might they be, by today's definition? Romances, saints' lives, lyrics, carols? Do we need a new category for them, something like *un*ballads, or unsung ballads? Perhaps we should follow W. P. Ker's example of "definition by inspection": "A ballad is *The Milldams of Binnorie*, *Sir Patrick Spens* and *The Douglas Tragedie* and *Lord Randal* and *Child Maurice*, and things of that sort."[43] Likewise we could say of the pre-1500 verses, "a ballad is 'Judas,' and 'Saint Stephen and Herod,' and 'Robin Hood and the Monk,' and things of that sort," but this really would not do.

Yet in fact, we have all the necessary material for a medieval definition at hand in *Piers Plowman*, when Sloth remarks, "I kan rymes of Robyn hood and Randolf, Erl of Chestre" (B-text, V.395). The reference to "rymes" would normally (but not always: *Havelok the Dane* is defined as a "rime") exclude romances and hint at shorter verse. Chaucer generally uses the word "romance" for a long narrative: "Upon my bed I sat upright / And bad oon reche me a book, / A romaunce..." (*Book of the Duchess*, line 48), whereas "rymes" were short rhyming verses: "His reson, as I may my rymes holde, / I wol yow telle" (*Troilus and Criseyde*, III, 90–91). The word could also refer to a tale in rhyme: "For other tale certes kan I noon, / But of a rym I lerned longe agoon" (*Canterbury Tales*, B² 708–09). Here the "rym" is Chaucer's *Sir Thopas*, a romance, though thankfully a short one. Nor would Sloth, doing the unexpected, necessarily have sung and danced to verses of Robin Hood, else he would have used the word "carol." Further, these "rymes" were not lyrics in our modern sense, since they retold the activities of popular heroes. Therefore, they were narrative verses, or tales in verse. Also, Robin Hood and Randolph Earl of Chester were traditional heroes whose exploits were evidently known in the popular mind. Sloth does not need to explain who these men were; both Langland and Repentance knew them from hearsay and recognized that their verses were not primarily didactic but, rather, meant to entertain. And so, the literary evidence and textual terms themselves would define the thirteenth-, fourteenth-, and fifteenth-century ballad as simply "short, traditional narrative rhymes." This definition can include "Judas" without a problem, and also "Saint Stephen and Herod," "Twelfth Day," and the Robin Hood songs. Though the printed "Geste" is rather long, it is probably an artificial patchwork of shorter ballads rather than an integral whole. Any narrower definition, however, would become exclusive and unworkable for the ballad before 1500.

We must repeat, though, that to define in this manner is to retroact. Sloth himself would not have known or cared about the genre of the rhymes he knew. Fowler makes the same point, that "in the early, formative period, ballads identified as such by Child tend to resemble one or another of several medieval forms: the carol, lyric, riddle, chanson d'aventure, romance, or metrical tale."[44] I would go one step further and say that at this time the ballad *was* the lyric, carol, romance, and things of that sort. And since it was not until the sixteenth century, according to Fowler, that the ballad achieved its identity, this is one evolutionary crux which—luckily—we do not have to deal with here.

It should be possible, however, by analyzing a romance and ballad that have the same story and that seem both to have originated in the fifteenth century to learn something about the transfer of literary favor. There is only one romance/ballad pair that meets these requirements: the narratives of Gawain and the loathly lady, in the above-mentioned romance "The Weddynge of Sir Gawen and Dame Ragnell" and the ballad "The Marriage of Sir Gawaine" (Child no. 31). It may be possible to establish a priority of origin for one work over the other, though obviously the result cannot be used to generalize for the types as a whole. Still, the fact remains that when we have ballads and romances with a common narrative (few as they are) the romance text always precedes the ballad text by at least a hundred years, with the one possible exception being "The Lord of Lorn and the False Steward" (Child no. 271) from the Percy Folio, ca. 1650, based on the romance "Rosewall and Lillian," printed in 1663 but probably composed in the later fifteenth century. This normal order of textual precedence is also seen in the two Gawain stories under discussion, the romance, MS. Rawlinson C.86 being dated ca. 1500 by Helaine Newstead and 1480–1508 by Mortimer Donovan, the ballad appearing in the Percy Folio.[45] On the putative composition, however, the two seem to be contemporary in the fifteenth century. Linguistic evidence puts the romance composition at ca. 1450.[46]

The skeleton plot of both romance and ballad, analogues to Chaucer's *Wife of Bath's Tale* and Gower's *Tale of Florent*, is as follows. King Arthur, meeting a bold baron while on a hunt, is challenged to a fight. The king refuses but promises to return in a year with the answer to the question, "What is it women most desire" or love best in this world? Arthur returns to Carlisle, where Gawain commiserates with him, and they both ride off to seek the answer. After collecting many suggestions, Arthur meets a loathly lady, and, in return for a promise that she may wed Gawain, she gives him the only true answer: "A woman will have her will" (ballad) or "Women desire sovereignty" over the manliest man (romance). The baron curses his sister for telling Arthur the correct solution, and Gawain keeps his promise of marriage. On their wedding night she asks whether Gawain wants her fair by day and ugly by night, or the reverse. He leaves the decision up to her, whereupon she is transformed into a beautiful young woman, the spell of her wicked stepmother having been broken because she had her will and has received sovereignty over the manliest man in England. The romance is 852 lines long with one leaf missing; the ballad, an incomplete version lacking a total of two-and-a-half pages and nine stanzas, runs to 57 four-line stanzas, 51 being complete.

MS. Rawlinson C.86 is a reading text written in a legible cursive hand. It contains a miscellany of secular, religious, and didactic works, the story of Dido, "Sir Landevale," and other shorter pieces, a one-volume general household library. Although the romance was composed in a six-line tail-rhyme stanza, which breaks down occasionally, the manuscript copy is in straight columns with no indentation or spaces, probably to save paper, and this is the way it is usually printed. There are several scribal corrections made in the same hand:

lines 230–31 "Her face was ['red' inserted above the line] her nose snotyd withall/ Her mowith wyde her ['teth' inserted above the line] yalowe on all."

line 244 "There is no ['thyng' deleted] tung may tell soturly"

lines 440–41 "The king rode forth a great shake / As fast as he might ['shake' deleted] gate"

line 467 "of fre and bond" is repeated from line above and deleted.

We can infer from these corrections that the scribe was copying the romance from another written source. Probably his attention wandered occasionally, which seems more likely than that he was correcting a corrupt exemplar; otherwise he would have emended silently. The manuscript shows a scribe commissioned to copy collected materials, writing in some hurry, pausing to sharpen his pen at folio 135, and then plodding on as the sand grains diminished in the glass. There was probably no great interest in the works themselves on his part, but the scribe had a professional pride in presenting an accurate copy.

The romance starts like a minstrel product: "Lythe and listenythe the life of a lord riche," and it was recited: "Nowe wylle ye lyst a whyle to my talking" (line 13). It was composed in prison:

> Ffor he is be-sett withe gaylours many,
> That kepen hym fulle sewerly,
> Withe wyles wrong and wraste.
> Nowe God as thou art veray kyng royalle,
> Help hym oute of daunger that made this tale,
> Ffor therin he hathe bene long.
>
> (lines 844–49)

The romance must have been intended by the poet to be presented orally at some later, and he hoped, liberated, time, either by himself or by another minstrel. The author drew on many Irish sources and Gawain legends in order to create his poem, though possibly the narrative had been in circulation before the prisoner reproduced the romance story from memory. Since it is conjectured that there is no direct link between romance ("Weddynge") and ballad ("Marriage"), in spite of the very close similarities, it is possible that other manuscripts or oral versions were known at the time.[47]

The differences, on the other hand, between romance and ballad are, it is fair to say, striking and significant. The romance, though humorous and unheroic, is a courtly tale of gentilesse both on Arthur's part and Gawain's. I would not count this one among the debased Gawain romances of the fifteenth century. To the contrary, the story is logically told, very consistent within itself as to characterization and action, and at times even surprisingly poignant and moving. The author, if not the Rawlinson scribe, appears quite involved in the story he tells. Admittedly, he dwells at length on the loathliness of the lady (lines 228-45, 548-56, 595-98), but in general there is a controlled elegance to the whole and real pathos at the end. In contrast, the ballad consciously moves toward the burlesque and a definite degradation of Arthur, with a tendency toward bawdiness shown in the puns of the ballad riddle answer: "A woman will have her will and that is all her chief desire."

In the romance Arthur logically refuses to fight the baron because he is himself unarmed, dressed only in hunting clothes: "Shame thou shalt haue to sle me in venere / Thou armyd and I clothed butt in grene, perde" (lines 82-83). In the ballad, however, his reason is frank cowardice:

> To fight with him I saw noe cause
> Methought it was not meet
> For he was stiffe and strong withal
> His strokes were nothing sweete.
> (stanza 11)

Although this first challenge is missing from the ballad, Arthur repeats his reason to Gawain later, as he does in the romance. Also, the whole marriage promise is handled very differently in the two works. In the romance Dame Ragnell asks the favor and Arthur answers that the choice must lie with Gawain alone. In fact, Arthur mourns the fact that he must put Gawain in jeopardy, and that he must make the request, knowing that Gawain "will be lothe to saye naye" (line 305). This is appropriate to the courtly Arthur, who swears to the baron that he will keep his promise and not betray him: "Vntrewe knyghte shalt thou neuere fynd me / To dye yett were me lever" (lines 116-17). The king's heart is heavy for Gawain's future, and later he is even ready to kill himself:

> Alas, I am in poynt my-self to spylle.
> (line 331)

> She sayd to me my life she wold saue,
> Butt fyrst she wold the to husbond haue,
> Wherfor I am wo begon,
> Thus in my hartt I make my mone.
> (lines 338-41)

Indeed, after the first challenge, the king had refused to tell anyone the reason for his sorrow until Gawain, sensing his grief, asked what was the matter. When Arthur returned from the loathly lady it was Gawain again who inquired how he had fared. Told of the proposed bargain, Gawain wholly, even joyfully, offers his service, himself in marriage. This section, lines 342–53, reflects Arthur's worthiness as much as do the king's own actions, just as Lancelot's continual "forbearance" of Arthur in Malory's last book proves Arthur's past greatness even in his decline.

In the ballad, Arthur's sorrow, as he tells it to Gawain, is only for his own predicament. When he meets the loathly lady he churlishly forgets his manners and fails to greet her until she reproaches him. When she hints that she might be able to help the king he immediately, and gratuitously, volunteers his cousin in marriage.

> "Giue thou ease me, lady," he said,
>   "or helpe me any thing,
> thou shalt haue gentle Gawaine, my cozen,
>   & marry him with a ring."
>                                    (stanza 21)

Later, when Sir Kaye and other knights make fun of the hag in the forest (an incident missing in the romance), Gawain reveals that one of the knights must marry her. Thereupon "some tooke vp their hawkes in hast, / & some tooke vp their hounds" (stanza 38), and Arthur, nervously, fearing that Gawain might back out of the agreement, tries to belittle the problem:

> And then be-spake him noble king Arthur
>   & sware there by this day,
> for a little foule sight & misliking. . . .
>                                    (stanza 39)

Here a half page is missing, but the noble Arthur, who boorishly forgot to greet her and does not have to marry her, obviously tries to assure the knights, specifically Gawain, that the old hag really isn't half so bad!

Many points in both romance and ballad remind us of *Sir Gawain and the Green Knight*: the description of the hag is an extension of the portrait of Morgan; in both romances Gawain volunteers his services; and in both there is great mourning and grief for Gawain at the courts. Even Arthur's somewhat cynical advice to Gawain, before he strikes the Green Knight,

'Kepe þe, cosyn,' quoþ þe kyng, 'þat þou on kyrf sette,
And if þou redeȝ hym ryȝt, redly I trowe
Þat þou schal byden þe bur þat he schal bede after . . .'
                                                (lines 372–74)

has echoes in the king's smug reassurance in the ballad. The tradition of the decline of a heroic Arthur and the parallel rise of the sympathetic but not necessarily heroic Gawain certainly began in the fourteenth century, and it accelerated in the fifteenth century as part of a general tendency toward satire and burlesque. In the post-Chaucer era of fifteenth-century turmoil it must have been difficult to worship heroes blindly. Arthur was of the past, and this romance and ballad were written, in a subtle and light-hearted way, to honor Gawain, a kind of antihero. Dame Ragnell was enchanted, we must remember, "Euyn tylle the best of England / Had wedyd me verament" (lines 695–96). Obviously, at this time the "best" was no longer Arthur.

Sumner attempted to establish a chronological priority for ballad and romance and concluded that the former was older. In general, she saw the romance as more "diffuse" than the ballad. She thought the chivalrous, courtly Arthur was "characteristic of later romance, the older conception of him being that of a warlike and rather brusque hero, as we see him in the ballad."[48] But the Arthur of the ballad is cowardly rather than warlike. Sumner's description fits better the Arthur of Layamon's *Brut* than the king who shows typical characteristics of the degeneration of the hero. For other evidence of the archaism of the ballad Sumner copies, somewhat closely, the reasoning of Görbing, who saw the alliterative tags in the ballad and the repetition, sometimes of whole lines, as evidence that it belonged to the early period of balladry.[49] Yet we know, as Leach noted, that repetition is "a general characteristic of folk literary style,"[50] and alliteration was an ongoing process: the very late fifteenth-century romances *The Taill of Rauf Coilyear* and the Middle Scots *Golagrus and Gawain* were written in the alliterative style, not to mention the fact that alliterative ballad refrains and clichés are a trademark of the type. Thus Sumner's evidence would lead more easily to a conclusion of priority for the romance over the ballad.

There is, however, an additional internal narrative point that would seem to prove conclusively that the romance "Wedding" preceded the ballad "Marriage" in composition. In the romance Arthur and Gawain go about collecting two books of answers to the riddle, but Arthur is not satisfied and seeks further until he meets the hag. He is, as noted, greatly disturbed that Gawain must marry her to save his life, if her answer proves to be the correct one. Even though Gawain willingly agrees to the marriage, the king can take no delight in the decision. Thereupon, on meeting Sir Gromer Somerjour, Arthur first desperately shows the books of answers. His action in attempting to save Gawain is consistent here with his previous reluctance to grant the hag's wish. The baron, however, sees no correct reply in the books, and Arthur must give the answer she provided. In the ballad also, although the sections are missing, it is obvious that Arthur has collected answers which he first presents to the knight: "And then he tooke King Arthurs letters in his hands, / And away he cold them fling" (stanza 24). Why would Arthur have collected these at all when the implication is that the king, having granted the hag's wish, received her answer immediately? And there is no additional reason in the ballad for Arthur to delay presenting the hag's answer, since he himself had voluntarily granted her Gawain in marriage. The motive, so obvious and touching in the romance, consistent with Arthur's character there, is lacking completely in the ballad. The ballad-maker, by including an irrelevant incident, shows that he did not understand his source or used a corrupt one some distance removed from the original romance. He would himself not have composed nonsense. Although we cannot rule out the possibility that a corrupt early "Marriage" ballad was refined by a later "Weddyng" romance, it does seem as if the total evidence leads to the conclusion that the ballad followed the romance.

What can we, in general, learn from this? We can say that, normally, burlesque and satire in popular literature imply the sophistication of an increasingly literate audience, not exclusive to the upper level of society. The impetus which Chaucer gave in the later fourteenth century, with *Sir Thopas*, or *The Nun's Priest's Tale*, to satire and a general wry, ironic look at the world, gained momentum in the fifteenth century.[51] The temper of the age needed, with textual proof, English (or Scottish) antiheroes, men not beyond the reach of the people and who were of them, like Gawain or even Mak the sheepstealer or Robin Hood, who feasted on the King's venison. Also, long romances, often with foreign worthies, became less popular, to be replaced by condensed, fast-moving shorter narrative verses about folk heroes at home. In fact, the whole evolution of *courtoisie* and gentilesse to a matter-of-factness, even a kind of prosaic view of things, was an ongoing process of Anglicization.

Although the debt of English romance to French sources and French *courtoisie* was overwhelming, the change in interest toward a national literary type was inexorable.[52] It came to a head in the fifteenth century with Malory's *Morte Darthur*, with the burlesque romances, the parody (*The Tournament at Tottenham Court*), the popular antihero, and finally, the rise from underground obscurity of the ballad. In its textual form, temperament, pace, and subject this was fully a British product. Therefore, what the great individual writers produced in isolation in the fourteenth century—a different view of the world, less grand and medieval—was carried forward in the fifteenth by a public that exhibited increasing impatience with a lengthy and outmoded form and a loss of interest in borrowing from abroad. Malory, of course, drew on French sources, but what he produced saved Arthur for Britain and from a French death.

The focus in the burlesque romance and ballad on the single narrative element, the ironic tone, the less than heroic stature of the hero, indeed the exemplary mode itself, here describing Gawain's selfless friendship rewarded, are all aspects of what Burrow calls "Ricardian" poetry. Many ballads carry part of this tradition forward, though Burrow would not attribute Ricardian characteristics to them.[53] Yet what we have seen here, in our discussion of these works, is the heritage of Chaucer and the *Gawain*-poet, among others, and without these the process of Anglicization would have been retarded.

Surely, the truth (and beauty) of all this was probably infinitely more complex than any theory, and I have indulged myself here to a greater extent than I set out to do. The problem of relationships between romance, ballad, and the confluence of form is teasing and seductive, but, in the absence of any new textual discovery, also vexing and incapable of resolution. It seems inevitable, however, that critics will ever and again be seduced into scholarly fantasy, feeling no doubt kinship to Keats's "happy melodist unwearied, / Forever piping songs forever new!"

## Notes

1. Holger Nygard, "Popular Ballad and Medieval Romance," in *Folklore International: Essays in Traditional Literature, Belief, and Custom in Honor of Wayland Debs Hand*, ed. Donald Knight Wilgus (Hatboro, Pa.: Folklore Associates, 1967), pp. 161–73.

2. M. J. C. Hodgart, *The Ballads* (London: Hutchinson, 1950), p. 73.

3. Lajos Vargyas, *Researches into the Medieval History of Folk Ballad*, trans. Arthur H. Whitney (Budapest: Akadémiai Kiado, 1967), pp. 275, 279.

4. David C. Fowler, *A Literary History of the Popular Ballad* (Durham, N.C.: Duke University Press, 1968), p. 18.

5. Holger Nygard, "Ballads," *Encyclopaedia Britannica*, 1968 ed.
6. Vargyas, *Researches*, p. 269.
7. John C. Holt agrees with Hodgart that the ballads "were related in their origins to both the romances and the French *caroles*, to literary and artistic forms which were alien to the English peasantry and which can only have been imported by their masters." See his "Origins and Audience of the Ballads of Robin Hood," in *Peasants, Knights, and Heretics: Studies in Medieval Social History*, ed. R. H. Hilton (Cambridge and New York: Cambridge University Press, 1976), p. 253.
8. Nygard, "Ballads," p. 20.
9. Francis J. Child, ed., *The English and Scottish Popular Ballads*, 5 vols. (Boston and New York: Houghton Mifflin, 1886–98). In this study, the numerals in parentheses indicate numbers of poems as published in Child's collection.
10. Helaine Newstead, "Romances," in *A Manual of the Writings in Middle English*, ed. J. Burke Severs (Hamden, Conn.: Archon Books/Shoe String Press for the Connecticut Academy of Arts and Sciences, 1967), 1:15–16.
11. W. J. Courthope, *History of English Poetry*, 6 vols. (New York and London: Macmillan, 1897–1911), 1:445.
12. Albert C. Baugh, "Improvisation in the Middle English Romance," *Proceedings of the American Philosophical Society* 103 (1959): 440.
13. Baugh (ibid.) noted: "As for the ballad, most of us I suppose have given up the romantic ideas that *das Volk dichtet*, but the late Professor Gerould once remarked that, if the people did not write the ballads, at least they rewrote them."
14. Albert C. Baugh, "The Middle English Romance: Some Questions of Creation, Presentation, and Preservation," *Speculum* 42 (1967): 18–21.
15. Nygard, "Popular Ballad," pp. 167, 170–71.
16. Ibid., p. 171.
17. Albert Friedman, "Ballads," *Encyclopaedia Britannica*, 1974 ed.
18. Fowler, *Literary History*, p. 10. In his "Ballads," in *A Manual of the Writings in Middle English*, ed. Albert E. Hartung, (Hamden, Conn.: Archon Books/Shoe String Press for the Connecticut Academy of Arts and Sciences, 1980), 6:1763, however, Fowler straddles the fence. Referring to Child no. 119 he says, "Like other tales in this manuscript, it is called a 'talking' (stanza 90), and there is little evidence that it ever had a tune (see Bertrand Bronson, *The Traditional Tunes of the Child Ballads*, 4 vols. [Princeton, N.J.: Princeton University Press, 1959]). The best indication that it may nevertheless have been a ballad is the striking lyrical character of the two opening stanzas."
19. Bronson, *Traditional Tunes*, 1:ix.

20. Ibid., p. 297.
21. Bronson, *Traditional Tunes* (1966), 3:17.
22. Derek Pearsall, "The Development of Middle English Romance," *Mediaeval Studies* 27 (1965): 91–92.
23. Baugh, "Middle English Romance," p. 17.
24. See also the introduction by Frances McSparran and P. R. Robinson to their edition of *Cambridge University Library MS. Ff.2.38* (London: Scolar Press, 1979), pp. vii–xii.
25. See the debate on the peasant or gentry origins of the Robin Hood ballads between R. H. Hilton, J. C. Holt, and Maurice Keen in Hilton, *Peasants*, pp. 221ff. The beginning of the *Gest* shows that the audience is gentle, and its other themes and chief topic are evidence "that it was primarily the literature of the county landowners, of the knights and gentry" (Holt, "Origins," p. 244).
26. MacEdward Leach, ed., *The Ballad Book* (New York: Barnes, 1955), p. 28.
27. Friedman, "Ballads," p. 643.
28. M. Stewart, "King Orphius," *Scottish Studies* 17 (1973): 1–16.
29. Fowler, "Ballads," p. 1759.
30. Nygard, "Popular Ballad," p. 171.
31. Newstead, "Romances," p. 65.
32. Carleton Brown, ed., *English Lyrics of the Thirteenth Century* (Oxford: Clarendon Press, 1932), p. 62.
33. Richard L. Greene, *The Early English Carols,* 2nd ed. (Oxford: Clarendon Press, 1977), p. 274.
34. Fowler, "Ballads," p. 1758.
35. See Brown, *English Lyrics*, p. 39, and Fowler, "Ballads," p. 1758.
36. Peter Dronke, "Learned Lyric and Popular Ballad in the Early Middle Ages," *Studi Medievali* 17 (1976): 1.
37. Ibid., p. 38.
38. Ibid., p. 4.
39. Ibid., pp. 37–38.
40. George Gregory Smith, "Ballads," *Encyclopaedia Britannica*, 1961 ed.
41. Vargyas, *Researches*, p. 275.
42. Fowler, "Ballads," p. 1760.
43. W. P. Ker, "On the History of the Ballads," *Proceedings of the British Academy, 1909–10* (1910): 179; also quoted in Nygard, "Ballads."
44. Fowler, "Ballads," p. 1757, and also Nygard, "Popular Ballad," p. 171.
45. Newstead, "Romances," p. 247; Mortimer J. Donovan, in Severs,

ed., *Manual*, p. 296.

46. Newstead, "Romances," pp. 65–66. See also Laura Sumner's edition of "The Weddynge of Sir Gawain and Dame Ragnell," *Smith College Studies in Modern Languages* 5 (1924): i–xiii.

47. Sumner, "Weddynge," pp. xxiii–xxiv.

48. Ibid., p. xxiv.

49. F. Görbing, "Die Ballade *The Marriage of Sir Gawain* in ihren Beziehungen zu Chaucers *Wife of Bath's Tale* und Gowers Erzählung von Florent," *Anglia* 23 (1901): 409.

50. Leach, *Ballad Book*, p. 18.

51. Pearsall, "Development," p. 92.

52. Baugh, "Improvisation," p. 431, and Pearsall, "Development," p. 97, n. 11.

53. John A. Burrow, *Ricardian Poetry* (London: Routledge and Kegan Paul, 1971), p. 10.

# James Ryman and the Fifteenth-Century Carol

## David L. Jeffrey

The medieval English carol is preeminently a gift of the fifteenth century. Indeed, as Carleton Brown suggested in his edition *Religious Lyrics of the Fifteenth Century*, very few carols from even the fourteenth century are preserved, while more than five hundred fifteenth-century texts survive.[1] Of these, nearly a quarter, or 119 carols, are in a single manuscript of 166 lyrics attributed to James Ryman, a Franciscan friar of Canterbury.[2] The character of Ryman's carols and the extent of his experimentation in vernacular hymnody suggest that increased acceptability of the popular carol form and its adaptability to the elaborate or "decorated" style of the macaronic hymn have combined to create in the fifteenth-century carol a significant evolution from the more "meditative" earlier English religious lyrics.[3]

There has been some question as to whether Ryman was the composer or merely the collector of the verse in MS. Cambridge Library Ee.I.12, and it is perhaps difficult to decide this matter definitively, even by an appeal to the stylistic similarity of many of the pieces in the later portion of the book with those of the former. Certain points, however, may be observed. First, at the conclusion of the song no. 110, "O Quene of pitee, moder of grace"—a carol with rhyme-royal stanzas—occurs the following inscription:

> Explicit liber ympnorum et canticorum, quem composuit frater Iacobus Ryman ordinis Minorum ad laudem omnipotentis dei et sanctissime matris eius Marie omniumque sanctorum anno domini millesimo cccc.$^{mo}$ lxxxxij°.[4]

In the same hand as the verse, this may be either signature to a holograph manuscript, or a scribal witness: in either case it seems to ascribe composition of the first 110 "hymns" and "songs" to Ryman, but does not address the question of the 56 additional lyrics. Zupitza believed that the new hand which commenced at song no. 112 and continued to the end was that of the poet himself, since it was the same hand that made corrections throughout the manuscript. This seems a plausible view, and though it still does not entirely prove the poems to be Ryman's own composition, together with the rubric at carol no. 110 and the stylistic similarities which do persist it argues for Ryman as composer at least as strongly as for Ryman as collector. In any case, the form of the collection suggests that the first 110 pieces represent a *compilatio* of sorts, more than a mere *collectio*, since the lyrics, translated hymns, and carols are largely organized by the theme and liturgical occasion or calendar, concentrating especially on the seasons Advent, Nativity, and Epiphany. In this light it might seem that the remaining poems, in the looser form of *collectio*, are additional to the matter of the first part, and that they could have been added on by Ryman, number by number, some time after the initial *explicit* was written. It is interesting that the first section ends with what is probably Ryman's most elegant address to the Virgin—an appropriate conclusion for a medieval Franciscan *compilatio*.

The first additional song is an early version of the song of the thieving fox (which still survives as a popular children's song). In this version it should be considered a representative of antifraternal satire:

> The fals fox came to oure halle dore
> And shrove our gese there in the flore
> With how, fox, et cetera . . .
>
> The fals fox came into oure halle
> And assoyled our gese both grete and small.
> With how, fox, et cetera. . . .

Beginning at stanza sixteen (though Zupitza's divisions make this hard to discern) is another version of the song, in which there is a conversation between the fox and the goose. This version is left unfinished: the notation seems to be simply a *memento*. That antifraternal satire should be collected by a friar is not surprising—there are other examples.[5] What is curious about this "fox" song is that it is the first additional lyric, the only "secular" song to be included in the collection, and the *Alma redemtoris mater* which follows does not by its form suggest that the song was included to index a tune to be associated with the subsequent lyric.

There are a variety of ways to characterize the content of the entire collection. One of these is to respect the address or function of the songs. The largest group—more than fifty numbers—concerns the Virgin or addresses her in sung prayers. A slightly smaller group—about thirty-five numbers—has Christ as a focus, either by way of sung prayers or in dramatic dialogue poems in which Christ speaks from the cross or converses, sometimes as a child, with his mother. More than a dozen poems concern themselves with the Trinity—an unusual feature of this collection. But a fairly large number of the songs are specifically catechal (thirty-five) or liturgical (ten). What all of this suggests is that the *explicit* "liber ympnorum et canticorum" ought perhaps to be taken quite literally in the modern sense of the terms, and Ryman's work seen as a deliberate contribution to vernacular hymnody, the book as a whole being a kind of forerunner of the modern hymnbook—as opposed to a medieval psalter, or even an earlier medieval "song book."[6]

We might come to this point in another way. Despite the eleven direct translations of traditional Latin hymns and thirty-odd religious lyrics of other forms which inhabit these pages, the volume is dominated by carols. The carol, as Greene and others have made clear, is an old pagan and popular form associated specifically with the ring dance in its origins.[7] Yet it was possible even for such a stringent moralist as Wyclif to approve of Christianized carolling, including the dance, as a festive recreation for "ʒonge wymmen."[8] What in the late fourteenth century were inevitably conjoined—the song and the dance—may have begun to separate somewhat in the late fifteenth. While "carol" maintained its association with the dance in Ryman's time, later it clearly became possible to imagine settings for the carol in which the dance was not a part of its performance.[9] With Ryman the carol as a song form was in any case acquiring another—and distinctly more modern—association.

A cursory examination of Ryman's carols will show that far the greater portion concern themselves with the Annunciation, Nativity, and Epiphany. That is, most of them are already "Christmas carols," associated with that season to which we now automatically direct the term (albeit often in misappropriation). Ryman devotes more space to Christmas season carols than is the overall pattern for his contemporaries in the genre, and heralds, accordingly, the future of the carol. In Ryman's signal anticipation of a trend we may fairly see the intimate association of the whole genre with what Greene calls "Franciscanism," which he feels virtually invites specialization of the carol as a Christmas song.[10] Indeed, we should expect Ryman to reflect especially Franciscan concerns and interests at least as much as his thirteenth- and fourteenth-century confrères. Yet their own concern for the Christmas events did not express itself notably in the carol, but most often in other verse and song forms. We would not normally think of these as hymns, in fact, but rather as poems of meditation or, at the most, songs in aid of popular mendicant homiletics.[11] There is another interesting point here, I think, and it bears particularly on a significant departure in Ryman from the actual poetics of his forebearers.

The macaronic hymn tradition enjoyed a particular vigor in the fifteenth century. William O. Wehrle has shown that in England it became then "a vogue as definite as the vogue of the sonnet among the renaissance Italians."[12] While macaronic lines were often employed in the systematic translation of the Latin hymns, they could also be used as the basis for creating new hymns. Wehrle makes it clear that the composition of macaronic hymns was a literate and especially clerical vocation:

> The skill of interlacing a definite Latin line into a poem so as to make it fit into the meter and often into the rhyme of the English poem required great skill in handling both languages, besides a thorough knowledge of both the liturgy and hymnody of the Church.[13]

It has already been pointed out by Karl Hammerle that Ryman is an outstanding figure in the macaronic hymn tradition.[14] Further, Wehrle's study reveals that the predominant themes of the macaronic hymn, from its inception, are the Nativity, followed by poems on the Blessed Virgin and then the saints whose feasts fall in the Christmas season.[15] That is, the Christmas season is the central subject matter for macaronic hymns. These facts, and one further consideration, suggest that Ryman was explicitly about the business of hymnody, as opposed to the collection or creation of meditative poetry or traditional Franciscan "gospel song."

In Ryman's macaronic lyrics, apart from Latin tags and "connective" phrases composed for a particular carol, most of the remaining lines come from the liturgy itself, especially its metrical portions. As Greene has shown, the hymn is nearest in likeness to the carol, both in its division into stanza and its being sung to a "repetition of the same musical setting."[16] With the exception of his "Te Deum" translations and adaptations (nos. 71-76), which show influence of the subject and not the metrical form of their source, Ryman is typical in that the direct contribution of the subject matter of the Latin to his English carols is, if anything, less evident than his retention of the four-stress line and four-stress stanza of the Latin hymns in many numbers. This suggests that familiar hymn tunes accompanied the vernacular composition, and not popular tunes a religious song or translated hymn.[17] The use of the four-stress line and stanza in each of the other carols that is not a translation as such (for example, no. 83) suggests that these songs too were probably entuned to the setting of familiar hymns or Latin carols.[18] That this choice indicates Ryman's specific interest in hymnody is already clear, I think. That it represents a different address to vernacular lyric poetry than was customary in the thirteenth and fourteenth centuries, even among Franciscans, may be made equally evident.

I have written elsewhere of the tendency of mendicants in the thirteenth and fourteenth centuries to write vernacular lyrics as preaching aids, sometimes setting these to music as a kind of baptised popular song.[19] Indeed, this pattern, along with the creation of a specifically meditational poetry for lay-readers, seems to have characterized the bulk of religious lyric-making in those centuries. On the other hand, where the audience for poetry was chiefly clerical in that period, it seems that much of the poetry remained traditional and latinate. It is interesting to consider the case of another Franciscan friar from Canterbury, Richard Ledrede, a fourteenth century compiler of lyrics. While he was Bishop of Ossory he wrote and collected songs for the use of vicars, priests, and clerks—not laymen—to be sung in festive seasons.[20] These songs, from their rubrics, "annotated" with scraps of English and French secular songs, were to be allowed popular tunes, not sung to hymn tunes. But the lyrics themselves are in Latin. That is, for a clerical audience the "baptism" was also a conversion of secular to religious language. The results are not, strictly speaking, hymns—but rather, spiritual songs for the recreation of the clergy. In Ryman's collection it is often just the other way around: the Latin is at least partially construed in simple vernacular, it is often a hymn which is directly translated or artfully adapted, and the resulting songs and carols are—at least some of the time—hymns as well as religious songs. Whom, one wonders, did Ryman expect to do the singing?

Almost everyone agrees that Ryman intended his poems to be sung. Beyond that, there has been less assurance. For Helmut Gneuss, "ob sie jemals gesungen wurden, ist eine andere Frage."[21] For Rossell Hope Robbins, in his edition *Secular Lyrics of the XIVth and XVth Centuries*, the carols are a kind of "closet hymn."[22] But the fact is that the manuscript itself contains musical notation, albeit faded, for several songs, and one of these is recognizable as a version of the Sarum hymn, *Salvator mundi*.[23] Moreover, two carols are based on the Latin carol "Ecce quod natura/mutat sua jura" (see no. 83), which is the only carol in English or Latin to survive with music in three separate manuscripts. And in the mid-sixteenth century, both in carols discovered transcribed among the papers of Henry Bradshaw and in the carolbook anthology printed by Richard Kele in 1550, some of Ryman's work continued to find audience.[24] That many of the carols were sung by some persons or other seems then most probable. Were they, as in the case of the fourteenth-century collection by Ledrede, entuned by clerics? Or, as in the case of some other religious songs of the earlier period, by groups of laypersons?[25] The evidence of Ryman's manuscript argues, I think, for both kinds of singers and customs of use for his hymns and carols.

It is evident from their predominant form that Ryman's lyrics were not intended for meditative, reflective use, as in books of hours or other meditational guides. This fact alone will account for the criticism, often levelled against a majority of poems in the collection, that they are lacklustre, unoriginal, and uninspired. Indeed, if they were intended as religious poetry in the manner of MS. Harley 2253, the commonplace book of Franciscan Friar John Grimestone, or the collection of Friar William Herebert, largely speaking they would deserve the unenthusiastic comment so far received. On the other hand, if the expectations which more properly accord to hymnody are introduced, our response ought to be somewhat different. For example, while in the former poetry attributes of the litany are tedious, in hymnody they may be essential to good effects. The same might be said for other kinds of repetitiveness, such as the burden or refrain of the carol, or the simple four-stress meter and line which predominate in these pieces so evidently intended to be sung heartily by groups, rather than mused over quietly by reflective individual readers.

Some of Ryman's songs require, nonetheless, a greater sophistication, and evidence more verbal complexity, than we would expect from the popular carol. In Ryman's experimentation, these numbers often stand out, such as is the case of no. 16, "Rarissima in delicijs / Iam veni: coronaberis," in which the dominant imagery involves conceit and jargon of a clerical kind:

> Come, my myelde dove, into thy cage,
> With ioye and blis replete which is;
> For whyit is thyne heritage.
> *Iam veni: coronaberis.*

> Thy stature is assymylate
> To a palm tree, and thy bristis
> To grapes, spowse immaculate.
> *Iam veni: coronaberis.*

In other cases the clue may be in the verse form itself. A pair of lyrics, nos. 84 and 85, clearly derive from a popular song, rather than from a hymn. (That is, they resemble the earlier pattern of Richard Ledrede's *Red Book of Ossory*.) In no. 84 it is specific to the first stanza, perhaps almost in unaltered form:

> Atte sumtyme mery, at sume tyme sadde;
> At symtyme wele, at symtyme woo;
> At symtyme sory, at symtyme gladde;
> At symtyme frende, at symtyme foo;
> At symtyme richess *and* welthe is hadde,
> At symtyme it is gone vs froo;
> Truly, he is not wyse, but madde,
> That aftur worldly welthe will goo.

The simple verse form *abababab* is maintained throughout the balance of an eight-stanza, homiletical lyric. The verse is unaffected and graceful with the rhetoric of good preaching. It continues:

> As medowe floures of swete odoures
> Vadeth to erthe by theire nature,
> Likewise richness *and* grete honoures
> Shall vade fro euery creature;
> Therfore to suffre grete doloures
> I holde it best to do oure cure
> And to forsake Castill*is and* toures,
> So that of blisse we may be sure.
>
> *In Genesi and* Iob we fynde
> *Et in Ecclesiastico*,
> Though art but erthe, man, by thy kynde
> And into erthe ayene shalt goo.
> On erthely good sette not thy myende,
> For erthely good shall passe the fro;
> Naked thou camest, though man so blynde,
> And into erthe naked shalte goo.
>
> . . .
>
> Crist seith hym self in the gospell:
> 'What preuayleth it a man vntill,

> Yf that his sowle in daungere dwell,
> Thow be alle this worlde haue at wille.'
> Therfore do by goostely counsell,
> For worldely welthe thy soule not spille;
> For, yf it come but ones in helle,
> Truly, it shall dwell therein still.

> . . .

> Fro endeles deth god vs defende
> And graunt vs alle by his grete grace,
> Out of this worlde when we shall wende,
> In heuen blisse to haue a place
> Therin to dwelle w*ith*outen ende
> And hym to see there face to face,
> Whoes ioye no tunge can comprehende,
> That ay shall be, is, *and* ay wace.

We feel this poem as a traditional meditative exercise, or perhaps a song with an application to the enterprise of a mendicant preacher. That is, we can at least imagine it being sung *to* a popular audience, if not likely *by* them. The lyric with which it is paired is a different proposition. It begins:

> Remembre well, thou man mortall,
> And Pryente wele in thy myende
> This worlde is mutabilite,
> That transitorious is.
> Beholde wele thy begynnyng
> And ondre wele thy kyende;
> Then calle to thy remembraunce
> Eternall ioye and blis.

> . . .

> Truly, the orient Phebus
> And the tenebrat nyght
> In nature be full different:
> So by mekenesse *and* pryde;
> Sorowe forto compare, truely,
> *With* ioye it is no right;
> This lyfe vnto celestiall
> Is but a mynute tyde.

*James Ryman and the Fifteenth-Century Carol*

The lyric continues for twice the length of the first, concluding in two stanzas that make clear both the connection with the tune of no. 84 and the predominant address to friars or other clerics themselves, as *exhortatio*:

> At sumtyme for thy synnes wepe,
> Moorne *and* make lamentacion;
> At symtyme rede, at symtyme syng
> To avoide vice and synne;
> At symtyme pray vpon thy knee
> For goostely inspiracion:
> And so gostely the victorie
> Of thy foo though shalt wynne.
>
> By nyght *and* day, yf that thou may,
> Vse devoute meditacion;
> Pray for thy frende, pray for they foo
> And pray for alle they kynne;
> Also, I rede, for the more mede,
> Vse goostely contemplacion:
> And than to blisse, that endeles is,
> Thy soule shalle entre in.

We see that while the tune may have been popular and easily recalled, Ryman makes no comparable effort in no. 85 for the lyric itself. The rhyme scheme, if it can be called that, is experimental and difficult: *abcdebfd*. The language is learned and latinate, and the form of the whole poem is as an examination of conscience.

But these poems are in fact the smallest part of Ryman's collection. By far the largest number are carols, and most of these specifically "Christmas carols," whose form and meter immediately suggest group singing that would be highly accessible even to the laity. The first song in the manuscript is, in this respect I think, exemplary of Ryman's primary intention. It is taken from the hymn "Alma redemptoris mater," one of the best known of Latin hymns, and the rhyme scheme is the simple, easily teachable *aaab/bb*. Thus:

> The aungell seyde, of high degree:
> 'Haile, full of grace: god is with the;
> Of alle women blessed thou bee,
> *Alma redemptoris mater!*'

with the refrain:

> *Alma redemptoris mater,*
> *Quem de celis misit pater.*

The meter is natural and yet hymnic, the rhythm jolly, almost boisterous, and the simple narrative of the Annunciation story has the magic of the well-known story of repentance simply told. The same lilt and cheer attach to nos. 2 and 3, another pair in which the first has the simple refrain "*inquit Marie Gabriell / 'concipies Emanuel,'* " and the second suggests a group of brothers singing the stanzas, perhaps, with all present joining in on an extended burden or *ripressa*:

> *Nowel, nowel, nowel, nowel*
> *Nowel, nowel, nowel, nowel!*
> *Inquit Marie Gabriel:*
> *'Concipies Emanuel.'*

In addition to the translated hymns, there are liturgical adaptations of Sarum use (no. 77, "Pater Noster," "Magnificat") and hymns for which one can only imagine a connection with the mass or other divine service. Number 56, a carol in form, is a hymn on the sacrament with the refrain:

> Ete ye this brede, ete ye this brede
> And ete it so, ye be not dede.
>
> This brede geveth eternall lyfe
> Bothe vnto man, to chielde *and* wyfe;
> It yeldeth grace *and* bateth stryfe:
> Ete ye it so, ye be not ded.
>
> It semeth white, yet it is rede,
> And it is quik and semeth dede,
> For it is god in fourme of brede:
> Ete ye it so, ye be not ded.
>
> This blessed brede is aungell*is* foode,
> Mannes also perfecte and goode;
> Therfore ete ye it *with* myelde moode:
> Ete ye it so, ye be not dede.

> This brede fro heven did descende
> Vs fro alle ille for to defende
> And to geve vs lyfe *with*oute ende:
> Ete ye it so, ye *be not dede.*
>
> In virgyne Mary this brede was bake,
> Whenne Criste of her manhoode did take
> Ere of alle synne mankkyende to make:
> Ete ye it so, ye *be not dede.*
>
> Ete ye this brede *with*outen synne,
> Eternall blis thanne shall ye wynne.
> God graunte vs grace to dwell therin.
> Ete ye it so, ye be not dede.

Such hymns and songs we can imagine being sung by friars as a means of making divine service itself more accessible to the laity, an increasingly important concern of the friars and others in the fifteenth century. But for simple, expository carols such as no. 38, "Be we mery now in this fest," no. 40, "To Criste singe we, singe we, singe we / In clennes and in charite," no. 41, "A meyden myelde a chielde hath bore / Mankyende to blis forto restore," it is difficult to imagine that Ryman did not intend the carols for general festive singing by the laity themselves as well as the brothers. Number 42, in simple *abab* stanza with refrain for a chorus, simplifies its narrative and catechal content and is like the songs which immediately precede it, short (seven stanzas) and teachable:

> And in a stalle this chielde was born
> Bitwene bothe oxe and asse
> To save, for synne that was forlorn,
> Mankyende, as his wille wasse.[26]

. . .

> The prophecy of Isay
> And prophetes alle *and* sume
> Now ended is thus finally,
> For god is man become.

These carols are an entirely different enterprise from the rhyme-royal ode to Henry VI (no. 96) or the elegant and sophisticated "Wisdom" poem which immediately follows it. These sorts of poems, a minority in the volume, seem to be squarely within established traditions of religious lyric poetry. Ryman's use of the carol, on the other hand, should be evaluated as an explicit innovation in hymnody and the vernacular, largely directed toward the Christmas season, and hence toward a wider participation and community of song.

What of the quality of Ryman's *liber ympnorum et canticorum*? At their worst, it must be admitted, Ryman's carols can embody the garishness and maudlin extremes of late fifteenth-century spirituality. One winces a little, in respect of the often used double-entendre in *yerde*, for example, at constructions such as the one Ryman offers in no. 20, "There sprung a yerde of Iesse moore":

> As Aaron yerde *with*oute moistoure
> Hath florisshed and borne a flou*re*,
> So hath she borne ou*re* savyou*re*
> *With*outen touche of dishonou*re*
> Of ma*n*nes sede;
> For god his self in her did brede.
>
> King Assuere was wrothe, i-wis,
> Whenne quene Vasty had done amys,
> And of her crowne priuat she is;
> But, when Hester his yerde did kis,
> By hir mekenes
> She chaunged his moode into softnes.[27]

But it can hardly be charged fairly, once we see the bulk of this work as a hymnbook, that his songs are merely boring. At their best Ryman's carols, with respect to their lyrics, are a blend of simplicity and unstudied elegance; with respect to meter and measure they are often "catchy" and eminently tunable; their spirit, unlike that of much earlier Franciscan or other religious poetry, is almost entirely joyous and celebratory even when a carol may move on from the season of Christ's nativity to anticipate the Cross:

> A Roose hath borne a lilly white,
> The whiche flou*re* is moost pure *and* bright.

To this roose aungell Gabriell
Seide: 'Thou shalt bere Emanuell,
Both god *and* man *with* vs to dwell';
The which flou*re* is moost pure *and* bright.

This roose, the *pro*phete Ysaye
Seyde, shulde conceyve *and* bere Messy
*With*outen synne or velonye;
The which flou*r* is moost pure *and* bright.

As the sonne beame goth thurgh the glas,
Thurgh this roose that lilly did pas
To save mankynde, as his wille was;
The whiche flou*re* is *moost pure and bright.*

This roose so myelde aye vndefielde
Hath borne a childe for man so wilde
By fraude begiled, from blis exiled;
The whiche flo*ur* is moost pure *and* bright.

This roose so good at the cros stode
*With* wofull moode, when Crist, our*e* foode,
Shed his hert bloode for man so woode;
The which flou*r* is moost pure *and* bright.

This swete roose pray bothe nyght *and* day,
*With*oute denay that we come maye
To blis for ay the redy waye;
The which flou*r* is moost pur*e and bright.*

It has been argued that there is a general tendency in the fifteenth-century lyric to etherealize and to lose the sight and touch of human reality.[28] If the argument is to be sustained it will not be, I think, by an appeal to the example of James Ryman. In his poetry and hymnody there is a definite rootedness of divine mystery and beauty in the tangibility of Christ's and the Virgin's humanity, in which we all join, singing not only with the angels but also with the magi and the shepherds. It is as if the traditional message of the Franciscans—that Christ's humble incarnation elevates and glorifies creation and our common humanity—has applied itself again in a marriage of music and verse forms. The humble and earthy ring-dance song of carollers combines, sometimes in lines alternating with those of Latin hymns, to sing the "new song" of Christmas—hymns and anthems to "the chielde borne to be kynge" and to "mary myelde," his mother. The macaronic hymn tradition, dedicated to making the hymnody of Christmas especially accessible to unlatinate laymen, by happy accidents of metrics and measure becomes, as we see in Ryman, a chief force in the specialization of the carol to the season with which we now associate it.

Ryman offers in one of his poems a kind of accidental *apologia* for the work that he has been doing, by way of encouraging others to participate in its larger intention. Here his choice of matter for "translation" and composition is not a traditional hymn of the Church, but the eighth chapter of the Book of Proverbs. In this chapter the voice of Wisdom speaks, identifying herself with the Spirit of the Lord, which was with God from the beginning, "set up from everlasting before ever the earth was," and present at the creation of the universe: she is the delight of the Lord of creation, "daily his delight and playing [ludens] always before him" (Proverbs 8:30). This *hokma*, or *sapientia*, is made to be the "voice" of Ryman's poem with several actual verses of the chapter woven into her address (verses 2-4, 10, 12, 14, 15, 17, 20, 21, and 34-36, for example). At the outset Ryman has her say:

'For cause alle men shall vnderstonde
My lordes preceptes iuste and right,
He hath me made to euery londe
In theire owne speche them to endite
And in this fourme them for to wright.
Therfore take hede bothe sume *and* alle
To his preceptis, bothe grete *and* small.

Later in the poem the audience he has in mind for Wisdom's general precepts in this matter of "translation" is clearly specified:

Nowe, dene of chapell *and* of quere,
Deuoutely do youre diligence,
Chaunters also *and* chapeleynes dere,
So in you be no negligence.

Also youre scilence, loke, ye kepe.
Wake not to late, rise not to sone.
When ye wolde laugh, lest that ye wepe.
Serue god *and* pley, when ye haue done.

The last injunction, not from the Scripture itself but Ryman's own, is to stewards of divine service, both to serve God and, in an allusion to verses not quoted (verses 30–31), perhaps to "pley." Ryman's *liber hymnorum et canticorum* offers the opportunity for exercise in both service and play by just such folk, and for the sake of "translation." The collection is a major document in the history of the fifteenth-century lyric, but more that that, it is also a signal contribution to the development in England of an accessible vernacular hymnody.*

# Notes

*Portions of this paper appeared in Canada under the title "Early English Carols and the Macaronic Hymn," *Florilegium: Carlton University Annual Papers on Classical Antiquity and the Middle Ages* 4 (1982): 210–27.

    1. Carleton Brown, *Religious Lyrics of the Fifteenth Century* (Oxford: Clarendon Press, 1939, reprint, 1952), p. xix; but cf. David L. Jeffrey, *The Early English Lyric and Franciscan Spirituality* (Lincoln: University of Nebraska Press, 1975), pp. 242–44, 255–56.

    2. Edited by J. Zupitza, "Die Gedichte des Franziskaners Jacob Ryman," *Archiv für das Studium der Neueren Sprachen und Literaturen* 89 (1892): 167–338, from MS. Ee.I.12 of the Cambridge University Library. Cf. Richard Leighton Greene, in his landmark edition, recently revised and updated, *The Early English Carols* (Oxford: Clarendon Press, 1977), p. clv. Ryman was ordained as an acolyte in 1476, so that one assumes him to be doing most of his composing or collecting during his twenties and early thirties. See A. G. Little, "James Ryman: A Forgotten Kentish Poet," in *Archaeologia Cantiana* 54 (1941): 1–4.

    3. Greene, *Early English Carols*, p. xlix. The term "meditation" is, of course, Rosemary Woolf's, from her excellent survey, *The English Religious Lyric in the Middle Ages* (Oxford: Clarendon Press, 1968).

    4. After no. 110, at f. 79 (Zupitza, "Gedichte," p. 284).

    5. E.g., MS. Harley 913, the "Kildare Book." See the edition by W. Heuser, "Die Kildare Gedichte," *Bonner Beiträge zur Anglistik* 14 (1904): 128–29.

    6. In his *Hymnar und Hymnen in Englischen Mittelalter* (Tübingen: Neimeyer, 1968), Helmut Gneuss makes the point that English, unlike German, does not distinguish between "Hymne und Kirchenlied," thus making it

difficult for modern hymnologists to keep fresh the distinction which ought to pertain between "die Dichtungen des Ambrosius und Prudentius ebenso bezeichnet wie die Lieder Martin Luthers und Charles Wesleys" (p. 207). Without reference to his specific examples, I should like to acknowledge that the linguistic problem he identifies affects my own discussion here to the degree that not all carols of Ryman's are hymns, in the strict sense, nor all hymns carols, of course. But some of Ryman's hymns are not direct translations of preexisting Latin hymns, either, and some of his macaronic "translations" of hymns grow so expansive or adopt forms diverse enough from their original that the English song is more properly *Kirchenlied* than *Hymn*. Mostly I must call this latter type "songs," in an effort to preserve the distinction I take to pertain to Ryman's *canticorum*.

    7. See Greene's *Early English Carols*, chap. 1, "The Carol as a Genre," for a definitive discussion. Breughel's painting *Elde danse*, or "Village Dancers," approximates the popular performance of a carol. Greene's frontispiece, from a fifteenth-century MS., affords an earlier illustration.

    8. Cited in ibid., p. clviii.

    9. See Eric Routley, *The English Carol* (New York: Oxford University Press, 1957).

    10. Greene, *Early English Carols*, p. clviii. Cf. Jeffrey, *Early English Lyric*, pp. 255-56.

    11. See Jeffrey, *Early English Lyric*, chaps. 4-5; and Woolf, *English Religious Lyric*.

    12. William Otto Wehrle, *The Macaronic Hymn Tradition in Medieval English Literature* (Washington: Catholic University of America Press, 1933), p. 167.

    13. Ibid.

    14. Karl Hammerle, "Die Mittelenglische Hymnodie," *Anglia* 55 (1931): 419.

    15. Wehrle, *Macaronic Hymn Tradition*, p. 171. Ryman is the first of the macaronic hymn writers to add a saint from a feast out of the Christmas season, namely Saint Francis, for whom he has four songs. It is noteworthy that Ryman, despite his Canterbury address, did not compose a carol for Thomas à Becket, whose feast day is December 29 and for whom several other carols are extant. (Some of these are published by Greene.)

    16. Greene, *Early English Carols*, p. lxxxv.

    17. Besides the *Te Deum* sequence, *Conditor alme siderum* (no. 22); *Verbum supernum prodiens* (no. 23); *Vox clara, ecce, intonat* (no. 24); *A solis ortus cardine* (nos. 25 and 26); *A Patre Unigenitus* (no. 28); *Christe, qui lux es et dies* (no. 29); *Salvator mundi, Domine* (no. 30); *Hostis Herodes impie* (no. 58); and *Christe,*

*redemptor omnium* (no. 27).

18. See John Stevens, *Music and Poetry in the Early Tudor Court* (London: Methuen, 1961), pp. 48-49.

19. Cf. n. 9.

20. The Latin note at the bottom of the first page of Ledrede's collection reads: "Be advised, reader, that the Bishop of Ossory has made these songs for the vicars of the cathedral church, for the priests and for his clerks, to be sung on important holidays and at celebrations, in order that their throats and mouths, consecrated to God, may not be polluted by songs which are lewd, secular, and associated with revelry, and since they are trained singers, let them provide themselves with suitable tunes according to what these sets of words require." Editions of Ledrede's poems may be had in R. L. Greene's edition. *The Lyrics of the Red Book of Ossory, Medium Aevum* Monographs, n.s. 5 (Oxford: Blackwell, 1974); and Edmund College, O.S.A., *The Latin Poems of Richard Ledrede, O.F.M.*, Pontifical Institute of Mediaeval Studies, Studies and Texts, no. 30 (Toronto, 1974).

21. Gneuss, *Hymnar und Hymnen*, p. 218.

22. Rossell Hope Robbins, *Secular Lyrics of the XIVth and XVth Centuries* (Oxford: Clarendon Press, 1955), p. xxi.

23. See Stevens, *Music and Poetry*, pp. 56, 48.

24. R. H. Robbins, "The Bradshaw Carols," *PMLA* 81 (1966): 308-10; Greene, *Early English Carols*, p. clv.

25. Greene (*Early English Carols*, p. clviii) seems to wish to hold out for both possibilities, in general practice, while seeing the carol as squarely within the Franciscan tradition, which he feels Ryman exemplifies.

26. The reference to ox and ass in connection with messianic prophecy is neither, as has sometimes been thought, a misreading of Jeremiah 11:19 ("I was brought as a lamb or an ox to the slaughter") nor simply, as Greene suggests, evidence of "the love of dumb creatures [to] which Francis preached and for which he is particularly remembered" (*Early English Carols*, p. clviii). Saint Francis was not unique, in his Christmas pageant, in using the *bovi et asino*. Here, as in medieval visual representations of the Nativity, the animals are an exegesis of Isaiah 1:3, "The ox knows his owner, and the ass his master's crib."

27. One can imagine thus how reflexive could be early sixteenth-century satire on this aspect of Franciscan carollry: Robbins ("The Bradshaw Carol") prints an irreverent rejoinder to one of Ryman's carols which describes a Grey Friar who "offered the Nunne to lerne her to synge . . ." and concludes:

> Thus the fryer lyke a prety man
> *inducas*
> Ofte rokkyed the Nunnys Quoniam
> *in temptacionibus*
>                               ffinis short and swete.

But Ryman, for all the vulnerability of some of his confrères, is not nearly so given to ambiguous imagery as many of them.

    28. Brown, *Religious Lyrics*, p. xx.

# The Ironic Art of William Dunbar

## Edmund Reiss

While acknowledging that William Dunbar may well be the first writer in the English language whose body of work consists almost entirely of short poems, we can hardly help but notice that these more-than-eighty pieces offer such diversity that it is exceedingly difficult to describe the body of poetry itself or the achievement demonstrated by it. Traditional classifications of these poems into such categories as allegories, love poems, invectives, petitions, moralizings, and hymns may give a sense of order, but they actually confirm our impression that Dunbar's poetic offering lacks both unity and a sustained purpose.[1]

We can hardly help but feel that whatever Dunbar may be at one moment, he is apt to be something quite different—unpredictably different—at the next. Though he can put on the garb of the priest—which he was—he can don as easily the motley of the court fool—which, though he was not, he certainly gives the distinct impression of being. And for all the sense we have of his being a sober and serious investigator of the human condition, we have just as great a sense of his being frivolous and zany, indeed a buffoon. We can hardly be blamed for thinking of so protean a poet as the elephant and his readers as the blind men trying to make sense of the strange object before them. With Dunbar's poetry, understanding the parts does not necessarily result in understanding the whole.

Even when we recognize the pervasiveness of the ludic in late medieval literature and the fact the *homo ludens* was at his zenith in the early sixteenth century, we may still have problems knowing just how to view Dunbar.[2] Though we may be able to appreciate much medieval mirth and game and to accept, for instance, Chaucer's bawdy Miller's Tale as a companion-piece to his elegant *Knight's Tale*, we may have difficulty finding in the body of Dunbar's poetry an equally happy marriage of the grave and humorous, the religious and the bawdy, the eloquent and the scatological. We may be more than a little offended that Dunbar, who was capable of writing the perfectly respectable epithalamion *The Thrissill and the Rois* and the technically brilliant hymn to the Virgin "Hale, sterne superne," would also pen the embarrassingly vulgar *Flyting of Dunbar and Kennedie* and the childishly bawdy "In secreit place."

The sense of a schizophrenic division within Dunbar's poetry has been perpetuated by the superficially attractive view of his two voices, one, as John Leyerle would have it, eldritch given to pasquinade, and the other aureate given to panegyric.[3] Neat as this distinction may seem, it is unfortunately simplistic and finally misleading. Not only are dozens of Dunbar's poems not accounted for in any kind of meaningful way by Leyerle's two voices, but even Leyerle himself, though maintaining a distinction between them, acknowledges that rarely does Dunbar employ one voice to the complete exclusion of the other. Rather than think that we should speak of two, or for that matter ten, voices—say, one for each mode or genre represented in his work—we should realize that, notwithstanding the various expressions it takes, there is but one main voice in Dunbar's poetry and that is the voice of irony.

No matter whether he is reiterating moral conventions or creating *tours de force* of language, the common denominator in most of Dunbar's eighty-odd poems is his sense of irony. It is this sense that allows for all of the incongruities, for his being both secular and religious, vulgar and aureate; and although he may seem to go from one to the other, we have this impression only because our view is necessarily influenced by our reading one poem at a time. Dunbar is most properly to be understood as blending as well as juxtaposing, offering simultaneously, as it were, the sacred and the profane. His procedure is such that he provides an excellent illustration of what that influential medieval literary theorist Geoffrey of Vinsauf had termed "the conjurer," the poet who transforms the normal order and nature of things. As Geoffrey states it, the poet's art "causes the last to be first, the future to be present, the oblique to be straight, the remote to be near; what is rustic becomes urbane, what is old becomes new, public things are made private, black things white, and worthless things are made precious."[4] Such is also what the perceptive recent theorist of irony Vladimir Jankélévitch has termed *le confusionisme ironique*, where the play with words consciously distorts their sense: it joins together what is different and separates what is similar.[5] Both Jankélévitch and Geoffrey could easily be describing Dunbar's poetry.

But while Dunbar's irony might be most apparent to us through his manipulations of language, we should realize that this irony itself is far more than a matter of surface effects or of tone injected sporadically by the poet into his writing. We may best think of this irony as not so much a particular point, theme, or solution as a general attitude. Hardly what was characterized later in sixteenth-century England by George Puttenham as "dry mock" or "perverse negativity," this irony is more what Cicero had termed *perpetuae facetiae*, a pervasive and continuous play that may be seen reflecting the essentially ironic world view of the Middle Ages, and one that was actually quite positive.[6]

Although our modern sense of irony may be the result of doubt about man and the future of this world, irony in the Middle Ages—including Scotland in the late fifteenth and early sixteenth centuries—may be thought of as the result of a sense of certainty.[7] Incongruous as such a notion may appear, we should recognize that Dunbar and his audience knew that regardless of how chaotic and incomprehensible things might seem to be, God was in his heaven and all was right with the world. All things really existed in harmony, and discord was more apparent than real, an aberration created by those unable to see with God's ubiquitous eye. Instead of relying on his faculty of reason, man should realize its limitations. As Nicholas of Cusa had reaffirmed in the mid-fifteenth century, reason was actually a matter of differentiating; and since its primary rule was noncontradiction, it could never take man to an understanding of the whole, where the ambiguities, confusions, and distortions that fill man's consciousness are resolved.[8]

Not only must man learn to view things *in specie aeternitatis*, he must also appreciate the ultimate harmony of everything, as expressed in the concept of the *connexio rerum*—the joining together of all creation—which, as derived by Thomas Aquinas from Pseudo-Dionysius,[9] led to the formulation by Nicholas that all things, however different they may appear to be, are really linked together in a *concordantia oppositorum*, which stemmed from and relied on a real delight in the diversity of creation.[10] In Aquinas's terms, it is man's awareness of the "heterogeneous whole" as well as the "homogeneous whole" that leads him to praise the *numerositas* and *varietas* of creation.[11] Precisely because of their recognition of the desirability of plenitude and of the real compatibility of apparently disparate entities, as well as their sense of certainty that truth could not be affected by man's confusions or purposeful distortions of it, Dunbar and his audience could delight in the celebration of the ambiguous and the incongruous. The linking together of the improbable as well as the ostensibly contradictory not only provides a basis for the element of counterpoint spoken of by Paul Zumthor in his reference to "the constant possibility of irony" in medieval literature, but also indicates the hallmark of Dunbar's ironic art.[12]

Whereas Dunbar's ironic distortions and plays of antitheses may be seen most readily in such dream fantasies as the *Dance of the Sevin Deidly Synnis* and the *Tournament*,[13] they should also be recognized in the fictions created by his blendings of the animal and human worlds—in the two James Dog poems, the so-called "Dance in the Quenis Chalmer," and the account of the king's amorous escapades in "This hyndir nycht in Dumfermeling."[14] And whereas the irony is obvious in such mythologizings of his contemporary world as the *Devillis Inquest*, with its depiction of the marketplace of this world, and in such allegorizations of contemporary events as the two John Damian pieces,[15] it is just as pervasive in his begging poems with their special pleading and all-consuming concern with material gain.[16] The fact that elsewhere Dunbar offers conventional moralizing about man's proper attitude toward earthly wealth may be taken as indicating not his inability to apply this wisdom to himself but rather his ironic use of the personal and the ostensibly autobiographical.

Dunbar's play with conventional attitudes takes a variety of shapes: in "Sanct salvatour" he curses money at the same time as he begs for it; in "He that hes gold," he notes man's predicament in this world and concludes by unpredictably counselling merriment instead of concern; and in "This waverand warldis wretchidnes," while addressing the fact of mutability in twenty-five stanzas, he responds in each with the refrain, "to consider is ane pane."[17] Elsewhere he is purposely outrageous in other ways, as when he refers to the lord treasurer of Scotland as "my awin lord thesaurair" and thinks of him as existing for the poet's benefit alone; when he tells the king that he hopes he will be Joan Thompson's man, that is, one who is dominated by his wife; when he urges the king while he is on a religious retreat to quit his purgatory and return to the paradise that is the court; and when he alternates drunken Scottish irreverence and serious Latin liturgical sequences.[18] Still elsewhere Dunbar is purposely contradictory in his treatment of the same subject or issue in several poems: besides begging insistently for advancement and reward while also advocating "discretioun" and the need to be content with little, he presents women as both nonpareils and harridans and both condones all sorts of earthly love and declares that "All lufe is lost bot upone God allone."[19]

Although Dunbar may combine humor and didacticism in a way never imagined by Horace, whose dictum that the poet should both delight and instruct was a commonplace in the early sixteenth century, his didacticism is real.[20] Like the second-century Greek writer Lucian—who, perhaps not coincidentally, became known to Northern Europe in Dunbar's lifetime—Dunbar might seem to be an unlikely source of moral and ethical instruction, but we should not assume that ironic fictions are necessarily inimical to eternal values and ultimate truths. If Dunbar had been called upon to define his ironic play, he might have replied as his contemporary Erasmus did when he explained that in his *Praise of Folly* he was taking the *via diversa* and presenting obliquely what he elsewhere presented directly.[21] In being oblique, Dunbar, like Lucian and Erasmus, presents the ridiculous with gravity and the grave ridiculously. Moreover, he may be seen exhibiting vividly the several kinds of humor found in Lucian, which, as described by Erasmus, include "All the dark humor men attribute to Momus and all the light they ascribe to Mercury."[22]

We may also see in the emphasis on "non-sense" in Dunbar's writing an expression of the compelling notion of learned ignorance (*docta ignorantia*), which while originating with Socrates and developed by Saint Paul and a host of subsequent Christian writers, became in its restatement by Nicholas of Cusa the mark of the age.[23] What this concept emphasized was, paradoxically, the need for man to become the *idiota* so that he might be open to the discovery of truth. Given the sense of the inadequacy of reason and traditional knowledge, the way to wisdom was increasingly seen to lie in accepting the apparently discordant and incomprehensible. By demonstrating the failures of the rational and by emphasizing "unknowing," the poet as well as the philosopher could go beyond the inadequacies of language and the trivialities of its manipulation.

Part of our difficulty in assessing what Dunbar is doing in his poetry comes from our ignorance not only of why a late medieval cleric would even turn to poetry but of what a sixteenth-century Scottish audience expected of its poets. What seems clear, however, is that as a purveyor of sanctity and morality, the court poet was necessarily less effective than the homilist, whose eye was wholly on the sermon and whose writing could be free of such distractions as rhetoric and prosody. The truths expressed by the court poet, though perhaps justifying his work, are hardly original with him, and they certainly do not depend on his poetry for either their existence or their validity. Because these truths are givens, Dunbar is able to employ traditional doctrine without being concerned about validity. Instead of wrestling with doctrinal problems, he can, as ironist, project both the problem and its solution and use the interplay as the structure of his poem.

We can see instances of this procedure in the several moralizings of Dunbar that concern the need for man to understand mutability as the way of the world and turn to that which is unchanging. In "I seik about this warld unstabille," the recognition of mutability leads to the wisdom of the last line, "Sa is this warld, and ay hes bein"; and elsewhere this insight takes the form of a refrain that drives home the lesson of the stanzas: "All erdly joy returnis in pane" and "Into this warld may none assure."[24] These expressions should be regarded not as instances of fatalism but as Dunbar's equivalents to the biblical and liturgical phrases that provide the refrains of other poems: "Vanitas vanitatum et omnia vanitas," "Quod tu in cinerem reverteris," and "Timor mortis conturbat me."[25]

While all these poems have as their premise man's inability or unwillingness to face the fact of mutability, all conclude with full recognition of it and, moreover, with a sense of resolution. In the "makaris" poem that has *timor mortis* as its refrain, the initial sickness of the narrator is seen to be due to his recognition of the transitoriness of human life (lines 5-8). The awareness that death takes everyone, not only the noble, powerful, and learned but also the "makaris," extends over twenty-four stanzas as Dunbar shows in instance after instance both the inexorable fact of death and the helplessness of man. But then in the last stanza we are offered the recognition that since there is no remedy for death, it is best for man to prepare for it so that he may live afterwards: "Sen for the ded remeid is none / Best is that we for dede dispone / Eftir our deid that lif may we" (lines 97-99). The *timor mortis* of the refrain, which had begun as a threat to man, becomes by the end of the poem a means of preparing him for his afterlife. Rather than suppose that the last stanza represents an afterthought which Dunbar tacked on to a catalogue of the victims of death, we should realize that it is what the poem has been pointing toward from its outset.

In like manner, other mutability poems of Dunbar offer refrains that, stemming from the recognition of mutability, affirm how man should respond to his new awareness: "For to be blyth me think it best," "Without glaidnes avalis no tresure," and "He hes anewch that is content."[26] What is significant in these pieces is that in all instances comprehension leads to peace of mind and even to happiness: it is hardly accidental that these refrains focus on such terms as "blyth," "glaidnes," and "content." What is ironic is not the transitoriness of life or the inadequacy of this world, or even the awareness of such seen in the course of the poem, but Dunbar's stance in relation to his subject. His simultaneous recognition of the problem and its solution allows him to manipulate the conflict between man's fears and traditional doctrine and to give the sense of a process of discovery even while we recognize that truth has been obvious all along.

To see further how Dunbar's ironic art transforms conventional moralizing into poetry, we may look at one other work, the poem on life, which, taking the form of a single Chaucerian stanza, may be quoted in its entirety:

> Quhat is this lyfe bot ane straucht way to deid,
>   Quhilk hes a tyme to pas and nane to duell;
> A slyding quheill us lent to seik remeid,
>   A fre chois gevin to paradice or hell,
>   A pray to deid, quhome vane is to repell;
> A schoirt torment for infineit glaidnes—
> Als schort ane joy for lestand hevynes.

Though ostensibly beginning as a question, the poem is actually a series of affirmations that take the shape of a definition which is a declaration and not at all an interrogative. That is, while creating a dilemma, Dunbar also offers a reaffirmation of traditional doctrine. His ironic approach to his subject allows him to suggest simultaneously the negative view, that life is the way to "lestand hevynes," and the positive view, that it is the way to "infineit glaidnes." While Dunbar insists that man can make of life what he will, his greatest concern here seems to be with the creation of his paradox, which he brings about through presenting a combination of, on the one hand, contrasting elements and, on the other hand, parallelism of syntax and vocabulary.

The point is that inasmuch as truth is immutable and even obvious, Dunbar is able to play with its shapes and use it as the basis of fictions whose particular significance may be seen to reside less in the traditional doctrine being revealed than in the poetic effort itself. In his various moralizings, as in his other more overtly ironic pieces, Dunbar may be regarded as not so much the preacher or teacher as the poetic craftsman who is concerned with exploring the possibilities of the word and with manipulating its various forms. But, ironically, while appreciating the beauties of language and the potentials of his Scottish vernacular, Dunbar also recognized the essential inadequacy of his writing and the triviality of the poet's activity. Even though the "makar" may seek to imitate the art of his own Maker, he must necessarily be inferior since he has only words to use, and these are both his tools and the products of his creation.

Moreover, as poets are at the mercy of death—they "Playis heir ther pageant, syne gois to graif;/Sparit is nought ther faculte"[27]—so poetry itself is fragile and ephemeral, at the mercy of a host of extraneous factors. As Dunbar's poem on his headache makes clear, even though the poet may intend "to dyt," he can very well be too "dullit" to proceed. Or again, as he shows in "Sanct salvatour," even though he would be delighted to write poems, a lack of spirit prevents him from doing so: "Quhen I wald blythlie ballattis breif/ Langour thairto givis me no leif."[28] As he makes clear elsewhere, even harsh weather can take away his desire to write—"Nature all curage me denyis/ Off sangis, ballattis and of playis"—and as he indicates in his so-called "Complaint against Mure," the poet's meter may easily be "dismemberit" and his rhetoric turned to "discordis."[29]

Beyond this, as we may see in the *Flyting of Dunbar and Kennedie*, what comes out of the poet's mouth is not necessarily gold. In fact, although Dunbar may elsewhere affirm that he "will no lesingis put in vers/ Lyk as thir jangleris dois rehers,"[30] the poet may well be, as Dunbar himself appears in the *Flyting*, a raw-mouthed ribald (line 27), whose "wit is thin" (line 354), and who is "imperfyte" in his poetry (line 498). In fact, the actual activity of the poet may be suspect. In the address to the king beginning "Schir, ʒit remember," although the narrator protests that since he can only write poems—"Allace, I can bot ballattis breif"—he is different from court sycophants who flatter and feign, it is clear that like the flatterers he is asking for preferment.[31] Dunbar may here be ironically linking the activity of the poet with the deceptions of hypocrites and the frauds of the unworthy. As the narrator goes on to complain, even the stable boy who is preferred over him has a false card up his sleeve that is worth all of his poems (lines 68–69).

Whereas, on the other hand, the *Goldyn Targe* would seem to offer unambiguous praise of poets and their craft, we should realize that in praising Chaucer's "fresch anamalit termes celicall"—that is, his freshly enameled heavenly phrases—and in noting that Gower and Lydgate "Oure rude langage has clere illumynate,/ And fair ourgilt oure spech that imperfyte/ Stude," Dunbar treats the famous English triumvirate as though they were painters whose excellence lay in their covering with a gilt veneer that which was crude and ugly.[32] But while the poet may transform what is before him, his powers are clearly limited. The idealized setting of the *Goldyn Targe*, for instance, cannot be described even by Homer, no matter how "fair" he could write and notwithstanding all his "ornate stilis so perfyte." Nor, Dunbar adds, could the art of Cicero, for all of its rhetoric, suffice to depict fully this paradise (lines 67–72). Such references indicate that far from being a seer, philosopher, or theologian the poet in Dunbar's view is at best a painter of words and a craftsman of language. Though in offering traditional doctrine he can go beyond being the "lear," the "tratlar," and the "janglar," and though in his singing he may even occasionally participate in the universal hymn of praise to the Creator—"All *Gloria in excelsis* cry, / Hevin, erd, se, man, bird and best"[33]—he most customarily offers his wit, rhetoric, and play for what they are worth in and of themselves.

Dunbar's ironic art, far from being an impediment or alternative to truth, is actually a means of taking his audience to truth. But along with noting the nature and practice of Dunbar's irony, we must do far more if we are to understand fully his poetic achievement. For all of his individuality, Dunbar is also very much a man of his age, and we must examine his individual effort in relationship to those of his contemporaries. How, for instance, is his ironic art distinct not only from that of such early sixteenth-century writers as Skelton, Erasmus, More, and Ulrich von Hutten, with their focus on the foolish and the ridiculous, but also from that of such contemporary artists as Holbein, Dürer, Bosch, and Breughel, with their emphasis on the grotesque and the distorted? Though we can hardly hope to investigate this matter here, we should recognize that, notwithstanding the particular achievements of these poets, thinkers, and artists, they all reveal a "non-sense" that is not a misguided effort but the expression of the natural and the fecund, and as such the way to wisdom. Once we understand Dunbar's place in what may be termed this "age of non-sense," we may most fully appreciate his ironic art.

# Notes

1. Though the eight categories in *The Poems of William Dunbar*, ed. W. Mackay Mackenzie (London: Faber and Faber, 1932) are reduced to five in *The Poems of William Dunbar*, ed. James Kinsley (Oxford: Clarendon Press, 1979), the classification itself is still arbitrary.

2. See Johan Huizinga, *Homo Ludens: A Study of the Play Element in Culture* (Boston: Beacon, 1955).

3. John Leyerle, "The Two Voices of William Dunbar," *University of Toronto Quarterly* 31 (1962): 316-38.

4. Geoffrey of Vinsauf, *Poetria nova* 2.121; trans. Margaret F. Nims (Toronto: Pontifical Institute of Mediaeval Studies, 1967), p. 20.

5. Vladimir Jankélévitch, *L'ironie* (Paris: Alcan, 1964), p. 146.

6. George Puttenham, *The Art of English Poesie* 3.18.186-96; Cicero, *De oratore* 2.60.243.

7. For a discussion of medieval irony, see Edmund Reiss, "Medieval Irony," *Journal of the History of Ideas* 42 (1981): 209-26.

8. Nicholas of Cusa, *De docta ignorantia* 1.1ff.

9. Thomas Aquinas, *Summa contra gentiles* 2.68; Pseudo-Dionysius, *De divinis nominibus* 70.

10. Nicholas, *De docta ignorantia* 3.1.

11. Aquinas, *Summa Theologiae*, I., q. 11, art. 2.2

12. Paul Zumthor, *Essai de poétique médiévale* (Paris: Editions du Seuil, 1972), p. 106.

13. Because Dunbar's poems have been known by various titles, I will cite them not only by their popular titles but in all instances by their first line and by their number in the Kinsley edition. In this edition, these two poems—"Off Februar the fyiftene nycht" and "Nixt that a turnament wes tryid"—have been integrated as the first two parts of a larger poem. See no. 52.

14. See "The wardraipper of Venus boure" (no. 29), "O gracious Princes, guid and fair" (no. 30), "Sir Jhon Sinclair begowthe to dance" (no. 28), and "This hinder nicht" (no. 37).

15. See "This nycht in my sleip I wes agast" (no. 56), "Lucina schynning in silence of the nicht" (no. 53), and "As ʒung Awrora with cristall haile" (no. 54).

16. See in particular "Schir, lat it never in toune be tald" (no. 43). This is the piece that begins in Mackenzie's edition with "Now lufferis cummis with larges lowd" (no. 22).

17. "Sanct salvatour, send silver sorrow" (no. 19), "He that hes gold and grit riches" (no. 70), and "This waverand warldis wretchidnes" (no. 39).

18. "I thocht lang quhill sum lord come hame" (no. 47), "Schir, for ʒour grace bayth nicht and day" (no. 25), "We that ar heir in hevins glory" (no. 22), and "I maister Andro Kennedy" (no. 38).

19. With begging poems like "Schir, ʒit remember as befoir" (no. 42) and "Schir, ʒe have mony servitouris" (no. 44), cf. the three poems *Of Discretioun* (nos. 78–80) and "Quho thinkis that he hes sufficence" (no. 66).

20. Horace, *Ars poetica*, line 333.

21. Erasmus, *Epistola* 337.

22. Preface to *Alexander*; quoted in Christopher Robinson, *Lucian* (Chapel Hill: University of North Carolina Press, 1979), p. 168.

23. Nicholas, *De docta ignorantia*, e.g., 1.1

24. See "I seik" (no. 58), line 20; "Off Lentren in the first mornyng" (no. 59); and "Quhome to sall I complene my wo" (no. 63).

25. See "O wreche, be war: this warld will wend the fro" (no. 60), "Memento homo quod cinis es" (no. 61), and "I that in heill wes and gladnes" (no. 62).

26. See "Full oft I mus and hes in thocht" (no. 64), "Be mery, man, and tak nocht fer in mynd" (no. 65), and "Quho thinkis that he hes sufficence" (no. 66).

27. "I that in heill wes" (no. 62), lines 46–47.

28. "My heid did 3ak 3ester nicht" (no. 21), lines 7, 10; "Sanct salvatour" (no. 19), lines 6–7.

29. "In to thir dirk and drublie dayis" (no. 69), lines 4–5; "Schir, I complane of injuris" (no. 26), lines 8, 11. Cf. *The Thrissill and the Rois* ("Quhen Merche wes with variand windis past," no. 50), where May says the lark should have inspired the narrator's "curage to indyt" and that he should be glad "sangis to mak" (lines 26, 28).

30. "This hindir nycht in Dumfermeling" (no. 37), lines 43–44. Cf. the *Flyting* ("Schir Johine the Ros, and thing thair is compild," [no. 23]).

31. "Schir, 3it remember" (no. 42), line 48.

32. "Ryght as the stern of day begouth to schyne" (no. 10), lines 257, 266–68.

33. See "Be 3e ane luvar, think 3e nocht 3e suld" (no. 11), lines 9–11; and "Rorate celi desuper" (no. 1), lines 53–54.

# Lydgate's Canterbury Tale
## *The Siege of Thebes*
## and Fifteenth-Century Chaucerianism

### A. C. Spearing

> Poetic history, in the book's argument, is held to be indistinguishable from poetic influence, since strong poets make that history by misreading one another, so as to clear imaginative space for themselves.

That sentence forms the second paragraph of the introduction to Harold Bloom's provocative book *The Anxiety of Influence*.[1] Bloom's argument is of great assistance in thinking about English literature in the fifteenth century. If he is right in identifying poetic history with poetic influence, then the fifteenth century is the first age in which it is possible to speak of the history of English poetry. Before then, as N. F. Blake has noted, texts in English "seem to appear quite fortuitously without past or future; they are not part of a native vernacular tradition." Later writers are not usually aware of the work of earlier writers; where they are aware of it, they do not see it as the property of individual precursors; they may incorporate parts of it in their own writing by adaptation or modernization, but without intending to produce recognizable quotation or allusion.[2]

With Chaucer, however, came a crucial change. As early as *The House of Fame*, under the impact of his reading of Dante, we find evidence in his work of a new sense of the possibility that writing in English might lay claim to inspiration and survival.[3] But of greater importance is that later passage, near the end of *Troilus and Criseyde*, in which he dismisses his work to posterity. His thought here may have originated in a sense of what he was doing in this longest and grandest of his narratives that shaped itself only as he actually wrote the poem. As the leaves of manuscript accumulated on his desk, I imagine that it came home to Chaucer with new force that he had created not merely an entertainment for transient courtly performance, but, in the fullest sense of the word, a book—a book, possessing something of the potentiality for permanence that had hitherto been associated only with Latin writing, one that might continue to exist in a future that he could only dimly envisage. And so he wrote:

> Go, litel bok, go, litel myn tragedye,
> Ther God thi makere yet, er that he dye,
> So sende myght to make in som comedye!
> But litel bok, no makyng thow n'envie,
> But subgit be to alle poesye;
> And kis the steppes, where as thow seest pace
> Virgile, Ovide, Omer, Lucan, and Stace.
>
> And for ther is so gret diversite
> In Englissh and in writyng of oure tonge,
> So prey I God that non myswrite the,
> Ne the mysmetre for defaute of tonge.
> And red wherso thow be, or elles songe,
> That thow be understonde, God I biseche!
> (V. 1786–98)

Probably no earlier writer in English had referred to his own work by either of the grand titles of "tragedye" or "comedye"; indeed, except for Chaucer's own use of the word *tragedye* shortly before this in his translation of Boethius, perhaps neither word had previously been used in English at all. I suppose too that no earlier writer in English had related his work to "poesye" as Chaucer does here—*poesye*, as opposed to the native word *makyng*, evidently meaning classical literature, all that is represented by the catalogue "Virgile, Ovide, Omer, Lucan, and Stace." Though strongly influenced by Dante (from whom the catalogue probably derives), Chaucer is doing something quite new in this stanza: he is inventing the conception of a history of literature in which a work in English may have a place, however modest, alongside the great writers of the classical past.[4] His book is "litel," to be sure, and it is to be subject to its precursors, to kiss the footsteps of the classics; but for all that it can be mentioned in the same breath as Virgil, Ovid, and the rest.[5]

In one stanza, then, Chaucer relates his book to the past; in the next he relates it to the future, and once more with a new conception of the possibilities for writing in English. Unlike Latin, the English language is for Chaucer diverse in its dialectal forms and in its spelling, so it will be difficult for an English poem to hold its shape against the errors of scribes. But Chaucer does imagine a future in which his book will go on being copied, even though miswritten and mismetered. Unable to foresee the invention of printing, what he imagines is a future of continued scribal copying and textual corruption; yet to do that was an astonishing act of imagination for a medieval English writer, who would normally think of his work as serving the purposes of entertainment or instruction only for the present: what Chaucer is doing in this stanza is virtually to invent the possibility of a history of English poetry. His fifteenth-century imitators looked back to him, we know, as "maister deere and fadir reverent";[6] and we have learned to discard the cliché of Chaucer as "the father of English poetry," because we are aware that there was poetry of major importance in English many centuries before Chaucer. But Chaucer surely *was* the father of English literary history: the first English poet to conceive of his work as an addition, however humble, to the great monuments of the classical past and as continuing to exist in a future over which he would have no control.

Chaucer then invented the idea of a poetic history for English: yet he rejected as far as possible the influence of existing English literature on his own work. There was no question of recovering the names and works of his English precursors, and he left it to his successors to enact the history he had invented. In the generations of English poetry, Chaucer established himself as the first father—for example, by using the lists of his own compositions which he gives in the prologue to *The Legend of Good Women*, in *The Man of Law's Prologue*, and at the end of *The Canterbury Tales* (the first such lists in English) as a means of marking out as his own property a certain area of poetic achievement. To his successors it would appear that, as father, he made possible their very existence as English poets, and yet that, as his successors, they inevitably came too late. Chaucer had done too much: the extraordinarily varied body of work he left behind seemed coextensive with what was possible for English poetry, so that it could be felt that his death "Despoiled hath this land of the swetnesse/Of rethorik."[7] A sense of inadequacy when confronted with Chaucer's achievement was common enough among fifteenth-century poets. John Walton, for example, introducing his verse translation of Boethius, writes:

> To Chaucer, that is floure of rethoryk
> In Englisshe tong and excellent poete,
> This wot I wel, no thing may I do lyk,
> Thogh so that I of makynge entyrmete.[8]

And John Lydgate, in his *Flower of Courtesy*, laments that

> We may assay for to countrefete
> His gaye style, but it wyl not be.[9]

Such passages are example of the rhetorical *topos* of modesty, but there is no reason to dismiss them as merely that. They appear to support Bloom's argument that poetic influence is accompanied by anxiety, though not his assumption that Shakespeare and his predecessors belonged to "the giant age before the flood, before the anxiety of influence became central to poetic consciousness."[10] The beginnings of English poetic history in the fifteenth century really do seem to be marked by anxiety of influence.

The example of Chaucerian influence to be considered here is, nevertheless, one of those least marked by overt anxiety.[11] Lydgate's *Siege of Thebes* was consciously and carefully composed as an addition to *The Canterbury Tales*. A major advantage of Chaucer as precursor was that so much of his work was left incomplete. It might not be possible for successors to contemplate matching his overall achievement or even to discover a literary field which he had not already appropriated, but some of the fields he had made his own were at least so large that he had not had time to finish ploughing them. Bloom, borrowing a term from Lacan, defines one type of poetic influence as "*tessera* or the link," in which "the later poet provides what his imagination tells him would complete the otherwise 'truncated' precursor poem and poet."[12] *The Canterbury Tales* is or appears to be genuinely truncated. The most yawning gap, if we can take the Host's proposals in the *General Prologue* as Chaucer's plan for the whole work, is the absence of any tales for the homeward journey. It is this gap that *The Siege of Thebes* is designed to fill, or rather to begin filling, since it is offered only as the first tale of the first day of the work's missing second half. In his prologue Lydgate recalls the tale-telling of *The Canterbury Tales*, following Chaucer in treating the pilgrimage as a real event of which the latter was merely "Chief registrer" (line 48).[13] He explains that, visiting Canterbury, "The holy seynt pleynly to visite, / Aftere siknesse my vowes to aquyte" (lines 71-72), he happened by chance to take lodgings in the very same inn as Chaucer's pilgrims. There he was accosted by "her governour, the Host" (line 79) and invited to join them for supper and for the return journey next morning, when he would be obliged to join the tale-telling competition. He agreed and was called on to tell the first tale, and *The Siege of Thebes* is the outcome.

In attaching to *The Canterbury Tales* a story told by a pilgrim not belonging to the original group that set off from the Tabard, Lydgate is already imitating Chaucer.[14] It will be recalled that "At Boghtoun under Blee" (VIII 556) Chaucer's pilgrims had been overtaken by "A man that clothed was in clothes blake" (VIII 557), and that his unexpected arrival led to the telling of an additional tale. It seems clear that Lydgate, also dressed in the black garb appropriate to his religious order (*Siege*, line 73), is a figure parallel to the Canon. Lydgate says that he was accompanied by "My man to-forn with a voide male" (line 76),[15] and he seems to have arrived at this detail by combining two elements from *The Canon's Yeoman's Prologue*: the Canon is also accompanied by "his yeman" (VIII 562), and we are told, in a couplet that a careless reader might well relate to the servant rather than the master, that "A male tweyfold on his croper lay;/It semed that he caried lite array" (VIII 566-67).[16] One further indication that Lydgate may have had the *Canon's Yeoman's Prologue* as his model for attaching *The Siege of Thebes* to *The Canterbury Tales* occurs when he makes the Host assert that none dare refuse to obey his command to tell a tale, "Knyght nor knave, *chanon*, prest, ne nonne" (*Siege*, line 137).

A far more important connection of the *Siege* with the *Tales* lies in its relationship with *The Knight's Tale*. This is, of course, the first tale of the outward journey, and immediately follows the *General Prologue*; *The Siege of Thebes* is presented as the first tale of the homeward journey, and is given a prologue manifestly modelled in style on the opening of the *General Prologue*. Appropriately, then, the *Siege* is intimately linked with *The Knight's Tale* in subject matter. It "completes" Chaucer's first tale by recounting the earlier stages of the Theban legend, to which there are so many allusions in its predecessor, and it ends by taking us up to the beginning of *The Knight's Tale*, "as my mayster Chaucer list endite" (*Siege*, line 4501), with the appeal of the Theban widows to Theseus. In the two hundred or so lines of narrative from the assembly of the widows, "alle in clothes blake" (line 4417)—symmetrically matching the teller of the prologue "In a cope of blak" (line 73)—I count allusions to no fewer than thirty separate lines occurring in *The Knight's Tale* I 878-1010. Evidently Lydgate now had a manuscript of the *Tale* in front of him, and as he constructs a mosaic of his own from Chaucer's words and phrases, his part of the Theban story merges into that of his master. Lydgate may have persuaded himself that not only *The Canterbury Tales* as a whole but also *The Knight's Tale* was "truncated": he would have found some warrant for this in the Knight's sharp abridgment of his story at its very beginning, and his modest excuse that

> I have, God woot, a large feeld to ere,
> And wayke been the oxen in my plough.

> The remenant of the tale is long ynough.
> (I 886–88)[17]

Whatever Lydgate's real opinion, on this one occasion he summoned up courage to use *"tessera* or the link" as a means of seizing back, or at least reinfiltrating, some of the ground already occupied by his poetic father. The surprising absence of Chaucer himself from the company of pilgrims that Lydgate encounters at Canterbury is worth notice: the implicit claim of the *Siege* is that in it Lydgate *becomes* the father whose place he usurps.

The purpose of what follows will be to examine the nature of Lydgate's Chaucerianism in *The Siege of Thebes*, while at the same time attempting to identify the merit of the later poet's work. Lydgate, in common with other fifteenth-century Chaucerians, sees the essence of Chaucer's achievement as consisting in the eloquence by which he first raised the English language to the level of a rhetorical high style. It was for this that he had praised him in the *Troy Book*:

> Noble Galfride, poete of Breteyne,
> Amonge oure Englisch that made first to reyne
> The gold dewe-dropis of rethorik so fyne,
> Oure rude langage only t'enlumyne.[18]

He praises him in similar terms in the first passage of *The Siege of Thebes* that alludes to Chaucer:

> ... hym that was, yif I shal not feyne,
> Floure of poetes thorghout al Breteyne,
> Which sothly hadde most of excellence
> In rethorike and in eloquence.
> (lines 39–42)

(This very passage, which identifies Chaucer without naming him, at once illustrates the rhetorical figure of *circumlocutio* and, by omitting the name, provides a verbal equivalent to Chaucer's physical absence from the company in Lydgate's poem.) Before offering a more detailed account of this ventriloquially produced Chaucerian eloquence, I must note that it would be an error to suppose that it is merely a matter of verbal style. For Lydgate, as evidently for Chaucer, genuine eloquence was a matter of high meaning as well as high style, or perhaps it would be better to say that elevated thought and feeling could be seen as one component of high style.[19] Thus he goes on to praise Chaucer for faithfully recording all the pilgrims' tales,

> Be rehersaile of his sugrid mouth,
> Of eche thyng keping in substaunce
> The sentence hool withoute variance,
> Voyding the chaf, sothly for to seyn,
> Enlumynyng the trewe piked greyn
> Be crafty writing of his sawes swete.
> (lines 52–58)

*The Siege of Thebes* tells a story and Lydgate may have had as deep and as unjustified a contempt as some twentieth-century critics for the mere art of storytelling; but it converts that story into eloquence not just by applying to it the "gold dewe-dropis of rethorik so fyne" but also by extracting from it a fruitful moral doctrine. The actual relation between narrative and moral generalization in Chaucer is more complex than Lydgate grasped; but for him doubtless nothing could be more unquestionably Chaucerian than, for example, to copy the verbal and moral eloquence of a stanza near the end of *Troilus and Criseyde* in some lines near the end of the *Siege*:

> Lo her, the fyn of contek and debat,
> Lo her, the myght of Mars, the froward sterre;
> Lo, what it is for-to gynne a werre.
> (lines 4628–30)[20]

Robert W. Ayers, in one of the few substantial published studies of the *Siege*, rightly emphasizes that Lydgate's purpose was "to teach some moral and political lessons." However, when he goes on to speak of the "moral—and thus extraliterary—relevance and application" of the *Siege*, he draws a distinction that I believe Lydgate would have thought false.[21] On the other hand, it must be admitted that the same distinction often holds good of Lydgate's practice in the *Siege*. The literary and the moral harmonize subtly in genuine Chaucerian eloquence; but in Lydgate, as we shall see, each is developed and indeed exaggerated on its own terms, and the result is sometimes painful or odd discord.

I turn first to the verbal aspects of the style of *The Siege of Thebes*. The Chaucerian high style which Lydgate aims to reproduce is that not only of *The Knight's Tale* but also of other courtly poems of Chaucer's maturity, and especially of the two that with *The Knight's Tale* form a group of what may be called "classical romances," *Troilus and Criseyde* and *The Franklin's Tale*. In all three poems Boccaccio is the source for an imaginative re-creation of the classical past; Boethius is the source for philosophical speculations that are generally compatible with Christianity yet can appropriately be attributed to pagan characters; and a high style is used that mediates between the native tongue and the classical eloquence of Latin poetry. A single example will show how Lydgate can move outside *The Knight's Tale* to imitate such effects. Amphiorax, the Greek high priest or "bishop," disappears with his chariot into the earth in the final battle at Thebes. This is an incident referred to in *Troilus and Criseyde* (II 104–05), but Lydgate chooses to describe it in lines adapted from a quite different context in *The Franklin's Tale*. Compare the following—

> For he ful lowe is discendid doun
> Into the dirk and blake regyoun
> Wher that Pluto is crownyd and ystallyd
> With his quene, Proserpina i-callyd
> *(Siege,* lines 4041–44)

—with the passage in which Chaucer's Aurelius begs Apollo to intercede with Lucina, the moon-goddess, in her role as Proserpina:

> Prey hire to synken every rok adoun
> Into hir owene dirke regioun
> Under the ground, ther Pluto dwelleth inne.
> (V 1073–75)

Lydgate's *circumlocutio* (for the underworld, or hell) elevates the stylistic level and at the same time has an elegant appropriateness to the pagan subject-matter. (It would be more elegant still if Lydgate had not already asserted, with an unChaucerian pious vehemence, that "thus the devel for his old outrages,/Lich his decert, paied hym his wages" [lines 4039–40] — a characteristic example of discord between rhetoric and moralism.)

The extent to which Lydgate's verbal eloquence in *The Siege of Thebes* can be considered as authentically Chaucerian is extremely difficult to determine, for two reasons in particular. One is that the more he imitates Chaucer, the less, in one sense, he is like Chaucer, who was not after all imitating himself. Further, it is hard to decide how far Lydgate intended his adaptations of specific Chaucer passages to be recognized as such. Did he hope to be the Chaucer of his time, or to practice a recognizably secondary art, one of skillful allusion to familiar sources? There is perhaps no simple answer to this question. Blake urges that in general "fifteenth-century writers who . . . wanted to imitate Chaucer went in for a Chaucerian style rather than for deliberate echoes of his poems," but in the case of the *Siege*, a poem manifestly designed as a counterpart to *The Knight's Tale*, it seems likely that Lydgate would have expected his audience to recognize at least some echoes of Chaucer's work.[22] At times, no doubt, his aim is no more than to create a generally Chaucerian texture by weaving together fragments from different passages in Chaucer. Thus his description of the army Adrastus gathers to assist Polymytes begins as follows:

> Ther men may see many straunge guyses
> Of armyng newe and uncouth devyses,
> Every man after his fantasye.
>
> (lines 2661–63)

These lines largely consist of words and phrases from two different arming scenes in *The Knight's Tale*, the first describing the knights gathered by Palamon (I 2118–89), the second describing the preparations on the morning of the tournament (I 2491–2536). *Guyses, newe*, and *Every . . . after his* come from the first; *Ther . . . may see, uncouth*, and *devyses* from the second. At other times Lydgate is challenging comparison with Chaucer passages that he must surely expect us to remember, as in the imitation in the *Siege*'s opening lines of the opening of *The Canterbury Tales*, or the imitation at *Siege* 4565–4602 of Chaucer's showpiece *occupatio* on Arcite's funeral rites (I 2919–66). *The Siege of Thebes* is poised somewhat uneasily between being simply another Canterbury tale, comparable with Chaucer's, and being an acknowledged pastiche of the master's methods.

The second difficulty is that the Chaucer Lydgate copied was the Chaucer he saw, a poet different in many ways from the Chaucer we see. In particular, Chaucer, "the firste that ever enluminede owre langage with flowres of rethorike and of elloquence" (as Lydgate himself put it), was responsible for the beginnings of a tradition of eloquence which runs centrally through English poetry at least down to the nineteenth century.[23] We therefore take for granted, as normal features of literary English, stylistic features that in Lydgate's time were admirable innovations, deserving to be copied for their own sake. There are perhaps four chief aspects of poetic style in which, alongside Chaucer's continuing use of many phrases from popular English verse, his "classical romances" and other mature courtly works break sharply with the Middle English poetry of his predecessors. These are the predominance of Latinate diction; the use of highly complex syntactical structures, often accompanied by an artificial word order, on the model of Latin poetry; a general concern for local beauty of thought and sound; and the substitution of figurative for literal and straightforward modes of expression. These are precisely the aspects of Chaucer's verbal style that Lydgate most persistently copies and in some cases exaggerates; and indeed one of the unexpected uses of his work is to enable us to recognize a dimension of Chaucer's achievement that time has flattened. I will consider each of the four aspects separately.

The Latinate or "aureate" diction of fifteenth-century poetry has been much discussed and needs little further comment.[24] However many or few Latinate words Chaucer actually added to the English language, it seems likely that he added many to English poetry, and Lydgate followed in his footsteps. It has been pointed out that many such words introduced by Lydgate have now become "so much part of the English language that we can hardly imagine how it managed without them."[25] An example from *The Siege of Thebes* which shows Lydgate as an authentic Chaucerian, using Chaucer in the way in which Chaucer used earlier nonpoetic writings, occurs in a *chronographia* which itself imitates a common Chaucerian device:[26]

> Whan Phebus passyd was merydyen
> And fro the south westward gan hym drawe,
> His gylte tressys to bathen in the wawe.
> (lines 4256–58)

In Chaucer, *merydyen* is used only in scientific prose; Lydgate creatively transfers it to the idiom of classically inspired poetic circumlocution.[27] "Aureate diction," however, is not an especially noticeable feature of the style of the *Siege*.

The ambitious clumsiness of Lydgate's attempts at complex Chaucerian syntax has also been discussed elsewhere, with the opening of the *Siege* as a salient example.[28] This is another *chronographia*, plainly composed in imitation of what is now perhaps the most famous passage in Chaucer, the opening sentence of *The Canterbury Tales*.[29] We scarcely notice the syntactic complexity or unEnglish word order of Chaucer's opening sentence, even though it is extended over eighteen lines by a whole series of adverbial clauses of time, each compound in structure and many containing further subordinate clauses. Lydgate's opening sentence, like Chaucer's, begins with *Whan* . . . and proceeds through a series of adverbial clauses of time; and the intention is doubtless that we should wait eagerly for the long-deferred main clause. If we do, our wait is long, for Lydgate takes a subsequent *whan*—

## Lydgate's Canterbury Tale

> The tyme in soth whan Canterbury talys
> Complet and told at many sondry stage
> Of estatis in the pilgrimage
> 
> (lines 18-20)

—as a cue to embark on a rambling sketch of Chaucer's poem and an eulogy of Chaucer. This does eventually, it is true, return to "the tyme that thei deden mete" (line 58), but the sentence peters out at last, about line 65, without ever having achieved a main clause at all.

The syntax of *The Siege of Thebes* is by no means always as inept as in this extraordinary opening. Indeed, even that is mildly pleasing in its soporific way: Lydgate has learned mellifluousness from Chaucer if not syntactical power, and he jogs gently and vaguely along, with an irregularity of meter that seems unobtrusively natural and not inappropriate to a slow-moving procession of pilgrims. Again, there are times when Lydgate puts his meandering diffuseness to expressive purposes with surprising dramatic power. When Tydeus goes to Thebes on Polymytes' behalf to persuade Ethyocles to keep his agreement to share the kingship, he begins with a lengthy profession of brevity that catches well the note of diplomatic negotiation:

> 'Sir,' quod he, 'unto your worthynesse
> My purpoos is breefly to expresse
> Th'effecte only, as in sentement,
> Of the massage why that I am sent.
> It were in veyn longe processe forto make,
> But of my mater the verrey ground to take,
> In eschewyng of prolixité,
> And voyde away al superfluyté,
> Sith youre-silf best ought to understond
> The cause fully that we han on hond,
> And ek conceyve th'entent of my menynge,
> Of rightwisnesse longgyng to a kynge.
> 
> (lines 1901-12)

When Ethyocles answers, "Dyssimulyng under colour feyned" (line 1958), his slow-moving indirection admirably suggests hypocrisy (lines 1965-92), with feigned astonishment gradually giving way to the threat that such a request

> ... were no token as of brotherhede,
> But a signe rather of hatrede,
> To interrupte my possessioun
> Of this litil pore regioun.
>
> (lines 1989–92)

But in general, when Lydgate aims at Chaucerian grandeur by means of hypotaxis, his style lacks the firm logical underpinning that it needs and that could be triumphantly achieved by later Chaucerians such as Gavin Douglas.

Local beauty of thought and sound is again something we take entirely for granted as a characteristic of English poetry: it reaches its culmination perhaps in late-Victorian poets such as Swinburne, in whom indeed it achieves an autonomy against which much twentieth-century poetry has reacted harshly. Yet before Chaucer this was not so: the beauty of poems such as *Havelok* or *Sir Orfeo* derives from the larger contours of narrative, not from the concentrated effect of single lines or phrases.[30] Pearsall notes how 'Often it seems that a particular cadence in Chaucer's verse has stuck in Lydgate's mind, so that he keeps coming back to it, trying to catch it himself;'[31] and Lydgate and other early disciples clearly recognized and attempted to imitate this new musicality, in which the garment of eloquence seems scarcely distinguishable from the body of sense. Thus we find in Hoccleve such lines as "My well, adew! farwell, my good fortune!" or "Excesse at bord hath layd his knyf with me."[32] Lydgate has been criticized for his failure to grasp Chaucerian metrics, but *The Siege of Thebes* is full of lines in which beauty of sound matches elegance of sense. I give two examples, chosen at random—"Thy byrth and blood ar bothe two unwist" (line 494) and "Wrong, wrouht of olde, newly to amende" (line 3700)—and then stop short, for the alternative would be a critical analysis of the whole poem.

I turn now to the fourth feature of Chaucer's poetic style, which must detain us for longer. One type of figuration that Lydgate learned from Chaucer is the substitution of learned metaphor for literal statement. This may be illustrated by the instances of *circumlocutio* quoted above from the *Siege*: lines 4042–44 meaning "into hell" or lines 4256–58 meaning "when the sun was setting." Again, one might mention the substitution of "Mercury" and "Mars" in the following passage for "persuasion" and "force," together with the metonymic use of "harp" and "sword" to represent the special powers of the two gods:

> Wherfor me semeth mor is fortunat
> Of Mercurye the soote sugred harpe
> Than Mars swerd, whetted kene and sharpe.
> (lines 272–74)

This passage has a special felicity in its context, because it is the means by which Lydgate returns from a digression about persuasion and force to his original topic of Amphion's employment of the literal harp given him by Mercury to raise up the city of Thebes. One more example is the extended metaphor (or small-scale allegory) Lydgate uses to convey the meaning that the news reached Ethyocles:

> But wel wote I the newe fame ran
> This mene while with ful swift passage
> Unto Thebes of this mariage;
> And by report trewe and not yfeyned
> The soune therof the erres hath atteyned,
> Myn auctour writ, of Ethyocles.
> (lines 1674–79)

Such figures seem perfectly normal elements of literary English, but before Chaucer they were not so, and they are used far more frequently by Lydgate than by his master.

Another type of figuration is the use of the various types of *mora* treated by writers on rhetoric as means of amplification. In a sense these are all "natural" devices of eloquence, which can be found in elementary forms even in speech; but Chaucer's widespread and elaborate use of them marked a new departure in English poetic style, and one that deeply impressed his successors. I mentioned above Lydgate's use of *occupatio* (in theory a means of abbreviation, in practice often used to amplify) at lines 4565–4602 in emulation of *Knight's Tale* I 2919–66. A similar case is the following passage about the wedding of Adrastus's daughters:

> But to telle all the circumstances
> Of justes, revel, and the dyvers daunces,
> The feestes riche and the gyftes grete,
> The pryvé sighes and the fervent hete
> Of lovys folk brennyng as the glede,
> And devyses of many sondry wede,
> The touches stole and the amerous lookes

> By sotyl craft leyd oute lyne and hokes
> The jalous folk to traysshen and begyle
> In their awayt with many sondry wile—
> Al this in soth descryven I ne can.
>                                         (lines 1663-73)

This was probably suggested by a series of parallel refusals to describe the details of Cambuskyan's birthday feast in *The Squire's Tale*. Or there is *apostrophatio*, "O cruel Mars . . ." (line 2553), with which Lydgate begins Part III of the *Siege*.[33] Another *mora* is *circumlocutio*, of which some examples have already been given; another is *digressio*, self-consciously introduced by Lydgate, in the form of *digressio ad aliam partem materiae*,[34] as follows:

> But now most I make a digressioun
> To telle shortly, as in sentement,
> Of thilke knyght that Tydeus hath sent.
>                                         (lines 2466-68)

Though it would be tedious and unprofitable to attempt an exhaustive survey of Lydgate's employment of the rhetorical devices he found in Chaucer, I must pause over his use of one means of amplification, and that perhaps the commonest in medieval poetry generally—*descriptio*. The strongly pictorial quality of much later medieval narrative poetry is well known, and is certainly prominent in *The Knight's Tale*, with its elaborate descriptions of people and places—above all of the two knights' champions and of the temples of the gods. There is nothing in *The Siege of Thebes* that corresponds very closely to these lengthy formal *descriptiones*, but on the other hand Lydgate, to a greater extent perhaps than Chaucer himself, does seem to have had a genuinely pictorial imagination. A typical example of the amplification to which this leads can be found in the scene in which King Adrastus (like the Theseus of *Knight's Tale* I 1696-1713) finds two knights fighting "Withoute juge her querel to depart" (line 1382). He orders them to stop and reconciles them; and when they disarm, Lydgate's apparent source says that they were provided with "deux manteaulx."[35] In the *Siege* this becomes:

> Tweyne mantels unto hem wer broght,
> Frett with peerle and riche stonys, wroght
> Of cloth of golde and velvyt cremysyn,
> Ful richely furred with hermyn,

> To wrap hem inne ageyn the colde morowe,
> After the rage of her nyghtes sorwe,
> To take her reste til the sonne arise.
>
> (lines 1439–45)

Lydgate imagines not only the luxurious external detail but the comforting warmth of fur in the cold morning that follows the angry night of their combat. A special piquancy is given to the scene by the reversal of the expected association of darkness with cold and light with warmth. Here indeed "pictorial" is far from covering the full range of sensory suggestion evoked. A different kind of descriptive effect occurs at the end of the scene mentioned above, in which Tydeus goes as ambassador to Ethyocles. Ethyocles angrily rejects his proposal; Tydeus defies him on behalf of Polymytes and calls on his lords to accept Polymytes as their king the following year, and then,

> As he that list no lenger ther sojourne,
> Fro the kyng he gan his face tourne—
> Nat astouned, nor in his hert afferde,
> But ful proudly leyde hond on his swerde,
> And, in despit who that was lief or loth,
> A sterne pas thorgh the halle he goth,
> Thorgh-out the courte, and manly took his stede,
> And out of Thebes faste gan hym spede,
> Enhastyng hym til he was at large,
> And sped hym forth touard the londe of Arge.
>
> (lines 2113–22)

At this moment of dramatic public action, Lydgate is perfectly in control of his syntax, and he creates a scene in which movement, gesture, facial expression, and even the vague sense of stunned onlookers ("in despit who that was lief or loth") are coordinated to produce a fine spectacle of heroic dignity.

Lydgate's most remarkable and characteristic descriptive skill depends on the evocation of space, light, and color, often with haunting delicacy, to produce picturesque effects of a kind comparable to those found in some of the masterpieces of late-medieval manuscript illumination.[36] One such scene is that in which Polymytes rides away from Thebes after it has been agreed that his brother shall reign first. The solitary journey is a common theme of romance, and its setting here is the wild forest that is the usual background to such knightly wanderings. Here however it is realized in greater detail than usual:

> ... a forest joynyng to the see, ...
> Ful of hilles and of hegh mounteyns,
> Craggy roches and but fewe playns,
> Wonder dredful and lothsom of passage,
> And ther-with-al ful of beestis rage.
> (lines 1163–68)

As night falls, a great storm blows up, with drenching rain and roaring both from the sea and from the forest beasts:

> ... the wooful sownes
> Of tygres, beres, boores, and lyounes,
> Which for refut, hem-silve forto save,
> Everich in hast drogh unto his cave.
> (lines 1179–82)

Polymytes, however, finds no shelter,

> Til it was passed almost mydnyght hour,
> A large space that the sterres clere,
> The clowdes voyde, in hevene did appere,
> (lines 1186–88)

and then he emerges from the forest, finds the city of King Adrastus, and falls asleep outside the palace. I am not sure of the syntactic function of the phrase "A large space," but its poetic effect is to evoke the opening up of the heavens as the clouds are blown away, and, beyond that, the removal of oppression and the escape into a new freedom of adventure. The landscape and weather evoked by Lydgate surely have some kind of connection—all the more engaging because not clearly defined—with the inner experience of Polymytes, as he passes from the cursed city of Thebes to the welcoming land of Argos.

Dorothy Everett once quoted W. P. Ker's definition of romance as "the name for the sort of imagination that possesses the mystery and spell of everything remote and unattainable," and went on to deny that the English medieval romances possessed that imaginative quality.[37] It seems clear that Lydgate at least did possess it, and to a greater degree than Chaucer. In other poems, Lydgate's love for picturesque detail can be merely confusing: so it is in allegorical narratives such as *The Temple of Glass*, where we seek in vain for the larger significance of moonlight or passing clouds.[38] But a romance-like historical narrative such as *The Siege of Thebes*, being exemplary rather than allegorical, can sustain almost any amount of such descriptive elaboration, for there is no generic expectation that every detail must convey some other meaning.

The most powerful of all the *descriptiones* in the *Siege* again begins at night. After Tydeus's departure described above, Ethyocles sends a party to ambush him; his first suspicion of them comes when he

> Thoght he saugh ageyn the mone shyne
> Sheldes fressh and plates borned bright,
> The which environ casten a gret lyght.
> (lines 2168-70)

They attack; Tydeus kills all but one, but is left

> Hym-silf yhurt and ywounded kene,
> Thurgh his harneys bledyng on the grene.
> (lines 2221-22)

The implied contrast between blood and grass, red and green, becomes a *leitmotiv* in what follows. He rides away, weak with loss of blood, till he comes to a great castle, once more glimpsed by moonlight:

> Conveyed thider be clernesse of the ston,
> That be nyght ageyn the moone shon,
> On heghe toures with crestes marcyal.
> (lines 2271-73)

The castle has "joyneaunt almost to the wal" (line 2274) a garden "lich a paradys" (line 2280)—a configuration juxtaposing two opposite aspects of aristocratic life, repeated from *The Knight's Tale* (I 1056-61). Within the paradisal garden, amid grass and flowers, the wounded knight lets his horse wander, and lies asleep, dreaming, on the ground.

> Ther he lay til the larke song
> With notes newe hegh up in the ayr,
> The glade morowe rody and right fayr,

> Phebus also castyng up his bemes,
> The heghe hylles gilte with his stremes,
> The sylver dewe upon the herbes rounde;
> Ther Tydeus lay upon the grounde
> At the uprist of the shene sunne,
> And stoundemele his grene woundes runne
> Round about, that the soyl was depeynt
> Of the grene with the rede meynt.
>                               (lines 2296-2306)

In this brilliantly pictorial scene, we find not only the pathetic contrast, common enough in heroic poetry, between an idyllic natural setting and human suffering, but an actual mingling of the two in the mingling of green with red on the ground. Lydgate has already mentioned "grene gras" (line 2288) and "herbes grene, whit, and red" (line 2290); now "green" wounds drip with red blood which stains green grass. The material Lydgate is using is supplied, of course, by literary tradition rather than by observation of life, but it undergoes an imaginative transformation which constantly provides surprises. For example, "painting" is a term used by Chaucer in *The Franklin's Tale*, in describing a paradisal garden, to refer metaphorically to the seasonal adornment of the earth:

> ... May hadde peynted with his softe shoures
> This gardyn ful of leves and of floures.
>                               (V 907-08)

In Lydgate's passage, the similar metaphorical use of *gilte* (line 2300) predisposes us to interpret *depeynt* (line 2305) in this sense, yet the line which follows indicates that *depeynt* here has its other metaphorical sense of "smeared (with blood)."[39] As the two senses fuse, the Monk of Bury brings us surprisingly close to the horrifying sensory acuteness of Marlowe's "Besmeared with blood that makes a dainty show."[40]

Before leaving the subject of Lydgate's poetic style, I must mention two other topics which deserve fuller discussion, but which I can touch on here only briefly. First, though Lydgate is aiming at a Chaucerian high style, he rightly recognizes that in Chaucer himself stylistic level is not governed by a rigid decorum. Thus, not only does he attempt in his prologue to match the low style of many of Chaucer's link passages (Pearsall writes well of Lydgate's "clumsy playfulness" here[41]), but he also imitates successfully in the main body of the poem those sharp turns into dismissive derision which may shock the reader of *The Knight's Tale*. Thus:

> But lete his brother blowen in an horn
> Wher that hym lyst, or pypen in a red
> (*Siege*, lines 1790–91)

clearly derives from *The Knight's Tale:*

> That oon of you, al be hym looth or lief,
> He moot go pipen in an yvy leef,
>                                                     (I 1837–38)

daringly fortified by "Absolon may blowe the bukkes horn" (*Miller's Tale* I 3387). Second, it is difficult to tell how far Lydgate grasped the ironic aspects of Chaucer's narratorial technique, a difficulty redoubled if we feel doubt (as I think we should) as to how securely we grasp them ourselves. At times it would appear that he misses the shimmer of irony that surrounds Chaucer's use of traditional narratorial devices such as the profession of ignorance. Thus Chaucer's

> But wheither that she children hadde or noon,
> I rede it naught, therfore I late it goon
> (*Troilus* I 132–33)

(shocking us by provoking speculation about Criseyde's earlier life and responsibilities) reappears as

> And whether that he had a wif or noon,
> I fynde not, and therfor lat it goon
> (*Siege*, lines 465–66)

(referring to Oedipus's foster-father, and apparently without any special significance). Yet at other times Lydgate's professions of ignorance are unmistakably intended ironically, as when he concludes his account of how Tydeus and Polymytes fell in love with Adrastus's daughters by writing:

> Withoute tarying to bedde streght they gon.
> Touchyng her reste, wher that thei slepte or non,
> Demeth ye lovers, that in such maner thing

> B'experience han fully knowlecchyng,
> For it is nat declared in my boke.
> (lines 1501–05)

Here of course the situation is more straightforward, and it must have been an easy step from Chaucer's pose of uncourtly inexperience in love to the inexperience appropriate to Lydgate's role as monk. Lydgate's Chaucerianism does extend to narratorial irony, but, on the whole, only of simple kinds.

I remarked above that it would be an error to draw a sharp distinction between the literary and the moral, at least so far as Lydgate's likely intentions in *The Siege of Thebes* are concerned. Many of the most striking rhetorical devices—*digressio, apostrophatio, sententia,* and so on—are employed to expound and generalize the meaning of his story as much as to elevate its style. That meaning is directed especially to rulers: Ayers has observed that Lydgate's purpose in the *Siege* was "to provide an historical 'mirror' wherein kings and governors particularly might observe the social effects of their actions,"[42] and his message to them is that they must rule mercifully and lovingly, and that resort to warfare is likely to lead to disastrous consequences for all: "Lo, what it is for–to gynne a werre" (line 4630). He ends his poem with a passage, possibly reflecting the Treaty of Troyes, in which he prays to Christ to send peace to this life as well as salvation in the next. Lydgate may well have seen himself as a true Chaucerian in this moral aspect of his poem. He will have remembered that in *Troilus and Criseyde*, if not in *The Knight's Tale*, a pagan story is given an explicitly Christian ending. He must have noted the importance of kingship in *The Knight's Tale*, as personified in Theseus, the virtuous but fallible pagan prince. He may well have thought that the *Tale* implied, if it did not state, that the resort to arms as a means of settling political and personal problems must lead to disaster, as in Theseus's well-meaning destruction of Thebes when he took it by assault, "And rente adoun bothe wall and sparre and rafter" (I 990), and his equally well-meaning organization of the tournament which ends in the gruesome death of Arcite. In these ways Lydgate may well have persuaded himself that he was "completing" his predecessor's "truncated" work, not just by supplying the absent beginnings of the narrative of Thebes, but by making explicit a moral significance that was left implicit by Chaucer, and that demanded clarification. Many recent interpreters of *The Knight's Tale* have in fact adopted similar attitudes, though they have not gone so far as to write poems to complete it, and would probably not wish to think of themselves as twentieth-century Lydgates.

In fact, Lydgate has performed upon Chaucer one of those acts of "misreading or misprision" that Bloom sees as necessary in the relation of poets to their precursors.[43] It is true that Chaucer is not centrally a celebrator of martial heroism, and that *The Knight's Tale* does not flinch from horror in its depiction of Mars and his influence over men—"The toun destroyed, ther was no thyng laft" (I 2016). But the *Tale* presents the aggressive instinct as being, like the erotic, an inevitable part of human nature, as productive of genuine chivalric splendor, and as capable of being controlled by justice, *pitee*, and brotherly love. Thus, for all its sombreness and its questioning philosophical scope, *The Knight's Tale* can still be thought of as a chivalric romance. *The Siege of Thebes* cannot, for Lydgate's opposition to the very substance of romance, the proof of worth by chivalric adventure, is so strong and explicit as to be destructive of the form in which he is writing. When Palamon and Arcite fight together in the grove near Athens, Theseus is humorously critical of their motives—"Now looketh, is nat that an heigh folye?" (I 1798)—but in the parallel scene of the encounter between Polymytes and Tydeus the narrator himself is far more absolute in his criticism:

> And thus thies knyghtes, pompous and ellat,
> For litil cause fillen at debat;
> And as they ranne to-gider on horsbak
> Everich on other first his spere brak;
> And after that, ful surquedous of pride,
> With sharpe swerdes they to-gyder ryde,
> Ful yrously, thise myghty champiouns,
> In her fury lik tygres or lyouns.
>               (lines 1349–56)

Although Tydeus is described, apparently admiringly, as "Lich Mars hymsilf, in stiel y-armed bright" (line 1882), Jocasta later has a lengthy speech attempting to persuade Ethyocles not to take up arms against Polymytes, in which, in effect, she argues against the part played by Mars in chivalric life:

> And it is foly be short avisement
> To putte a strif in Martys jugement;
> For hard it is, whan a juge is wood,
> To tret aforn hym with-out loos of blood;
> And yif we put our mater hool in Marte,
> Which with the swerd his lawes doth coarte,
> Than may hit happe, wher ye be glad or loth,

> Thow and thy brother shal repente both,
> And many a-nother that is her present,
> Of youre trespas that ben innocent;
> And many thousand in cas shal compleyn
> > For the debat only of yow tweyn,
> > And for your strif shal fynde ful unsoote.
> > (lines 3661–73)[44]

In part Lydgate, as a monk, is simply ignorant of and bored with the details of soldiership—after the passage quoted above in which he begins to imitate the arming scenes from *The Knight's Tale*, he breaks off abruptly, declining to "specifie" any further such "derk" matters (lines 2664, 2668)—but above all he strongly disapproves of human aggressiveness.

In this matter and in others, Lydgate resorts quickly and frequently to Christian moralization of his narrative. He opens Part III with an indignant address to "cruel Mars" (line 2553) and goes on to trace back the destruction of Thebes to that "ynfeccioun called Orygynal" (line 2565), which is the source of all the evils of life. The passage itself is finely eloquent, but, in a very unChaucerian way, it closes too quickly the fundamental issues of the story by means of this utterly comprehensive explanation. The rapid resort to moralization is seen at its worst in Lydgate's treatment of the Oedipus story. This begins, charmingly enough, by being accommodated to the conventions of romance. Oedipus kills Laius unwittingly in a tournament; the Sphinx is one of many monsters inhabiting "a wylde and a waast contré" (line 611), placed there "I suppose by enchauntement" (line 626). Then, however, the Sphinx's riddle is posed in such diffusely simple terms as to deprive it of all enigmatic force, and Oedipus's answer is equally tediously drawn out: both suggest that Lydgate was determined not to let his audience's imaginations wander. Finally, the significance of Oedipus's incestuous marriage is reduced to a series of trite moral lessons. Incest "is neither feire ne good, / Nor acceptable" to God (lines 787–88), and always leads to evil consequences, as is shown by the exemplum of Herod's marriage to his brother's wife and the subsequent slaying of John the Baptist:

> Therfor I rede every man take hede,
> Wherso he be prynce, lorde, or kyng,
> That he be war t'eschewe such weddyng.
> > (lines 802–04)

After the dreadful conclusion with Oedipus's self-blinding, Lydgate tells us what we are to learn:

> For which shortly to man and child I rede
> To be wel war and to taken hede
> Of kyndely right and of conscience
> To do honur and due reverence
> To fader and moder, of what estat thei be,
> Or certeyn ellis they shul nevere the.
> (lines 1019-24)

He continues in this strain for another nineteen lines. It would be difficult to imagine a more inept explanation of one of the most haunting myths of Western man; indeed, Lydgate's only tribute to its power is to be found in his determination to defuse it.

Lydgate's treatment of the Oedipus story is an extreme but not untypical example of his "misreading" of Chaucer's greatest imaginative achievement in *The Knight's Tale*. In this poem above all, though also to a lesser extent in his other "classical romances," Chaucer, guided by his reading of Boccaccio, attempted with extraordinary success to reimagine a classical pagan culture in its own terms, as possessing its own integrity, its own world-view—a culture imaginable because it had much in common with that of medieval Christianity, but interesting because it was also crucially different. Here the "high style" in which, also under Italian influence, Chaucer attempted to produce a vernacular equivalent to the classical eloquence of Latin is of crucial importance; for it enabled him to overcome, at least partly and intermittently, what Panofsky called the "law of disjunction" governing the medieval arts. As he put it,

> medieval art and, to a somewhat lesser extent, medieval literature, consistently separated classical form from classical subject matter: Madonnas or patriarchs could borrow their appearance from classical statues or reliefs while the classical gods or heroes appeared in the guise of medieval knights and scholars, and it was left to the Renaissance to reintegrate what the Middle Ages had set asunder.

Panofsky went on to argue that,

> Looking back at the pagan world from a quasi-historical point of view much as the Renaissance artists looked at the visible world from a perspective point of view, and projecting this image onto an ideal projection plane, the Renaissance humanists learned to think of classical civilization as a totality.[45]

That, I believe, is what Chaucer was at least feeling his way toward doing in his "classical romances"; and in his attempt to interpret the pagan world as an autonomous totality the part played by Boethius is of special importance. The *De Consolatione Philosophiae*, compatible with Christianity and yet excluding the truths known only through the Christian revelation, provided Chaucer with a way of thought that a Christian poet could appropriately attribute to pagan characters. In *The Knight's Tale* the highest interpretation of events from within the poem is in Boethian, not specifically Christian, terms, and indeed Theseus's references in his final speech to the "grace" of Jupiter, though noble, are in fact erroneous so far as the Saturnine world of his poem is concerned.[46]

It was precisely this achievement of the historical imagination, so remarkable in an English poet of the fourteenth century, that most of Chaucer's followers, and certainly Lydgate, were least able to grasp and develop.[47] The reasons for this inability doubtless lie not only in their individual capacities but at a deeper level in the culture of fifteenth-century England; whatever they were, the consequence was a retreat from Chaucer's most original achievement by the very poets who most saw themselves as his descendants. Ultimately, the work of creating an English Renaissance, begun by Chaucer because he was able to respond so intelligently to his reading in Italian, was virtually abandoned, and had to be recommenced in the sixteenth century.

Boethius, so effective a mediator in *The Knight's Tale* between pagan story and Christian narrator, is absent from *The Siege of Thebes*, and there pagan and Christian grind jarringly against each other.[48] Lydgate's only way of avoiding friction between them is an unChaucerian resort to allegory: pagan myth is reinterpreted to produce religious or moral meaning, whereas Chaucer's tendency is always to allow classical myth and legend their own value as narrative.[49] As we have seen, Lydgate allegorizes the story of Amphion, a "derke poesye" (line 214) interpreted in accordance with Boccaccio's *De Genealogia Deorum* to mean that Amphion built Thebes by means of the persuasive power of "rethorik" (line 219). Later Lydgate explains that Martianus Capella's *De Nuptiis Philologiae et Mercurii* treats symbolically of the union of wisdom with eloquence (lines 837–44), a piece of information not supplied by Chaucer in the passage from *The Merchant's Tale* (IV 1732–35) from which Lydgate is borrowing.

Lydgate, however, does not attempt to allegorize his whole story, only to make it point a Christian moral; and here serious problems arise. He has learned something from Chaucer's willingness to imagine a pagan past on its own terms, but he lacks either the imagination or the courage to follow him all the way, especially in the crucial matter of pagan religion.⁵⁰ The result is a tendency to hover between the normal medievalization of classical antiquity and a fascinated horror with what he imagines it to have been in itself. Terdymus, chosen by the Greeks to succeed Amphiorax as high priest, can be described as "a bisshop mytred in his stalle" (line 4186) when he is "confermed and stallyd in his se" (line 4189), though the rites are performed before him "in many uncouth wyse" (line 4187). Horror is expressed most strikingly in relation to the death of his predecessor Amphiorax—

> Lo her, the mede of ydolatrie,
> Of rytys old and of fals mawmetrye!
> Lo, what avayllen incantaciounis
> Of exorcismes and conjurisouns?
> What stood hym stede his nigromancye,
> Calculacioun or astronomye?
> What vaylled hym the hevenly manciouns,
> Diverse aspectis or constellaciouns?
> The ende is nat but sorowe and meschaunce
> Of hem that setten her outre affiaunce
> In swiche werkes supersticious
> Or trist on hem: he is ungracious
> (lines 407–58)

—and earlier in relation to Oedipus's resort to the oracle of Apollo:

> And with-in a spirit ful unclene,
> Be fraude only and false collusioun,
> Answere gaf to every questioun,
> Bryngyng the puple in ful gret errour
> Such as to hym dyden fals honour
> Be rytys used in the olde dawes
> Aftere custome of paganysmes lawes.
> (lines 538–44)⁵¹

Lydgate doubtless thought he saw good precedent in Chaucer for such condemnation of paganism as fraudulent and vain: the passage about Amphiorax recalls a passage from *Troilus and Criseyde*: "Lo here, of payens corsed olde rites, / Lo here, what alle hire goddes may availle" (V 1849–50). That about the oracle is generally reminiscent of the attitude expressed in *The Franklin's Tale* toward "swiche illusiouns and swiche meschaunces / As hethen folke useden in thilke dayes" (V 1292-93). But the *Troilus* passage is briefer, comes from a narrator shocked into repugnance by the end of his tale, and modulates at once into a gentler, more wistful attitude toward "the sad story that human history tells": "Lo here, the forme of olde clerkis speche / In poetrie, if ye hire bokes seche" (V 1854-55).[52] And the nervous attitude of *The Franklin's Tale* seems clearly to be associated with its socially and intellectually insecure narrator: we are meant to be amused by the Franklin's anxious insistence. Chaucer was not really worried that his audience might think (or think he thought) that there was some truth in pagan religion; Lydgate, I believe, really was, and there is no possibility of detaching the gratuitous denunciation from the poet himself—its vehemence appears to have had no equivalent in his sources. For all its reverent imitation of Chaucer, *The Siege of Thebes* is fundamentally unChaucerian in its lack of imaginative openness toward the classical pagan past.[53]

I began by quoting Harold Bloom, and I return to him for my conclusion. Bloom sees the poetic influence which for him constitutes poetic history in Freudian, Oedipal terms. The literary son feels that his authority is lessened by the imaginative area already occupied by the literary father, and he *must*, if he is himself a "strong poet" or "major aesthetic consciousness," adopt one or more of a variety of modes of "misprision or misreading" in order to gain for himself this already occupied space.[54] Father Chaucer left behind him a reputation for tolerant amiability which Lydgate himself well described:

> For he that was gronde of wel-seying
> In al his lyf ne hindred no makyng,
> My maister Chaucer, that founde ful many spot:
> Hym liste nat pinche nor gruche at every blot,
> Nor meve hym-silf to parturbe his rest
> (I have herde telle), but seide alweie the best,
> Suffring goodly of his gentilnes
> Ful many thing enbracid with rudnes.
> 
> (*Troy Book* V 3519-26)

The position of such a father must have been especially difficult to usurp: indeed, it might have been better for Chaucer's poetic descendants if he had been a more tyrannical parent, of the kind who stimulates adolescent rebellion in his children. The "strong" way out of the son's relation to him is the kind of respectful repudiation practiced by Robert Henryson from the safe distance of Scotland, beginning with admiration but proceeding to the simple question, "Quha wait gif all that Chauceir wrait was trew?"[55] But that is rare among the fifteenth-century poets, partly, I suspect, because Chaucer was so undominating a father even of his own works that it was difficult to determine what, if anything, he intended to convey as truth. Lydgate's practice of *tessera* is more common. It is worth bearing in mind, however, that *The Siege of Thebes* partly consists of a retelling of the story of Oedipus. It is difficult, perhaps, to see the Monk of Bury as a "major aesthetic consciousness," engaged in a life-or-death struggle to win authority from his powerful ancestor; but then Oedipus did not know that it was his father whom he had killed. Harold Bloom might argue that in the early part of *The Siege of Thebes* Lydgate was dramatizing, no doubt unconsciously, precisely the innocent because unknowing destructiveness that he had to engage in himself in order to survive such a powerful yet unassertive father. In order to live as a poet, he had to kill Chaucer, first by removing him silently from among the Canterbury pilgrims, then by casting him in the role of Laius; and in order for him to be able to kill such a "well-saying" and tolerant father, it was essential that he should conceal from himself what he was doing. The truth may be less sensational than such an argument would suggest, but it is undoubtedly true that both the shortcomings and the merits of *The Siege of Thebes* can best be understood through investigation of Lydgate's intricate and uneasy relation with his precursor.[56]

# Notes

1. (London and New York: Oxford University Press, 1973), p. 5. I had supposed that I was the first to see Bloom's theory as applicable to later medieval England, but in 1979 I discovered that Louise Fradenburg, then of the University of Virginia, was thinking along similar lines. I benefited from discussing the matter with her, and may now well have been influenced by her. Since the fifteenth century such problems of influence have been inescapable. For a proposal as to the applicability of Bloom's theory to Boccaccio's influence on Chaucer, see Donald R. Howard, "Fiction and Religion in Boccaccio and Chaucer," *Journal of the American Academy of Religion* 47/2 supplement (June, 1979): 307-28.

2. *The English Language in Medieval Literature* (London: Dent; Totowa, N.J.: Rowman and Littlefield, 1977), pp. 14-15 and chap. 1, passim. Blake's

argument is of great interest, though in my view he seriously underestimates the difference between the fifteenth century and earlier periods.

3. Lines 518–28, 1091–1109. Chaucer references and quotations are from *The Works of Geoffrey Chaucer*, ed. F. N. Robinson, 2nd ed. (Boston: Houghton Mifflin, 1957).

4. At *Inferno* 4. 102 Dante is greeted as the sixth in a company of poets of whom the other members are Virgil, Ovid, Homer, Lucan, and Horace. Here and in *The Knight's Tale* Chaucer suppresses the crucial part played by his reading in Italian as a bridge between the classical past and himself as vernacular poet. Himself the first major source of poetic influence in English, he conceals the influence of Dante and especially of Boccaccio, which made that role possible for him.

5. Cf. the phrase "this lytel laste bok" in *House of Fame*, line 1093. The combination of humility with a new pride in authorship is characteristic of both poems.

6. Thomas Hoccleve, *Regement of Princes*, line 1961, in *Works*, ed. F. J. Furnivall, vol. 3, Early English Text Society, ES 72 (London, 1897).

7. Ibid., lines 2084–85.

8. *English Verse between Chaucer and Surrey*, ed. Eleanor P. Hammond (Durham, N.C.: Duke University Press, 1927), p. 42.

9. *Minor Poems of John Lydgate*, ed. H. N. MacCracken, vol. 2, Early English Text Society, OS 192 (London, 1934), lines 239–40.

10. Bloom, *Anxiety*, p. 11.

11. Derek Pearsall (*John Lydgate* [London: Routledge and Kegan Paul, 1970], p. 153) notes the surprising absence of "the usual professions of modesty" from the prologue to *The Siege of Thebes* and suggests that Lydgate's recent successful completion of the *Troy Book* had produced in him an "access of confidence."

12. Bloom, *Anxiety*, p. 66.

13. I quote *The Siege of Thebes* from the edition of Axel Erdmann and Eilert Ekwall, Early English Text Society, ES 108, 125 (London 1911, 1930). With this and other medieval texts, I have normalized spelling (þ, ȝ, i/j, u/v) and repunctuated according to modern usage. The reference to Chaucer in the notes of the EETS edition are helpful but by no means exhaustive; in the present paper, wherever possible, I have taken my material from parallels not noted by Erdmann and Ekwall. I have deliberately not attempted to relate the *Siege* to its source, because the specific redaction of the *Roman de Thèbes* used by Lydgate has not yet been identified. If the assumption is correct that the 1491 *Ystoire de Thèbes* is closely similar to Lydgate's source, then most of the passages I discuss are his own additions.

14. Blake would presumably argue that he was imitating an earlier imitation that formed part of *The Canterbury Tales* as he had read it: see "The Relationship between the Hengwrt and the Ellesmere Manuscripts of the *Canterbury Tales*," *Essays and Studies*, n.s. 32 (1979): 1–18.

15. It is interesting that Pearsall (*John Lydgate*, p. 66) should class this line among the "touches of revealing description and observation" in the prologue. Like many such touches in Lydgate (and in Chaucer too, of course), its "observation" is of earlier literature.

16. Hammond (*English Verse*, p. 417) notes the specific parallel between *Siege*, line 76, and *Canon's Yeoman's Prologue* 566–67, but without suggesting any more general similarity in the two scenes. The errors in Lydgate's recollections of *The Canterbury Tales* in the prologue to the *Siege*, such as the utter confusion of Miller, Pardoner, and Summoner in lines 32–35, indicate that he was indeed a careless reader of Chaucer.

17. Alain Renoir (*The Poetry of John Lydgate* [London: Routledge and Kegan Paul, 1967], p. 113) notes that Lydgate has a passage imitating this near the end of the *Troy Book* (V 2927–31). It is at least possible that Lydgate also had in mind to supply the "geste / Of the siege of Thebes" read to Criseyde and her ladies at *Troilus* II 81–84.

18. Ed. H. Bergen, Part 1, Early English Text Society, ES 97 (London, 1906) II 4697–4700.

19. Compare the continuation of the first passage from Hoccleve quoted above:

> O maister deere and fadir reverent!
> Mi maister Chaucer, flour of eloquence,
> Mirour of *fructuous entendement*.

20. Cf. *Troilus and Criseyde* V 1849–55. Pearsall (*John Lydgate*, p. 53) notes that "Again and again, he echoes this sequence," and quotes an example from *Troy Book* III 4224–26.

21. "Medieval History, Moral Purpose, and the Structure of Lydgate's *Siege of Thebes*," *PMLA* 73 (1958): 463–74; see especially pp. 463, 468.

22. Blake, *English Language*, p. 32.

23. *The Serpent of Division*, ed. Henry Noble MacCracken (London: Frowde; New Haven, Conn.: Yale University Press, 1911), p. 65.

24. E. g., John C. Mendenhall, *Aureate Terms* (Lancaster, Pa.: Wickersham, 1919); Elfriede Tilgner, *Die 'Aureate Terms' als Stilelement bei Lydgate* (Berlin: E. Eberling, 1936); John Norton-Smith, ed., *John Lydgate: Poems* (Oxford: Clarendon Press, 1966), pp. 192–95.

25. Pearsall, *John Lydgate*, pp. 50–51.

26. Compare *Troilus* V 8: "The gold-ytressed Phebus heighe on-lofte" and V 1107–09:

> The laurer-crowned Phebus, with his heete,
> Gan, in his course ay upward as he wente,
> To warmen of the est see the wawes weete.

But Chaucer does not arrive at the beautiful image of Apollo bathing his golden hair in the sea.

27. *Astrolabe* II. 39, 7, etc. Chaucer begins the adaptation to poetic purposes at *Squire's Tale* V 263: "Phebus hath laft the angle meridional." Compare Chaucer's own transfer of *orizonte* from scientific (*Astrolabe*, prologue 9, etc.) to poetic contexts (*Troilus* V 276; *Merchant's Tale* IV 1797, alongside *ark diurne, latitude,* and *hemysperie; Franklin's Tale* V 1017).

28. E. g., Hammond, *English Verse,* p. 415; Pearsall, *John Lydgate,* pp. 58–59.

29. An opening was doubtless felt to be a specially appropriate place for a display of rhetorical skill: compare the opening stanza of *Troilus and Criseyde,* where the subject and verb do not enter until the fifth line. As C. S. Lewis pointed out (*The Discarded Image* [Cambridge: Cambridge University Press, 1964], p. 195), "at no period of the English language would such a sentence have been possible in conversation."

30. Cf. John A. Burrow, *Ricardian Poetry* (New Haven and London: Yale University Press, 1971), p. 43: "This strict subordination of the local and concentrated effect to the demands of a larger context marks the style of Ricardian poetry as essentially a long-poem style."

31. *John Lydgate,* p. 52.

32. *Complaint*, line 267 and *Male Regle*, line 112, in *Hoccleve's Minor Poems,* ed. F. J. Furnivall, Early English Text Society, ES 61 (London, 1892).

33. The substance of this passage may be influenced, as Erdmann and Ekwall suggest, by *Anelida and Arcite,* lines 50–53, but its rhetorical form parallels Palamon's "O cruel goddes" (*Knight's Tale* I 1303).

34. For *digressio ad aliam partem materiae* see Geoffroi de Vinsauf, *Documentum,* in *Les arts poétiques du XIIe et du XIIIe siècle,* ed. Edmond Faral (Paris: Champion, 1926), pp. 274–75, discussed by Eugéne Vinaver, ed., *The Works of Sir Thomas Malory* (Oxford: Clarendon Press, 1947), I: li–lii. Lydgate appears to have misunderstood Chaucer's use of *sentement* to mean "personal, inner experience" (e.g., *Troilus* II 13); here, and in *Siege,* line 1903, quoted above, as the EETS glossary explains, he used it to mean "substance."

35. *Roman de Edipus,* C.iiii, front: quoted in EETS edition, II. 109, note

to lines 1430–35.

36. E.g., *Le Livre du Cueur d'Amours Espris* of René d'Anjou, ed. Franz Unterkircher, trans. Sophie Wilkins (London: Thames and Hudson, 1975), ff. 2, 12v, 47v, 55; or the *Grandes Heures* of Anne of Brittany, f. 68v (ed. John Harthan as *Books of Hours* [New York: Crowell, 1977]).

37. *Essays on Middle English Literature*, ed. P. M. Kean (Oxford: Clarendon Press, 1955), p. 7, quoting Ker, *Epic and Romance* (London: Macmillan, 1908), p. 321.

38. Cf. A. C. Spearing, *Medieval Dream-Poetry* (Cambridge: Cambridge University Press, 1976), p. 173.

39. Cf. *Legend of Good Women*, line 875: "How with his blod hirselve gan she peynt."

40. I *Tamburlaine* I. i. 80.

41. *John Lydgate*, p. 66.

42. Robert W. Ayers, "Medieval History, Moral Purpose and the Structure of Lydgate's *Siege of Thebes*," *PMLA* 73 (1958): 467.

43. Harold Bloom, *A Map of Misreading* (London and New York: Oxford University Press, 1975), p. 3.

44. Amphiorax too denounces "The wooful wrath and the contrariousté / Of felle Mars in his cruelté (lines 2898–99).

45. Erwin Panofsky, "Artist, Scientist, Genius: Notes on the *Renaisance-Dämmerung*," in *The Renaissance: Six Essays,* ed. Wallace K. Ferguson et al. (New York: Harper and Row, 1962), pp. 128–29. Panofsky's interpretation is set out more fully in his *Renaissance and Renascances in Western Art* (New York: Harper and Row, 1972).

46. I have argued this case more fully in my edition of *The Knight's Tale* (Cambridge: Cambridge University Press, 1966), pp. 75–78. See also Elizabeth Salter, *Chaucer: The Knight's Tale and the Clerk's Tale* (London: Arnold, 1962), pp. 35–36; Robert B. Burlin, *Chaucerian Fiction* (Princeton, N. J.: Princeton University Press, 1977), pp. 98–99; and J. D. Burnley, *Chaucer's Language and the Philosophers' Tradition* (Ipswich: Boydell Press, 1979), pp. 79–80.

47. Henryson in *The Testament of Cresseid* may well be an exception; this, significantly, is a poem which owes almost as much to *The Knight's Tale* as it does to *Troilus and Criseyde,* as I have argued in *Criticism and Medieval Poetry*, 2nd ed. (London: Arnold, 1972), pp. 174–76.

48. Ayers writes ("Medieval History," p. 465) that "The moral and philosophical framework outlined by Lydgate in the almost countless moral passages of the poem appears to be essentially Boethian in character." Perhaps this is so, if one generalizes sufficiently, but I find nothing specifically

reminiscent of Boethius in *The Siege of Thebes*.

49. The most obvious instance is the absence of allegorizing comment from *The Legend of Good Women*.

50. Cf. the discussion of Lydgate's knowledge and appreciation of antiquity in C. David Benson, "The Ancient World in John Lydgate's *Troy Book*," *American Benedictine Review*, 24 (1973): 299–312.

51. Renoir's argument that in this passage among others Lydgate "presents classical antiquity in a much more appealing light" than in his source (*The Poetry of John Lydgate*, pp. 119, 121–23) seems to me quite unconvincing, even if we could be sure that his source was identical with the extant *Roman de Edipus*. For a similar denunciation by Lydgate of pagan superstition, see *Troy Book* I 909–11 (cited by Pearsall, *John Lydgate*, p. 131).

52. Quoted from the brilliant analysis of this stanza by E. Talbot Donaldson, "The Ending of *Troilus,*" in his *Speaking of Chaucer* (New York: Norton, 1970), pp. 98–99.

53. It will be seen that my emphasis is quite different from that of Renoir, who finds in the *Siege* and other later works of Lydgate "a somewhat unmediaeval attitude towards classical antiquity," an attitude which approaches that of "Renaissance humanism" (*The Poetry of John Lydgate*, p. 126). He even sums up the *Siege* as "a French mediaeval romance translated into an English Renaissance epic" (p. 135). Renoir, in my view, sees the *Siege* in a false perspective through not considering the nature of its relationship to Chaucer's work.

54. Bloom, *Anxiety*, p. 6.

55. *The Testament of Cresseid*, line 64, in *The Poems of Robert Henryson*, ed. Denton Fox (Oxford: Clarendon Press, 1981).

56. This essay was completed in 1981, before the publication of the important book by A. J. Minnis, *Chaucer and Pagan Antiquity* (Cambridge and Totowa, N. J.: D. S. Brewer and Rowman and Littlefield, 1982), which throws valuable light on some of the issues raised here. It also antedates my article, "Chaucerian Authority and Inheritance," in *Literature in Fourteenth-Century England*, ed. Pieor Boitani and Anna Torti (Gunter Narr Verlag and D. S. Brewer, Tübingen and Cambridge, 1983), which is concerned with some of the same issues.

# Contributors

R. F. YEAGER is Professor of English (faculty unranked) at Warren Wilson College.

A. S. G. EDWARDS is Associate Professor of English at the University of Victoria.

JEROME MITCHELL is Associate Professor of English at the University of Georgia.

LOUISE O. FRADENBURG is Assistant Professor of English at Dartmouth College.

FLORENCE H. RIDLEY is Professor of English at the University of California at Los Angeles.

DEREK PEARSALL is Professor of English at the University of York.

THOMAS W. ROSS is Professor of English (retired) at Colorado College.

JOHN H. FISHER is John C. Hodges Professor of English at the University of Tennessee.

DONALD C. BAKER is Professor of English at the University of Colorado.

C. DAVID BENSON is Professor of English at the University of Connecticut.

LARRY D. BENSON is Professor of English at Harvard University.

JOHN BURROW is Winterstoke Professor of English at the University of Bristol.

DENTON FOX is Professor of English at Victoria College, University of Toronto.

THOMAS J. GARBÁTY is Professor of English at the University of Michigan.

DAVID L. JEFFREY is Professor of English at the University of Ottawa.

EDMUND REISS has written several books on late medieval literature, including *William Dunbar* (1979).

A. C. SPEARING is Professor of English at Queen's College, Cambridge University.

LIBRARY OF DAVIDSON COLLEGE